"CONSIDER HISTORY WITH·THE BEGINNINGS · OF· IT·STRETCHING DIMLY·INTO·THE REMOTE · TIME; E- MERGING· DARK LY· OVT· OF· THE MYSTERIOVS ETERNITY: THE· TRVE·EPIC POEM· AND· VNI VERSAL·DIVINE SCRIPTVRE. ·"

CARLYLE

A·HISTORY·of
THE·ITALIAN
REPUBLICS
BEING·A·VIEW
of the ORIGIN
PROGRESS·&
FALL·OF
ITALIAN
FREEDOM
BY·J.C.L.DE
SISMONDI

EDITOR'S INTRODUCTION

THE life of Sismondi is the history of a great enthusiasm. Born at Geneva in 1773, John Charles Leonard Simonde de Sismondi very early showed the master faculty that directed him: he was a lover and servant of mankind, gentle, wise and indefatigable. Before everything he was a student of the history of men, whether in the literary past, or in his own time and in the living course of affairs. If his first claim is that of an able and original historian, he was also the first political economist of his time; it was he who inaugurated the great change from the old economy to the new; it was he who first saw the fallacy of that fatal maxim of the earlier French political economists, " Laissez faire et laissez passer !" and combated it with a vigour that found its last expression in the words of one of his disciples : " Laissez faire la misère, laissez passer la mort !"

Thus Sismondi was no academic historian; he was of the ardent type who can recreate in the imagination people long dead; he continually sought to discover the motive and the cause lying beneath the apparent result. His "History of the Italian Republics," here presented in little, was written in the earliest vigour of his faculties. It was begun in 1803, when he was a man of thirty. After many disappointments, the first two volumes were published at Zürich in 1807. The last and sixteenth volume was finished in 1818.

The work was originally written in French. Although descended from an old and noble family of Pisa, Sismondi was Swiss by birth and education, his family having been driven from Italy in the year 1524, and obliged to seek an asylum first in France and later at Geneva. Even at Geneva this much-tormented family were not safe. There revolution stripped them of all they possessed, and drove them to England, where they stayed for some time. While in England Sismondi made good use of his time: he made a characteristic study of the English, their laws and institutions, and their ways, and he thoroughly learned the language. But Madame de Sismondi, his mother, one of the most remarkable women of her day, was seized with homesickness, and they returned to Geneva, only to be driven forth again, and to find an asylum in Northern France. Here M. de Sismondi, by his mother's advice, commenced his arduous work as a historian. The work was shown presently to Madame de Staël, his lifelong friend, and to his mother, whose advice was always his safeguard.

"Take care," wrote she, "to avoid everything which approaches at ever so great a distance the manner of the philosophical haranguers of 1789, who thunder as soon as they open their mouth: warmth must come from development."

Later, when combating her son's adherence to fixed opinions, his often destructive religious criticism, she writes:

"You must not thus throw about fire and flame; reflect on it, you who require love so much. It is not merely enemies of a day that are made by this decided tone; they are exasperated, and for life."

Sismondi was fortunate in having the criticism of some of the finest minds of the day to help him in the work as it progressed. He never worked, he tells us, less than eight hours a day. In apologising for his style, he writes: "I have been obliged to live, in some sort, out of my maternal tongue. I have been obliged habitually to write and think in Italian or in Latin, and occasionally in German, Spanish, Greek, English, Portuguese, Provençal. I have been obliged to pass from one of these languages to another, without reflecting on the form in which thought was clothed, almost without perceiving the substitution of one dialect for another."

When published, this book brought him a wide fame, and many and brilliant friendships. Hardly had he laid down his pen when he took it up again to write his " History of the French "—a work which cost him twenty-four years of ceaseless labour. Its conclusion was written only five weeks before his death. " It will soon be two years," he writes in finishing, "since I enjoyed a single day of health. They were not common efforts that have been required, not to be diverted one day from my work. . . . There is one testimony that I dare to render to myself: the work I am finishing is that of a conscientious writer. I have always sought for truth, and I have spared neither labour nor expense to discover it.'

During the last five weeks of his life he worked on heroically, suffering the last tortures of an internal cancer with perfect fortitude. On June 25, 1842, he died at his country house, near the village of Chêne, a league and a half from Geneva.

The following is the table of his published works:

Tableau de l'agriculture toscane, 1801; De la richesse commerciale, ou principes d'économie politique, etc., 1803; De la vie et des écrits de P. H. Mallet, 1807; Histoire des républiques italiennes au moyen âge, 16 vols., 1809-18, 1818; (an abridgment of this work was contributed to Lardner's Cyclopædia); Du Papier-monnaie dans les États autrichiens et des moyens de le supprimer, 1810; De la littérature du midi de l'Europe, 4 vols., 1813; Sur les Lois éventuelles, 1814; Considérations sur Genève dans ses rapports avec l'Angleterre, etc., with a treatise on the Philosophy of History, 1814; De l'intérêt de la France à l'égard de la traité des nègres, 1814; Nouvelles réflexions sur la traité des nègres, 1815; Examen de la constitution française, 1815; article on Political Economy for Dr. Brewster's Edinburgh Encyclopædia, 1815; Nouveaux principes d'économie politique, ou de la richesse dans ses rapports avec la population, 2 vols., 1819, 1827; Progetti dell' Austria sull' Italia, translated from the French, 1821; Histoire des Français (continuation by A. Renée), 31 vols., 1821-44; Julia Severa, ou l'an quatre cent quatre-vingt douze (a novel), 1822; Considérations sur la guerre actuelle des Grecs et sur ses historiens, 1825; Histoire de la rénaissance de la liberté en Italie, de ses progrès, de sa décadence, et de sa chute, 1832; Des espérances et des besoins de l'Italie, 1832; Histoire de la chute de l'Empire Romain et du déclin de la civilisation de l'an 250 à l'an 1000, 1835, 1842; Études sur les constitutions des peuples libres, 1836; Études des sciences sociales, 1836-38; Études sur l'Économie politique, 1837, 1838; Précis de l'histoire des Français, 1839; Della condizione degli agricoltori in Toscana; Della condizione degli agricoltori nell' Agro Romano; Del modo di rinstaurare la popolazione e l' agricoltura nella Campagna di Roma (three articles in the Biblioteca dell' Economista, second series, vol. ii.), 1860. Sismondi also contributed articles on the History of Italy to the Biographie Universelle, and numerous articles to the Revue Encyclopédique, others

to Annales de Législation, La Bibliothèque Universelle, the Protestant, Pallas, and the Atti della Academia Italiana.   Sismondi's
notes are among those of others in the edition of Ricardo's works,
1847; and in the Biblioteca dell' Economista, first series, vol. ii.,
on his Principles of Political Economy, 1856; Adam Smith's
Recherches sur la nature et la cause de la richesse des nations,
1843, has also notes by Sismondi; Chenevière Fragments du
journal et de la correspondance de J. C. L. S. de S., 1857;
Fragments du journal et de sa correspondance avec Mdlle. de
Sainte-Aulaire, 1863; Saint-Réné Taillandier, Lettres inédites de
J. C. L. de Sismondi (and others) à Mme. la Comtesse d'Albany,
1863.

1907.

HISTORY OF THE ITALIAN REPUBLICS

INTRODUCTION

THE republics which flourished in Italy during the middle ages have neither been attached by ancient alliances, nor opposed by long rivalries and wars, to the powers which divide Europe at this day. From this it might be supposed that their history is altogether of secondary importance, and that each people, after having studied its own, should give precedence over that of the Italians to the history either of hereditary allies, or of those who, by a prejudice of barbarism, are called natural enemies. It would be a great error: history has no true importance but as it contains a moral lesson. It should be explored, not for scenes of carnage, but for instructions in the government of mankind. The knowledge of times past is good only as it instructs us to avoid mistakes, to imitate virtues, to improve by experience: but the pre-eminent object of this study,—the science of governing men for their advantage, of developing their individual faculties, intellectual and moral, for their greater happiness,—that political philosophy, began in modern Europe only with the Italian republics of the middle ages, and from them diffused itself over other nations.

After the destruction of the Roman empire, which carried away ancient civilisation with it in its fall, power henceforth, through many generations, belonged only to barbarians, exercising with their brutal passions the rights of conquest over human society. There was no longer a government, no longer an association of all

A

the inhabitants of a country organised for the common good: society was divided between the conquerors and the conquered. The former, indeed, had a spirit of independence: they were companions united under their chief, to satisfy in common their rapacity and luxury; it was their glory to be feared, to be obeyed, and to be revenged. After having exhausted their caprices on the vanquished, they delighted in hearing such feats celebrated by their poets at festivals, as great deeds in which they took pride. For those, on the contrary, who had fallen under the yoke of the barbarians, there was no protection to be expected, there was no government formed even partly for their advantage—in short, there was no social bond. They were compelled to labour, that their conquerors might enjoy,—to suffer and be humiliated, that those might pride themselves on their domination. Such was the state of Europe for a long period after the fall of the Roman empire,—a state of which the history offers but little real instruction, and on which perhaps it may be as well not to dwell. We are easily seduced by the display of energy: the courage of the barbarians, employed only in crime and devastation, attracts us; long rivalries sometimes appear to us as a reason for hatred between descendants; and a poetic hue still disguises ages which can only teach us one lesson—to avert at all price their return.

Useful history, that of which the knowledge should be universally diffused, begins only with the period when the victors and vanquished, inhabitants of the same country, were fused into one people; and still more decisively when they became united by a single bond, the public good, at the period when the government belonged to the people, and not the people to the government. The fusion of conquerors and conquered was more or less rapid in the different states of Europe: in some it lowered the former, in others it raised the latter; and public order cannot be considered as having been established till the people were no longer confounded with the property which they created for the use of their masters. After the invasion of the barbarians, the people everywhere belonged, in the first instance, to the army; but, as the army must preserve its organisation to remain powerful, it could not exist without a chief: the power of the chief was often confounded with that of his soldiers, who sometimes found it advantageous to invest him with almost despotic authority. Thus it frequently happened that the chief, called by the barbarians king, from having been no more than the deputy chosen by the army, became its master. He had ruled for the army, by the army, and finally he ruled the army itself: government from being military became patrimonial; the people and the army belonged alike to the king, and were governed solely for the advantage of the king. In the midst of these governments, either military or patrimonial, when Gaul belonged to the Franks, Spain to the Visigoths, England to the Saxons, and at a later period to the Normans, or when each of these countries belonged to a king of the dominant race, Italy began early to feel, and to declare, that she belonged only to herself—to assume authority, and to exercise it for her own advantage. Italy, invaded by the barbarians, like the other western states, pillaged, oppressed, and disorganised, could, no more than they, repel the invaders or expel them, and constitute herself a single state. There, as elsewhere, the ancient social body was annihilated; but there, more than elsewhere, the principle of life remained in the fragments of the broken colossus: the Italians succumbed as a nation, but the component parts of their grand social union, their cities and towns, the first elements in some sort of what forms a nation, arose and defended themselves on their own account; every smaller association of men, which had survived the great one, had the courage to exist for itself—to feel that it had interests to protect, sentiments above fear, and virtues that deserved success. The Italians sought the good of all, not that of masters at the expense of slaves. Their hearts first told them, and their reason confirmed, that they had still a country: for her they set the first example of those public virtues which became the pattern of Europe. From the moment they formed their own governments, and formed them for the common good, they prospered: while every other nation suffered, they rose in intelligence as well as virtue. The exercise of commerce and the arts augmented their wealth, and fixed on them the attention of other nations; their example enlightened the smaller associations framed in the towns of the rest of Europe, and imitating them at a distance; their experience directed the meditations of some superior minds formed in the government of the Italian republics, who rose from the practice to the theory of civil society, and showed, not only to their own country, but to future nations and ages, the object to which all human associations should tend, and the best means by which to attain it.

In the mean time, while the Italian republics increased in population, intelligence, virtue, and wealth, the patrimonial governments of the rest of Europe advanced also, but in another manner. Nations made some slow progress in civilisation; their chiefs increased in power, not by the development of the resources of their people, but by the agglomeration of new states; their kingdoms, subject to the laws of inheritance and primogeniture, which always cause, and in no long period, the extinction of rich families, had grown, as the patrimony of the wealthy grows, by inheritance, by marriage, and by the abuse of power. The ancient sovereign families had, for the most part, become extinct, if not in all their branches, at least in the eldest; and their territories had accumulated on a few survivors in the younger branches. About ten powerful succeeded a hundred feeble princes. Towards the end of the fifteenth century, the chiefs of the French, German, and Spanish nations were tempted to invade Italy, allured by the marvellous opulence of a country where the plunder of a single town afforded sometimes greater riches than they could wrest from millions of their own subjects. The most frivolous pretexts sufficed; and, during forty years of war, that prosperous and beautiful country was ravaged by all the various nations which could find their way into Italy. The insatiable brigandage of these new barbarians at length destroyed the opulence which had allured them; but the soldiers of the north and west carried into their own countries, along with the treasures of the Italians, the instruction and example of a more advanced civilisation: numerous germs of a better state of things, carried away from the Italian republics of the middle ages, were spread over the rest of Europe. Let us not, while we now reap the harvest, forget the parent soil.

Introduction

It is this first developement of the Italian nation, thus instructive to every other, that we here purpose shortly to retrace. We have endeavoured to include in a single volume a summary of the events of which the Italian peninsula was the theatre, from the fall of the Roman empire to the end of the Middle Age. This summary will not satisfy the philosopher, who wishes to distinguish in the mass of general history the peculiar genius of each people, to follow institutions from their birth, to know their action and their defects, to study man in his various circumstances, and to see depicted individuals as well as nations. We refer those who can bestow time and attention on historical studies to the much larger work which we have already published on the same subject: they will there find ample details, and they will be put in the way to obtain still more. Proposing to ourselves here only a summary of facts, and a more luminous view of the ideas they suggest, in order to satisfy the curiosity of those who can give only a limited time and attention to the study of history, we have abstained from all references; we have considered it useless to cite authorities which we have made known elsewhere; and, above all, we have endeavoured to make the following pages universally intelligible without the aid of any other book.

CHAPTER I

STATE OF THE POPULATION OF ITALY AT THE FALL OF THE ROMAN EMPIRE IN THE FIFTH CENTURY—ITALY TORMENTED DURING FIVE CENTURIES BY THE SUCCESSIVE INVASIONS OF BARBARIANS —FIRST EFFORTS OF TOWNS IN THE TENTH CENTURY TO DEFEND AND GOVERN THEMSELVES

ANCIENT Italy lost her freedom in the conquests of the Roman republic. Her numerous and warlike people had long defended themselves, either in the chain of mountains which, issuing from the southern Alps, crosses the whole length of Italy; or in the vast and rich plains to the east of that chain, formerly occupied by the Cisalpine Gauls. This people disappeared; their cities, enlarged and embellished by the Romans, lost all independence, all remembrance of nationality; the land was no longer cultivated but by slaves; when the Roman republic itself in its turn also lost its freedom. Rome held sway over the greatest part of the known world; but, under the necessity of employing despotic authority, in order to secure the obedience of the army, and the distant provinces, she finally became herself the property of the master whom she had imposed on others. One of the early successors of Augustus had granted to every Italian the rights of citizenship in Rome; but those rights had ceased to confer a participation in the sovereignty of the republic. On the other hand, the inhabitants of the municipalities of Italy, in becoming Roman citizens, renounced no one of the rights of their native cities, of which they might be either jealous or proud.

Italy continued to decline rapidly under the emperors: the component parts were no longer in due proportion. Rome contained about two or three thousand senatorial families, whose luxury and splendour surpassed all the pomp now displayed by the greatest nobles of our richest monarchies; but whose effeminacy and pusillanimity shrunk from all the active offices of life. These families were often decimated by despotism; their property was frequently confiscated; and they became rapidly extinct: but others arrived from the provinces to take their place. They were surrounded by an immense population, lodged in miserable houses, almost the only property they possessed. Rome contained several millions of inhabitants: the smallest number only exercised the necessary arts and employments of life, and even this more active part of the population (composed chiefly of foreigners and freedmen) left the manual work entirely to slaves; the remainder, all those who gloried in the title of Roman citizen, who had long despised every vocation but the military service, henceforward rejected even that, and lived in absolute idleness: supported by distributions of corn and largesses from the public treasury, they passed their days in the bath, the circus, and the amphitheatre. The state not only supported them, but took upon itself the charge of amusing them by gratuitous public spectacles. Whole families became extinct from the vices engendered by idleness; but their place was continually supplied by the crowd which flocked from the provinces to enjoy a life of indolence, largesses, immunities, and public shows.

Italy was covered with cities: the greater number of those now existing flourished in at least equal splendour in the time of the Roman empire; some, such as Milan, Verona, Bologna, Capua, were so considerable as to present an image of Rome, with their circus, their amphitheatre, their tumultuous and idle population, their riches, and their poverty. Their administration was nearly republican, most commonly composed, after the example of Rome, of a *curia*, or municipal senate elected by the people, and of duumvirs, or annual consuls. In all these towns, among the first class of inhabitants were to be found the proprietors of the neighbouring land, lodged in palaces with their slaves and freedmen; secondly, the artisans and shopkeepers whom their consumption established around them; lastly, a crowd of idle people, who had preserved just enough of land to supply, with the strictest economy, the means of existence. It does not appear that there was any prosperous manufactory in Italy. All manual labour, as well in towns as in the country, was executed by slaves. Objects of luxury, for the most part, came from Asia. War had for a long time been the only occupation of the Italians; for a long period, too, the legions had been levied partly among the Romans, and partly among their allies in Italy: but, under the emperors, the distrust of the master seconded the luxurious effeminacy of the subject, the Italians finally renounced even war; and the legions were recruited only in Pannonia, Gaul, and the other provinces bordering on the Rhine and the Danube. At a later period, the barbarians who menaced Rome were seduced by liberal pay to engage in its defence; and in the Roman armies the enemies of Rome almost entirely replaced the Romans. The country could not, as in modern states, supply the place of cities in recruiting the armies with a class of men accustomed to the inclemencies of the weather, and inured to toil. The only labourers to be found were an oppressed foreign race, who took no interest in public affairs. The Romans cultivated their land either by slaves purchased from the barbarians, and forced by corporal punishment to labour, or by *coloni partiarii*, to whom was given a small share in the harvest as wages : but, in order to oblige these last to content themselves with the least possible share, they were attached to the land, and nearly as much oppressed as slaves themselves. The proprietors of land varied between these two systems, according as the price of slaves varied, or the *colons* (peasants, labourers) were more or less numerous: no cultivator of the land had any property in it. The greatest part was united in immense domains, sometimes embracing whole provinces, the administration of which was intrusted to freedmen, whose only consideration was, how to cultivate the land with the least possible expense, and how to extract from their labourers the greatest degree of work with the smallest quantity of food. The agriculturists, as well what were called freedmen as slaves, were almost all barbarians by birth, without any interest in a social order which only oppressed them, without courage for its defence, and without any pecuniary resources for themselves ; their numbers also diminished with an alarming rapidity, partly from desertion, partly from new invasions of barbarians, who carried them off to sell as slaves in other Roman provinces, and, finally, from a mortality, the necessary consequence of poverty and starvation.

Italy, nevertheless, was supposed to enjoy a constant prosperity. During the entire ages of Trajan and the Antonines, a succession of virtuous and philosophic emperors followed each other ; the world was in peace ; the laws were wise and well administered ; riches seemed to increase ; each succeeding generation raised palaces more splendid, monuments and public edifices more sumptuous, than the preceding ; the senatorial families found their revenues increase ; the treasury levied greater imposts. But it is not on the mass of wealth, it is on its distribution, that the prosperity of states depend : increasing opulence continued to meet the eye, but man became more miserable ; the rural population, formerly active, robust, and energetic, were succeeded by a foreign race ; while the inhabitants of towns sunk in vice and idleness, or perished in want, amidst the riches they had themselves created.

It was into this Italy, such as despotism had made it, that the barbarians penetrated. Eager for the booty which it contained and could not defend, they repeatedly ravaged it during the last two centuries of the western empire. The mercenary troops that Rome had levied amongst them for its defence, preferring pillage to pay, frequently turned their arms against those they were engaged to defend. They vied with the Romans in making and unmaking emperors ; and generally chose them from their own ranks, in order to secure to the soldier a greater share of the property of the citizen. The booty diminished as the avidity of these foreigners increased. The pomp of the western empire soon appeared, to an army thus formed, an useless expense. Odoacer, of the nation of the Heruli, chief of the mercenaries who then served in Italy, suppressed it by deposing, in 476, the last emperor. He took upon himself the title of king, and distributed amongst his soldiers one-third of the land in the most fertile provinces : he governed during seventeen years this still glorious country, as a rich farm which the barbarians had a right to cultivate for their sole use.

The mercenaries united under the sceptre of Odoacer were not sufficiently strong to defend Italy against a new invasion of barbarians. The Ostrogoths, encouraged by the Grecian sovereign of new Rome, the emperor of the east, arrived in 489, under the command of Theodoric, from the countries north of the Euxine to the borders of Italy : they completed the conquest of it in four, and retained possession of the Peninsula sixty-four years, under eight successive kings. These new barbarians, in their turn, demanded and obtained a portion of land and slaves: they multiplied, it is true ; but became rapidly enervated in a delicious climate, where they had suddenly passed from the severest privations to the enjoyment of every luxury. They were at last conquered and subdued, in the year 553, by the Romans of Constantinople, whom they despised as the degenerate successors of the same nation which their ancestors had vanquished.

The invasion of the Lombards, in 568, soon followed the destruction of the monarchy of the Ostrogoths. Amongst the various hordes which issued from the north of Germany upon the southern regions, the Lombards were reputed the most courageous, the most cruel, and the proudest of their independence ; but their number was inconsiderable, and they scarcely acknowledged any social tie sufficient to keep them united : accordingly, they never completed the conquest of Italy. From 568 to 774, twenty-one Lombard kings, during 206 years, succeeded each other without establishing their dominion either on the Lagunes, at the extremity of the Adriatic gulf, where such of the inhabitants of upper Italy as were personally the most exposed had taken refuge and founded the Venetian republic ; or on the shores of the Adriatic, now called Romagna, governed by a lieutenant of the emperor of Constantinople, under the title of exarch of the five cities of Pentapolis ; or on Rome, de-fended only by the spiritual arms of the patriarch of the western church ; or on the southern coast, where the Greek municipalities of Naples, Gaëta, and Amalfi governed themselves almost as independent republics. The Lombards, nevertheless, founded a kingdom in northern Italy, of which Pavia was the capital ; and in southern Italy the duchy of Beneventum, which still maintained its independence two centuries after the kingdom was subjugated.

From the middle of the eighth century the Lombards, masters of a country where the great towns still con-tained much wealth, where the land had lost nothing of its fertility, where the example of the vanquished had taught the vanquishers the advantage of reviving some agricultural industry, excited the envy of their neigh-bours the Franks, who had conquered and oppressed the Gauls, who despised all occupation but war, and desired no wealth but what the sword could give. They by repeated invasions devastated Italy ; and at length, in 774, completed the destruction of the Lombard monarchy. For more than twenty years the popes or bishops of Rome had been in the habit of opposing the kings of France to the monarchs of Lombardy, who were odious to them, at first as pagans, and afterwards as heretics. Chief of the clergy of the ancient capital, where the power of the emperors of Constantinople had been nominally established but never felt, they confounded their pretensions with those of the empire; and the Lombards having recently conquered the exarchate of Ravenna, and the Pentapolis, they demanded that these provinces should be restored to Rome. The Frank kings made themselves the champions of this quarrel, which gave them an opportunity of conquering the Lombard monarchy; but Charles, the king who accomplished this conquest, and who was the greatest man that barbarism ever produced, in treating with Rome, in subjugating Italy, comprehended all the beauty of a civilisation which his predecessors had seen only to destroy: he conceived the lofty idea of profiting by the barbarian force at his disposal to put himself at the head of the civilisation which he laboured to restore. Instead of considering himself as the king of the conquerors, occupied only in enriching a barbarous army with the spoils of the vanquished, he made it his duty and his glory to govern the country for its best interests, and for the common good: he did more. In concert with Pope Leo III., he re-established the monarchy of the conquered as a western Roman empire, which he considered the representative of right, in opposition to barbaric force: he received from the same pope, and from the Roman people, on Christmas-day in the year 800, the title of Roman emperor, and the name of Charlemagne, or Charles the Great, which no one before had ever so well deserved. As king, and afterwards as emperor, he governed Italy, together with his other vast states, forty years: he pursued with constancy, and with increasing ability, the end he proposed to himself, viz., establishing the reign of the laws, and a flourishing civilisation: but barbarism was too strong for him; and when he died, in 814, it was re-established throughout the empire.

Italy had eight kings of the family of Charlemagne, reckoning his son and grandson, who reigned under him, and were, properly speaking, his lieutenants. Charles le Gros, great grandson of Charlemagne, was deposed in 888; after which ten sovereigns, either Italian or Burgundian, but allied to the race of the Franks, disputed, for seventy years more, the crown of Italy and the empire. In 951, Otho I. of Saxony, king of Germany, forced Berenger II., who then reigned, to acknowledge

himself his vassal: in 961, Otho entered Italy a second
time with his Germans, was crowned at Rome with the
title of emperor, and sent Berenger II. to end his days in
a fortress in Germany.

Thus, nearly five centuries elapsed from the fall of the
ancient Roman empire to the passing over of the renewed
empire to the Germans. For a long space of time Italy
had been pillaged and oppressed, in turn, by barbarians
of every denomination, who wantonly overran the country
only to plunder, and believed themselves valiant because,
though in small numbers, they spread terror over a vast
extent, and imagined by bloodshed to give a dignity to
their depredations. The country, thus exposed to so
many outrages, did not remain such as the Romans had
left it. The Goth, Lombard, Frank, and German warriors,
who had successively invaded Italy, introduced several of
the opinions and sentiments of the barbarian race, particularly the habit of independence and resistance to authority.
They divided with their kings the country conquered by
their valour. They caused to be ceded to them vast
districts, the inhabitants of which they considered their
property equally with the land. The Lombard monarchy
comprehended thirty dukedoms, or marquisates; their
number diminished under Charlemagne and his successors: but, at the same time, there rose under them
a numerous class of counts and *vavasors*, amongst whom
every duke divided the province that had been ceded to
him, under condition that they should swear fealty and
homage, and follow him to the wars. The counts, in
their turn, divided among the warriors attached to their
colours the land apportioned to them. Thus was the
feudal system, which made the possession of land the
warrior's pay, and constituted an hereditary subordination, founded on interest and confirmed by oath, from
the king down to the lowest soldier, established at the
same time throughout Europe. The Lombards had carried
into Italy the first germs of this system, which had been
developed by the Franks, and invigorated by the civil
wars of Charlemagne and his successors: these wars
rendered it necessary that every feudatory should fortify
his dwelling to preserve his allegiance to his lord; and
the country, which till then had been open, and without

defence, became covered with castles, in which these
feudal lords established their residence.

About the same time,—that is to say, in the ninth
century,—cities began to rebuild their ancient walls; for
the barbarian kings who had everywhere levelled these
walls to the ground no longer opposed their reconstruction,
the danger of being daily invaded by the rival princes who
disputed the throne made them necessary; besides, at
this epocha new swarms of barbarians from all parts
infested Europe; the inhabitants of Scandinavia, under
the name of Danes and Normans, ravaged England and
France; the Hungarians devastated Germany and Upper
Italy; the Saracens, masters of Africa, infested the
southern coasts of Italy and the isles: conquest was
not the purpose of any of these invaders; plunder and
massacre were their only objects. Permission to guard
themselves against continual outrages could not be withheld from the inhabitants of towns. Several thousand
citizens had often been obliged to pay ransom to little
more than a hundred robbers: but, from the time they
were permitted by their emperors to rebuild their walls,
to purchase or manufacture arms, they felt themselves in
a state to make themselves respected. Their long suffering
had hardened them, had accustomed them to privations
and danger, and had taught them it was better to defend
their lives than yield them up to every contemptible
aggressor; at the same time, the population of cities, no
longer living in idleness at the expense of the provinces
of the empire, addicted themselves to industry for their
own profit: they had, accordingly, some wealth to defend.
The ancient curiæ and municipalities had been retained
in all the towns of Italy by their barbarian masters, in
order to distribute more equally the burdens imposed by
the conquerors, and reach individuals more surely. The
magistrates were the chiefs of a people who demanded
only bread, arms, and walls.

From the time when towns were secured by walls, their
power rapidly increased; the oppressed from all parts
sought refuge in them from the oppressors: they carried
with them their industry, and arms to protect the walls
that defended them. Everywhere they were sure of a
good reception; for every city felt it had strength only

in proportion to the number of its citizens: each vied with its neighbour in efforts to augment the means of defence, and in the reception given to strangers. The smaller towns imitated the greater, the villages those in their turn; and each had a castle, or at least a tower, where the population, in case of a sudden attack, might retire with the most precious of their effects.

In the mean time the dukes, marquisses, counts, and prelates, who looked on these cities as their property, on the inhabitants as men who belonged to them, and laboured only for their use, soon perceived that these citizens were ill disposed to obey, and would not suffer themselves to be despoiled; since they had arms, and could defend themselves under the protection of their walls: residence in towns thus became disagreeable to the nobles, and they left them to establish themselves in their castles. They became sensible that to defend these castles they had need of men devoted to them; that, notwithstanding the advantage which their heavy armour gave them when fighting on horseback, they were the minority; and they hastened to enfranchise the rural population, to encourage their growth, to give them arms, and to endeavour to gain their affections. The effect of this change of rule was rapid: the rural population in the tenth and eleventh centuries increased, doubled, quadrupled in exact proportion to the land which they had to cultivate.

Otho I., his son Otho II., and his grandson Otho III., were successively acknowledged emperors and kings of Italy, from 961 to 1002. When this branch of the house of Saxony became extinct, Henry II. of Bavaria, and Conrad the Salic of Franconia, filled the throne from 1004 to 1039. During this period of nearly eighty years, the German emperors twelve times entered Italy at the head of their armies, which they always drew up in the plains of Roncaglia near Placentia: there they held the states of Lombardy, received homage from their Italian feudatories, caused the rents due to be paid, and promulgated laws for the government of Italy. A foreign sovereign, however, almost always absent, known only by his incursions at the head of a barbarous army, could not efficaciously govern a country which he hardly knew, and where his yoke was detested. During these five reigns, the social power became more and more weak in Italy. The emperors were too happy to acknowledge the local authorities, whatever they were, whenever they could obtain from them their pecuniary dues: sometimes they were dukes or marquisses, whose dignities had survived the disasters of various invasions and of civil wars; sometimes the archbishops and bishops of great cities, whom Charlemagne and his successors had frequently invested with duchies and counties escheated to the crown, reckoning that lords elected for life would remain more dependent than hereditary lords; sometimes, finally, they were the magistrates themselves, who, although elected by the people, received from the monarch the title of imperial vicars, and took part with the nobles and prelates in the *Plaids* (Placita), or diets of Roncaglia.

After a stay of some months, the emperor returned with his army into Germany; the nobles retired to their castles, the prelates and magistrates to their cities: neither of these last acknowledged a superior authority to their own, nor reckoned on any other force than what they could themselves employ to assert what they called their rights. Opposite interests could not fail to produce collision, and the war was universal. In the time of Conrad the Salic, the prelates almost throughout Lombardy joined the cities against the nobles; and from 1035 to 1039 there was a general war between these two orders of society. Conrad put an end to it, by a constitution which is considered to be the basis of feudal law. By this the inheritance of fiefs was protected from the caprices of the lords and of the crown,—the most oppressive conditions of feudal dependence were suppressed or softened,—and the few remaining slaves of the land were set free.

The crown of Conrad the Salic passed in a direct line to his son, grandson, and great-grandson. The first, Henry III., reigned from 1039 to 1056; the second, Henry IV., from 1056 to 1106; the third, Henry V., from 1106 to 1125. The last two reigns were troubled by the bloody quarrel between the Empire and the court of Rome, called the war of investitures. Rome had never made part of the monarchy of the Lombards. This ancient capital of the world, with the territory appertaining to it, had, since the conquest of Alboin, formed a dukedom, governed by a patrician or Greek duke, sent from Constantinople. The bishop of Rome, however, who, according to the ancient canonical forms, was elected by the clergy, the senate, and the people of his diocese, had much more authority over his flock than this foreign magistrate. He considered himself, too, as patriarch of the West, and the head of all the Latin churches. This authority, it is true, was not indisputably acknowledged by orthodox prelates ; and the barbarians, who professed either paganism or Arianism, held it in contempt. The pontiff, however, who now began to take exclusively the name of Pope, had more than once successfully defended Rome with his spiritual arms when temporal ones had failed. When, in the year 717, an *iconoclast*, or enemy of images, filled the throne of Constantinople, the popes, under the pretence of heresy, rejected his authority altogether : a municipality, at the head of which were a senate and consuls, then governed Rome nearly as an independent state ; the Greeks, occupied with their own dissensions, seemed to forget it ; and Rome owed to this forgetfulness fifty years of a sort of liberty. The Romans found once more a faint image of their past glory : sometimes even the title of Roman republic was revived. They approved, notwithstanding, of pope Stephen II. conferring on the princes of the Franks the dignity of patricians, in order to transfer to them the authority which the Greek magistrate exercised in their city in the name of the emperor of Constantinople ; and the people gladly acquiesced when, in the year 800, Leo III. crowned Charlemagne as Augustus, and restorer of the western empire. From that period Rome became once more the capital of the empire. At Rome the chiefs of the empire were henceforth to receive the golden crown from the hands of the pope, after having received the silver one of the kingdom of Germany at Aix-la-Chapelle, and the iron crown of Lombardy at Milan.

Great wealth and much feudal power were, by the gratitude of the emperors, attached to the see of Rome. The papacy became the highest object of ambition to the whole sacerdotal order ; and, in an age of violence and anarchy, barons notorious for their robberies, and young libertines recommended only by the favour of some Roman ladies, not unfrequently filled the pontifical chair. The other bishops selected were often no better. The German emperors, on arriving at Rome, were sometimes obliged to put an end to such a scandal, and choose among the competitors, or depose a pope who put all Christendom to the blush. Henry III. obliged the people to renounce the right which they had hitherto exercised, and so greatly abused, to take part in the election of popes. He named, himself, four successively, whom he chose among the most learned and the most pious of the clergy of Italy and Germany; and thus powerfully seconded the spirit of reform which began to animate the church from the eleventh century.

Amidst the convulsions to which society was exposed, the wealth of the clergy had remained intact. The kings whom it tempted dared not seize it for themselves; but they distributed it, with the dignities of the church, among their favourites—their creatures,—servile priests, who had nothing ecclesiastical but the name. These promotions excited a general clamour. Religious men pretended that kings introduced corruption into the body of the clergy—that they destroyed the independence which ought to belong to the ministers of God. An ardent desire to purify the priesthood, by preventing these dignities from being distributed in purely temporal views, was manifested; but it belonged to one of the greatest characters produced in the middle age to agitate all Christendom for the attainment of this end.

Hildebrand, born at Soana, in Tuscany, a man of the most obscure condition, but from the moment when he entered into orders distinguished for his talents, was sent by his convent to pursue his studies at Cluny, in France. He conceived, in his solitude, the plan of revolution, by which he proposed to himself the subjugation of the world to the sacerdotal power. In the universe he saw but God, the priest his sole minister, and mankind obedient. He designed that the whole priesthood should be moved by one single will, should know only one passion—that of establishing the power of Heaven. The whole church appeared to him corrupted: he undertook to reform it in its head, in its members, in the whole body of the faithful under its control. He anathematised all intervention of the secular power in the distribution of the dignities of the church; it was, he said, simony—making a commerce of the gifts of the Holy Spirit. The crime was the same, whether the people in their public assemblies, or nobles, or kings, took part in the election of prelates, or attempted to confer on them the investiture of even the temporal power attached to their bishoprics. In 1059, he obtained of the council of Lateran that the election of popes should be vested in the cardinals; and the nomination of all prelates in the chapters, jointly with the pope. To detach the clergy from human society, he proscribed and punished with severity the marriage of priests, which, till then, had been permitted or tolerated by some provincial councils, particularly in Lombardy. Finally, concentrating all the power of the church in the pope, he taught the priests to consider him as an unerring being, who became holy by his election—who could alone name and depose bishops—assemble, preside over, and dissolve councils: he was, he said, in short, a god upon earth—absolute master of all princes, who were bound to kiss his feet, and whom he could depose at will, by releasing their subjects from their oaths of fidelity.

Hildebrand accomplished, at least for a time, the immense revolution which he had undertaken: he changed the spirit of the popedom, of the clergy, and the people; and he enslaved kings. He procured, by his influence, the election of the four popes who preceded him in the chair of St. Peter, which he ascended himself in the year 1073, taking the name of Gregory VII. The popes his successors continued, after his death in 1085, to act upon his maxims, and seemed as if still animated by his spirit. Nevertheless, he experienced from the clergy, above all from those of Lombardy, a prodigious resistance. He tormented Italy and Germany with a constant civil war; he called in against Rome the Normans, who burnt the city, and sold almost all the inhabitants into slavery; he compelled his heroic rival, the emperor Henry IV., to do penance before him in the open court of Canosa, whilst the ground was covered with snow; he obliged him to remain three days and three nights in the habit of a penitent, barefooted and fasting, before he would grant him

absolution. The successors of Gregory VII. excited the
two sons of Henry IV. successively to revolt against him,
and depose him. Henry soon died of a broken heart.
Henry V., the second of these unnatural children, whose
cause the pope had espoused, after having obtained the
crown by the aid of the priests, became their enemy in
his turn. During sixteen years he made war against the
church, to maintain the independence of the imperial
crown, and the rights of secular sovereigns over the fiefs
held by the clergy. The people at length, wearied and
exhausted, forced these two rival powers to an agreement,
in which the rights of both were curtailed. In the diet
of Worms, 1122, the emperor abandoned to the pope the
investiture of bishops by the ring and crosier; while he
reserved to himself the transmission of the regal rights
attached to each bishopric by the concession of the sceptre.
These were only exterior ceremonies; in fact, the people
alone were deprived of their rights in the choice of their
pastor. Sovereigns retained almost exclusively the nomination of prelates in their respective dominions.

The war of investitures, which lasted more than sixty
years, accomplished the dissolution of every tie between
the different members of the kingdom of Italy. Civil
wars have at least this advantage,—that they force the
rulers of the people to consult the wishes of their subjects,
oblige them to gain affections which constitute their
strength, and to compensate, by the granting of new
privileges, the services which they require. The prelates,
nobles, and cities of Italy obeyed, some the emperor,
others the pope; not from a blind fear, but from choice,
from affection, from conscience, according as the political
or religious sentiment was predominant in each. The
war was general, but every where waged with the national
forces. Every city armed its militia, which, headed by
the magistrates, attacked the neighbouring nobles or towns
of a contrary party. While each city imagined it was fighting either for the pope or the emperor, it was habitually
impelled exclusively by its own sentiments: every town
considered itself as a whole, as an independent state, which
had its own allies and enemies; each citizen felt an ardent
patriotism, not for the kingdom of Italy, or for the empire,
but for his own city.

At the period when either kings or emperors had granted to towns the right of raising fortifications, that of assembling the citizens at the sound of a great bell, to concert together the means of their common defence, had been also conceded. This meeting of all the men of the state capable of bearing arms was called a *parliament*. It assembled in the great square, and elected annually two consuls, charged with the administration of justice at home, and the command of the army abroad. The militia of every city was divided into separate bodies, according to local partitions, each led by a *gonfaloniere*, or standard bearer. They fought on foot, and assembled round the *carroccio*, a heavy car drawn by oxen, and covered with the flags and armorial bearings of the city. A high pole rose in the middle of this car, bearing the colours and a Christ, which seemed to bless the army, with both arms extended. A priest said daily mass at an altar placed in the front of the car. The trumpeters of the community, seated on the back part, sounded the charge and the retreat. It was Heribert archbishop of Milan, contemporary of Conrad the Salic, who invented this car in imitation of the ark of alliance, and caused it to be adopted at Milan. All the free cities of Italy followed the example : this sacred car, intrusted to the guardianship of the militia, gave them weight and confidence. The nobles who committed themselves in the civil wars, and were obliged to have recourse to the protection of towns, where they had been admitted into the first order of citizens, formed the only cavalry.

The parliament, which named the consuls, appointed also a secret council, called a *Consilio di Credenza*, to assist the government, composed of a few members taken from each division; besides a grand council of the people, who prepared the decisions to be submitted to the parliament. The *Consilio di Credenza* was, at the same time, charged with the administration of the finances, consisting chiefly of entrance duties collected at the gates of the city, and voluntary contributions asked of the citizens in moments of danger. As industry had rapidly increased, and had preceded luxury,—as domestic life was sober, and the produce of labour considerable,—wealth had greatly augmented. The citizens allowed themselves no other use of their riches than that of defending or embellishing their country. It was from the year 900 to the year 1200 that the most prodigious works were undertaken and accomplished by the towns of Italy. They began by surrounding themselves with thick walls, ditches, towers, and counter guards at the gates; immense works, which a patriotism ready for every sacrifice could alone accomplish. The maritime towns at the same time constructed their ports, quays, canals, and custom-houses, which served also as vast magazines for commerce. Every city built public palaces for the *Signoria*, or municipal magistrates, and prisons; and constructed also temples, which to this day fill us with admiration by their grandeur and magnificence. These three regenerating centuries gave an impulse to architecture, which soon awakened the other fine arts.

The republican spirit which now fermented in every city, and gave to each of them constitutions so wise, magistrates so zealous, and citizens so patriotic, and so capable of great achievements, had found in Italy itself the models which had contributed to its formation. The war of investitures gave wing to this universal spirit of liberty and patriotism in all the municipalities of Lombardy, in Piedmont, Venetia, Romagna, and Tuscany. But there existed already in Italy other free cities, of which the experience had been sufficiently long to prove that a petty people finds, in its complete union and devotion to the common cause, a strength often wanting in great states. The free cities which flourished in the eleventh century rose from the ruins of the western empire; as those in Italy which preceded them in the career of liberty rose from the ruins of the empire of the East.

When the Greeks resigned to the Lombards Italy, which a few years before they had conquered from the Ostrogoths, they still preserved several isolated ports and fortified places along the coast. Venice, at the extremity of the Adriatic; Ravenna, at the south of the mouth of the Po; Genoa, at the foot of the Ligurian mountains; Pisa, towards the mouths of the Arno; Rome, Gaëta, Naples, Amalfi, Bari, were either never conquered by the Lombards, or in subjection too short a time to have lost their ancient walls, and the habit of guarding them. These cities served as the refuge of Roman civilisation. All those who had preserved any fortune, independence of mind, or hatred of oppression, assembled in them to concert the means of resisting the insolence of their barbarian masters. The Grecian empire maintained itself at Constantinople in all its ancient pride; but, with oriental apathy, it regarded these remains as still representing its province of Italy, while it did nothing for their defence. From time to time, a duke, an exarch, a patrician, a catapan, or other magistrate, was sent, with a title announcing the highest pretensions, but unaccompanied by any real force. The citizens of these towns demanded money and soldiers to repair and defend their fortifications; whilst the emperors, on the contrary, demanded that the money and soldiers of Italy should be sent to Constantinople. After some disputes, the Greek government found it prudent to abandon the question, and shut its eyes on the establishment of a liberty which it despised, but which perhaps might be useful in the defence of these distant possessions; finally, the magistrates, whom these towns themselves nominated, became the acknowledged depositories of the imperial authority. The disposal of their own money and soldiers was allowed them, on condition that nothing should be demanded of the emperors, who were satisfied to see their names at the head of every act, and their image on the coin, without exacting other acts of submission. This policy was not, however, exactly followed with respect to Ravenna, or afterwards to Bari. In these cities the representative of the emperor had fixed his residence with a Greek garrison. Ravenna, as well as the cities appertaining to it, denominated the Pentapolis, was conquered by the Lombards between 720 and 730. Bari became then the capital of the *thema* of Lombardy, which extended over a great part of Apulia. We have already shown how Rome passed from the Greek to the western empire: we suspect, rather than know, that Genoa and Pisa, after having been occupied by the Lombards, preserved their relations with Constantinople. The *pallium*, or silk flag, presented for some time to the emperors, was considered by them as a sort of tribute; but Venice on the upper sea, Gaëta, Naples, and Amalfi, on the lower, advanced more openly to independence.

From the invasion by Attila in 452, the marshes called *Lagune*, formed at the extremity of the Adriatic by the slime deposed by seven or eight great rivers, amidst which arose innumerable islands, had been the refuge of all the rich inhabitants of Padua, Vicenza, Verona, Treviso, and other great cities of Venetia, who fled from the sabres of the Huns. The Roman empire of the west survived this great calamity twenty-four years; but it was only a period of expiring agony, during which fresh disasters continually forced new refugees to establish themselves in the *Lagune*. A numerous population was at length formed there, supported by fishing, the making of salt, some other manufactories, and the commerce carried on by means of these many rivers. Beyond the reach of the barbarians, who had no vessels, forgotten by the Romans, and their successors the Ostrogoths, they maintained their independence under the administration of tribunes, named by an assembly of the people in each of the separate isles. The Venetians looked upon the Ostrogoths, and their successors the Lombards, as heretics; so that religious zeal strengthened their aversion to the dominant powers of Italy. On the other hand, the population of each island forming a little separate republic, jealousies arose; their tribunes disagreed. To put an end to these factions, the citizens of every island met in a single assembly at Heraclea in 697, and elected a chief of maritime Venetia, whom they called doge, or duke. This title, borne by the Greek governors of the provinces of Italy, seems to indicate that the doge was considered a lieutenant of the emperor of Constantinople. The Venetians, in fact, persisting in regarding themselves as members of the eastern empire, never acknowledged the pretensions of Charlemagne and his successors to the dominion of all Italy. It was in 809, in a war against Pepin, son of Charlemagne, that the Venetians made choice of the island of the Rialto, near which they assembled their fleet, with their wealth collected on board, and built the city of Venice, the capital of their republic. Twenty years afterwards they transported thither, from Alexandria, the body of St. Mark, the evangelist. They chose him patron of their state. His lion figured in their arms, and his name in their language, whenever they would designate with peculiar affection their country or government.

While the Venetians disputed with the Lombards, the Frank and the German emperors, the little land on which stood their houses, they had also to dispute the sea that bathed them with the Slavonians, who had established themselves for the purpose of piracy on the eastern side of the Adriatic. Amidst them, on the same coast, several little cities inhabited by Greeks, but forgotten by the empire, endeavoured in vain to defend their liberties and municipal governments. In 997, these small towns of Istria and Dalmatia made alliance with Venice; consented to receive judges chosen by the doge, and to fight under his banner. With their aid Venice vanquished the pirates of Narenta and Croatia; and the doge from that period took the title of duke of Venice and Dalmatia.

The first magistrate of the republics of Naples, Gaëta, and Amalfi bore likewise the title of doge. These three cities, forgotten by the Greek emperors, and receiving no aid from them, still held by the ties of commerce to Greece. The inhabitants had devoted themselves with ardour to navigation; they trafficked in the Levant, and covered southern Italy with its rich merchandise. The country situated beyond the Tiber had been exposed to fewer invasions than upper Italy. It had not, however, entirely escaped. A Lombard chief entered it in 589, and founded the great duchy of Benevento, which comprehended nearly the whole southern part of the peninsula. This dukedom maintained itself independent of the kingdom of the Lombards at Pavia, and had not been involved in its fall. It defended itself with valour against Charlemagne and his successors, who attempted its conquest; but in 839, at the end of a civil war, it was divided into the three principalities of Benevento, Salerno, and Capua. The Saracens had established colonies, in the year 828, in Sicily, which till then had been subject to the Greek empire: these Saracens, a few years afterwards, passed into southern Italy. The three republics of Naples, Gaëta, and Amalfi preserved their independence by exciting enmity between the Lombards and Saracens,

who equally menaced them ; but these barbarians soon
sank into the languor produced by the charms of a
southern climate.   It seemed as if they had no longer
courage to risk a life to which so many enjoyments were
attached.   When they fought it was with effeminacy ;
and they hastened the termination of every war, to plunge
again into the voluptuous ease from which it had roused
them.   The citizens of the republics had the advantage
over them of walls and defiles ; and, without being braver
than the Lombards, maintained their independence against
them for six centuries.

Southern Italy, till the year 1000, was disturbed only
by the petty wars between the Lombard principalities,
the republics under the protection of the Greek empire,
the *catapans* of Bari, and the wandering bands of Mussulmans, whom love of plunder more than religious zeal had
brought into Italy.   But about this epoch their arrived
at Salerno, and afterwards in Apulia, Norman adventurers, the second or third generation of those terrible
Danish corsairs who had so long and so cruelly ravaged
France, and who were already, in 912, established in
Neustria, where they adopted Christianity and the French
language.   They retained the valour of their ancestors,
their love of adventure, and passion for voyages.   They
first came in great numbers to visit as pilgrims the
sanctuaries of southern Italy, and afterwards entered as
soldiers into the armies either of the princes of Lombardy,
the republics, or the Greeks of Bari, who had recently
reconquered the whole of Apulia.   They proved so
superior in valour to all those to whom they were
opposed, that these mercenaries soon made all the small
states, among which they had come to seek adventures,
tremble.   In 1041, they conquered Apulia from the
Greeks ; in 1060, Calabria ; from 1061 to 1090, Sicily :
about the same time they subjugated the three Lombard
principalities of Beneventum, Salerno, and Capua.   The
three republics were the last states in southern Italy
which fell under the Norman yoke.   We do not, indeed,
know the date of the conquest of Gaëta, the records of
the history of the town being very scanty.   But Amalfi,
illustrious for the foundation, in the Holy Land, of the
hospital and military order of St. John of Jerusalem, for

the invention of the compass, and for the preservation of
the pandects of Justinian, surrendered to the Normans in
1131.   The leader of these last was then Roger II.; to
whom the antipope Anacletus had, the preceding year,
given the title of king of the Two Sicilies.   Roger
besieged, in 1138, the city of Naples; which though, in
turns, succoured by the emperor of Germany and the
republic of Pisa, was compelled also to surrender.

The republic of Pisa, which vainly sought to save from
ruin these first Italian republics of the middle ages, was
a city which navigation and commerce had enriched.
Genoa, which soon became its rival, had escaped the
pillage of these northern conquerors, and had preserved
a constant intercourse with Constantinople and with
Syria; from whence the citizens brought the rich merchandise which they afterwards dispersed throughout
Lombardy.   The Pisans and Genoese, invigorated by
a seafaring life, were accustomed to defend with the
sword the merchandise which they conveyed from one
extremity to the other of the Mediterranean.   They were
often in conflict with the Saracens, like them addicted to
maritime commerce, to which these last frequently added
piracy.   The Saracens pillaged Genoa in the year 936.
In 1005 they entered a suburb of Pisa; and again
invested that city in the year 1012.   Their colonies in Sardinia, Corsica, and the Balearic Isles, constantly menaced
Italy.   The Pisans, seconded by the Genoese, in their
turn attacked Sardinia, in the year 1017; but completed
the conquest only in 1050.   They established colonies
there, and divided it into fiefs, between the most illustrious families of Pisa and Genoa.   They also conquered
the Balearic Isles from the Saracens, in the year 1113.

When, towards the end of the eleventh century, the
western world took up the dispute with the Saracens for
the sepulchre of Jesus Christ, Venice, Pisa, and Genoa
had already reached a high point of commercial power;
these three cities had more vessels on the Mediterranean
than the whole of Christendom besides.   They seconded
the Crusaders with enthusiasm.   They provisioned them
when arrived off the coast of Syria, and kept up their
communication with the west.   The Venetians assert
that they sent a fleet of 200 vessels, in the year 1099, to

second the first crusade. The Pisans affirm that their archbishop Daimbert, who was afterwards patriarch of Jerusalem, passed into the east with 120 vessels. The Genoese claim only twenty-eight galleys and six vessels: but all concurred with equal zeal in the conquest of the Holy Land; and the three maritime republics obtained important privileges, which they preserved as long as the kingdom of Jerusalem lasted.

Such were the changes which the space of six centuries from the fall of the Roman empire accomplished in Italy. Towards the end of the fifth century, the social tie, which had made of the empire one body, became dissolved, and was succeeded by no other. The citizen felt nothing for his fellow-citizen; he expected no support from him, and offered him none. He could nowhere invoke protection; he every where saw only violence and oppression. Towards the beginning of the twelfth century, the citizens of the towns of Italy had as little to expect from abroad. The emperor of the Germans, who called himself their sovereign, was, with his barbarian army, only one enemy more. But universally, where the circle of the same wall formed a common interest, the spirit of association was developed. The citizens promised each other mutual assistance. Courage grew with liberty; and the Italians, no longer oppressed, found at last in themselves their own defence.

CHAPTER II

FREDERICK BARBAROSSA ENDEAVOURS TO ABRIDGE THE LIBERTIES
OF THE TOWNS OF ITALY—THEIR RESISTANCE—THE LEAGUE OF
LOMBARDY—TRUCE OF VENICE—AND PEACE OF CONSTANCE—
WHICH FIXES THEIR RIGHTS

WHEN the inhabitants of the cities of Italy associated for their common defence, their first necessity was to guard against the brigandage of the barbarian armies, which invaded their country and treated them as enemies; the second, to protect themselves from the robberies of other barbarians who called themselves their masters. Their united efforts soon ensured their safety; in a few years they found themselves rich and powerful; and these same men, whom emperors, prelates, and nobles considered only as freed serfs, perceived that they constituted almost the only public force in Italy. Their self-confidence grew with their power; and the desire of domination succeeded that of independence. Those cities which had accumulated the most wealth, whose walls enclosed the greatest population, attempted, from the first half of the twelfth century, to secure by force of arms the obedience of such of the neighbouring towns as did not appear sufficiently strong to resist them. These greater cities had no intention to strip the smaller of their liberty; their sole purpose was to force them into a perpetual alliance, so as to share their good or evil fortune, and always place their armed force under the standard of the dominant city.

The long war of the *investitures*, between the Franconian emperors and the popes, had given the first impulse to this ambition : as general interests were involved, as it was a question of distant operations and common danger, the cities felt the necessity of alliances, and of an active correspondence, which soon extended from one extremity of Italy to the other. The smaller towns soon found that this general policy was beyond their means, and that the great cities, in which commerce and wealth had accumulated knowledge, and which alone received the communications of the pope or of the emperor, naturally placed themselves at the head of the league formed in their provinces, either for the empire or for the church. These two leagues were not yet known in Italy by the names of Guelph and Ghibeline, which in Germany had been the war-cry of the two parties at the battle of Winsberg, fought on the 21st of December, 1140, and which had previously distinguished, the former the dukes of Saxony and Bavaria, devoted to the pope ; the latter, the emperors of the house of Franconia. But although these two names, which seem since to have become exclusively Italian, had not yet been adopted in Italy, the hereditary affection respectively for the two parties already divided the minds of the people for more than a century, and faction became to each a second country, often served by them with not less heroism and devotion than their native city.

Two great towns in the plains of Lombardy surpassed every other in power and wealth: Milan, which habitually directed the party of the church; and Pavia, which directed that of the empire. Both towns, however, seem to have changed parties during the reigns of Lothario III. and Conrad II., who, from the year 1125 to 1152, placed in opposition the two houses of Guelphs and Ghibelines in Germany. Milan, having during the first half of the twelfth century experienced some resistance from the towns of Lodi and Como, rased the former, 'dispersing the inhabitants in open villages, and obliged the latter to destroy its fortifications. Cremona and Novara adhered to the party of Pavia; Tortona, Crema, Bergamo, Brescia, Placentia, and Parma, to that of Milan. Among the towns of Piedmont, Turin took the lead, and disputed the authority of the counts of Savoy, who called themselves imperial vicars in that country. Montferrat continued to have its marquises. They were among the few great feudatories who had survived the civil wars; but the towns and provinces were not in subjection to them, and Asti was more powerful than they were. The family of the Veronese marquises, on the contrary, who from the time of the Lombard kings had to defend the frontier against the Germans, were extinct; and the great cities of Verona, Padua, Vicenza, Treviso, and Mantua, nearly equal in power, maintained their independence. Bologna held the first rank among the towns south of the Po, and had become equally formidable on the one side to Modena and Reggio, and on the other to Ferrara, Ravenna, Imola, Faenza, Forli, and Rimini. Tuscany, which had also had its powerful marquises, saw their family become extinct with the countess Matilda, the contemporary and friend of Gregory VII. Florence had since risen in power, destroyed Fiesole, and, without exercising dominion over the neighbouring towns of Pistoja, Arezzo, San Miniato, and Volterra, or the more distant towns of Lucca, Cortona, Perugia, and Sienna, was considered the head of the Tuscan league; and the more so that Pisa at this period thought only of her maritime expeditions. The family of the dukes of Spoleto had also become extinct, and the towns of Ombria regained their freedom; but their situation in the mountains prevented them from rising into importance. In fine, Rome herself indulged the same spirit of independence. An eloquent monk, the disciple of Abelard, who had made himself known throughout Europe, preached in 1139 a twofold reform, in the religious and political orders; the name borne by him was Arnold of Brescia. He spoke to men of the antique liberty which was their right; of the abuses which disfigured the church. Driven out of Italy by pope Innocent II. and the council of Lateran, he took refuge in Switzerland, and taught the town of Zurich to frame a free constitution; but in the year 1143 he was recalled to Rome, and that city again heard the words " Roman republic," " Roman senate," " comitia of the people." The pope branded his opinions with the name of " heresy of the politicians "; and Arnold of Brescia, having been given up to him by the emperor, was burnt alive before the gate of the castle of St. Angelo, in the year 1155. But his precepts survived, and the love of liberty in Rome did not perish with him. In southern Italy, the conquests of the Normans had finally smothered the spirit of liberty; and the town of Aquila in the Abruzzi alone preserved any republican privileges.

Such was the state of Italy, when the Germanic diet, assembled at Frankfort in 1152, conferred the crown on Frederick Barbarossa, duke of Swabia, and of the house of Hohenstaufen. This prince was nephew to Conrad III., whom he succeeded; he was allied to the two houses of the Guelphs and Ghibelines, which had contended with each other for the empire, and was regarded, with good reason, by the Germans as their most distinguished chief. Frederick Barbarossa was not only brave, but understood the art of war, at least so far as it could be understood in an age so barbarous. He made himself beloved by the soldiers, at the same time that he subjected them to a discipline which others had not yet thought of establishing. He held his word sacred; he abhorred gratuitous cruelty, although the shedding of human blood had in general nothing revolting in it to a prince of the middle ages; but the prerogatives of his crown appeared to him sacred rights, which from pride, and even from conscience, he was disposed to preserve and extend. The Italians he considered in a state of revolt against the imperial

throne and the German nation ; and he believed it to be
his first duty to reduce them to subjection.

Frederick Barbarossa, accordingly, in the month of
October, 1154, entered Italy with a powerful German
army, by the valley of Trent. He proposed to himself
not only receiving there the crowns of Italy and the empire, and reducing to obedience subjects who appeared to
him to forget their duty to their sovereign ; but also to
punish in particular the Milanese for their arrogance ; to
redress the complaints which the citizens of Pavia and
Cremona had brought against them ; and to oblige Milan
to render to the towns of Lodi and Como, which it had
dismantled, all the privileges which Milan itself enjoyed.
On arriving at Roncaglia, where the diets of the kingdom of Italy were held, he was assailed by complaints
from the bishops and nobles against the towns, as well
as by complaints against the Milanese from the consuls
of Pavia, of Cremona, of Como, and of Lodi ; while
those of Crema, of Brescia, of Placentia, of Asti and
Tortona, vindicated them.   Before giving judgment on
the differences submitted to his decision, Frederick
announced his intention of judging for himself the state
of the country, by visiting in person Piedmont and
Montferrat.   Having to pass through the Milanese territory on his way to Novara, he commanded the consuls
of Milan to supply him with provisions on the road.
The towns acknowledged that they owed the emperors
upon their journeys the dues designated by the feudal
words "*foderum, parata, mansionaticum,*" forage, food, and
lodging : but the Germans, retarded in their march by
heavy and continual rain, took two days to reach a stage
which the Milanese supposed they would reach in one :
provisions of course failed ; and [the Germans avenged
themselves on the unhappy inhabitants by pillaging and
burning the villages wherever sufficient rations were not
found.   Frederick treated with kindness the towns of
Novara and Turin ; but those of Chieri and Asti had
been denounced to him as entertaining the same sentiments as Milan ; the inhabitants fled at his approach,
and he plundered and burnt their deserted houses.
Arrived next before Tortona, he ordered the inhabitants
to renounce their alliance with the Milanese ; but they,

trusting to the strength of the upper town, into which they had retreated, while Frederick occupied the lower part, had the courage to refuse. The Germans began the siege of Tortona on the 13th of February, 1155. They could not prevent the entrance of 200 Milanese, to assist in its defence. For sixty-two days did this brave people resist the attacks of the formidable army of Frederick, the numbers of which had been increased by the armed force of Pavia, and the other Ghibeline towns. The want of water compelled them at last to surrender ; and the emperor allowed them to retire to Milan, taking only the few effects which each individual could carry away ; every thing else was given up to the pillage of the soldiers, and the houses became a prey to the flames. The Milanese received with respect these martyrs of liberty, and every opulent house gave shelter and hospitality to some of the unhappy inhabitants of Tortona. Frederick meanwhile placed on his head, in the temple of Pavia, the iron crown of the kings of Lombardy ; and began his march to Rome, to receive there the golden , crown of the empire.

But the Germans who accompanied the emperor, notwithstanding the ardour with which they had undertaken this distant expedition, began to be tired of so long an absence from their home. The licence extended to their pillage and debauchery no longer appeared to them a sufficient compensation for tedious marches and the dangers of war. They pressed the emperor to advance towards Rome, and to avoid all quarrel with the great towns by which they passed, although almost all refused to admit them within their walls,—providing subsistence and lodging for them in the suburbs only. The impossibility of maintaining discipline in a rapacious army, which beheld for the first time the unknown riches of commerce and the arts; the difficulty of avoiding quarrels between two nations, neither of which understood the language of the other, perhaps justified this precaution. Frederick thus passed by Placentia, Parma, Bologna, and Florence. He was not received even into Rome ; his troops occupied what was styled the Leonine city, or the suburb built round the Vatican : he was there crowned by the pope, Adrian IV.; while his army was obliged to repel the Romans who advanced by the bridge of St. Angelo and the *borgo* [1] of Trastevere to disturb the ceremony. Frederick withdrew from Rome the following day ; conducting his army into the mountains, to avoid the great heat of summer. The citizens of Spoleto, not having supplied with sufficient haste the provisions he demanded, he attacked, took, and burnt their city : sickness, however, began to thin the ranks of his soldiers ; many also deserted, to embark at Ancona. Frederick, with a weakened army, directed his march on Germany by the valleys of the Tyrol. The citizens of Verona, who would not admit the Germans within their walls, constructed for him a bridge of boats on the Adige, which he hastily passed over, but had hardly gained the opposite bank, when enormous pieces of wood, carried down by the impetuosity of the current, struck and destroyed the bridge. Frederick had no doubt that the Lombards had laid this snare for him, and flattered themselves with the breaking of the bridge whilst he should be in the act of passing over ; but he was no longer sufficiently strong to avenge himself.

The emperor at length returned into Germany with his barbarian soldiers. He everywhere on his passage spread havoc and desolation ; the line by which he marched through the Milanese territory was marked by fire ; the villages of Rosate, Trecale, and Galiata, the towns of Chieri, Asti, Tortona, and Spoleto were burnt. But whilst he thus proved his barbarism, he also proved his weakness. He did not dare to attack the stronger and more populous cities, which congratulated themselves on having shut their gates, and refused submission to him. Thus a year's campaign sufficed to destroy one of the most formidable armies that Germany had ever poured into Italy ; and the example of ancient times encouraged the belief that it would be long before the emperor could again put the Germans in motion. The Milanese felicitated themselves on having preserved their liberty by their courage and patriotism. Their treasury was indeed empty ; but the zeal of their opulent citizens, who knew no other luxury than that of serving their country, soon

[1] Borgo is the communication between Trastevere and the Vatican.

replenished it. These men, who poured their wealth into
the treasury of the republic, contented themselves with
black bread and cloaks of coarse stuff. At the command
of their consuls, they left Milan to join their fellow-
citizens in rebuilding, with their own hands, the walls
and houses of Tortona, Rosate, Trecale, Galiata, and
other towns, which had suffered in the contest for the
common cause. They next attacked the cities of Pavia,
Cremona, and Novara, which had embraced the party of
the emperor, and subjected them to humiliating conditions; while they drew closer their bonds of alliance
with the towns of Brescia and Placentia, which had
declared for liberty.

But Frederick had more power over Germany than
any of his predecessors : he was regarded there as the
restorer of the rights of the empire and of the German
nation. He obtained credit for reducing Italy from what
was called a state of anarchy and revolt, to order and
obedience. His vassals accordingly flocked with eagerness to his standard, when he summoned them, at the
feast of Pentecost, 1158, to compel the submission of
Italy. The battalions of Germany entered Lombardy at
the same time by all the passes of the Alps. Their
approach to Brescia inspired the inhabitants with so
much terror, that they immediately renounced their
alliance with Milan, and paid down a large sum of
money for their ransom. The Milanese, on the contrary, prepared themselves for resistance. They had
either destroyed or fortified all the bridges of the Adda ;
flattering themselves that this river would suffice to stop
the progress of the emperor; but a body of German
cavalry dashed boldly into the stream, and, swimming
across the river, gained in safety the opposite bank.
They then made themselves masters of the bridge of
Cassano, and the whole army entered into the Milanese
territory. Frederick, following the course of the Adda,
made choice of a situation about four miles from the
ruins of the former Lodi. Here he ordered the people
of Lodi to rebuild their town, which would in future
secure to him the passage of the Adda. He summoned
thither also the militias of Pavia and Cremona, with
those of the other towns of Lombardy, which their

jealousy of Milan had attached to the Ghibeline party;
and it was not till after they had joined him that he
encamped, on the 8th of August, 1158, before Milan.
His engines of war, however, were insufficient to beat
down the walls of so strong and large a town; and he
resolved to reduce the Milanese by famine. He seized
their granaries, burnt their stacks of corn, mowed down
the autumnal harvests, and announced his resolution not
to raise the siege till the Milanese had returned to their
duty. The few nobles, however, who had preserved
their independence in Lombardy proceeded to the camp
of the emperor. One of them, the count de Blandrate,
who had before given proofs of his attachment to the town
of Milan, offered himself as a mediator, was accepted, and
obtained terms not unfavourable to the Milanese. They
engaged to pay a tribute to Frederick of 9000 marks of
silver, to restore to him his legal rights, and to the towns
of Lodi and Como their independence. On their side,
they were dispensed from opening their gates to the
emperor. They preserved the right of electing their
consuls, and included in their pacification their allies of
Tortona and Crema. This treaty was signed the 7th of
September, 1158.

Frederick, in granting an honourable capitulation to
revolted subjects, whom he had brought back to their
obedience, had no intention of renouncing the rights of
his empire. He considered that he had preserved, untouched, the legislative authority of the diet of his kingdom of Italy. The Milanese, on the contrary, regarded
their treaty as definitive; and were both astonished and
indignant when Frederick, having assembled, towards the
11th of November following, the *placita* or diets of the
kingdom at Roncaglia, promulgated by this diet a constitution which overthrew their most precious rights. It
took the administration of justice from the hands of the
consuls of towns, to place it in those of a single judge, and
a foreigner, chosen by the emperor, bearing the name of
podestà; it fixed the limits of the regal rights, giving them
much more importance than had been contemplated by
the Milanese when they agreed to acknowledge them;
it deprived cities, as well as the other members of the
empire, of the right of making private war; it changed

the boundaries of territories appertaining to towns, and in particular took from Milan the little town of Monza, and the counties of Seprio and of Martesana, which the inhabitants had always regarded as their own property. Just motives had made the emperor and the diet consider these innovations necessary for the public peace and prosperity; but the Milanese regarded them only as perfidious violations of the treaty. When the podestà of the emperor arrived at Milan to take possession of the tribunal, he was sent contemptuously away. The Milanese flew to arms; and making every effort to repossess the different passes of the Adda, prepared to defend themselves behind this barrier. Frederick, on his side, assembled a new diet of the kingdom of Italy at Bologna, in the spring of 1159, and placed Milan under the ban of the empire.

The emperor did not yet attempt to reduce the Milanese by a regular siege. His army was neither sufficiently numerous to invest so large a town, nor his engines of war of sufficient force to make a breach in such strong walls; but he proclaimed his determination to employ all his power, as monarch of Germany and Italy, to ruin that rebellious town. The Milanese, accordingly, soon saw their corn mowed down, their autumn harvests destroyed, their vine stocks cut, the trees which covered their country either cut down or barked, their canals of irrigation broken: but the generous citizens of this new republic did not allow themselves to be discouraged by the superior force of such an enemy, or by the inevitable issue of such a contest. They saw clearly that they must perish; but it would be for the honour and the liberty of Italy: they were resolved to leave a great example to their countrymen, and to future generations.

. The people of Crema had remained faithful to the Milanese in their good and evil fortune; but the siege of that town presented fewer difficulties to the emperor than the siege of Milan. Crema was of small extent, and could be invested on every side; it was also more accessible to the engines of war, though surrounded by a double wall and a ditch filled with water. The Cremonese began the siege on the 4th of July; and on the 10th, Frederick arrived to direct it in person. Four hundred

Milanese had thrown themselves into the town, to partake the combats and dangers of their allies. The emperor, who regarded the besieged only as revolted subjects, sought to terrify them by the spectacle of punishments. Hostages had been sent to him by Milan and Crema : he ordered several of them to be hung before the walls of the town. Some were children of the most distinguished families : he caused them to be bound to a moving tower, which was brought so close to the attack that the besieged could not repel it without killing or wounding their own children. A cry of despair resounded along the walls of Crema. The wretched parents implored death from their fellow-citizens, to escape witnessing the agony of their children, and at the same time cried out to their children not to fear giving up their lives for their country. The battle, in fact, was not interrupted ; and the moving tower was repelled, after nine of the young hostages who covered it with their bodies had been killed. During six entire months did the small town of Crema resist the whole army of the emperor. Famine at length accomplished what force could not ; and on the 26th of January, 1160, the heroic inhabitants capitulated, abandoning their wealth to pillage, and their houses to the flames. For themselves, wasted by famine and fatigue, they obtained permission to withdraw to Milan.

The siege of Crema exhausted the patience of the German army. At this period, soldiers were unaccustomed to such protracted expeditions. When they had accomplished their feudal service, they considered they had a right to return home. The greater number, accordingly, departed ; but Frederick, with immovable constancy, declared he would remain, with the Italians only of the Ghibeline towns, to make war against the Milanese ; and placing himself at the head of the militias of Pavia, Cremona, and Novara, carried on the war a whole year, during which his sole object was to destroy the harvests, and prevent the entrance of any kind of provision into Milan. In the month of June, 1161, a new army arrived from Germany to his aid. His subjects began to feel ashamed of having abandoned their monarch in a foreign country, amongst a people whom they accused of perfidy and rebellion. They returned with redoubled

animosity, which was soon manifested by ferocious deeds:
they tortured and put to death every peasant whom they
surprised carrying provisions of any kind into Milan.
The rich citizens of the republic had aided the government in making large magazines, which were already
in part exhausted: an accidental fire having consumed
the remainder, hunger triumphed over courage and the
love of liberty. For three entire years had the Milanese,
since they had been placed under the ban of the empire,
supported this unequal contest; when, in the beginning
of March, 1162, they were reduced to surrender at discretion. In deep despair they yielded up their arms and
colours, and awaited the orders of the emperor. Frederick,
harsh and haughty, was not ferocious: never had he put
to death by the executioner rebels or enemies whom he
had vanquished. He suffered nearly a month to elapse
before he pronounced his final determination; perhaps to
augment the anxiety of the subdued,—perhaps, also, to
pacify his own wrath, which he at last vented on walls
and inanimate objects, while he pardoned man. He
ordered the town to be completely evacuated, so that
there should not be left in it a single living being. On
the 25th of March, he summoned the militias of the rival
and Ghibeline cities, and gave them orders to rase to
the earth the houses as well as the walls of the town,
so as not to leave one stone upon another.

Those of the inhabitants of Milan whom their poverty,
labour, and industry attached to the soil, were divided
into four open villages, built at a distance of at least two
miles from the walls of their former city. Others sought
hospitality in the neighbouring towns of Italy; even in
those which had shown most attachment to the emperor.
Their sufferings, the extent of their sacrifices, the recollection of their valour, and the example of their noble
sentiments, made proselytes to the cause of liberty in
every city into which they were received. The delegates
of the emperor also (for he himself had returned to his
German dominions), the podestas whom he had established in every town, soon made those Lombards who
had fought with him feel only shame and regret at having
lent their aid to rivet his yoke on their own necks. All
the privileges of the nation were violated; justice was

sacrificed to party interest. Taxes continually augmenting had increased six-fold; and hardly a third part of
the produce of the land remained to the cultivator. The
Italians were universally in a state of suffering and
humiliation; tyranny at length reached even their con-
sciences. On the death of pope Adrian IV., in September, 1159, the electing cardinals had been equally divided
between two candidates; the one a Siennese, the other a
Roman. Both were declared duly elected by their separate
parties; the first, under the name of Alexander III.; the
second, under that of Victor III. Frederick declared for
the latter, who had shown himself ready to sacrifice to
him the liberties and independence of the church. The
former had been obliged to take refuge in France, though
almost the whole of Christendom did not long hesitate
to declare for him. While one council assembled by
Frederick at Pavia rejected him, another assembled at
Beauvais not only rejected but anathematised Victor.
Excommunication at length reached even the emperor;
and Alexander, to strengthen himself against Frederick,
endeavoured to gain the affections of the people, by ranging
himself among the protectors of the liberties of Italy.

Frederick re-entered Italy in the year 1163, accompanied
not by an army, but by a brilliant retinue of German
nobles. He did not imagine that in a country which he
now considered subdued, he needed a more imposing
force; besides, he believed that he could at all times
command the militias of the Ghibeline towns; and, in
fact, he made them this year rase to the ground the walls
of Tortona. He afterwards directed his steps towards
Rome, to support by his presence his schismatic pontiff:
but, in the mean time, Verona, Vicenza, Padua, and
Treviso, the most powerful towns of the Veronese marches,
assembled their consuls in congress, to consider of the
means of putting an end to a tyranny which overwhelmed
them. The consuls of these four towns pledged themselves
by oath in the name of their cities to give mutual support
to each other in the assertion of their former rights, and
in the resolution to reduce the imperial prerogatives to
the point at which they were fixed under the reign of
Henry IV. Frederick, informed of this association,
returned hastily into northern Italy, to put it down. He

assembled the militias of Pavia, Cremona, Novara, Lodi, and Como, with the intention of leading them against the Veronese marches ; but he soon perceived that the spirit of liberty had made progress in the Ghibeline cities as well as in those of the Guelphs ; that the militias under his command complained as much of the vexations inflicted by his podestas as those against whom he led them ; and that they were ill disposed to face death only to rivet the chains of their country. Obliged to bend before a people which he considered only as revolted subjects, he soon renounced a contest so humiliating, and returned to Germany, to levy an army more submissive to him. Other and more pressing interests diverted his attention from this object till the autumn of 1166. During this interval his anti-pope, Victor III., died ; and the successor whom he caused to be named was still more strongly rejected by the church. On the other side, Alexander III. had returned from France to Rome ; contracted an alliance with William, the Norman king of the Two Sicilies ; and armed the whole of southern Italy against the emperor.

When Frederick, in the month of October, 1166, descended the mountains of the Grisons to enter Italy by the territory of Brescia, he marched his army directly to Lodi, without permitting any act of hostility on the way. At Lodi, he assembled towards the end of November, a diet of the kingdom of Italy, at which he promised the Lombards to redress the grievances occasioned by the abuses of power by his podestas, and to respect their just liberties ; he was desirous of separating their cause from that of the pope, and the king of Sicily ; and to give greater weight to his negotiation, he marched his army into central Italy. The towns of Romagna and Tuscany had hitherto made few complaints, and manifested little zeal in defence of their privileges. Frederick hoped that by establishing himself amongst them, he should revive their loyalty, and induce them to augment the army which he was leading against Rome. But he soon perceived that the spirit of liberty, which animated the other countries of Italy, worked also in these : he contented himself, accordingly, with taking thirty hostages from Bologna, and having vainly laid siege to Ancona, he, in the month of July, 1167, marched his army towards Rome.

The towns of the Veronese marches, seeing the emperor and his army pass without daring to attack them, became bolder : they assembled a new diet, in the beginning of April, at the convent of Pontida, between Milan and Bergamo. The consuls of Cremona, of Bergamo, of Brescia, of Mantua and Ferrara met there, and joined those of the marches. The union of the Guelphs and Ghibelines, for the common liberty, was hailed with universal joy. The deputies of the Cremonese, who had lent their aid to the destruction of Milan, seconded those of the Milanese villages in imploring aid of the confederated towns to rebuild the city of Milan. This confederation was called the League of Lombardy. The consuls took the oath, and their constituents afterwards repeated it, that every Lombard should unite for the recovery of the common liberty ; that the league for this purpose should last twenty years ; and, finally, that they should aid each other in repairing in common any damage experienced in this sacred cause, by any one member of the confederation : extending even to the past this contract for reciprocal security, the league resolved to rebuild Milan. The militias of Bergamo, Brescia, Cremona, Mantua, Verona, and Treviso arrived the 27th of April, 1167, on the ground covered by the ruins of this great city. They apportioned among themselves the labour of restoring the enclosing walls ; all the Milanese of the four villages, as well as those who had taken refuge in the more distant towns, came in crowds to take part in this pious work ; and in a few weeks the new-grown city was in a state to repel the insults of its enemies. Lodi was soon afterwards compelled, by force of arms, to take the oath to the league ; while the towns of Venice, Placentia, Parma, Modena, and Bologna voluntarily and gladly joined the association.

Frederick, meanwhile, arrived within sight of Rome. The Romans dared to await him in the open field; he defeated them with great slaughter, and made himself master of the Leonine city. The inhabitants still defending themselves in the Vatican, he dislodged them by setting fire to Santa Maria, the adjoining church ; Alexander, in his fright, escaped by the Tiber. After his retreat, the Romans took the oath of fidelity to the emperor, without,

D

however, receiving his army within their walls; but fever, and the suffocating heat of the Campagna, soon began, by its ravages, to avenge the Italians: from the first days of August an alarming mortality broke out in the camp of the emperor. The princes to whom he was most attached, the captains in whom he had most confidence, two thousand knights, with a proportional number of common soldiers, were carried off in a few weeks. He endeavoured to flee from the destructive scourge; he traversed in his retreat Tuscany and the Lunigiana; but his route was marked with graves, into which every day, every hour, he deposited the bodies of his soldiers. He was no longer strong enough to vanquish even the opposition of the little town of Pontremoli, which refused him a passage; and it was by roads almost impracticable that he at length crossed the Apennines. He arrived at Pavia about the middle of September, and attempted to assemble a diet; but the deputies of Pavia, Novara, Vercelli, and Como alone obeyed his summons. He harangued the assembly with great vehemence; and, throwing down his glove, challenged the rebellious cities to a pitched battle. He passed the winter in combating, with his small remaining army, the league of Lombardy; but in the month of March, 1168, he escaped from the Italians, and repassed Mount Cenis, to return and arm the Germans anew against Italy. After his departure, Novara, Vercelli, Como, Asti, and Tortona also entered into the confederation, which resolved to found, as a monument of its power, and as a barrier against the Ghibelines of Pavia and Montferrat, a new city, on the confluence of the rivers Tanaro and Bormida. The Lombards named it Alexandria, in honour of the chief of the church, and of their league. They collected in it all the inhabitants of the different villages of that rich plain, which extends from the Po to the Ligurian Alps, and secured to them all the liberty and privileges for which they themselves had fought.

Frederick had sacrificed more time, treasure, and blood, to strengthen his dominion over Italy than any of his predecessors: he had succeeded for a long period in associating the German nation in his ambition. He persuaded the Germans that their interest and their

honour were concerned in the submission of the Italians.
They began, however, to feel tired of a long contest, from
which they derived no advantage: other interests, affairs
more pressing, demanded the presence of the emperor at
home; and Frederick was obliged to suspend for five
years his efforts to subdue Italy. During this period
the towns of Lombardy, in the plenitude of their power
and liberty, corrected their laws, recruited their finances,
strengthened their fortifications, and finally placed their
militias on a better war establishment. Their consuls
met also in frequent diets, where they bound themselves
by new oaths to the common defence, and admitted fresh
members into the confederation, which at length reached
to the extremity of Romagna.

Frederick, however, did not entirely abandon Italy.
He sent thither Christian, the elected archbishop of
Mentz, and arch-chancellor of the empire, as his representative. This warlike prelate soon felt that there was
nothing to be done in Lombardy; and he proceeded to
Tuscany, where the Ghibeline party still predominated.
His first pretension was to establish peace between the
two maritime republics of Genoa and Pisa, which disputed with arms in their hands the commerce of the
East. As he found a greater spirit of pride and independence in the Pisans, he caused to be thrown into a
dungeon their consuls, who had presented themselves at
the diet of the Tuscan towns convoked by him at San
Ginasio, in the month of July, 1173; he arrested, at the
same time, the consuls of the Florentines their allies,
while he studiously flattered those of Lucca, of Sienna,
of Pistoia, and the nobles of Tuscany, Romagna, and
Ombria; promising to avenge them on their enemies:
but, said he, "to do so more effectually, you must
first co-operate with me in crushing the enemies of
the emperor." He thus succeeded in persuading
them to second him in the attack which he meditated for the following spring on Ancona. This city,
the most southern of all those attached to the league
of Lombardy, contained about twelve thousand inhabitants, enriched by maritime commerce, and confident in
the strength of their almost unassailable position. Their
town, beautifully situated on the extremity of a promon-

tory, which surrounded a magnificent port, presented on
the side open to the continent only precipitous rocks,
with the exception of a single causeway. The citizens
had accordingly repulsed successfully for ages all the
attacks of the barbarians, and all the pretensions of the
emperors. The archbishop, Christian, arrived before
Ancona in the beginning of April, 1174, and invested the
city with an army levied among the Ghibelines of Tuscany
and Ombria. The people of Ancona repulsed their attack
with their accustomed bravery. But hunger, more formidable than the sword, soon menaced them. The preceding harvests had failed; their granaries were empty;
and an enemy's fleet closed their port. They saw the
harvest ripen, without the possibility of a single sack of
corn reaching them. All human subsistence was soon
exhausted: undismayed, however, they tried to support
existence with the herbs and shell-fish which they
gathered from their rocks, or with the leather which
commerce had accumulated in their magazines. Such
was the food on which had long subsisted a young and
beautiful woman. Observing one day a soldier summoned to battle, but unable from hunger to proceed, she
refused her breast to the child whom she suckled; offered
it to the warrior; and sent him, thus refreshed, to shed
his blood for his country. But to whatever distress the
people of Ancona were reduced, they rejected every pro-
posal to capitulate. At length the succour invoked from
the Guelphs of Ferrara and Romagna approached; Christian saw the fires which they lighted on the mountain of
Falcognara, about four miles from Ancona; and, unable
to give them battle with an army exhausted by the
fatigues of a long siege, he hastily retreated.

In the beginning of October, 1174, Frederick, at the
head of a formidable army, again re-entered Italy. He
passed from the county of Burgundy into Savoy, and
descended by Mont Cenis. Suza, the first town to which
he came on his passage, was taken and burnt; Asti, in
alarm, opened its gates, and purchased its security from
pillage by a heavy contribution; but Alexandria stopped
the progress of the emperor. This city, recently founded
by the league of Lombardy, did not hesitate to enter into
a contest with the imperial power, for the sake of its

confederates; although its mud walls were an object of
derision to the Germans, who first gave this town the
surname of Alexandria *della paglia*, or of straw. Nevertheless these walls of mud and straw, but defended by
generous and devoted citizens, resisted all the efforts of
the most valiant army and the most warlike monarch of
Germany. Frederick consumed in vain four months in
a siege, which was prolonged through the winter. The
inundation of rivers more than once threatened him with
destruction, even in his camp; sickness also decimated
his soldiers. Finally, the combined army of the Lombard
league advanced from Placentia to Tortona; and on
Easter Sunday of the year 1175 Frederick found himself
obliged to raise the siege, and to march for Pavia, to
repose his army.

This last check at length compelled the emperor to
acknowledge the power of a people which he had been
accustomed to despise. The chiefs of the Lombard army
showed themselves well prepared for battle; but still
respecting the rights of their monarch, declined attacking
him. He entered into negotiation with them : all professed their ardent desire to reconcile the prerogatives of
the emperor and he rights of the Roman church with
those of liberty. Six commissioners were appointed to
settle the basis of a treaty which should reconcile these
several claims. They began by demanding that the
armies on each side should be disbanded. Frederick did
not hesitate to comply: he dismissed his Germans, and
remained at Pavia, trusting solely to the fidelity of his
Italian Ghibelines. Legates from the pope arrived also
to join the commissioners; and the negotiations were
opened. But the demands of Frederick were so high as
to render agreement almost impossible. He declared
that he desired only his just rights; "but they must be
those," said he, "which have been exercised by my
predecessors, Charlemagne, Otho, and the emperors
Henry III. and Henry IV." The deputies of the towns
opposed to this the concessions of Henry V. and Lothario;
but even these could no longer satisfy them. For the
Italians, liberty had advanced with civilisation; and they
could not now submit to the ancient prerogatives of their
masters, without returning to their own ancient barbarism.

The negotiations were broken off, and Frederick sent to Germany for another army, which, in the spring of 1176, entered the territory of Como, by the Grisons. The emperor joined it about the end of May, after traversing, without being recognised, the territory of Milan. It was against this great town that he entertained the most profound resentment, and meditated a new attack. He flattered himself that he should find the citizens still trembling under the chastisement which he had before inflicted on their city. On the 29th of May, he met the Milanese army between Lignano and Barano, about fifteen miles from Milan. Only a few auxiliaries from Placentia, Verona, Brescia, Novara, and Vercelli had yet joined them. An impetuous charge of the German cavalry made that of the Lombards give way. The enemy pressed forward so near the *carroccio*, as to give great alarm lest this sacred car should fall into their hands. But in the army of the Milanese there was a company of 900 young men, who had devoted themselves to its defence, and were distinguished by the name of " the company of death." These brave youths seeing the Germans gain ground, knelt down ; and invoking God and St. Ambrose, renewed their vow to perish for their country ; then rising, they advanced with such impetuosity that the Germans were disconcerted, divided, and driven back. The whole army, reanimated by this example, hastily pressed forward. The Germans were put to flight ; their camp was pillaged ; Frederick was separated from his companions in arms, and obliged to conceal himself ; and it was not till he had passed several days, and encountered various dangers, that he succeeded in reaching Pavia, where the empress was already mourning his death.

The defeat at Lignano at length determined Frederick to think seriously of peace, and to abandon pretensions which the Lombards resisted with so much energy. New negotiations were opened with the pope ; and Venice was chosen, in concert with him, as the place for holding a congress. This town had withdrawn its signature from the league of Lombardy ; it was acknowledged foreign to the Western empire, and might be considered neutral, and indifferent in the quarrel between the emperor and

the free towns.   The pope, Alexander III., arrived at
Venice on the 24th of March, 1177.   The emperor, whose
presence the Venetians feared, first fixed his residence at
one of his palaces, near Ravenna ; approached afterwards
as far as Chiozza, and finally came even to Venice.   The
negotiation bore upon three different points,—to reconcile
the emperor to the church, by putting an end to the
schism ; to restore peace between the empire of the
West and that of the East, and the king of the Two
Sicilies ; and finally to define the constitutional rights of
the emperor and of the cities of Lombardy.   Frederick
was ready to submit to the church ; and he had few subjects of dispute with the Grecian emperor, or the Norman
king of the Sicilies : these parts of the treaty were not
difficult to terminate.   But that part which related to the
league of Lombardy must be founded on a new order of
ideas : it was the first pact that Europe had seen made
between a monarch and his subjects ; the first boundary
line traced between authority and liberty.   After long and
vain attempts, the negotiators separated, contenting themselves only with obliging the emperor and the Lombards
to conclude a truce of six years, bearing date from the
1st of August, 1177.   During its existence, the rights on
each side were to remain suspended ; and the freedom of
commerce was re-established between the cities which
remained faithful to the emperor, and those which drew
still closer their bonds of union by a renewal of the league
of Lombardy.

The six years of repose, however, which this truce
guaranteed, accustomed the emperor to submit to limita-
tions of his authority.   Thirty years had passed since the
contest had begun between him and the Italian nation ;
age had now tempered his activity and calmed his pride.
New incidents had arisen to fix his attention in Germany.
His son, Henry VI., demanded to be associated in the
sovereignty of his two kingdoms of Germany and Italy.
A definitive peace only could restore to Frederick his
rights and revenues in Lombardy, which his subjects
there did not dispute, but which the truce held suspended.
The adverse claims were honestly weighed at the diet of
Constance; reciprocal concessions were made both by
the monarch and his subjects, and the peace of Constance,

the basis of new public rights for Italy, was at length
signed on the 25th of June, 1183. By this peace the
emperor renounced all regal privileges which he had
hitherto claimed in the interior of towns. He acknow
ledged the right of the confederate cities to levy armies,
to enclose themselves within fortifications, and to exercise
by their commissioners within their own walls both civil
and criminal jurisdiction. The consuls of towns acquired
by the simple nomination of the people all the prerogatives of imperial vicars. The cities of Lombardy were
further authorised to strengthen their confederation for
the defence of their just rights, recognised by the peace
of Constance. But, on the other side, they engaged to
maintain the just rights of the emperor, which were
defined at the same time ; and in order to avoid all disputes, it was agreed that these rights might always be
bought off by the annual sum of 2000 marks of silver.
Thus terminated, in the establishment of a legal liberty,
the first and most noble struggle which the nations of
modern Europe have ever maintained against despotism.

CHAPTER III

PROGRESS OF THE CITIES TOWARDS INDEPENDENCE, FROM THE PEACE
OF CONSTANCE TO THE DEATH OF FREDERICK II —RELENTLESS
ENMITY BETWEEN THE GUELPHS AND GHIBELINES—FIRST PARTY
CHIEFS WHO ATTAINED TYRANNICAL POWER

THE generous resistance of the Lombards, during a war
of thirty years, had conquered from the emperors political
liberty for all the towns of the kingdom of Italy. The
right of obeying only their own laws, of being governed
by their own magistrates, of contracting alliances, of
making peace or war, and, in fine, of administering their
own finances, with the exception only of a certain revenue
payable into the imperial treasury, was more particularly
secured by the peace of Constance to the confederate
cities of the league of Lombardy. But the Germans
easily comprehended the impossibility of refusing to their
allies the privileges which their enemies had gained by

conquest ; the liberties, therefore, stipulated by the peace
of Constance, were rendered common to all the towns of
Italy : and those which had been most distinguished by
their attachment to the Ghibeline party, were often found
the most zealous for the establishment and preservation
of all the rights of the people. The cities, however, did
not consider themselves independent. They were proud
of the title of members of the empire : they knew they
must concur in its defence, as well as in the maintenance
of internal peace ; reserving only that it must be in pursuance of their free choice and deliberation. They were
in a manner confederates of an emperor, who acted on
them rather by persuasion than orders ; rather as a party
chief than as a monarch : and as he was habituated to
this compromise with public opinion in his relations with
the princes of the empire, he yielded with the less repugnance to his Italian subjects. It is a circumstance highly
honourable to the princes of the house of Hohenstaufen,
which continued to reign sixty-seven years after the peace
of Constance, that during this long period they made no
attempt to infringe the conditions of the compact. They
admitted, with good faith, all the consequences of the
concessions made ; they pardoned liberty, which the
vulgar order of kings always regarded as a usurpation of
the subjects on the rights of the crown.

It was not long, however, before the struggle was
renewed between the emperor and most of the towns.
It was supported with not less devotion and not fewer
sacrifices ; it caused not less calamity, whilst it endured ;
and it was crowned, at its close, with results not less
happy. But the cities did not, as in the preceding
struggle, engage in it for their own immediate interest ;
they rather seconded the policy of the holy see, which
sought the independence of the church and of Italy, and
did not cease to fight for the attainment of this object till
the extinction of the house of Hohenstaufen.

Frederick I. survived the peace of Constance seven
years. During this period he visited Italy with his son
Henry VI. : he remained some time at Milan, where he
was received with respect, and gained the affection of all
the inhabitants, towards whom he testified the utmost
trust, confidence, and kindness. Instead of endeavouring

to intimidate Lombardy, and recover by intrigues his former power, he was occupied only with the marriage of his son Henry, whom he had previously crowned king of Germany, with Constance, sole heiress of the Norman kings who had conquered the Two Sicilies. The union of this crown with that of Germany and of Lombardy would have reduced the pope to be no more than the first bishop of his states ; it would have disarmed the two auxiliary powers which had supported the league of Lombardy against the emperor ; and it alarmed the church, in proportion as it flattered his ambition. The endeavours to prevent or dissolve this union gave rise to all the wars of the period embraced in the present chapter. Frederick Barbarossa did not see the commencement of them. When the news of the taking of Jerusalem by Saladin, on the 2nd of October, 1187, had thrown all Europe into consternation, Frederick, listening only to his religious and chivalric enthusiasm, placed himself at the head of the third crusade, which he led into the East by land, and died the 10th of June, 1190, of a stroke of apoplexy, caused by the coldness of the waters of the little river Salef in Asia Minor.

Henry VI. had worn for five years the German and Italian crowns, when he received in Germany, where he then was with his wife, news of the death of William II., king of the Two Sicilies, to whom Constance was successor ; and a few months after, that of his father, Frederick I. He immediately began his journey towards southern Italy. Tancred, a bastard of the race of the Norman kings, but in opposition to him by the Sicilians, defended, for some time with success, the independence of those provinces, but died in 1194 ; and Henry, who had entered the kingdom as conqueror, and had made himself detested for his cruelty, also died there suddenly, on the 28th of September, 1197. He left by his marriage with Constance only one son, Frederick II., hardly four years old, who lost his mother in the following year ; and was, under the protection of the pope, acknowledged, child as he was, king of the Two Sicilies : but the imperial and Lombard crowns were withheld from him for several years.

From the peace of Constance to the death of Henry VI.

the free cities of Italy had, for the space of fifteen years,
no contest to maintain against the emperors; but their
repose and liberty were, during this period, constantly
endangered by the pretensions of the nobility. The
growing grandeur of the cities, and the decay of the
imperial power, had left the nobles of Italy in a very
ambiguous position.

They in some measure had no longer a country; their
only security was in their own strength; for the emperor
in resigning his power over the towns had not thought
of giving an organisation to the nobles dispersed in
castles. All the families of Italian dukes, and almost
all those of marquises and counts, had become extinct;
those who remained had lost all jurisdiction over their
inferiors; no feudal tenure was respected; no vassal
appeared at the baronial court, to form the tribunal of
his lord. The frontiers of the kingdom of Lombardy
were called *marches*, after a German word adopted into
almost all the European languages, and the commander
of these frontiers was called marquis; but the families of
the powerful Tuscan marquises were extinct, as well as
those of the marquises of Ancona, of Fermo, of Camerino,
of Ivrea, and of those of the Veronese and Trevisan
marches. There remained, however, on these frontiers
some families which bore the same title, and had preserved some wrecks of these ancient and powerful marquisates: such was the marquis d'Este, in the Veronese
march; the marquises of Montferrat, Palavacino,
Malaspina, in the march of Ivrea; but they were not
acknowledged as lords paramount, or lords of counties
and baronies: there was moreover no other organisation
than that created by the spirit of party. The nobles were
not united by the hierarchical connection of the feudal
system, but by the affections or antipathies of the Guelphs
or Ghibelines. In general, the most powerful families
among the nobles, those who had castles sufficiently
strong, lands sufficiently extensive, and vassals sufficiently numerous to defend themselves, listening only to
the ambition of courts, were attached to the Ghibeline
party. Those families, on the contrary, who possessed
castles capable of but little resistance, situated on accessible eminences, or in plains; those whose castles were

near great towns, and too weak to support a contest with
them, had demanded to be made citizens of the towns;
they had served them in the wars of the league of Lombardy ; they had since taken a principal share in the
government, and they thus found themselves attached by
common interests to the party of the Guelphs. Independent nobles were no more to be found in all the plains
of Lombardy; there was not one who had not become
citizen of some republic ; but every chain of mountain
was thick-set with castles; where a nobility choosing
obedience to an emperor rather than to citizens, maintained themselves independent : these, too, attracted
sometimes by the wealth and pleasures of towns, and
sometimes desirous of obtaining influence in the counsels
of powerful republics, in order to restore them to the
emperor, demanded to be made citizens, when they
thought it would open the way to a share in the government ; and as war was their sole occupation, they were
often gladly received by the republics, which stood in
need of good captains. It was thus the Ghibeline family
of Visconti, whose fiefs extended from the Alps to the
Lago Maggiore, became associated with the republic of
Milan. The house of Este, allied to the Guelphs of
Saxony and Bavaria, and devoted to the pope, possessors
of several castles built on the fertile chain of the Euga-
nean hills, joined the republic of Ferrara ; the parallel
chain, which serves as a base to the Tyrolese Alps,
was crowned with the castles of Ezzel, or Eccelino, of
Romano, a family enriched by the emperors, entirely
devoted to the Ghibeline party, and in process of time
attached to the republics of Verona and Vicenza. In
like manner were situated on the northern side of the
Apennines the fortresses of the Ghibeline nobles, who
excited revolutions in the republics of Placentia, Parma,
Reggio, and Modena : on the southern side were the
castles of other Ghibelines, in turns citizens and enemies
of the republics of Arezzo, Florence, Pistoia, and Lucca :
lower in the valleys of the Po, or in the upper vale of
Arno, were the castles of the Guelphs, who had become
decidedly citizens of the same republics.

The more the social tie was weakened in the kingdom
of Lombardy, the more eager the nobles became to be

admitted into the cities. Their wealth and military education soon led them, by the suffrages of their fellow-citizens, to the magistracy in this their new country. But if they displayed more talent for war and politics, they evinced much less subordination or submission to the laws. Their aversions were more virulent, and they gloried in cherishing them as a family inheritance. Accustomed in their castles to decide every question by the sword, they brought the same habits to the towns. Retaining, when they became inhabitants of cities, the wild independence of their ancient fastnesses, their houses were fortresses; thick walls, high and narrow windows, a massive door of oak, secured with iron bars, promised to resist more than one attack; and if they were at last forced, a high square tower still served for refuge. From these palaces of the nobles bands of assassins were often seen issuing, to rob or murder citizens, who were treated as enemies : chains were prepared to be thrown across the streets, and in an instant form barricades ; behind which were seen ranged several hundred warriors. The peaceable citizens, to whom these quarrels were indifferent, never knew whether the peace they then saw reign around them should not in a few hours be changed into a general war. The power of the consuls seemed insufficient to repress these fiery passions. All the towns saw the necessity of adopting the institution of the *podestà*, which they had received from Frederick Barbarossa. Their custom was accordingly to choose annually, by their *consiglio di credenza*, a foreign knight of arms, a warrior chosen from one of the confederate cities. This knight, whom they named *podestà*, was accompanied by two or three doctors in civil and criminal law, dependent on him, and acting under him as judges. The podesta received at the same time the command of the militia, and the power of the sword of justice, or of pronouncing and causing to be executed sentences on criminals. He was bound to render, at the end of the year, an account of the manner in which he had performed his functions to commissioners chosen by the people, and called *syndics*, before whom he remained a certain number of days amenable to justice. The towns believed that this foreign judge would remain impartial

amidst their factions; but the podesta himself rarely
escaped participating in the deep hatred of the Guelphs
or Ghibelines : he needed also a hand of iron to maintain
order among nobles, so turbulent and so vindictive ; he
was accordingly invested with almost unlimited authority,
the republics preferring rather to submit to his despotic
sway than to anarchy.   The violence of faction, nevertheless, and its natural consequence, a severe administration of justice, inspired the citizens universally with
a deep hatred of the nobles, who were alone accused of
having introduced disorder within their walls ; and before
the end of the twelfth century all the Lombard cities rose
successively against the nobles, excluded them from all
public functions, and even expelled them from the towns.
Brescia, Padua, and Modena were the first to set the
example ; but, after a few months, private affection
triumphed over public resentment, and the nobles were
recalled.

The death of Henry VI. was followed by a general
war throughout the empire, which gave fresh activity to
the passions of the Italian nobles, and greater animosity
to the opposing parties.   The two factions in Germany
had simultaneously raised to the empire the two chiefs
of the houses of Guelph and Ghibeline.   Philip I. duke
of Swabia, and brother of Henry VI., had been named
king of the Romans by the Ghibelines ; and Otho IV.,
son of Henry the Lion, duke of Bavaria and Saxony, by
the Guelphs.   Their contest was prolonged to the 22nd
of June, 1208, when Philip was assassinated by a private
enemy.   The Germans, wearied with eleven years of
civil war, agreed to unite under the sceptre of his rival,
Otho IV., whom they crowned anew.   The following
year he passed into Italy, to receive from the pope the
golden crown of the empire.   But though Otho was the
legitimate heir of the Guelphs of Bavaria, so long chiefs
of the opposition to the imperial prerogatives, yet now
wearing himself the crown, he was desirous of possessing
it with these disputed rights : every one was denied him,
and all his actions controlled by the pope.   There was
soon a declared enmity between the emperor and the
pontiff, who, rather than consent to any agreement, or to
abate any of his pretensions, raised against the Guelph

emperor the heir of the Ghibeline house, the young
Frederick II., grandson of Frederick I., hardly eighteen
years of age, and till then reigning under the pope's
tutelage over the Two Sicilies only. Frederick, excited
and seconded by the pope, boldly passed through Lombardy in 1212, and arrived at Aix la Chapelle, where the
German Ghibelines awaited, and crowned him king of
the Romans and Germans. Otho IV. in the mean time
returned to Germany, and was acknowledged by Saxony.
The civil war, carried on between the two chiefs of the
empire, lasted till the 19th of May, 1218, when Otho died,
without any attempt by either party to despoil his rival
of his hereditary possessions. It was this civil war that
caused the names of Guelphs and Ghibelines to be
exclusively substituted for those of party of the church,
and party of the empire. In fact, each noble family, and
each city, seemed to consult only their hereditary affection,
and not their political principles, in ranging themselves
under either standard. The Guelphs placed themselves
in opposition to the pope, to repel his Ghibeline candidate;
and Milan, Placentia, and Brescia braved even excommunication to resist him: while, on the contrary, the
Ghibelines of Pavia, Cremona, and of the March armed
themselves with zeal against an emperor of the Guelph
blood.

During this period, while the minority of Frederick II.
left so much to the cities of Italy to consolidate their
independence, and to form real republics, the person
most influential and most prominent in history was the
pope, Innocent III., who reigned from 1197 to 1216. He
was a Roman noble, count of Signa, and only thirty-
seven years of age when he ascended the papal chair: he
had been raised to it by his reputation for sanctity and
learning. A worthy successor of Gregory VII., he
elevated, like him, the sovereignty of the popes; but he
seemed to labour for that purpose with a fanaticism more
religious, and a pride less worldly: all his efforts tended
much more to confirm the power of the church and of
religion than his own. Like Alexander III. he did not
refuse to join the people in their efforts to obtain liberty,
provided that liberty bowed with awe before the authority
of the church, and admitted no private judgment in

matters of faith.   He founded the two mendicant orders
of Franciscans and Dominicans; new champions of the
church, who were charged to repress all activity of mind,
to combat growing intelligence, and to extirpate heresy.
He confided to the Dominicans the fearful powers of the
inquisition, which he instituted: he charged them to discover and pursue to destruction the new reformers, who,
under the name of *paterini*, multiplied rapidly in Italy.
He roused the fanatics of France to exterminate, in the
Albigenses, the same reformers; and to destroy not only
heretics, but all who, in the population of Languedoc,
had any wealth or independence.   He addressed his orders
to the kings of Europe with a haughtiness worthy of
Gregory VII.; but always fixing his attention much more
on discipline and the maintenance of morality than on
the augmentation of his temporal power.   Finally, he
gained a triumph over the eastern church, which he had
not sought, but of which he knew how to profit, in subjecting to his authority, and attaching to the Latin
church, the patriarch of Constantinople, till then his rival
and antagonist.

In the beginning of his pontificate, 1198, a crusade had
been preached in France by Fulk de Neuilly.   The
crusaders, having resolved to go by sea to the Holy
Land, borrowed vessels of the republic of Venice; and
finding themselves afterwards too poor to pay the freight
on which they had agreed, they offered instead of it their
military services.   After having subdued Zara, which
had revolted against the republic, they bore up to Constantinople in concert with old Andrea Dandolo, doge of
Venice.   On the 12th of April, 1204, they took by assault
the capital of the Grecian empire.   They named a Frenchman, Baldwin, count of Flanders, emperor of Constantinople, and elected under him a Latin patriarch.   They
gave the kingdom of Thessalonica to an Italian, the
marquis of Montferrat; and they abandoned to the
Venetians, for their share of the conquest, one fourth
and a half of the Roman empire.   The doge was named
lord of this portion of the empire, but the conquests of
the republic were in reality limited to the island of
Candia, some other isles, Achaia, and the Morea.   These
possessions beyond the sea diverted for a long period the

republic of Venice from any participation in the affairs of Italy.

While Innocent III. caused his power to be felt in the remotest parts of Christendom, he suffered to be constituted at Rome, under his own eye, a republic, the liberty of which he respected, and over which he assumed no authority. The thirteen districts of Rome named each annually four representatives or *caporioni;* their meeting formed the senate of the republic, who, with the concurrence of the people, exercised the sovereignty, with the exception of the judicial power. This power belonged, as in other republics, to a foreign military chief, chosen for one year, and assisted by civil judges, dependent on him, but bearing the name of *senator*, instead of podesta. We have still extant the form of oath taken by the first of these senators, named in 1207. By it he engages to guarantee security and liberty to the pope as well as to his brothers the cardinals, but promises no submission to him for himself.

In the beginning of the pontificate of Innocent III., two German generals, to whom Henry VI. had given the titles of duke of Spoleto, and marquis of Ancona, held in dependence and subjection the provinces nearest Rome. Innocent, to revive the spirit of liberty, sent thither two legates; and by their interference, the cities of these provinces, built for the most part in the mountains, and without any means of becoming either wealthy or populous, threw off the German yoke, and made alliance with those cities which from the preceding period had entered into the league of Lombardy: thus two Guelph leagues were formed, under the protection of the pope; one in the March, comprehending the cities of Ancona, Fermo, Osimo, Camerino, Fano, Jesi, Sinigallia, and Pesaro; the other in the duchy, comprehending those of Spoleto, Rieti, Assisa, Foligno, Nocera, Perugia, Agobbio, Todi, and Città di Castello. These leagues, however, in accustoming the cities of these two provinces to regard the pope as their protector, led them afterwards to submit without resistance to the sovereignty of the church.

Other legates had been about the same time sent into Tuscany by the pope: they convoked at St. Ginasio, a borough situated at the foot of the mountain of San

Miniato, the diet of the towns of that country. These
provincial diets were in the habit of assembling frequently,
and had till then been presided over by an officer belonging to the emperor, in memory of whom the castle in
which he resided is still called San Miniato al Tedesco.
These diets settled the differences which arose between
cities, and had succeeded in saving Tuscany from the
civil wars between the Guelphs and Ghibelines. Pisa,
which had been loaded with favours by the sovereigns of
the house of Hohenstaufen, and which had obtained from
them the dominion of sixty-four castles or fortified towns
on the shores of Tuscany, and over the isles of Corsica,
Elba, Capraia, and Pianosa, proclaimed its determination
of remaining faithful to the Ghibeline party, and its
consuls withdrew from the diet convoked at San Ginasio;
but those of the cities of Florence, of Sienna, of Arezzo,
of Pistoia and of Lucca, accepted the protection of the
pope, offered by his two legates, and promised to coalesce
in defence of their common liberty. Numerous noble
families in these towns, both Guelphs and Ghibelines,
had demanded the rights of citizenship. Hitherto the
magistrates succeeded in maintaining peace, and one of
the objects of the league was to preserve it; but, in 1215,
a Guelph noble of the upper Vale of Arno, named
Buondelmonte, who had been made citizen of Florence,
demanded in marriage a young person of the Ghibeline
house of Amidei, and was accepted. While the nuptials
were in preparation, a noble lady of the family Donati
stopped Buondelmonte as he passed her door, and, bringing him into the room where her women were at work,
raised the veil of her daughter, whose beauty was ex-
quisite. "Here," said she, "is the wife I had reserved
for thee. Like thee, she is Guelph; whilst thou takest
one from the enemies of thy church and race." Buondelmonte, dazzled and enamoured, instantly accepted the
proffered hand. The Amidei, looked upon his inconstancy as a deep affront. All the noble Ghibeline families
of Florence, about twenty-four in number, met, and agreed
that he should atone with his life for the offence.
Buondelmonte was attacked on the morning of Easter
Sunday, just as he had passed the Ponte Vecchio, on
horseback, and killed at the foot of the statue of Mars,

which still stood there. Forty-two families of the Guelph party met and swore to avenge him; and blood did indeed atone for blood. Every day some new murder, some new battle, alarmed Florence during the space of thirty-three years. These two parties stood opposed to each other within the walls of the same city; and although often reconciled, every little accident renewed their animosity, and they again flew to arms to avenge ancient wrongs.

The death of Innocent III., and, two years afterwards, of Otho IV., broke the unnatural alliance between a pope and the heir of a Ghibeline family. The Milanese, ex-communicated by Innocent for having fought against Frederick II., did not the less persist in making war on his partisans; well convinced that the new pope, Honorius III., would soon thank them for it. They refused Frederick the iron crown of Lombardy, preserved at Monza, and contracted an alliance with the count Thomas of Savoy, and with the cities of Crema, Placentia, Lodi, Vercelli, Novara, Tortona, Como, and Alexandria, to drive the Ghibelines from Lombardy. The Ghibelines defeated them on the 6th of June, 1218, in a great battle fought against the militias of Cremona, Parma, Reggio, and Modena, before Ghibello. This reverse of fortune calmed for some time their military ardour. The citizens of every town accused the nobles of having led them into war from family enmities and interests foreign to the city: at Milan, Placentia, Cremona, and Modena, there were battles between the nobles and the people. Laws were proposed, to divide the public magistracy in due proportions between them; finally the Milanese, in the year 1221, expelled all the nobles from their city.

The young Frederick re-entered Italy; and, after some differences with Honorius III., received from him, on the 22nd of November, 1220, the crown of the empire. He afterwards occupied himself in establishing order in his kingdom of the Two Sicilies, where, during his minority, the popes had encouraged an universal in-subordination. Born in the march of Ancona, at Jesi, in December, 1194, he was Italian as well by language as by affection and character. The Italian language, spoken at his court, first rose above the *patois* in common

use throughout Italy, regarded only as a corruption of
Latin: he expressed himself with elegance in this
language, which, from his time, was designated by the
name of *lingua cortigiana;* he encouraged the first poets,
who employed it at his court, and he himself made
verses; he loved literature and encouraged learning; he
founded schools and universities; he promoted distinguished men; he spoke with equal facility Latin,
Italian, German, French, Greek, and Arabic; he had the
intellectual suppleness and finesse peculiar to the men of
the south, the art of pleasing, a taste for philosophy, and
great independence of opinion, with a leaning to infidelity;
hence he is accused of having written a book against the
three revelations of Moses, Jesus, and Mahomet, entitled
" De Tribus Impostoribus," which no one has ever seen,
and which perhaps never existed. His want of faith in
the sacred character of the Roman church, and the
sanctity of popes, is less doubtful; he was suspicious of
them, and he employed all his address to defend himself
against their enterprises. Honorius III., desirous of
engaging him to recover the Holy Land from the
Saracens, made him, in 1225, marry Yolanda de Lusignan,
heiress of the kingdom of Jerusalem; after which,
Honorius and his successor Gregory IX. pressed him to
pass into Palestine. A malady stopped him, in 1227,
just as he was about to depart: the pope, to punish him
for this delay, excommunicated him. He still pursued
him with his anathema when he went to the Holy Land
the year following, and haughtily testified his indignation,
because Frederick, in the year 1229, recovered Jerusalem
from the hands of the sultan by treaty, rather than exterminate the infidels with the sword.

Meanwhile the Guelph party again raised their standard
in Lombardy, the republics of Milan, Bologna, Placentia,
Verona, Brescia, Faenza, Mantua, Vercelli, Lodi, Bergamo, Turin, Alexandria, Vicenza, Padua, and Treviso,
assembled their consuls in council at San Zenone in the
Mantuan territory, on the 2nd of March, 1226. They
renewed the ancient league of Lombardy for twenty-five
years; and engaged to defend in concert, their own
liberty and the independence of the court of Rome.
Three years afterwards, they sent succour to Gregory IX.,

when he was attacked by Frederick II. on his return from the Holy Land; and they were included in the treaty of peace between the pope and the emperor in 1230.

The pope, however, though defended by the arms of the Lombards, made them pay dearly for the favour which he showed in naming them to the emperor as his allies. He consented to protect their civil liberty only so far as they sacrificed to him their liberty of conscience. The same spirit of reformation which animated the Albigenses had spread throughout Europe: many Christians, disgusted with the corruption and vices of the clergy, or whose minds revolted against the violence on their reason exercised by the church, devoted themselves to a contemplative life, renounced all ambition and the pleasures of the world, and sought a new road to salvation in the alliance of faith with reason. They called themselves *cathari*, or the purified; *paterini*, or the resigned. The free towns had, till then, refused permission to the tribunals of the inquisition, instituted by Innocent III., to proceed against them within their walls; but Gregory IX. declared the impossibility of acknowledging as allies of the holy see republicans so indulgent to the enemies of the faith; at the same time, he sent among them the most eloquent of the Dominicans, to rouse their fanaticism. Leo dà Perego, whom he afterwards made archbishop of Milan, had only a too fatal success in that city, where he caused a great number of *paterini* to be burnt. Saint Peter Martyr, and the monk Roland of Cremona, obtained an equal triumph in the other cities of Lombardy. The monk John of Vicenza had the cities of the March assigned to him as a province, where the heretics were in still greater numbers than in Lombardy, and included in their ranks some of the most powerful nobles in the country; among others, Eccelino II. of Romano. The monk John announced himself the minister of peace, not of persecution. After having preached successively in every town, he assembled, on the plain of Paquara, the 28th of August, 1233, almost the whole population of the towns of the March: he exhorted them to peace in a manner so irresistible, that the greatest enemies, setting aside their animosities, pardoned and embraced each other; and all, with tears of joy, celebrated the warm charity of this man of God. This man of God, however, celebrated the festival of this reconciliation by judging and condemning to the flames sixty cathari in the single town of Verona, whose sufferings he witnessed in the public square; and afterwards obtained full power from the towns of Vicenza and Padua to act there in the like manner.

It was only a short period after the peace of Paquara that Frederick II., believing he had sufficiently re-established his power in southern Italy, began to turn his attention towards Lombardy; he had no intention or disputing the rights guaranteed by his grandfather at the peace of Constance; but it was his will that the cities should remain, what they ought to be by the treaty, members of the empire, and not enemies of the emperor. He had raised an army, over which he feared neither the influence of the monks nor the pope. He had transported from the mountains of Sicily, into the city of Luceria, in the capitanate, and into that of Nocera, in the principato, two strong colonies of Saracens, which could supply him with 30,000 mussulman soldiers, strangers, by their language and religion, to all the intrigues of the court of Rome. There was in the Veronese march a man endowed with great military talents, ambitious, intrepid, and entirely devoted to the emperor,—Eccelino III., of Romano, already powerful by the great fiefs he held in the mountains, and the number of his soldiers, whom Frederick made still more so, by placing him at the head of the Ghibeline party in all the cities. Eccelino, born on the 4th of April, 1194, was precisely of the same age as the emperor. The pope had summoned him to arrest his father, and deliver him to the tribunal of the inquisition as a paterino: but though Eccelino knew neither virtue, pity, nor remorse, he was not sufficiently depraved for such a crime.

As Frederick was on the point of attacking the Guelphs of Lombardy on the south with the Saracens, while Eccelino advanced on the east, he learnt that his son Henry, whom he had in the year 1220 crowned king of Germany, in spite of his extreme youth, seduced by the Guelphs and the agents of the pope, had revolted against him. The Milanese, in 1234, sent deputies to offer him the iron crown, which they had refused to his father. The latter hastened into Germany, and ordered his son to meet him at Worms, where he threw himself at the feet of his father, and entreated forgiveness. Frederick deprived him of the crown, and sent him to Apulia, where he died a few years afterwards. The emperor was obliged to employ two years in restoring order in Germany : he after that returned into Italy by the valley of Trento, and arrived, on the 16th of August, 1236, at Verona with 3000 German cavalry. A senate of eighty members, nobles and Ghibelines, then governed that republic : Frederick, by his address in managing men, engaged them to name Eccelino captain of the people : this committed to him at the same time the command of the militia and the judicial power ; and, in the state of excitement in which the parties were, much more occupied with the triumph of their faction than with the security of their liberty, gave him almost sovereign power. Frederick, obliged to return to Germany, left under the command of Eccelino a body of German soldiers, and another of Saracens, with which this able captain made himself, the same year, master of Vicenza, which he barbarously pillaged, and the following year of Padua. This last was the most powerful city of the province, that in which the form of government was the most democratic, and in which the Guelphs had always exer-cised the most influence. Eccelino judged it necessary to secure obedience by taking hostages from the richest and most powerful families ; he employed his spies to discover the malcontents, whom he punished with torture, and redoubled his cruelty in proportion to the hatred which he excited.

The same year, 1237, Frederick approached Mantua ; and thus giving courage to the Ghibeline party, made them triumph over the Guelphs, who had, till then, the ascendant in the city : he was joined there by 10,000 Saracens, whom he summoned from Apulia, and after-wards advanced into the Cremonese territory to attack the confederate army of the Guelphs, commanded by the consuls of Milan, who knew no other art of war but the bravery evinced in battle. Frederick was a more able captain : by manœuvring between Brescia and Cremona,

he drew the Milanese beyond the Oglio, and finally succeeded, as they believed the campaign finished, in placing
himself between them and their country at Cortenuova,
near Crema. The Guelphs, although thus cut off from
retreat, boldly accepted battle on the 27th of November,
1237, and long disputed the victory. Their defeat was
only the more bloody: it cost them 10,000 men killed or
taken prisoners, with the loss of the *carroccio*. The
fugitives followed during the night the course of the
Oglio to enter the Bergamasque mountains; they would
all, however, have fallen into the hands of the Ghibelines,
if Pagan della Torre, the lord of Valsassina, and a Guelph
noble, had not hastened to their assistance, opened the
defiles covered by his fortresses, and brought them thus
safely to Milan. The citizens of this town never forgot
so important a service; and they contracted with the
house of della Torre an alliance which subsequently
proved dangerous to their freedom.

The defeat of the Guelphs at Cortenuova alarmed the
towns of Lombardy, the greater number of which detached
themselves from Milan. Frederick, entering Piedmont
the following year, gave preponderance to the Ghibeline
party in the cities of Turin, Asti, Novara, Alexandria,
and several others. The constitution was not changed
when the power in council passed from one party to
another; but the emperor generally reckoned his partisans
among the nobility, while the people were devoted to the
church: accordingly, the triumph of the aristocracy
generally accompanied that of the Ghibeline party. Four
cities only, Milan, Brescia, Placentia, and Bologna,
remained at the end of the year opposed to the imperial
power. Frederick began his attack on them by laying
siege to Brescia; but the Brescians dared to face the
storm: they supported, during sixty-eight days, the
repeated attacks of the emperor, rendered all his efforts
fruitless, and forced him at last to raise the siege with an
army weakened and discouraged.

In the mean time, Gregory IX. redoubled his efforts to
save the Guelph party from ruin. He saw, with alarm,
an emperor, master of the Two Sicilies and of Germany,
on the point of vanquishing all resistance in Upper Italy.
He anticipated that this monarch, whose mussulman

soldiers were constantly passing through the states of Rome, would escape the influence of the church, and soon evince no respect whatever for a religion which he was accused of not believing. Gregory had recourse to the two maritime republics of Venice and Genoa, which, in general occupied with their conquests and commerce in the East, seldom took any part in the politics of Italy. He represented to them, that they would be soon deprived of the freedom of the seas, if they did not make some effort to save the champions of liberty and of the church in Lombardy. He at length obtained their agreement to contract an alliance with the four only surviving cities of the league of Lombardy; and finally, towards the beginning of the year 1239, he fulminated another sentence of excommunication against Frederick. This had a greater effect than Gregory ventured to hope. A considerable number of nobles of Guelph origin, seduced by court favours, had been won over to the imperial party. They perceived that after the anathema of the pope, the emperor distrusted them. The marquis d'Este and the count di San Bonifacio were even warned that their heads were in danger, and they made their escape from the imperial camp : all the other Guelph nobles followed their example ; and the Guelph cities gained captains habituated to arms and familiarised with higher ideas of politics.

Gregory began to think he should give still greater weight to the anathemas which he launched against the emperor, if they were sanctioned by a council. In the year 1241 he convoked at Rome all the prelates of Christendom. Frederick, who had been established at Pisa since the autumn of the year 1239, exerted himself to prevent the meeting of a council which he dreaded. While the two other maritime republics had declared for the Guelphs, Pisa was entirely of the Ghibeline party. The people were enthusiastically attached to the emperor, and among the nobles, a few only, proprietors of fiefs in Sardinia, headed by the Visconti of Gallura, had forsaken him for the Guelphs. The Pisans, further excited by their jealousy of the Genoese, promised Frederick that they would brave for him all the thunders of the church, and assured him they knew well how to hinder the

E

meeting of the council. A considerable number of French prelates had embarked at Nice for Ostia, on board Genoese galleys. Ugolino Buzzacherino de Sismondi, admiral of the Pisans, lay in wait with a powerful fleet before Meloria, attacked them on the 3rd of May, 1241, sunk three vessels, took nineteen, and made prisoners all the French prelates who were to join the council at Pisa. The republic loaded them with chains, but they were chains made of silver, and imprisoned them in the chapter house of the cathedral. Gregory, alarmed at this reverse of fortune, survived only a few months: he died the 21st of August, 1241; and the college of cardinals, reduced to a very small number, passed nearly two years before they could agree on a new choice. At last, on the 24th of June, 1243, Sinibald de' Fieschi, of Genoa, who took the name of Innocent IV., was elected to the chair of St. Peter. His family, powerful in Genoa and in the Ligurian mountains, was also allied to many noble families, who possessed castles on the northern side of the Apennines; and this position gave him great influence in the neighbouring cities of Placentia, Parma, Reggio, and Modena. The elevation of a Fieschi to the pontificate gave courage to the Guelph party in all these cities.

Frederick had recourse in vain to the new pope to be reconciled to the church; Innocent IV. was determined to see in him only an enemy of religion, and of the pontifical power, and a chief of barbarians, who in turns summoned his Germans and his Saracens to tyrannise over Italy. He drew closer his alliance with the cities of the league of Lombardy, and promised them to cause the emperor to be condemned and deposed by an *œcumenical* council, as his predecessor would have done; but instead of convoking the council in Italy, he fixed for that purpose on the city of Lyons, one half of which belonged to the empire, and the other to the kingdom of France. He determined on placing himself with the prelates whom he had summoned under the protection of St. Louis, who then reigned in France. He went from Rome to Genoa by sea, escaping the Pisan fleet which watched to intercept his passage: he excited by his exhortations the enthusiasm of the Guelphs of Genoa, and of the cities of Lombardy and Piedmont, which he visited on his passage; and arriving at Lyons, he opened, on the 28th of June, 1245, in the convent of St. Just, the council of the universal church. He found the bishops of France, England, and Germany eager to adopt his passions; so that he obtained from them at their third sitting, on the 17th of July, a sentence of condemnation against Frederick II. The council declared, that for his crimes and iniquities God had rejected him, and would no longer suffer him to be either emperor or king. In consequence, the pope and the council released his subjects from their oath of allegiance; forbade them under pain of excommunication to obey him under any title whatever; and invited the electors of the empire to proceed to the election of another emperor, while the pope reserved to himself the nomination of another king of the Two Sicilies.

Frederick at first opposed all his strength of soul against the sentence of excommunication pronounced by the council on him. Causing his jewels to be brought him, and placing the golden crown of the empire on his head, he declared before a numerous assembly that he would still wear it, and knew how to defend it; but, notwithstanding the enthusiasm of the Ghibeline party, the devotion of his friends, and the progress of philosophical opinions, which he had himself encouraged, the man whom the church had condemned was in constant danger of being abandoned or betrayed. The mendicant monks every where excited conspiracies against him. They took advantage of the terrors inspired by sickness and age, to make sinners return, as they said, to the ways of salvation, and desired them to make amends for their past transgressions, by delivering the church of God from its most dangerous enemy. Insurrections frequently broke forth in one or other of the Two Sicilies; still oftener the emperor discovered amongst his courtiers plots to destroy him, either by the dagger or poison; even his private secretary, his intimate friend, Pietro delle Vigne, whom he had raised from abject poverty, to whom he had intrusted his most important affairs, gave ear to the counsel of the monks, and promised to poison his master. Frederick, on his part, became suspicious and cruel: his distrust fell on his most faithful friends; and the execu-

E 2

tions which he ordered sometimes preceded the proofs of guilt. He had confided Germany to his son Conrad, and the exclusive government of the Veronese marches to Eccelino. The hatred which this ferocious man excited by his crimes fell on the emperor. Eccelino imprisoned in the most loathsome dungeons those whom he considered his enemies, and frequently put them to death by torture, or suffered them to perish by hunger: he was well aware that the relatives of these victims must also be his enemies: they were, in their turn, arrested; and the more he sacrificed to his barbarity, the more he was called upon to strike. The citizens of Milan, Mantua, Bergamo, and Brescia every day heard of new and horrible crimes committed by the governor of the marches; they conceived the greater detestation of the Ghibeline party, and entertained the firmer determination to repel Frederick. He, on the contrary, had no thoughts of attacking them: he established himself during the council of Lyons at Turin, and thence entered into a negotiation with St. Louis, to obtain by his mediation a reconciliation with the church, to which he made, in token of his submission, the offer to accompany Louis to the Holy Land.

The revolt of Parma, on the 16th of June, 1247, obliged Frederick to resume his arms at a moment when he was least disposed. The friends and relatives of pope Innocent IV., the Guelph nobles of the houses of Corregio, Lupi, and Rossi, re-entering Parma, whence they had been exiled, triumphed over their adversaries, and in their turn expelled them from the city. Frederick was determined at any price to recover Parma. He sent for a numerous band of Saracens from Apulia, commanded by one of his natural sons, named Frederick, to whom he gave the title of king of Antioch. He assembled the Lombard Ghibelines, under the command of another of his illegitimate sons, named Hans or Hensius, called by him king of Sardinia, and whom he had made imperial vicar in Lombardy. Eccelino arrived too at his camp from the Veronese march, with the militias of Padua, Vicenza, and Verona; and the soldiers whom he had raised in his hereditary fiefs. On the other side, the Guelphs of Lombardy hastened to send succour to a

city which had just sacrificed itself for them. The
Milanese set the example; the militias of Mantua,
Placentia, and Ferrara followed it; and the Guelphs,
who had been exiled from Reggio, Modena, and other
Ghibeline cities, thinking they served their country in
fighting for their faction, arrived in great numbers to
shut themselves up in Parma. Frederick was prevented
from hanging the hostages given previous to the revolt,
before the walls of the city, by the militia of Pavia; who
declared it was with the sword of Ghibeline soldiers only,
and not with that of the executioner, that they would
secure the throne of the emperor. The siege made little
progress; the winter had begun, but Frederick persisted
in his attempt. He proclaimed his determination to rase
Parma to the ground, and to transfer those of the inhabitants who should be spared into his fortified camp, of
which he would make a new town, called Vittoria. This
camp, which he quitted on a hawking party, on the 8th
of February, 1248, was in his absence surprised by a
sortie of a Guelph army from Parma, taken, and pillaged,
his soldiers were dispersed, and the emperor had the
humiliation of being forced to raise the siege.

Before this event, he had sent his son, the king of
Antioch, into Tuscany with 1600 German cavalry, to
secure Florence to his party; where, since the death of
Buondelmonte, the Guelphs and Ghibelines, always in
opposition, had not ceased fighting. There was seldom
an assembly, a festival, a public ceremony, without some
offence given, either by one or other of the parties. Both
flew to arms; chains were thrown across the streets;
barricades were immediately formed, and in every quarter,
round every noble family; the more contiguous, who
had the most frequent causes of quarrel, fought at the
same time in ten different places. Nevertheless the
republic was supposed to lean towards the Guelph party;
and the Florentine Ghibelines, in their relations with
other people, had never sought to separate from their
fellow-countrymen, or to place themselves in opposition
to their magistrates. Frederick, fearing to lose Florence,
wrote to the Uberti, the chiefs of the Ghibeline faction,
to assemble secretly in their palace all their party, to
attack afterwards in concert and at once all the posts of

the Guelphs; whilst his son, the king of Antioch, should present himself at the gates, and thus expel their adversaries from the city. This plan was executed on the night of Candlemas, 1248: the barricades of the Guelphs were forced in every quarter, because they defended themselves in small bands against the whole of the opposite party. The Ghibelines, masters of the town, ordered all the Guelphs to quit it. They afterwards demolished thirty-six palaces belonging to the same number of the most illustrious families of that party; and intimidating the other cities of Tuscany, they constrained them to follow their example, and declare for the emperor.

Frederick II., after the check experienced by him at Parma, returned to his kingdom of the Two Sicilies, and left to his son Hensius, who established himself at Modena, the direction of the war in Lombardy. The pope, however, had sent a legate, the cardinal Octavian degli Ubaldini, to the Guelph cities, to engage them to pursue their victory, and punish the imperial party for what he called their revolt against the church. The powerful city of Bologna, already celebrated for its university, and superior to the neighbouring ones by its wealth, its population, and the zeal which a democratic government excites, undertook to make the Guelph party triumph throughout the Cispadane region. Bologna first attacked Romagna, and forced the towns of Imola, Faenza, Forli, and Cervia to expel the Ghibelines, and declare for the church. The Bolognese next turned their arms against Modena. The Modenese cavalry, entering Bologna one day by surprise, carried off from a public fountain a bucket, which henceforth was preserved in the tower of Modena as a glorious trophy. The war which followed furnished Tassoni with the subject of his mock-heroic poem, entitled " La Secchia Rapita." The vengeance of the Bolognese was, however, any thing but burlesque; after several bloody battles, the two armies finally met at Fossalta on the 26th of May, 1249. Philip Ugoni of Brescia, who was this year podestà of Bologna, commanded the Guelph army, in which was united a detachment from the militias of all the cities of the league of Lombardy. The Ghibelines were led by king Hensius: each army consisted of from fifteen to twenty thousand combatants. The battle was long and bloody, but ended with the complete defeat of the Ghibeline party ; king Hensius himself fell into the hands of the conquerors : he was immediately taken to Bologna, and confined in the palace of the podestà. The senate of that city rejected all offers of ransom, all intercession in his favour. He was entertained in a splendid manner, but kept a prisoner during the rest of his life, which lasted for twenty-two years.

This last check overwhelmed Frederick. He had now during thirty years combated the church and the Guelph party : his bodily as well as mental energy was worn out in this long contest. His life was embittered by the treason of those whom he believed his friends, by the disasters of his partisans, and by the misfortunes which had pursued him even in his own family. He saw his power in Italy decline ; while the crown of Germany was disputed with his son Conrad, by competitors favoured by the church. He appeared to be at length himself disturbed by the excommunications of the pope, and the fear of that hell with which he had been so incessantly menaced. He implored anew the assistance and mediation of St. Louis of France, who was then in the isle of Cyprus. He provided magnificently for the wants of the crusade army, which this king commanded : he solicited leave to join it. He offered to engage never to return from the Holy Land, and to submit to the most humiliating expiations which the church could impose. He succeeded in inspiring St. Louis with interest and gratitude. Frederick, while waiting the effect of St. Louis's good offices, seemed occupied solely in the affairs of his kingdom of the Two Sicilies, where he restored order, and established a prosperity not to be seen elsewhere in Europe. On the 13th of December, 1250, he was seized with a dysentery, of which he died, in the fifty-sixth year of his age, at his castle of Florentino, in the capitanate where he had fixed his residence.

CHAPTER IV

INTERREGNUM OF THE EMPIRE—DECLINE AND SUBJUGATION OF THE
LOMBARD REPUBLICS — CHARLES OF ANJOU CALLED TO THE
SUPPORT OF THE GUELPHS—HIS POWER—HIS CRUELTY—SICILIAN
VESPERS

THE Italian cities, which for the most part date the commencement of their liberty from the conflicts between
the sovereigns of Italy and Germany, or the invasion of
Otho the Great, in 951, had already, at the death of
Frederick II., enjoyed for three centuries the protection
and progressive improvement of their municipal constitutions. These three centuries, with reference to the rest
of Europe, are utterly barbarous. Their history is every
where obscure and imperfectly known. It records only
some great revolution, or the victories and calamities of
princes; the people are always left in the shade: a writer
would have thought it beneath him to occupy himself
about the fate of plebeians; they were not supposed to be
worthy of history. The towns of Italy, so prodigiously
superior to all others in wealth, intelligence, energy, and
independence, were equally regardless of preserving any
record of past times. Some grave chroniclers preserved
the memory of an important crisis, but in general the
cities passed whole centuries without leaving any written
memorial; thinking it perhaps good policy not to attract
notice, and to envelope themselves in obscurity. They,
however, of necessity, departed from this system in the
last century, owing to the two conflicts, in both of which
they remained victorious. From 1150 to 1183, they had
fought to obtain the peace of Constance, which they
regarded as their constitutional charter. From 1183 to
1250, they preserved the full exercise of the privileges
which they had so gloriously acquired: but while they
continually advanced in opulence, while intelligence and
the arts became more and more developed, they were led
by two passions, equally honourable, to range themselves
under two opposite banners. One party, listening only
. to their faith, their attachment, and their gratitude to a
family which had given them many great sovereigns, were

ready to venture their all for the cause of the Ghibelines ; the other, alarmed for the independence of the church, and the liberty of Italy, by the always increasing grandeur of the house of Hohenstaufen, were not less resolute in their endeavours to wrest from it the sceptre which menaced them. The cities of the Lombard league had reached the summit of their power at the period of this second conflict. During the interregnum which lasted from the death of Frederick II. to the entrance into Italy of Henry VII. in 1310, the Lombard republics, a prey to the spirit of faction, and more intent on the triumph of either the Guelph or Ghibeline parties, than on securing their own constitutions, all submitted themselves to the military power of some nobles to whom they had intrusted the command of their militias, and thus all lost their liberty.

On the death of Frederick II., his son, Conrad IV., king of Germany, did not feel himself sufficiently strong to appear in Italy, and place on his head, in succession, the iron crown at Monza, and the golden crown at Rome. He wished first of all to secure that of the Two Sicilies ; and embarked at some port in Istria for Naples, in a Pisan vessel, during the month of October, 1251. The remainder of his short life was passed in combating and vanquishing the Neapolitan Guelphs. He died suddenly at Lavello, on the 21st of May, 1254. His natural brother, Manfred, a young hero, hardly twenty years of age, succeeded by his activity and courage in recovering the kingdom which Innocent IV. had already invaded, with the intention of subduing it to the temporal power of the holy see. But Manfred, beloved by the Saracens of Luceria, who were the first to defend him, and admired by the Ghibelines of the Two Sicilies, was for a long time detained there by the attacks of the Guelphs, before he could in his turn pursue them through the rest of Italy. Conrad had left in Germany a son, still an infant, afterwards known under the name of Conradin ; he was acknowledged king of Germany, under the name of Conrad V., by a small party only. The electors left the empire without a head ; and when they afterwards proceeded to elect one, in the year 1257, their suffrages were divided between two princes, strangers to Germany,

F

where they had never set foot; one, an Englishman, Richard earl of Cornwall; the other, a Spaniard, Alphonso X. of Castile.[1]

Innocent IV. was still in France, when he learnt the death of Frederick II.; he returned thence in the beginning of the spring of 1251; wrote to all the towns to celebrate the deliverance of the church; gave boundless expression to his joy; and made his entry into Milan, and the principal cities of Lombardy, with all the pomp of a triumph. He supposed that the republicans of Italy had fought only for him, and that he alone would henceforth be obeyed by them; of this he soon made them but too sensible. He treated the Milanese with arrogance, and threatened to excommunicate them for not having respected some ecclesiastical immunity. It was the moment in which the republic, like a warrior reposing himself after battle, began to feel its wounds. It had made immense sacrifices for the Guelph party; it had emptied the treasury, obtained patriotic gifts from every citizen who had any thing to spare; pledged its revenues, and loaded itself with debt to the extent of its credit. For the discharge of their debts, the citizens resigned themselves to the necessity of giving to their podestà, Beno de' Gozzadini of Bologna, unlimited power to create new imposts, and to raise money under every form he found possible. The ingratitude of the pope, at a moment of universal suffering, deeply offended the Milanese; and the influence of the Ghibelines in a city, where, till then, they had been treated as enemies, might be dated from that period.

Innocent IV. pursued his journey towards Rome; but found the capital of Christendom still less disposed than the first city of Lombardy to obey him. The Romans, in 1253, called another Bolognese noble, named Brancaleone d'Andolo, to the government of their republic; and gave him, with the title of senator, almost unlimited authority. The citizens, continually alarmed by the quarrels and battles of the Roman nobles, who had converted the Coliseum, the tombs of Adrian, Augustus, and Cæcilia

---

[1] Until the end of the year 1256, William, Count of Holland, one of the competitors whom the Guelph party had given to Frederick II., bore the title of King of the Romans.

Metella, the arches of triumph, and other monuments of
ancient Rome, into so many fortresses, whence issued
banditti, whom they kept in pay, to pillage passengers,
and peaceable merchants, demanded of the government,
above all things, vigour and severity. They forgot the
guarantee due to the accused, in their attention to those
only which were required by the public peace. The
senator Brancaleone, at the head of the Roman militia,
successively attacked these monuments, become the
retreat of robbers and assassins; he levelled to the
ground the towers which surmounted them; he hanged
the adventurers who defended them, with their commanders the nobles, at the palace windows of the latter;
and thus established, by terror, security in the streets of
Rome. He hardly showed more respect to Innocent
than to the Roman nobility. The pope, in order to be at
a distance from him, had transferred his court to Assisi.
Brancaleone sent him word, that it was not decorous in a
pope to be wandering like a vagabond from city to city;
and that, if he did not immediately return to the capital
of Christendom, of which he was the bishop, the Romans,
with their senator at their head, would march to Assisi,
and send him out of it by setting fire to the town.

Thus, although the power of kings had given way to
that of the people, liberty was in general ill understood
and insecure. The passions were impetuous; a certain
point of honour was attached to violence; the nobles
believed they gave proof of independence by rapine and
outrage; and the friends of order believed they had
attained the highest purpose of government, when they
made such audacious disturbers tremble. The turbulence
and number of the noble criminals, the support which
their crimes found in a false point of honour, form an
excuse for the judicial institutions of the Italian republics,
which were all more calculated to strike terror into
criminals too daring to conceal themselves, than to protect the accused against the unjust suspicion of secret
crimes. Order could be maintained only by an iron
hand; but this iron hand soon crushed liberty. Nevertheless, among the Italian cities there was one which,
above all others, seemed to think of justice more than of
peace, and of the security of the citizen more than of the

punishment of the guilty. It was Florence: its judicial institutions are, indeed, far from meriting to be held up as models; but they were the first in Italy which offered any guarantee to the citizen; because Florence was the city where the love of liberty was the most general and the most constant in every class; where the cultivation of the understanding was carried farthest; and where enlightenment of mind soonest appeared in the improvement of the laws.

The Ghibeline nobles had taken possession of the sovereignty of Florence, with the help of the king of Antioch, two years before the death of his father, Frederick II.; but their power soon became insupportable to the free and proud citizens of that republic, who had already become wealthy by commerce, and who reckoned amongst them some distinguished literary men, such as Brunetto Latini, and Guido Cavalcante, without having lost their simplicity of manners, their sobriety of habits, or their bodily vigour. Frederick II. still lived, when, by an unanimous insurrection, on the 20th of October, 1250, they set themselves free. All the citizens assembled at the same moment in the square of Santa Croce; they divided themselves into fifty groups, of which each group chose a captain, and thus formed companies of militia: a council of these officers was the first-born authority of this newly-revived republic. The podestà, by his severity and partiality, had rendered himself universally detested: they deposed him, and supplied his place by another judge, under the name of captain of the people, but soon afterwards decreed that the podestà and the captain should each have an independent tribunal, in order that they should exercise upon each other a mutual control; at the same time, they determined that both should be subordinate to the supreme magistracy of the republic, which was charged with the administration, but divested of the judicial power. They decreed that this magistracy, which they called the *signoria*, should be always present, always assembled in the palace of the republic, ever ready to control the podestà or the captain, to whom they had been obliged to delegate so much power. The town was divided into six parts, each *sestier*, as it was called, named two *anziani*. These twelve

magistrates ate together, slept at the public palace, and
could never go out but together; their function lasted
only two months. Twelve others, elected by the people,
succeeded them; and the republic was so rich in good
citizens, and in men worthy of its confidence, that this
rapid succession of *anziani* did not exhaust their number.
The Florentine militia, at the same time, attacked and
demolished all the towers which served as a refuge to the
nobles, in order that all should henceforth be forced to
submit to the common law.

The new *signoria* was hardly informed of the death of
Frederick, when, by a decree of the 7th of January, 1251,
they recalled all the Guelph exiles to Florence. They
henceforth laboured to give that party the preponderance
throughout Tuscany. They declared war against the
neighbouring cities of Pistoia, Pisa, Sienna, and Volterra;
not to subjugate them, or to impose hard conditions, but
to force them to rally round the party which they considered that of the church and of liberty. The year 1254,
when the Florentines were commanded by their podestà,
Guiscardo Pietra Santa, a Milanese, is distinguished in
their history by the name of the "year of Victories."
They took the two cities of Pistoia and Volterra; they
forced those of Pisa and Sienna to sign a peace favourable to the Guelph party; they refused to profit by a
treason which had given them possession of the citadel
of Arezzo, and they restored it to the Aretini; lastly,
they built in the Lunigiana, beyond the territory of
Lucca, a fortress destined to shut the entry of Tuscany
on the Ligurian side, which, in the memory of their
podestà, bears to this day the name of Pietra Santa.
The signoria showed themselves also worthy to be the
governors of a city renowned for commerce, the arts, and
liberty. The whole monetary system of Europe was at
this period abandoned to the depredations of sovereigns
who continually varied the title and weight of coins,—
sometimes to defraud their creditors, at other times to
force their debtors to pay more than they had received,
or the tax-payers more than was due. During 150 years
more, the kings of France violated their faith with the
public, making annually, with the utmost effrontery,
some important change in the coins. But the republic

of Florence, in the year 1252, coined its golden florin, of 24 carats fine, and of the weight of one drachm. It placed the value under the guarantee of publicity, and of commercial good faith ; and that coin remained unaltered, as the standard for all other values, as long as the republic itself endured.

A conspiracy of Ghibelines to recover their power in Florence, and to concentrate it in the aristocratic faction, forced the republic, in the year 1258, to exile the most illustrious chiefs of that party. It was then directed by Farinata degli Uberti, who was looked upon as the most eloquent orator and the ablest warrior in Tuscany. All the Florentine Ghibelines were favourably received at Sienna, although the two republics had mutually engaged in their last treaty not to give refuge to the rebels of either city. Farinata afterwards joined Manfred, whom he found firmly established on the throne of the Two Sicilies ; and represented to him that, to guard his kingdom from all attack, he ought to secure Tuscany, and give supremacy to the Ghibeline party. He obtained from him a considerable body of German cavalry, which he led to Sienna. Hostilities between the two republics had already begun : the colours of Manfred had been dragged with contempt through the streets by the Florentines. Farinata resolved to take advantage of the irritation of the Germans, in order to bring the two parties to a general battle. He knew that some ignorant artisans had found their way into the *signoria* of Florence, and he tried to profit by their presumption. He flattered them with the hope that he would open to them one of the gates of Sienna, if they ordered their army to present itself under the walls of that city. At the same time, his emissaries undertook to excite the ill will of the plebeians against the nobles of the Guelph party, who, being more clear-sighted, might discover his intrigues. Notwithstanding the opposition of the nobles in council, the *signoria* resolved to march a Guelph army through the territory of Sienna. They demanded, for this purpose, succour from Bologna, Pistoia, Prato, San Miniato, San Gemignano, Volterra, and Colle. They appointed a meeting with the militias of Arezzo and of Orvieto at Monte Aperto, five miles from Sienna, on the other side of the Arbia. The whole power of the Guelph party in Tuscany, amounting to 30,000 infantry and 3,000 cavalry, was collected there. The Guelphs were only anxious how they should draw their enemies from within the walls of Sienna. They were themselves in a state of perfect security, when, on the 4th of September, 1260, they were unexpectedly attacked by Farinata degli Uberti, and by the generals of Manfred. The Ghibelines had not more than 13,000 men, reckoning the emigrants of Florence, the militias of Sienna and of Pisa, and the Germans; but they relied on a treacherous understanding in the Guelph camp. Bocca degli Abbati, placing himself at the head of the traitors, and suddenly seizing the great standard of the republic, threw it to the ground. The whole army was panic-struck when they saw the colours fall: they learned that the enemy was master of the head-quarters, without knowing their numbers. The Guelphs fled on all sides; but, unrelentingly pursued, left 10,000 dead on the field of battle, and a great number of prisoners in the hands of the enemy.

The Florentine Guelphs found themselves too much weakened by the defeat of Arbia to maintain themselves in Florence. The circumference of the walls was too vast, and the population too much discouraged by the enormous loss which they had experienced, to admit of defending the city. All those, accordingly, who had exercised any authority in the republic,—all those whose names were sufficiently known to discover their party,— left Florence for Lucca together, on horseback. The Guelphs of Prato, Pistoia, Volterra, and San Gemignano could not hope to maintain their ground, when those of Florence failed. All abandoned their dwellings, and joined the Florentines at Lucca. That city granted to the illustrious fugitives the church and portico of San Friano, and the surrounding quarter, where they pitched their tents. The Ghibelines entered Florence on the 27th of September; immediately abolished the popular government; and formed a new magistracy, composed entirely of nobles, who took the oath of fidelity to Manfred, king of the Two Sicilies.

At a diet of the Ghibeline cities, assembled at Empoli, the ambassadors of Pisa and Sienna strongly represented,

that whilst Florence existed, the preponderance of the
Ghibeline party in Tuscany could never be secure. They
affirmed, that the population of that proud and warlike
city was entirely devoted to the Guelph party; that
there was no hope of mitigating their hatred of the nobles
and of the family of the last emperor; that democratic
habits were become a sort of second nature to every one
of the inhabitants; they concluded with demanding that
the walls of Florence should be rased to the ground, and
the people dispersed among the neighbouring towns.
All the Ghibelines of Tuscany, all the deputies of the
cities jealous of Florence, received the proposition favourably. It was about to be adopted, when Farinata degli
Uberti rose, and repelled with indignation this abuse of
the victory which he had just gained. He protested that
he loved his country far better than his party; and
declared that he would, with those same companions in
arms whose bravery they had witnessed at the battle of
Arbia, join the Guelphs, and fight for them, sooner than
consent to the ruin of what was in the world most
dear to him. The enemies of Florence dared not answer
him; and the diet of Empoli contented itself with
decreeing that the league of Tuscany should take into
pay 1000 of the soldiers of Manfred, to support in that
province the preponderance of the Guelph party. Dante
has immortalised Farinata as the saviour of Florence,
and Bocca degli Abbati as the traitor who placed it on
the brink of destruction. His poem is filled with allusions
to this memorable epoch.

While the Ghibelines thus acquired the preponderance
in Tuscany, the tyrant fell who at the head of that party
had caused so much blood to flow in the Trevisan
march. Eccelino was hereditary lord of Bassano and
Pedemonte: he succeeded in making himself named
captain of the people by the republics of Verona, Vicenza,
Padua, Feltre, and Belluno. By this title he united the
judicial with the military power; he was subject only to
councils which he might assemble or not at his pleasure.
It does not appear that there was any permanent magistracy, like the *signoria* of Florence, to repress his abuse
of power. Accordingly, he soon changed the authority
which he derived from the people into a frightful tyranny:

fixing his suspicions upon all who rose to any distinction, who in any way attracted the attention of their fellow-citizens, he did not wait for any expression of discontent, or symptom of resistance, in the nobles, merchants, priests, or lawyers, who by their eminence alone became suspected, to throw them into prison, and there, by the most excruciating torture, extract confessions of crimes that might justify his suspicions. The names which escaped their lips in the agony of torture were carefully registered, in order to supply fresh victims to the tyrant. In the single town of Padua there were eight prisons always full, notwithstanding the incessant toil of the executioner to empty them; two of these contained each 300 prisoners. A brother of Eccelino, named Alberic, governed Treviso with less ferocity, but with a power not less absolute. Cremona was in like manner subject to a Ghibeline chief; Milan no longer evinced any repugnance to that party. In that city, as well as in Brescia, the factions of nobles and plebeians disputed for power.

Alexander IV., to destroy the monster that held in terror the Trevisan march, caused a crusade to be preached in that country. He promised those who combated the ferocious Eccelino all the indulgences usually reserved for the deliverers of the Holy Land. The marquis d'Este, the count di San Bonifazio, with the cities of Ferrara, Mantua, and Bologna, assembled their troops under the standard of the church; they were joined by a horde of ignorant fanatics from the lowest class, anxious to obtain indulgences, but unsusceptible of discipline, and incapable of a single act of valour. Their number, however, so frightened Eccelino's lieutenant at Padua, that he defended but feebly the passage of the Bacchiglione, and the town. The legate Philip, elected archbishop of Ravenna, entered Padua at the head of the crusaders, on the 18th of June, 1256; but he either would not or could not restrain the fanatic and rapacious rabble, which he had summoned to the support of his soldiers: for seven days the city was inhumanly pillaged, by those whom it had received as its deliverers. As soon as Eccelino was informed of the loss he had sustained, he hastened to separate and disarm the 11,000 Paduans belonging to his army; he confined them in prisons, where all, with the exception of 200, met a violent or lingering death. During the two following years, the Guelphs experienced nothing but disasters: the legate, whom the pope had placed at their head, proved incompetent to command them; and the crowd of crusaders whom he called to his ranks served only to compromise them, by want of courage and discipline. The Ghibeline nobles of Brescia even delivered their country into the hands of Eccelino after he had put the legate's army to flight, in the year 1258. The following year, this tyrant, unequalled in Italy for bravery and military talent, always an enemy to luxury, and proof against the seductions of women, making the boldest tremble with a look, and preserving in his diminutive person, at the age of sixty-five, all the vigour of a soldier, advanced into the centre of Lombardy, in the hope that the nobles of Milan, with whom he had already opened a correspondence, would surrender this great city to him. He passed the Oglio, and afterwards the Adda, with the most brilliant army he had ever yet commanded: but the marquis Palavicino, Buoso da Doara, the Cremonese chieftain, and other Ghibelines, his ancient associates, disgusted with his crimes, had secretly made an alliance with the Guelphs, for his destruction. When they saw him advance so far from his home, they rushed upon him from all sides. On the 16th of September, 1259, whilst he was preparing to retire, he found himself stopped at the bridge of Cassano. The Brescians, no longer obedient to his command, began their movement to abandon him; all the points of retreat were cut off by the Milanese, Cremonese, Ferrarians, and Mantuans: repulsed, pursued as far as Vimercato, and at last wounded in the foot, he was made prisoner, and taken to Soncino: there, he refused to speak, rejected all the aid of medicine; tore off all the bandages from his wounds, and finally expired, on the eleventh day of his captivity. His brother with all his family were massacred in the following year.

The defeat of Eccelino, and the destruction of the family of Romano, may be regarded as the last great effort of the Lombards against the establishment of tyranny in their country. About this time, the cities began to be accustomed to absolute power in a single person. In each republic, the nobles, always divided by hereditary feuds, regarded it as disgraceful to submit to the laws, rather than do themselves justice by force of arms : their quarrels, broils, and brigandage carried troubles and disorder into every street and public place. The merchants were continually on the watch to shut their shops on the first cry of alarm ; for the satellites of the nobles were most commonly banditti, to whom they gave shelter in their palaces, and who took advantage of the tumult to plunder the shops. At the same time that the nobles irritated the plebeians by their arrogance, they ridiculed their incapacity, and endeavoured to exclude them from all the public offices. The people often, in their indignation, took arms; the streets were barricaded, and the nobles, besieged in their town houses, were driven to take refuge in their castles ; but if the militias of the towns afterwards presumed to pursue in the plains of Lombardy the nobles whom they forced to emigrate, they soon found themselves sadly inferior. In the course of this century, the nobles had acquired the habit of fighting on horseback, with a lance, and covered with heavy armour. Continual exercise could alone render them expert in the manœuvres of cavalry, and accustom them to the enormous weight of the cuirass and helmet ; on the other hand, this armour rendered them almost invulnerable. When they charged with couched lance, and with all the impetuosity of their war-horses, they overthrew and annihilated the ill-armed infantry opposed to them, without experiencing themselves any damage. The cities soon felt the necessity of opposing cavalry to cavalry, and of taking into their pay either those nobles who made common cause with the people, or foreigners and adventurers, who about this time began to exchange their valour for hire. As the custom was prevalent of giving the command of the militia to the first officer of justice, in order to give him authority either to direct the public force against rebels or disturbers of order, or to discipline the soldier by the fear of punishment, no commander could be found who would undertake the military service or a town, without at the same time possessing the power of the judicial sword,—such power as was intrusted to the podestà or captain of the people. It became necessary then to deliver into his charge what was named the *signoria ;* and the more considerable this corps of cavalry, thus placed for a certain number of years at the service of the republic, the more this *signoria,* to which was attached the power of adjudging life or death in the tribunals, became dangerous to liberty.

Among the first feudal lords who embraced the cause of the people, and undertook the service of a town, with a body of cavalry raised among their vassals, or among the poor nobles, their adherents, was Pagan della Torre, the lord of Valsassina. He had endeared himself to the Milanese by saving their army from the pursuit of Frederick II. after the battle of Cortenuova. He was attached by hereditary affection to the Guelph party; and although himself of illustrious birth, he seemed to partake the resentment of the plebeians of Milan against the nobility who oppressed them. When he died, his brother Martino, after him Raymond, then Philip, lastly, Napoleon della Torre, succeeded each other as captains of the people, commanders of a body of cavalry which they had raised and placed at the service of the city; they were the acknowledged superiors of the podestà and the tribunals. These five lords succeeded each other in less than twenty years ; and even the shortness of their lives accustomed the people to regard their election as the confirmation of a dynasty become hereditary. Other Guelph cities of Lombardy were induced to choose the same captain and governor as Milan, because they believed him a true Guelph, and a real lover of the people. These towns found the advantage of drawing closer their alliance with the city which directed their party; of placing themselves under a more powerful protection; and of supporting their tribunals with a firmer hand. Martin della Torre had been elected podestà of Milan in 1256; three years later, he obtained the title of elder, and lord of the people. At the same time, Lodi also named him lord. In 1263, the city of Novara conferred the same honour on him. Philip, who succeeded him in 1264, was named lord by Milan, Como, Vercelli, and Bergamo. Thus began to be formed among the Lombard republics, without their suspecting that they divested themselves of their liberty,

the powerful state which a century and a half later
became the duchy of Milan. But the pope, jealous of the
house of Della Torre, appointed archbishop of Milan Otho
Visconti, whose family, powerful on the borders of the
Lago Maggiore, then shared the exile of the nobles and
Ghibelines. This prelate placed himself at the head of
their faction ; and henceforward the rivalry between the
families of Della Torre and Visconti made that between
the people and the nobles almost forgotten.

The bitter enmity between the two parties of the
Guelphs and Ghibelines was fatal to the cause of liberty.
With the former, the question was religion,—the independence of the church and of Italy, menaced by the
Germans and Saracens, to whom Manfred granted not
less confidence than Frederick II.; with the latter, honour
and good faith towards an illustrious family, and the
support of the aristocracy as well as of royalty ;—but
both were more intent on avenging offences a thousand
times repeated, and guarding against exile, and the confiscation of property, which never failed to follow the
triumph of the opposite party. These party feelings
deeply moved men who gloried in the sacrifices which
they or their ancestors had made to either party ; while
they regarded as entirely secondary the support of the
laws, the impartiality of the tribunals, or the equal participation of the citizens in the sovereignty. Every town
of Lombardy forgot itself, to make its faction triumph ;
and it looked for success in giving more unity and force
to power. The cities of Mantua and Ferrara, where the
Guelphs were far the more numerous, trusted for their
defence, the one to the count di San Bonifazio, the other
to the marquis d'Este, with so much constancy, that these
nobles, under the name of captains of the people, had
become almost sovereigns. In the republic of Verona,
the Ghibelines, on the contrary, predominated ; and as
they feared their faction might sink at the death of
Eccelino, they called to the command of their militia, and
the presidency of their tribunals, Mastino della Scala,
lord of the castle of that name in the Veronese territory ;
whose power became hereditary in his family. The
marquis Pelavicino, the most renowned Ghibeline in the
whole valley of the Po ; whose strongest castle was

San Donnino, between Parma and Placentia, and who had
formed and disciplined a superb body of cavalry, was
named, alternately with his friend, Buoso da Doara, lord
of the city of Cremona. Pavia and Placentia also chose
him almost always their captain; and this honour was at
the same time conferred on him by Milan, Brescia,
Tortona, and Alexandria. The Ghibeline party had,
since the offence given by Innocent IV. to the Guelphs
of Milan, obtained the ascendency in Lombardy. The
house of Della Torre seemed even to lean towards it;
and it was all powerful in Tuscany. The city of Lucca
had been the last to accede to that party in 1263; and the
Tuscan Guelphs, obliged to leave their country, had
formed a body of soldiers, which placed itself in the pay
of the few cities of Lombardy still faithful to the Guelph
party.

The court of Rome saw, with great uneasiness, this
growing power of the Ghibeline party, firmly established
in the Two Sicilies, under the sceptre of Manfred.
Feared even in Rome and the neighbouring provinces;
master in Tuscany, and making daily progress in
Lombardy,—Manfred seemed on the point of making the
whole peninsula a single monarchy. It was no longer
with the arms of the Italians that the pope could expect
to subdue him. The Germans afforded no support.
Divided between Richard of Cornwall and Alphonso of
Castile, they seemed desirous of delivering themselves
from the imperial authority, by dividing between foreigners
an empty title; while each state sought to establish a
separate independence at home, and abandon the supremacy of the empire over Italy. It was accordingly
necessary to have recourse to other barbarians to prevent
the formation of an Italian monarchy fatal to the power
of the pontiff. Alexander IV. died on the 25th of May,
1261 : three months afterwards, a Frenchman, who took
the name of Urban IV., was elected his successor; and
he did not hesitate to arm the French against Manfred.

His predecessor had already opened some negotiations,
for the purpose of giving the crown of Sicily to Edmund,
son of Henry III. king of England. Urban put an end
to them by having recourse to a prince nearer, braver,
and more powerful. He addressed himself to Charles

count of Anjou, the brother of St. Louis, sovereign in
right of his wife of the county of Provence. Charles had
already signalised himself in war; he was, like his brother,
a faithful believer, and still more fanatical and bitter
towards the enemies of the church, against whom he
abandoned himself without restraint to his harsh and
pitiless character. His religious zeal, however, did not
interfere with his policy; his interest set limits to his
subjection to the church; he knew how to manage those
whom he wished to gain; and he could flatter, at his
need, the public passions, restrain his anger, and preserve
in his language a moderation which was not in his heart.
Avarice appeared his ruling passion; but it was only the
means of serving his ambition, which was unbounded.
He accepted the offer of the pope. His wife Beatrice,
ambitious of the title of queen, borne by her three sisters,
pawned all her jewels to aid in levying an army of
30,000 men, which she led herself through Lombardy.
He had preceded her. Having gone by sea to Rome,
with 1000 knights, he made his entry into that city on
the 24th of May, 1265. A new pope, like his predecessor
a Frenchman, named Clement IV., had succeeded Urban,
and was not less favourable to Charles of Anjou. He
caused him to be elected senator by the Roman republic,
and invested him with the kingdom of Sicily, which he
charged him to conquer; under the condition, however,
that the crown should never be united to that of the
empire, or to the sovereignty of Lombardy and Tuscany.
A tribute of 8000 ounces of gold, and a white palfrey,
was, by this investiture, assigned to St. Peter.

The French army, headed by Beatrice, did not pass
through Italy till towards the end of the summer of
1265; and in the month of February of the following
year, Charles entered, at its head, the kingdom of
Naples. He met Manfred, who awaited him in the plain
of Grandella, near Benevento, on the 26th of February.
The battle was bloody. The Germans and Saracens
were true to their ancient valour; but the Apulians fled
like cowards, and the brave son of Frederick II., abandoned by them on the field of battle, perished. The
kingdom of the Two Sicilies was the price of this victory.
Resistance ceased, but not massacre. Charles gave up

the pillage of Benevento to his soldiers ; and they cruelly put to death all the inhabitants. The Italians, who believed they had experienced from the Germans and Saracens of Frederick and Manfred all that could be feared from the most barbarous enemies, now found that there was a degree of ferocity still greater than that to which they had been accustomed from the house of Hohenstaufen. The French seemed always ready to give as to receive death. The two strong colonies of Saracens at Luceria and Nocera were soon exterminated, and in a few years there remained not in the Two Sicilies a single individual of that nation or religion, nor one German who had been in the pay of Manfred. Charles willingly consented to acknowledge the Apulians and Sicilians his subjects; but he oppressed them, as their conqueror, with intolerable burdens. While he distributed amongst his followers all the great fiefs of the kingdom, he so secured, with a hand of iron, his detested dominion, that two years afterwards, when Conradin, the son of Conrad, and the nephew of Manfred, arrived from Germany to dispute the crown, few malcontents in the Two Sicilies had the courage to declare for him.

The victory of Charles of Anjou over Manfred restored the ascendant of the Guelph party in Italy. Philip della Torre, who for some time seemed to hesitate between the two factions, at last gave passage through the Milanese territory to the army of Beatrice. Buoso da Doara was accused of having received money not to oppose her on the Oglio. The count di San Bonifazio, the marquis d'Este, and afterwards the Bolognese, openly joined her party. After the battle of Grandella, the Florentines rose, and drove out, on the 11th of November, 1266, the German garrison, commanded by Guido Novello, the lieutenant of Manfred. They soon afterwards received about 800 French cavalry from Charles, to whom they intrusted, for ten years, the *signoria* of Florence; that is to say, they conferred on him the rights allowed by the peace of Constance to the emperors. At the same time they re-established, with full liberty, their internal constitution; they augmented the power of their numerous councils, from which they excluded the nobles and Ghibelines ; and they gave to the corporations of trade, into which all the industrious part of the population was divided, a direct share in the government.

It was about the end of the year 1267 that the young Conradin, aged only sixteen years, arrived at Verona, with 10,000 cavalry, to claim the inheritance of which the popes had despoiled his family. All the Ghibelines and brave captains, who had distinguished themselves in the service of his grandfather and uncle, hastened to join him, and to aid him with their swords and counsel. The republics of Pisa and Sienna, always devoted to his family, but whose zeal was now redoubled by their jealousy of the Florentines, made immense sacrifices for him. The Romans, offended at the pope's having abandoned their city for Viterbo, as well as jealous of his pretensions in the republic, from the government of which he had excluded the nobles, opened their gates to Conradin, and promised him aid. But all these efforts, all this zeal, did not suffice to defend the heir of the house of Hohenstaufen against the valour of the French. Conradin entered the kingdom of his fathers by the Abruzzi; and met Charles of Anjou in the plain of Tagliacozzo, on the 23rd of August, 1268. A desperate battle ensued: victory long remained doubtful. Two divisions of the army of Charles were already destroyed; and the Germans, who considered themselves the victors, were dispersed in pursuit of the enemy; when the French prince, who, till then, had not appeared on the field, fell on them with his body of reserve, and completely routed them. Conradin, forced to fly, was arrested, forty-five miles from Tagliacozzo, as he was about to embark for Sicily. He was brought to Charles, who, without pity for his youth, esteem for his courage, or respect for his just right, exacted, from the iniquitous judges before whom he subjected him to the mockery of a trial, a sentence of death. Conradin was beheaded in the market-place at Naples, on the 26th of October, 1268. With him perished several of his most illustrious companions in arms,—German princes, Ghibeline nobles, and citizens of Pisa; and, after the sacrifice of these first victims, an uninterrupted succession of executions long continued to fill the Two Sicilies with dismay.

The defeat and death of Conradin established the

preponderance of the Guelph party throughout the peninsula. Charles placed himself at the head of it : the pope named him imperial vicar in Italy during the inter-regnum of the empire, and sought to annex to that title all the rights formerly exercised by the emperors in the free cities. Clement IV. died on the 29th of November, 1268,—one month after the execution of Conradin. The cardinals remained thirty-three months without being able to agree on the choice of a successor. During this interregnum,—the longest the pontifical chair had ever experienced,—Charles remained sole chief of the Guelph party, ruling over the whole of Italy, which had neither pope nor emperor. He convoked, in 1269, a diet of the Lombard cities at Cremona, in which the towns of Placentia, Cremona, Parma, Modena, Ferrara, and Reggio, consented to confer on him the *signoria :* Milan, Como, Vercelli, Novara, Alexandria, Tortona, Turin, Pavia, Bergamo, and Bologna, declared they should feel honoured by his alliance and friendship, but could not take him for master. Italy already felt the weight of the French yoke, which would have pressed still heavier if the crusade against Tunis, to which Charles of Anjou was summoned by his brother, Saint Louis, had not diverted his projects of ambition.

The conclave assembled at Viterbo at length raised to the vacant chair Tebaldo Visconti, of Placentia, who was at that time in the Holy Land. On his return to Italy, in the year 1272, he took the name of Gregory X. This wise and moderate man soon discovered that the court of Rome had overreached itself : in crushing the house of Hohenstaufen, it had given itself a new master, not less dangerous than the preceding. Gregory, instead of seeking to annihilate the Ghibelines, like his predecessors, occupied himself only in endeavouring to restore an equilibrium and peace between them and the Guelphs. He persuaded the Florentines and Siennese to recall the exiled Ghibelines, for the purpose, as he announced, of uniting all Christendom in the defence of the Holy Land ; and testified the strongest resentment against Charles, who threw obstacles in the way of this reconciliation. He relieved Pisa from the interdict that had been laid on it by the holy see. He showed favour to Venice and

Genoa; both of which, offended by the arrogance and injustice of Charles, had made common cause with his enemies. He engaged the electors of Germany to take advantage of the death of Richard of Cornwall, which took place in 1271, and put an end to the interregnum by proceeding to a new election. The electors conferred the crown, in 1273, on Rodolph of Hapsburg, founder of the house of Austria. The death of Gregory X., in the beginning of January, 1276, deprived him of the opportunity to develop the projects which these first steps seem to indicate; but Nicolas III., who succeeded him in 1277, after three ephemeral popes, undertook more openly to humble Charles, and to support the Ghibeline party. He forced the king of Sicily to renounce the title of imperial vicar, to which Charles had no title except during the interregnum of the empire: he still further engaged him to resign the title of senator of Rome, and the dignity of the *signoria*, which had been conferred on him by the cities of Lombardy and Tuscany, by representing to him that his power over those provinces was contrary to the bull of investiture, which had put him in possession of the kingdom of Naples.

Rodolph of Hapsburg, who had never visited Italy, and was ignorant of the geography of that country, was, in his turn, persuaded by the pope to confirm the charters of Louis *le Débonnaire*, of Otho I., and of Henry VI., of which copies were sent to him. In these charters, whether true or false, taken from the chancery at Rome, the sovereignty of the whole of Emilia or Romagna, the Pentapolis, the march of Ancona, the patrimony of St. Peter, and the campagna of Rome, from Radicofani to Ceperano, were assigned to the church. The imperial chancery confirmed, without examination, a concession which had never been really made. The two Fredericks, as well as their predecessors, had always considered this whole extent of country as belonging to the empire, and always exercised there the imperial rights. A chancellor of Rodolph arrived in these provinces to demand homage and the oath of allegiance, which were yielded without difficulty; but Nicolas appealed against this homage, and called it a sacrilegious usurpation. Rodolph was obliged to acknowledge that it was in contradiction to his own diplomas, and resigned his pretensions. From that period, 1278, the republics, as well as the principalities situated in the whole extent of what is now called the States of the Church, held of the holy see, and not of the emperor.

A revolution, not long previous, in the principal cities of Lombardy, had secured the preponderance to the nobles and the Ghibeline party. These, having been for a considerable period exiled from Milan, experienced a continuation of disasters, and, instead of fear, excited compassion. While Napoleon della Torre, chief of the republic of Milan, was exasperating the plebeians and Guelphs with his arrogance and contempt of their freedom, he was informed that Otho Visconti, whom he had exiled, although archbishop of Milan, had assembled round him at Como many nobles and Ghibelines, with whom he intended making an attack on the Milanese territory. Napoleon marched to meet him ; but, despising enemies whom he had so often vanquished, he carelessly suffered himself to be surprised by the Ghibelines at Desio, in the night of the 21st of January, 1277. Having been made prisoner, with five of his relatives, he and they were placed in three iron cages, in which the archbishop kept them confined. This prelate was himself received with enthusiasm at Milan, at Cremona, and Lodi. He formed anew the councils of these republics, admitting only Ghibelines and nobles ; who, ruined by a long exile, and often supported by the liberality of the archbishop, were become humble and obsequious : their deference degenerated into submission ; and the republic of Milan, henceforth governed by the Visconti, became soon no more than a principality.

Nicolas III., of the noble Roman family of the Orsini, felt an hereditary affection for the Ghibelines, and every where favoured them. A rivalry between two illustrious families of Bologna, the Gieremei and the Lambertazzi, terminated, in 1274, in the exile of the latter, who were Ghibelines, with all their adherents. The quarrel between the two families became, from that period, a bloody war throughout Romagna. Guido de Montefeltro, lord of the mountains in the neighbourhood of Urbino, who had never joined any republic, received the Ghibelines into

his country; and in commanding them gained the reputation of a great captain. Nicolas III. sent a legate to
Romagna, to compel Bologna and all the Guelph republics
to recall the Ghibelines, and establish peace throughout
the province. He succeeded in 1279. Another legate on
a similar mission, and with equal success, was sent to
Florence and Sienna. The balance seemed at last on
the point of being established in Italy, when Nicolas died,
on the 19th of August, 1280.

Charles, who had submitted without opposition, and
without even manifesting any displeasure, to the depres-
sion of a party on which were founded all his hopes, and
to a reconciliation which destroyed his influence in the
Guelph republics, hastened to Viterbo as soon as he
learned the death of the pope, fully resolved not to suffer
another of his enemies to ascend the chair of St. Peter.
He caused three cardinals, relatives of Nicolas, whom he
regarded as being adverse to him, to be removed by force
from the conclave; and, striking terror into the rest, he
obtained, on the 22nd of January, 1281, the election of a
pope entirely devoted to him. This was a canon of Tours,
who took the name of Martin IV. He seemed to have
no higher mission than that of seconding the ambition of
the king of the Two Sicilies, and serving him in his
enmities. Far from thinking of forming any balance to
his power, he laboured to give him the sovereignty of all
Italy. He conferred on him the title of senator of Rome;
he gave the government of all the provinces of the church
to his French officers; he caused the Ghibelines to be
exiled from all the cities; and he encouraged, with all
his power, the new design of Charles to take possession
of the Eastern empire. Constantinople had been taken
from the Latins on the 25th of July, 1261; and the son of
the last Latin emperor was son-in-law of Charles of
Anjou. Martin IV. excommunicated Michael Paleologus,
the Greek emperor, who had vainly endeavoured to
reconcile the two churches. The new armament, which
Charles was about to lead into Greece, was in preparation at the same time in all the ports of the Two Sicilies.
The king's agents collected the taxes with redoubled
insolence, and levied money with greater severity. The
judges endeavoured to smother resistance by striking

terror. In the meanwhile, a noble of Salerno, named John da Procida, the friend, confidant, and physician of Frederick II., and of Manfred, visited in disguise the Two Sicilies, to reanimate the zeal of the ancient Ghibelines, and rouse their hatred of the French and of Charles. After having traversed Greece and Spain to excite new enemies against him, he obtained assurances that Michael Paleologus, and Constance, the daughter of Manfred and wife of don Pedro of Aragon, would not suffer the Sicilians to be destroyed, if these had the courage to rise against their oppressors. Their assistance was, in fact, promised,—it was even prepared; but Sicily was destined to be delivered by a sudden and popular explosion, which took place at Palermo, on the 30th of March, 1282. It was excited by a French soldier, who treated rudely the person of a young bride as she was proceeding to the church of Montreal, with her betrothed husband, to receive the nuptial benediction. The indignation of her relations and friends was communicated with the rapidity of lightning to the whole population of Palermo. At that moment the bells of the churches were ringing for vespers: the people answered by the cry, " To arms—death to the French !" The French were attacked furiously on all sides. Those who attempted to defend themselves were soon overpowered ; others, who endeavoured to pass for Italians, were known by their pronunciation of two words, which they were made to repeat—*ceci* and *ciceri*, and were, on their mispronunciation, immediately put to death. In a few hours, more than 4000 weltered in their blood. Every town in Sicily followed the example of Palermo. Thus the Sicilian vespers overthrew the tyranny of Charles of Anjou and of the Guelphs; separated the kingdom of Sicily from that of Naples; and transferred the crown of the former to don Pedro of Aragon, the son-in-law of Manfred, who was considered the heir to the house of Hohenstaufen.

CHAPTER V

ITALY NEGLECTED BY THE EMPERORS—ABANDONED BY THE POPES
—COUNT UGOLINO—THE BLANCHI AND NERI AT FLORENCE—
CLOSE OF THE GRAND COUNCIL AT VENICE — THE EMPEROR
HENRY VII.—HIS EXPEDITION INTO ITALY

HITHERTO we have found the connecting chain of the
events, of which we have undertaken the narrative, in a
common interest felt throughout Italy. In seeking to
trace the concurrent history of more than two hundred
small states, we have found their frequent revolutions
referable to the efforts made by the Italians to maintain
the balance between the rights of the empire, of the
church, and of each city. In the period on which we now
enter, politics become complex, interests more widely
spread ; and it is much more difficult to seize and follow
a dominant idea amidst the various revolutions to which
Italy was a prey. This difference results chiefly from
the fact, that no potentate existed in Italy at this time
superior to the republics ; such as the former kings of
Naples, the emperors, and popes, who succeeded in
acquiring the entire government of a faction, and in thus
directing to one end the opposite efforts of all the people
of the peninsula.

Charles of Anjou, the first French king of the Two
Sicilies, survived the Sicilian vespers only three years.
He died on the 7th of January, 1285, aged sixty-five
years. At this period, his son, Charles II., was a prisoner
in the hands of the Sicilians : he was set at liberty in 1288,
in pursuance of a treaty, by which he acknowledged the
separation and independence of the two crowns of Naples
and Sicily. The first was assigned to the Guelphs and
the house of Anjou ; the second to the Ghibelines, and the
house of Aragon : but Nicholas IV., by whose influence
the treaty was made, broke it, released Charles from his
oath, and authorised him to begin the war anew. This
war, which lasted twenty-four years, occupied without
lustre the whole reign of Charles II. This prince was
milder than his father, but weaker also. He had neither
the stern character of Charles of Anjou, which excited

hatred; nor his talents, which commanded admiration
or respect. He always called himself the protector of
the Guelph party, but ceased to be its champion; and
neither the court of Rome, nor the Guelph republics, any
longer demanded counsel, direction, or support from the
court of Naples. He died on the 5th of May, 1309; and
was succeeded by his son Robert. The influence of the
emperors, as protectors of the Ghibeline party, during
this period was almost extinct in Italy. Rodolph of
Hapsburg, who reigned with glory in Germany from
1273 to 1291, never passed the Alps to be acknowledged
emperor and king of the Lombards; after him, Adolphus
of Nassau, and his successor, Albert of Austria,—the one
assassinated in 1298, the other in 1308,—remained alike
strangers to Italy. The Ghibeline party was, accordingly,
no longer supported or directed by the emperors, but it
maintained itself by its own resources, by the attachment
of the nobles to the imperial name, and still more by the
self-interest of the captains; who, raised to the *signoria*
either by the choice of the people or of their faction,
created for themselves, in the name of the empire, a
sovereignty to which the Italians unhesitatingly gave the
name of tyranny.

Lastly, the third power, that of the pope, which till
then had directed the politics of Italy, ceased about this
time to follow a regular system, and consequently to give
a powerful impulse to faction. Martin IV., whose life
terminated two months after that of Charles I., had
always acted as his creature, had seconded him in his
enmities, in his thirst of vengeance against the Sicilians,
and in his efforts to recover his dominion over Italy.
But Honorius IV., who reigned after him, from 1285 to
1287, appeared to have no other thought than that of
aggrandising the noble house of Savelli at Rome, of
which he was himself a member: after him, Nicolas IV.,
from 1288 to 1292, was not less zealous in his efforts
to do as much for that of Colonna. His predecessor,
Nicolas III., had a few years previously set the example,
by applying all his power as pope to the elevation of the
Orsini. These are nearly the first examples of the
nepotism of the popes, who had hardly yet begun to feel
themselves sovereigns. They raised these three great

Roman families above all their ancient rivals: almost all the castles in the patrimony of St. Peter, and in the Campagna of Rome, became their property. The houses of Colonna, Orsini, and Savelli, to support their nobility, soon began to traffic in their valour, by hiring themselves out with a body of cavalry to such as would employ them in war; whilst the peasants, their vassals, seduced by the spirit of adventure, and still more by the hope of plunder, abandoned agriculture to enlist in the troops of their liege lord. The effect of their disorderly lives was, that the two provinces nearest Rome soon became the worst cultivated and the least populous in all Italy, although the treasures of Europe poured into the capital of the Faithful. After Nicolas IV., a poor hermit, humble, timid, and ignorant, was raised, in 1294, to the chair of St. Peter, under the name of Celestine V. His election was the effect of a sudden burst of religious enthusiasm, which seized the college of cardinals; although this holy senate had never before shown themselves more ready to consult religion than policy. Celestine V. maintained himself only a few months on the throne; all his sanctity could not serve as an excuse for his incapacity; and the cardinal Benedict Caietan, who persuaded him to abdicate, was elected pope in his place, under the name of Boniface VIII. Boniface, able, expert, intriguing, and unscrupulous, would have restored the authority of the holy see, which during the latter pontificates had been continually sinking, if the violence of his character, his ungovernable pride, and his transports of passion, had not continually thwarted his policy. He endeavoured at first to augment the power of the Guelphs by the aid of France; he afterwards engaged in a violent quarrel with the family of Colonna, whom he would willingly have exterminated; and, finally, taking offence against Philip le Bel, he treated him with as much haughtiness as if he had been the lowest of his vassals. Insulted, and even arrested, by the French prince, in his palace of Anagni, on the 7th of September, 1303, Boniface died a few weeks afterwards of rage and humiliation.

While the power of the kings of Naples, of the emperors, and of the popes, was as it were suspended in

Italy, innumerable small states, which had risen to
almost absolute independence, experienced frequent
revolutions, for the most part proceeding from internal
and independent causes. We can, at most, only indicate
shortly those of the republics, the most distinguished and
the most influential in Italy : but, before thus entering
within the walls of the principal cities, it is right to give
a sketch of the general aspect of the country, particularly
as the violent commotions which it experienced might
give a false idea of its real state. This aspect was one
of a prodigious prosperity, which contrasted so much the
more with the rest of Europe that nothing but poverty
and barbarism were to be found elsewhere. The open
country, designated by the name of *contado*, appertaining
to each city, was cultivated by an active and industrious
race of peasants, enriched by their labour, and not fearing
to display their wealth in their dress, their cattle, and
their instruments of husbandry. The proprietors, inhabitants of towns, advanced them capital, shared the
harvests, and alone paid the land-tax : they undertook
the immense labour which has given so much fertility to
the Italian soil,—that of making dikes to preserve the
plains from the inundation of the rivers, and of deriving
from those rivers innumerable canals of irrigation. The
naviglio grande of Milan, which spreads the clear waters
of the Ticino over the finest part of Lombardy, was
begun in 1179, resumed in 1257, and terminated a few
years afterwards. Men who meditated, and who applied
to the arts the fruits of their study, practised already
that scientific agriculture of Lombardy and Tuscany
which became a model to other nations ; and at this day,
after five centuries, the districts formerly free, and always
cultivated with intelligence, are easily distinguished from
those half-wild districts which had remained subject to
the feudal lords.

The cities, surrounded with thick walls, terraced, and
guarded by towers, were, for the most part, paved with
broad flag-stones ; while the inhabitants of Paris could
not stir out of their houses without plunging into the
mud. Stone bridges of an elegant and bold architecture
were thrown over rivers ; aqueducts carried pure water
to the fountains. The palace of the podestàs and *signorie*

united strength with majesty. The most admirable of
those of Florence, the *Palazzo-Vecchio*, was built in 1298.
The Loggia in the same city, the church of Santa Croce,
that of Santa Maria del Fiore, with its dome, so admired
by Michael Angelo, were begun by the architect Arnolfo,
scholar of Nicolas di Pisa, between the years 1284 and
1300. The prodigies of this first-born of the fine arts
multiplied in Italy : a pure taste, boldness, and grandeur
struck the eye in all the public monuments, and finally
reached even private dwellings; while the princes of
France, England, and Germany, in building their castles,
seemed to think only of shelter and defence.   Sculpture
in marble and bronze soon followed the progress of architecture : in 1300, Andrea di Pisa, son of the architect
Nicolas, cast the admirable bronze gates of the Baptistery
at Florence ; about the same time, Cimabue and Giotto
revived the art of painting, Casella music, and Dante
gave to Italy his divine poem, unequalled in succeeding
generations. History was written honestly, with scrupulous research, and with a graceful simplicity, by
Giovanni Villani, and his school ; the study of morals
and philosophy began ; and Italy, ennobled by freedom,
enlightened nations, till then sunk in darkness.
    The arts of necessity and of luxury had been cultivated
with not less success than the fine arts : in every street,
warehouses and shops displayed the wealth that Italy
and Flanders only knew how to produce.   It excited the
astonishment and cupidity of the French or German adventurer, who came to find employment in Italy, and
who had no other exchange to make than his blood
against the rich stuffs and brilliant arms which he coveted.
The Tuscan and Lombard merchants, however, trafficked
in the barbarous regions of the west, to carry there the
produce of their industry. Attracted by the franchises
of the fairs of Champagne and of Lyons, they went
thither, as well to barter their goods as to lend their
capital at interest to the nobles, habitually loaded with
debt; though at the risk of finding themselves suddenly
arrested, their wealth confiscated, by order of the king of
France, and their lives, too, sometimes endangered by
sanctioned robbers, under the pretext of repressing
usury. Industry, the employment of a superabundant

capital, the application of mechanism and science to the production of wealth, secured the Italians a sort of monopoly through Europe : they alone offered for sale what all the rich desired to buy ; and, notwithstanding the various oppressions of the barbarian kings, notwithstanding the losses occasioned by their own often-repeated revolutions, their wealth was rapidly renewed. The wages of workmen, the interest of capital, and the profit of trade, rose simultaneously, while every one gained much and spent little ; manners were still simple, luxury was unknown, and the future was not forestalled by accumulated debt.

The republic of Pisa was one of the first to make known to the world the riches and power which a small state might acquire by the aid of commerce and liberty. Pisa had astonished the shores of the Mediterranean by the number of vessels and galleys that sailed under her flag, by the succour she had given the crusaders, by the fear she had inspired at Constantinople, and by the conquest of Sardinia and the Balearic Isles.   Pisa was the first to introduce into Tuscany the arts that ennoble wealth : her dome, her baptistery, her leaning tower, and her Campo Santo, which the traveller's eye embraces at one glance, but does not weary of beholding, had been successively built from the year 1063 to the end of the twelfth century.   These *chefs-d'œuvre* had animated the genius of the Pisans : the great architects of the thirteenth century were, for the most part, pupils of Nicolas di Pisa.   But the moment was come in which the ruin of this glorious republic was at hand ; a deep-rooted jealousy, to be dated from the conquest of Sardinia, had frequently, during the last two centuries, armed against each other the republics of Genoa and Pisa : a new war between them broke out in 1282.   It is difficult to comprehend how two simple cities could put to sea such prodigious fleets as those of Pisa and Genoa.   In 1282, Ginicel Sismondi commanded thirty Pisan galleys, of which he lost the half in a tempest, on the 9th of September ; the following year, Rosso Sismondi commanded sixty-four ; in 1284, Guido Jacia commanded twenty-four, and was vanquished.   The Pisans had recourse the same year to a Venetian admiral, Alberto Morosini,

to whom they intrusted 103 galleys: but, whatever
efforts they made, the Genoese constantly opposed a
superior fleet.   This year, however, all the male population of the two republics seemed assembled on their
vessels: they met on the 6th of August, 1284, once more
before the Isle of Meloria, rendered famous forty-three
years before by the victory of the Pisans over the same
enemies.   Valour was still the same, but fortune had
changed sides; and a terrible disaster effaced the memory
of an ancient victory.   While the two fleets, almost
equal in number, were engaged, a reinforcement of
thirty Genoese galleys, driven impetuously by the wind,
struck the Pisan fleet in flank: seven of their vessels
were instantly sunk, twenty-eight taken; 5,000 citizens
perished in the battle, and 11,000 who were taken
prisoners to Genoa preferred death in captivity rather
than their republic should ransom them, by giving up
Sardinia to the Genoese.   This prodigious loss ruined
the maritime power of Pisa; the same nautical knowledge, the same spirit of enterprise, were not transmitted
to the next generation.   All the fishermen of the coast
quitted the Pisan galleys for those of Genoa.   The
vessels diminished in number, with the means of man-
ning them; and Pisa could no longer pretend to be more
than the third maritime power in Italy.

While the republic was thus exhausted by this great
reverse of fortune, it was attacked by the league of the
Tuscan Guelphs; and a powerful citizen, to whom it
had intrusted itself, betrayed his country to enslave it.
Ugolino was count of the Gherardesca, a mountainous
country situated along the coast, between Leghorn and
Piombino: he was of Ghibeline origin, but had married
his sister to Giovan di Gallura, chief of the Guelphs of
Pisa and of Sardinia.   From that time he artfully opposed
the Guelphs to the Ghibelines; and though several accused him of having decided the issue of the battle of
Meloria, others regarded him as the person most able,
most powerful by his alliance, and most proper, to reconcile Pisa with the Guelph league.   The Pisans, amidst
the dangers of the republic, felt the necessity of a dictator.
They named Ugolino captain-general for ten years: and
the new commander did, indeed, obtain peace with the

Guelph league; but not till he had caused all the fortresses of the Pisan territory to be opened by his creatures
to the Lucchese and Florentines, — a condition of his
treaty with them which he dared not publicly avow.
From that time he sought only to strengthen his own
despotism, by depriving all the magistrates of power,
and by intimidating the archbishop Roger degli Ubaldini, who held jointly with him the highest rank in the
city. The nephew of Ubaldini, having opposed him with
some haughtiness, was killed by him on the spot with his
own hand. His violence, and the number of executions
which he ordered, soon rendered him equally odious to
the two parties: but he had the art, in his frequent
changes from one to the other, to make the opposite
party believe him powerfully supported by that with
which he at the moment sided. In the summer of 1282
the Guelphs were exiled: but finding in the Ghibeline
chiefs, the Gualandi Sismondi and Lanfranchi, a haughtiness which he thought he had subdued, he charged his
son to introduce anew the Guelphs into the city. His
project was discovered and prevented; the Ghibelines
called the people on all sides to arms and liberty. On
the 1st of July, 1288, Ugolino was besieged in the palace
of the *signoria*: the insurgents, unable to vanquish the
obstinate resistance opposed to them by himself, his sons,
and his adherents, set fire to the palace; and, having
entered it amidst the flames, dragged forth Ugolino, two
of his sons, and two of his grandsons, and threw them
into the tower of the Sette Vie. The key was given to
the archbishop; from whom was expected the vigilance
of an enemy, but the charity of a priest. That charity,
however, was soon exhausted: the key after a few
months was thrown into the river; and the wretched
count perished in those agonies of hunger, and of
paternal and filial love, upon which poetry,[1] sculpture,
and painting have conferred celebrity.

The victory over count Ugolino, achieved by the most
ardent of the Ghibelines, redoubled the enthusiasm and
audacity of that party; and soon determined them to
renew the war with the Guelphs of Tuscany. Notwithstanding the danger into which the republic was thrown

---

[1] Dante.

by the ambition of the last captain-general, it continued
to believe, when engaged in a hazardous war, that the
authority of a single person over the military, the
finances, and the tribunals was necessary to its protection ; and it trusted that the terrible chastisement just
inflicted on the tyrant would hinder any other from
following his example. Accordingly Guido de Montefeltro was named captain. He had acquired a high
reputation in defending Forli against the French forces
of Charles of Anjou ; and the republic had not to repent
of its choice. He recovered by force of arms all the
fortresses which Ugolino had given up to the Lucchese
and Florentines. The Pisan militia, whom Montefeltro
armed with cross-bows, which he had trained them to
use with precision, became the terror of Tuscany. The
Guelphs of Florence and Lucca were glad to make
peace in 1293.

While the Pisans became habituated to trusting the
government to a single person, the Florentines became
still more attached to the most democratic forms of
liberty. In 1282 they removed the *anziani*, whom they
had at first set at the head of their government, to make
room for the *priori delle arti*, whose name and office was
preserved not only to the end of the republic, but even to
our day. The corporation of trades, which they called
the *arti*, were distinguished by the titles of major and
minor. At first only three, afterwards six, major *arti*
were admitted into the government. The college, consisting of six *priori delle arti*, always assembled, and living
together, during two months, in the public palace, formed
the *signoria*, which represented the republic. Ten years
later, the Florentines completed this *signoria* by placing
at its head the gonfaloner of justice, elected also for two
months, from among the representatives of the arts,
manufactures, and commerce. When he displayed the
gonfalon, or standard of the state, the citizens were
obliged to rise and assist in the execution of the law.
The arrogance of the nobles, their quarrels, and the
disturbance of the public peace by their frequent battles
in the streets, had, in 1292, irritated the whole population
against them. Giano della Bella, himself a noble, but
sympathising in the passions and resentment of the people,

proposed to bring them to order by summary justice, and to confide the execution of it to the gonfaloner whom he caused to be elected. The Guelphs had been so long at the head of the republic, that their noble families, whose wealth had immensely increased, placed themselves above all law. Giano determined that their nobility itself should be a title of exclusion, and a commencement of punishment; a rigorous edict, bearing the title of "ordinance of justice," first designated thirty-seven Guelph families of Florence, whom it declared noble and great, and on this account excluded for ever from the *signoria;* refusing them at the same time the privilege of renouncing their nobility, in order to place themselves on a footing with the other citizens. When these families troubled the public peace by battle or assassination, a summary information, or even common report, was sufficient to induce the gonfaloner to attack them at the head of the militia, rase their houses to the ground, and deliver their persons to the podestà, to be punished according to their crimes. If other families committed the same disorders, if they troubled the state by their private feuds and outrages, the *signoria* was authorised to ennoble them, as a punishment of their crimes, in order to subject them to the same summary justice. A similar organisation, under different names, was made at Sienna, Pistoia, and Lucca. In all the republics of Tuscany, and in the greater number of those of Lombardy, the nobility by its turbulence was excluded from all the magistracies; and in more than one, a register of nobles was opened, as at Florence, on which to inscribe, by way of punishment, the names of those who violated the public peace.

However rigorous these precautions were, they did not suffice to retain in subjection to the laws an order of men who believed themselves formed to rule, and who despised the citizens with whom they were associated. These very nobles, to whom was denied all participation in the government of the republic, and almost the protection and equality of the law, were no sooner entered into their mountain castles, than they became sovereigns, and exercised despotic power over their vassals. The most cultivated and wooded part of the Apennines belonged to the republic of Pistoia. It was a considerable district, bordering on the Lucchese, Modenese, Bolognese, and Florentine territory, and was emphatically designated by the name of the *Mountain*. It was covered with castles belonging either to the Cancellieri, or Panciatichi, the two families most powerful in arms and wealth in all Italy : the first was Guelph, the second Ghibeline ; and as the party of the former then ruled in Tuscany, they had obtained the exile of the Panciatichi from Pistoia. The Cancellieri took advantage of this exile to increase their power by the purchase of land, by conquest, and by alliance ; in their family alone they reckoned one hundred men at arms. This family was divided into two branches, of distant relationship and which were distinguished by the names of *Bianchi* and *Neri* (whites and blacks) ; a quarrel arose between them, and was maintained with all the perfidy and ferocity of which the Pistoiese nobility were then accused. Mutilations, assassinations, and desperate battles, from 1296 to 1300, followed each other with a frequency which at last alarmed all Tuscany. The Florentines, desirous of pacifying Pistoia, engaged that city to banish from its bosom all the Cancellieri, but at the same time opened their own gates to them, in the hope of being able to accomplish a reconciliation. This powerful family, allied to all the Guelph nobility of Italy, instead of forgetting their reciprocal injuries, drew their hosts into their quarrel: there were, it is true, already other causes of excitement in Florence. Corso Donati, a Guelph, possessed great influence over the ancient families who had from the beginning directed that party. Vieri de Cerchi, a Guelph also, was the chief of those who, like himself, had recently risen to wealth and power ; he reproached the former for not forgetting the ancient enmity between the Guelphs and Ghibelines ; for still troubling the republic with factions, when there was no longer any motive ; and proposed to substitute equal laws, for superannuated proscriptions. The Cancellieri of the Neri party sided with Corso Donati, the ancient nobles, and the most violent of the Guelphs. Those of the Bianchi, on the contrary, took part with Vieri de Cerchi, the moderate Guelphs, and subsequently with the Ghibelines and the Panciatichi. In this last party enlisted Dante,

H

the historian Dino Compagni, the father of Petrarch, and
all those who began about this time at Florence to
distinguish themselves in literature.

Boniface VIII. endeavoured to reconcile the two
parties who, under the names of Bianchi and Neri, began
to divide all Tuscany; but, violent and choleric, he was
ill calculated to make peace between men as intemperate
as himself. He soon espoused with zeal the party of the
Neri, the aristocracy, and the most zealous Guelphs.
He had called Charles de Valois, the brother of Philip
le Bel, to Italy, to place him at the head of an expedition
which he meditated against Sicily. He charged him to
pacify Tuscany in his way; and gave him to understand
that it would be easy, in states so rich, to repay himself
for his trouble. The republic of Florence dared not
refuse the mediation of Charles: it was accustomed to
regard the house of France as the protector of the church
and of the Guelph party. It, however, limited, in precise
terms, the authority allowed him, before receiving him,
and the 800 cavalry which he commanded, within the
city. But the French princes, at this period, neither
respected nor comprehended the liberty of the citizen:
they were incapable of forming any idea of the reciprocal
rights which they had to maintain. Charles, making no
account of the engagements which he had taken, formed
an intimate alliance with the Neri, whom he soon discovered to be the more aristocratic, and more virulent in
their enmities. Having agreed on his share of the booty,
he gave, from the 5th to the 11th of November, 1301, a
loose rein to their passions. He permitted them to pillage
and burn the houses of their enemies; to kill those who
were the most odious to them; to carry off the heiresses
of rich families, and marry them to their sons; to cause
sentences of exile and confiscation to be pronounced
against all the most illustrious families of the Bianchi
party by the podestà, a creature of Charles de Valois,
whom he had brought there. The French cavalry, and
the Guelphs of Romagna, whom Charles had also introduced into the city, assisted in all these outrages. It
was then that Dante, and Petracco dell' Ancisa, the
father of Petrarch, were exiled from their country, with
many hundred others. Charles at last quitted Florence,

on the 4th of April, 1302, carrying off immense wealth.
His cavalry were loaded with gold and precious stuffs;
but he carried with him also the curse of the Florentines,
which seemed to follow him in his unsuccessful expedition
against Sicily.   Benedict XI., the successor of Boniface,
vainly endeavoured, during his short pontificate, to
reconcile the Bianchi and Neri in the cities of Tuscany,
and to recall the latter from exile.   He died of poison, on
the 4th of July, 1304.   Some accuse Philip le Bel of the
crime; he at least reaped all the benefit.   This king
succeeded by fraud in getting a Frenchman elected pope,
under the name of Clement V., whom, to keep him more
subservient to his will, he always retained in France;
drawing thither, also, the college of cardinals, who were
recruited in that country, so that the successors of
Clement might also be Frenchmen.   It was the beginning of the long retirement, or, as the Italians call it,
exile of the popes, at Avignon, which terminated in 1377,
and soon after began anew with the great western schism.
This exile was favourable to the independence of Rome,
and of the other cities of the pontifical states; and at the
same time rendered the holy see almost indifferent to the
Guelph party, which it had often indecently seconded.

While the nobles of the Italian cities had, by their
turbulence, excited the resentment of all classes of the
people,—while, by their disobedience to the laws, contempt of the tribunals and of public peace, they had
drawn on themselves the exclusion not only from the
magistracies, but from the common rights, the most
precious to the citizens of a free state,—the nobility of
Venice rose in importance, and took possession of the
government.   Submissive to the laws, but shaping them
for their own use,—forgetting individuals and families, to
occupy themselves only about their corporate interests,—
they arrived, by insensible usurpations, to the sovereignty
of this ancient republic.   This nobility of Venice, which
appeared so docile to the laws, so patient, so skilful, was
the oldest in Europe.   It inherited the honours of the
Roman empire; and alone preserved, from the fifth to
the eleventh century, the family names, according to the
Roman custom, which had been abandoned by the rest
of Europe.   Like the nobles in the other cities of Italy,

they were in turn sovereigns in their fiefs, and subjects in the city. After the conquest of the Greek empire, the Venetians distributed among their nobles several islands in the Archipelago, of which they preserved the sovereignty, with the titles of dukes or counts, even after the Greeks had recovered Constantinople ; but they had not, and could not have, any fortresses in the vast plains that surround Venice. They had no devoted vassals, always ready to espouse their quarrels ; nor retreats, into which to withdraw from the power of the law. They acknowledged and submitted to the authority of the tribunals ; they conducted themselves as citizens, and thus soon became masters of the state.

It was by slow and artfully disguised encroachments that the nobility of Venice succeeded in substituting itself for the civic power, and investing itself with the sovereignty of the republic. During the earlier period, the doge was an elective prince, the limit of whose power was vested in assemblies of the people. It was not till 1032 that he was obliged to consult only a council, formed from amongst the most illustrious citizens, whom he designated. Thence came the name given them of *pregadi* (invited). The grand council was not formed till 1172, 140 years later, and was, from that time, the real sovereign of the republic. It was composed of 480 members, named annually on the last day of September, by twelve tribunes, or grand electors, of whom two were chosen by each of the six sections of the republic. No more than four members from one family could be named. The same counsellors might be re-elected each year. As it is in the spirit of a corporation to tend always towards an aristocracy, the same persons were habitually re-elected ; and when they died, their children took their places. The grand council, neither assuming to itself nor granting to the doge the judicial power, gave the first example of the creation of a body of judges, numerous, independent, and irremovable; such, nearly, as was afterwards the parliament of Paris. In 1179, it created the criminal *quarantia ;* called, also, the *vecchia quarantia*, to distinguish it from two other bodies of forty judges, created in 1229. The grand council gave a more complete organisation to the government formed from

among its members. It was composed of a doge ; of six
counsellors of the red robe, who remained only eight
months in office, and who, with the doge, formed the
signoria ; and of the council of pregadi, composed of
sixty members, renewed each year. The doge was
obliged, on entering office, to take a rigorously detailed
oath, which guaranteed all the public liberties. At his
death, a commission of enquiry was formed, to examine
whether he had not exceeded his powers ; and in case he
had, his heirs were responsible. In 1249, the sovereign
council renounced the election of the doge, and entrusted
it to a commission drawn by lot from among the whole
council. This commission named another ; which,
reduced by lot to one fourth, named a third ; and by
these alternate operations of lot and election, at length
formed the last commission of forty-one members, who
could elect the doge only by a majority of twenty-five
suffrages. It was not till towards the end of the
thirteenth century that the people began to discover that
they were no more than a cipher in the republic, and the
doge no more than a servant of the grand council,—
surrounded, indeed, with pomp, but without any real
power. In 1289, the people attempted themselves to
elect the doge ; but the grand council obliged him whom
the popular suffrages had designated to leave Venice,
and substituted in his place Pietro Gradenigo, the chief
of the aristocratic party. Gradenigo undertook to exclude
the people from any part in the election of the grand
council, as they were already debarred from any participation in the election of a doge. He represented it to
the grand council as notorious, that for more than a
century the same persons, or families, were invariably
re-elected ; that the twelve tribunes charged with the
annual election contented themselves with examining
only whether any of the ancient members merited exclusion from the sovereign council, and confirming all the
others ; that since the election was reduced only to the
condemnation of some individuals, it was more expedient
to confide that judgment to the equity of the same
tribunal to which the citizens intrusted their honour and
their lives, than to the arbitrary will of twelve individuals,
most frequently nominated by intrigue. He proposed,

accordingly, instead of election, the purification of the
grand council by the forty criminal judges. The decree
which he proposed and carried on the 28th of February,
1297, is famous in the history of Venice, under the name
of *serrata del maggior consiglio* (shutting of the grand
council). He legally founded that hereditary aristocracy,—so prudent, so jealous, so ambitious,—which
Europe regarded with astonishment; immovable in principle, unshaken in power; uniting some of the most
odious practices of despotism with the name of liberty;
suspicious and perfidious in politics; sanguinary in
revenge; indulgent to the subject; sumptuous in the
public service, economical in the administration of the
finances; equitable and impartial in the administration
of justice; knowing well how to give prosperity to the
arts, agriculture, and commerce; beloved by the people
who obeyed it, whilst it made the nobles who partook its
power tremble. The Venetian aristocracy completed its
constitution, in 1311, by the creation of the Council of
Ten, which, notwithstanding its name, was composed of
sixteen members and the doge. Ten counsellors of the
black robe were annually elected by the great council,
in the months of August and September; and of the six
counsellors of the red robe, composing a part of the
signoria, three entered office every four months. The
Council of Ten, charged to guard the security of the state
with a power higher than the law, had an especial commission to watch over the nobles, and to punish their
crimes against the republic. In this they were restrained
by no rule: they were, with respect to the nobility, the
depositaries of the power of the great council, or rather
of a power unlimited, which no people should entrust to
any government. Some other decrees completed the
system of the *serrata del maggior consiglio*. It was forbidden
to the quarantia to introduce any *new man* into power. In
1315, a register was opened, called the Golden Book, in
which were inscribed the names of all those who had sat
in the great council. In 1319, all limitation of number
was suppressed; and, from that period, it sufficed to
prove that a person was the descendant of a counsellor,
and twenty-five years of age, to be by right a member of
the grand council of Venice.

On the 25th of November, 1308, the diet of Germany named Henry VII. of Luxembourg as successor to Albert of Austria; and this election suddenly brought Italy back to the same struggle for her independence which she had so heroically supported against the two Fredericks. From the death of the second Frederick, fifty-eight years had passed since she had seen an emperor.   Rodolph of Hapsburg, Adolphus of Nassau, and Albert of Austria, had too much to do in Germany, to occupy themselves with this constantly agitated country, where they could demand obedience only with arms in their hands. Henry VII. was a brave, wise, and just prince; but he was neither rich nor powerful.   He secured to his son, by marriage, the crown of Bohemia, which had excited some jealousy among the Germans; and he believed it would be expedient, in order to avoid all quarrel in the empire, to quit it for some time.   To flatter the national vanity, he determined on an expedition to Italy.

Henry, himself a Belgian, had no power but in Belgium and the provinces adjoining France.   From Luxembourg he went through the county of Burgundy to Lausanne. Here he received, in the summer of 1310, the ambassadors of the Italian states, who came to do him homage.   He entered Piedmont, by Mont Cenis, towards the end of September, accompanied by only two thousand cavalry, the greater part of whom were Belgians, Franc-Comtois, or Savoyards.   This force would have been wholly in- sufficient to subdue Italy; but Henry VII. presented himself there as the supporter of just rights, of order, and, to a certain degree, of liberty.   The result of the violence of faction, and of the exhaustion of the citizens, had been, to subject almost all Lombardy to petty tyrants.   Every city had its lord, sometimes chief of the Guelph, some- times of the Ghibeline faction, whom his partisans had, for their own interests, invested with dictatorial power. Sometimes he was a neighbouring noble, who, seconded by a band of his vassals, had inspired terror, and whom the people respected, because he forced to obedience turbulent nobles who had never submitted to any law; and sometimes too he was a captain of foreign cavalry, called to the service of the republic by the council, with the title of lord assigned at the same time.   The name of liberty, and the cry of *popolo! popolo!* were every where frequently heard; but it was only to overthrow the existing power, and substitute another quite as arbitrary. These despotisms, it is true, were of short duration; but yet hardly one city enjoyed true liberty. The desire of tranquillity, resulting from the outrages committed by the nobles or by factions, was so great, that the citizens demanded, above all, of the lords and magistrates strength to make themselves feared,—to punish rapidly and severely whoever troubled the public peace. Every city submitted to a form of summary justice, preferring that to anarchy, although the sovereign lord often made an ill use of it, either to gratify his brutal passions, or to accumulate wealth which should be his resource in exile; an evil always to be expected.

The lords of all Lombardy and Piedmont came to present themselves to Henry; some at Turin, others at Asti. He received them with kindness, but declared his determination to establish legal order, such as had been settled by the peace of Constance, in all the cities of the empire; and to name in each an imperial vicar, who should govern in concert with the municipal magistrates. Philippone di Langusco, at Pavia; Simon da Colobiano, at Vercelli; William Brusato, at Novara; Antonio Fisiraga, at Lodi; in obedience to this intimation, laid down the sovereign power. At the same time, Henry every where recalled the exiles, without distinction of party : at Como and Mantua, the Ghibelines; at Brescia and Placentia, the Guelphs; leaving out, however, the exiles of Verona, a powerful city, which he did not visit, and which was governed by Can' Grande della Scala, the most able Ghibeline captain in Italy, the best soldier, the best politician, and the person whose services and attachment the emperor most valued. The rich and populous city of Milan required also to be treated with address and consideration. The archbishop, Otho Visconti, had retained the principal authority in his hands to a very advanced age. But long previously to his death, which took place in 1295, he had transferred to his nephew, Matteo Visconti, the title of captain of the people, and had accustomed the Milanese to consider him as his lieutenant and successor. Matteo did, in fact, govern

after him, and with almost despotic power, from 1295 to
1302. He was also named lord of several other cities of
Lombardy ; at the same time he strengthened his family
by many rich alliances. But Visconti had not the art to
conciliate either the remains of national pride, or the love
of liberty which still subsisted among his subjects, or the
jealousy of the other princes of Lombardy. A league to
give the preponderance to the Guelph party in this
province was formed by Alberto Scotto, lord of Placentia,
and by Ghiberto da Correggio, lord of Parma : they
forced the Viscontis to quit Milan, in 1302, and installed
in their place Guido della Torre and his family, who had
been exiles twenty-five years. When Henry VII. presented himself before Milan, he found it governed by
Guido della Torre and the Guelphs. Matteo Visconti
and the Ghibelines were exiled. Henry exacted their
recall ; he was crowned in the church of St. Ambrose, on
the 6th of January, 1311, and afterwards asked of the city
a gratuity for his army of one hundred thousand florins.
Till then, the Italians had seen in the monarch only a
just and impartial pacificator ; but when he demanded
money, the different parties united against him. A violent
sedition broke forth at Milan. The Della Torres and the
Guelphs were forced to leave that city. Matteo Visconti
and the Ghibelines were recalled, and the former restored
to absolute power. The Guelphs, too, in the rest of
Lombardy, rose, and took arms against the emperor.
Crema, Cremona, Lodi, Brescia, and Como revolted at
the same time. Henry consumed the greater part of the
summer in besieging Brescia, which at last, towards the
end of September, 1311, he forced to capitulate. He
granted to that town equitable conditions, impatient as
he was to enter Tuscany ; but, although Lombardy
seemed subdued to his power, he left more germs of
discontent and discord in it than he had found about a
year before.

Henry VII. arrived with his little army at Genoa, on
the 21st of October, 1311. That powerful republic now
maintained at St. Jean d'Acre, at Pera opposite to
Constantinople, and at Caffa in the Black Sea, military
and mercantile colonies, which made themselves respected
for their valour, at the same time that they carried on

the richest commerce of the Mediterranean. Several islands in the Archipelago, amongst others, that of Chios, had passed in sovereignty to Genoese families. The palaces of Genoa, already called the "superb," were the admiration of travellers. Its sanguinary rivalry with Pisa had terminated by securing to the former the empire of the Tyrrhene Sea. From that time, Genoa had no other rival than Venice. An accidental rencounter of the fleets of these two cities in the sea of Cyprus lighted up between them, in 1293, a terrible war, which for seven years stained the Mediterranean with blood, and consumed immense wealth. In 1298, the Genoese admiral, Lamba Doria, meeting the Venetian commander, Andrea Dandolo, at Corzuola or Corcyra the Black, at the extremity of the Adriatic Gulf, burnt sixty-six of his galleys, and took eighteen, which he brought into the port of Genoa, with 7,000 prisoners; suffering only twelve vessels to escape. The humbled Venetians, in the next year, asked and obtained peace. The Genoese, vanquishers in turn of the Pisans and Venetians, passed for the bravest, the most enterprising, and the most fortunate mariners of all Italy. The government of their city was entirely democratic; but the two chains of mountains which extend from Genoa, the one towards Provence, and the other towards Tuscany (called by the Italians *Le Riviere di Genoa*, because the foot of these mountains forms the shore of the sea), were covered with the castles of the Ligurian nobles; the peasantry were all dependent on them, and were always ready to make war for their liege lords. Four families were pre-eminent for their power and wealth—the Doria and the Spinola, Ghibelines; the Grimaldi and the Fieschi, Guelphs. These nobles, incensed against each other by hereditary enmity, had disturbed the state by so many outrages, that the people adopted, with respect to them, the same policy as that of the Tuscan republics, and had entirely excluded them from the magistracy. On the other hand, they had rendered such eminent and frequent services to the republic; above all, they had produced such great naval commanders, that the people, whenever the state was in danger, had always recourse to them for the choice of an admiral. Seduced by the glory of these chiefs, the people

often afterwards shed their blood in their private quarrels;
but often, also, wearied by the continual disturbances
which the nobles excited, they had recourse to foreigners
to subdue them to the common law. The people were
in this state of irritation against the Ligurian nobles,
when Henry VII. arrived at Genoa, in 1311; and to
oblige them to maintain a peace, which they were continually breaking, the Genoese conferred on that monarch
absolute authority over the republic for twenty years.
But when the emperor suppressed the podestà, and then
the abbate or defender of the people, and afterwards
demanded of the city a gift of 60,000 florins, the Genoese
perceived that they needed a government not only to
suppress civil discord, but also to protect rights not less
precious than peace ; an internal fermentation of increasing danger manifested itself; and Henry was happy to
quit Genoa in safety, on the 16th of February, 1312, on
board a Pisan fleet, which transported him with about
1,500 cavalry to Tuscany.

Henry VII., when he entered Italy, was impartial
between the Guelphs and Ghibelines. He owed his
election to the influence of the popes, and he was accompanied by cardinal legates, who were to crown him
at Rome. He had no distrust either of Robert, then
king of Naples, the son of Charles II., or of the Guelph
cities. He had no hereditary affection for the Ghibelines, the zealous partisans of a family long extinct.
He endeavoured, accordingly, to hold the balance fairly
between the two parties, and to reconcile them wherever
he was allowed ; but experience had already taught him
that the very name of elected emperor had a magic influence on the Italians, either to excite the devoted
affection of the Ghibelines, or the terror and hatred of
the Guelphs. It was with the latter that resistance to
him had begun in the preceding year in Lombardy ;
and that revolt had burst forth on all sides since his
departure. Robert, king of Naples, who assumed the
part of champion of the Guelph party, already testified
an open distrust of him ; and Florence, which by its prudence, ability, wealth, and courage, was the real director
of that party, took arms to resist him, refused audience to
his ambassadors, raised all the Guelphs of Italy against

him, and finally constrained him to place that city under the ban of the empire. The republic of Pisa, on the other hand, whose affection for the Ghibeline party was connected with its hopes, as well as its recollections, served him with a devotion, zeal, and prodigality, which he had not met elsewhere. The Pisans had sent him, when at Lausanne, a present of 60,000 florins, to aid him on his passage to Italy. They paid his debts at Genoa, and they gave him another present when he entered their city; finally, they placed at his disposal thirty galleys and 600 cross-bowmen, who accompanied him to Rome, where he received the golden crown of the empire from the hands of the pope's legate, in the church of St. John de Lateran, on the 29th of June, 1312. The Romans, who had taken arms against him, and had received within their walls a Neapolitan garrison, kept their gates shut during the ceremony, and would not suffer one of his soldiers to enter the city.

The coronation of the emperor at Rome was the term of service of the Germans : they took no interest afterwards in what was passing, or might be done, in that country. They were anxious to depart; and Henry found himself at Tivoli, where he passed the summer, almost entirely abandoned by his transalpine soldiers. Had the Neapolitan king Robert been bolder, Henry would have been in great danger. In the autumn, however, the Ghibelines and Bianchi of central Italy rallied round him, and formed a formidable army, with which he marched to attack Florence, on the 19th of September, 1312. The Florentines, accustomed to leave their defence to mercenaries, whose valour was always ready for pay, made small account of a military courage which they saw so common among men whom they despised ; but no people carried civil courage and firmness in misfortune farther. Their army was soon infinitely superior in numbers to that of Henry ; they carried on with perfect calmness their commerce and negotiations, as if their enemies had already departed for Germany, but they would not drive them out of their territory by giving battle ; they preferred bearing patiently their depredations, and waiting till they had worn out their enthusiasm, exhausted their finances, and should depart of themselves, which they did on the 6th of January, 1313, finding they could obtain no advantage. Henry, after having given some months of repose to his army, took the command of the militia of Pisa, and made war at their head against Lucca; at the same time, he solicited from his brother, the archbishop of Treves, a German reinforcement, which he obtained in the following month of July. On the 5th of August, 1313, Henry VII. departed from Pisa, commanding 2,500 ultramontane and 1,500 Italian cavalry, with a proportionate number of infantry. He began his march towards Rome, having been informed that Robert, called by the Florentines to their aid, advanced with all the forces of the Guelph party to oppose him. The declining military reputation of the Neapolitans inspired the Germans with little fear, and Robert had but a small number of French cavalry to give courage to his army; but the priests and monks, animated with zeal in defence of the ancient Guelph party and the independence of the church, seconded him with their prayers, and the report soon spread that they had seconded him in another manner and in their own way. The emperor took the road of San Miniato to Castel Fiorentino; arrived at Buon Convento, twelve miles beyond Sienna; and stopped there to celebrate the festival of St. Bartholomew. On the 24th of August, 1313, he received the communion from the hands of a Dominican monk, and expired a few hours afterwards. It was said the monk had mixed the juice of Napel in the consecrated cup. It was said, also, that Henry was already attacked by a malady which he concealed. A carbuncle had manifested itself below the knee; and a cold bath, which he took to calm the burning irritation, perhaps occasioned his sudden and unexpected death.

CHAPTER VI

THE POWER AND GREATNESS OF SOME OF THE GHIBELINE CHIEFS—
DISORGANISATION OF THAT PARTY, THROUGH THE INCONSISTENCY
AND PERFIDY OF THE EMPEROR LOUIS OF BAVARIA—EFFORT OF
THE FLORENTINES TO MAINTAIN AN EQUILIBRIUM BETWEEN THE
DIFFERENT POWERS OF ITALY—THE TYRANNY AND EXPULSION
OF THE DUKE OF ATHENS

THE electors of the empire were not convoked at Frankfort to name a successor to Henry VII. till ten months
after his death.   Ten, instead of seven, princes presented
themselves ; two pretenders disputed the electoral rights
in each of the houses of Saxony, Bohemia, and Branden-
burg.   The electors, divided into two colleges, named
simultaneously, on the 19th of October, 1314, two
emperors : the one, Louis IV. of Bavaria ; the other,
Frederick III. of Austria.   Their rights appeared equal ;
their adherents in Germany were also of nearly equal
strength ; the sword only could decide ; and war was
accordingly declared, and carried on till the 28th of
September, 1322 ; when Frederick was vanquished and
made prisoner at Muhldorf.

The church abstained, while the civil war lasted, from
pronouncing between the two pretenders to the empire.
Clement V. did not witness their double election ; he died
on the 20th of April, 1314.   It was necessary, two years
afterwards, to use fraud and violence, to confine the cardinals in conclave at Lyons, for the purpose of naming
his successor.   They at last elected the bishop of Avignon.
He was a native of Cahors, the devoted creature of king
Robert of Naples ; and took the name of John XXII.
He was the first who made Avignon, which was his
episcopal town, the residence of the Roman court, exiled
from Italy.   He was an intriguer, notoriously profligate,
scandalously avaricious : he fancied himself, however, a
philosopher, and took a part in the quarrel between the
realists and nominalists ; he made himself violent enemies
in the schools, on the members of which he sometimes
inflicted the punishment of death.   While he used such
violence towards his adversaries as heretics, he shook

the credit of the court of Rome, by being himself accused
of heresy.   His great object was to raise to high temporal power the cardinal Bertrand de Poiet, whom he
called his nephew, and who was believed to be his son.
For that purpose, he availed himself of the war between
the two pretenders to the empire, regarded by him as
a prolongation of the interregnum, during which he
asserted all the rights of the emperors devolved on the
holy see.   He charged cardinal Bertrand to exercise
those rights as legate in Lombardy, crush the Ghibelines, support the Guelphs ; but above all, subdue both
to the authority of the church and its legate.

The cardinal Bertrand de Poiet launched his excommunications, and employed the soldiers, whom his father
had raised for him in Provence, particularly against
Matteo Visconti, lord of Milan, one of the most able
and powerful of the Ghibeline chiefs.   Visconti made
himself beloved by the Milanese, whom he had always
treated with consideration.   Without being virtuous, he
had preserved his reputation unstained by crime.   His
mind was enlightened.   To a perfect knowledge of mankind, he added quick-sightedness, prompt decision, and
a certain military glory, heightened by that of four sons,
his faithful lieutenants, who were all distinguished among
the brave.   The Italians gave him the surname of Great,
at a period when, it is true, they were prodigal of that
epithet.   Matteo Visconti, in his war with the Lombard Guelphs, took possession of Pavia, Tortona, and
Alexandria.   He beseiged, in concert with the Genoese
Ghibelines, Robert king of Naples, who had shut himself
up in Genoa, desirous of making that city the fortress
of the Guelphs of Lombardy.   Visconti compelled the
retreat of Philip de Valois, who, before he was king, had
entered Italy at the solicitation of the pope, in 1320.
The following year he vanquished Raymond de Cardona,
a Catalonian, and one of the pope's generals ; he persuaded Frederick of Austria, who had sent his brother
to aid the pope, to recall his Germans, making him
sensible it could suit neither of the pretenders to the
empire to weaken the Ghibelines, who defended in Italy
the interests of whoever of the two remained conqueror.
But, after having made war against the church party

twenty years, without ever suspecting that he betrayed his faith, for he was religious without bigotry, age awakened in him the terrors of superstition ; he began to fear that the excommunications of the legate would deprive him of salvation ; he abdicated in favour of his eldest son, Galeazzo ; and died a few weeks afterwards, on the 22nd of June, 1322. The remorse and scruples of Matteo Visconti had carried trouble and disorder into his own party, and gave boldness to that of his adversaries. A violent fermentation at Milan at length burst forth ; Galeazzo was obliged to fly, and the republic was proclaimed anew : but virtue and patriotism, without which it could not subsist, were extinguished ; and, after a few weeks, Galeazzo was recalled, and reinvested with the lordship of Milan.

The two parties of the Guelphs and Ghibelines, since the death of Henry VII., no longer nearly balanced each other in virtue, talents, and patriotism. In the beginning of their struggle, there were almost as many republics on one side as the other ; and sentiments as pure, and a devotion as generous, equally animated the partisans of the empire and of the church. But, in the fourteenth century, the faction of the Ghibelines had become that of tyranny,—of the Guelphs that of liberty. The former displayed those great military and political talents which personal ambition usually develops. In the second were to be found, almost exclusively, patriotism, and the heroism which sacrifices to it every personal interest. The republic of Pisa alone, in Italy, united the love of liberty with the sentiments of the Ghibeline party. This republic had been thunderstruck by the death of Henry VII. at a moment when a career of glory and prosperity seemed to open on him. Pisa, exhausted by the prodigious efforts which she had made to serve him, was true to herself, when all the Guelphs of Tuscany rose at once, on the death of Henry, to avenge on her the terror which that monarch had inspired. She gave the command of her militia to Uguccione dà Faggiuola, a noble of the mountainous part of Romagna, which, with the March, produced the best soldiers in Italy. The Pisans, under the command of Faggiuola, obtained two signal advantages over the

Guelphs. They took Lucca, on the 14th of June, 1314,
while the Lucchese Guelphs and Ghibelines were engaged
in battle in the streets of that city; and, on the 29th of
August of the same year, they defeated, at Montecatino,
the Florentines, commanded by two princes of the house
of Naples, and seconded by all the Guelphs of Tuscany
and Romagna. But the Pisans soon perceived that they
were fighting, not for themselves, but for the captain
whom they had chosen. Almost immediately after his
victory, he began to exercise an insupportable tyranny
over Pisa and Lucca. Fearing much more the citizens
of these republics than the enemies of the state, he, on
the slightest suspicion, employed the utmost severity
against all the most illustrious families. At Lucca, he
threw into a dungeon Castruccio Castracani, the most
distinguished of the Ghibeline nobles, who had recently
returned to that city with a brilliant reputation, acquired
in the wars of France and Lombardy. A simultaneous
insurrection at Lucca and Pisa, on the 10th of April,
1316, delivered these cities from Uguccione dà Faggiuola,
and his son, while, at the head of their cavalry, they
were departing to join each other. This revolution re-
established the republic of Pisa; but left it exhausted
and ruined by long hostilities, and discontented with the
Ghibelines and with its own nobility, who, by a blind
spirit of party, had drawn it into continual war. In
the month of May, 1322, fifteen chiefs of noble Ghibeline
families, defeated in an obstinate battle, were exiled from
Pisa; and, in less than a year afterwards, all the Pisans
established in Sardinia were massacred on the same day,
in consequence of a plot, formed by a Pisan rebel, to
deliver Sardinia to Alphonso, the son of James II. of
Aragon. The war with the Aragonese, to defend the
island, completed the ruin of the republic; and hostilities
terminated with the abandonment of this important possession, on the 10th of June, 1326.

The revolution of Lucca, which had deprived Uguccione dà Faggiuola of power, conferred it on his prisoner,
Castruccio Castracani, who still bore the fetters on his
feet when the insurgents delivered him from his dungeon
to be proclaimed lord of Lucca. Castruccio was of the
ancient family of the Interminelli, so long exiled, with all

the Ghibelines, from that city, that it might well have
been believed that they had lost all influence; but the
emigrants of the Italian republics frequently acquired,
during their exile, new wealth and consideration.   Want
frequently forced them to labour with redoubled dili-
gence,—to devote themselves to commerce, or to military
studies.   Lucca had been esteemed the citadel of the
Guelph party in Tuscany during the latter part of the
thirteenth century : since its rich Ghibeline exiles had
been recalled, it was become entirely of the latter party.
The family of Castruccio had acquired its wealth in England; he had himself learned the art of war there, and
in France and Lombardy.   He had seen displayed, in
these countries, the bravery of the soldier; but he owed
to his own intellect and studies the art of leading and
disposing armies, which in Italy only began to deserve
the name of military science.   Signally brave himself, he
had the art of communicating to the soldier his courage
and enthusiasm.   No one had so quick and sure an eye on
the field of battle.   He was a no less able politician than
warrior; and whether he took part with the Ghibeline
chiefs of Lombardy, or the emperor Louis of Bavaria, he
became always the sole director of those who admitted
him into their council.   To such talents and acquirements
was added hardly one virtue: without fidelity in his
engagements, without pity for the people, without gratitude to those who had served him, he put to death, by
various cruel executions, all those who at Lucca excited
in him the slightest suspicion ; and, amongst others, the
Quartigiani and the Poggi, to whom he owed his elevation.   Castruccio was thirty-two years of age when he
obtained the sovereignty of his country.   He was tall,
with an agreeable countenance ; and his face, thin and
surrounded with long fair hair, was remarkable for its
paleness.
    The republic of Florence found itself called upon to
make head against Castruccio, and defend, against his
ambition, the independence of Tuscany.   Florence was
the Athens of Italy.   The genius displayed by some of
its citizens,—the talent and intelligence in business to be
found even in the mass of the people,—the generosity
which seemed the national character, whenever it was

necessary to protect the oppressed or defend the cause of liberty,—raised this city above every other. Sienna, Perugia, and Bologna were at this period, like Florence, attached to the Guelph party; and these four republics, with some weaker towns, formed the Guelph league of Lombardy. The democratic spirit of the Florentines, which imparted so much energy, had also its dangers. These republicans, jealous of all distinction, and passionately attached to equality, demanded it not only in obedience, but in command. They insisted that the greatest possible number of citizens should, in turn, arrive at the office of *priori*, which, for two months, represented the sovereignty. It, however, did not proceed from base cupidity: this office, as well as every other of the magistracy, was gratuitous. The republic provided the table of the *priori* only when they were in the palace. In the month of October, 1323, the Florentines introduced drawing by lot into the nomination of their first magistrates. They ordained that a general list of all the eligible citizens, Guelphs, and at least thirty years of age, should be formed by a majority of five independent magistracies, of which each represented a national interest: the *priori*, that of the government; the gonfaloner, that of the militia; the captains of the party,[1] that of the Guelphs; the judges of commerce represented the merchants; and the consuls of the arts, industry. Each of these had a right to point out the most eligible citizen. The list which they had prepared was submitted to the revision of a *balia* (a word signifying power), composed of the magistrates in office, and the thirty-six deputies chosen by the six divisions of the town. The balia effaced from the list the names of all those whom it considered incapable; and classed the others according as they appeared suitable to the different magistracies, to which they were finally to be raised by lot. Lastly, it divided the list of names by series; so that the destined purse from which to draw the signoria contained twenty-one tickets, on each of which was inscribed a gonfaloner and six priori; similar purses were prepared, from which to draw by lot the names of the twelve *buon' uomini*, the

[1] The Capitani di Parte were the elective heads of the Guelph party, three in number.

nineteen gonfaloniers of the companies, and all the other magistrates of the republic. All this arrangement was to last only three years and a half, after which a new balìa recommenced. Still, in our day, the municipal magistrates of Tuscany are drawn by lot, in the same manner. The activity, wisdom, and extensive views of the Florentine republic, while its supreme magistrates were changed by lot every two months, proves, at the same time, how much intelligence and patriotism there was in the people, and how worthily the *priori* appreciated statesmen, who, without having ostensible offices, directed the republic by their counsel.

This movable signoria, however, could not meet in war on equal terms with Castruccio, who united to high talents an energetic character, promptitude, secrecy, and unity of design. He began the war by taking from the Florentines Pistoia, where an abbot, by the little artifices of a monk, had obtained possession of the sovereignty. The abbot, on the 5th of May, 1325, sold his country to Castruccio. Florence took into its service Don Raymond de Cardona, a Catalonian general, whom the cardinal Bertrand de Poiet had introduced into Italy. But all who served the Florentines speculated on their wealth: Cardona remarked, that in the brilliant army which the republic had placed under his command, there were many rich merchants, who bore impatiently the fatigues and privations of the service: in order to sell them leave of absence at a higher price, he resolved to complete their disgust. He led them in the middle of summer round the marshes of Bientina, where he long detained them. Many merchants obtained leave of absence by rich presents; but many more died or fell sick. With his army thus weakened by his own fault, he engaged Castruccio at Alto Pascio, and was defeated, on the 23rd of September, 1325. Raymond was taken prisoner; the carroccio fell into the hands of the enemy; and these trophies of victory ornamented the triumphal pomp with which Castruccio returned to Lucca at the head of his army. A signal defeat of the Bolognese, at Monteveglio, on the 15th of November, 1325, completed the discouragement of the Guelph party. Bologna sought a protector in the cardinal de Poiet, on whom was conferred the

signoria. The Florentines had recourse to the king of
Naples, who agreed to aid them only on condition that
they would confer the signoria on his son, the duke of
Calabria. Intelligence that Castruccio had engaged the
emperor Louis of Bavaria to enter Tuscany, induced
them, though with the utmost repugnance, to adopt this
measure.

Louis of Bavaria had treated his prisoner Frederick of
Austria with magnanimity. He not only set him at
liberty, but associated him in his government. Louis
passed in Germany for a loyal and generous prince;
perhaps, only because violent and cruel actions inspired
there little horror; public opinion was not yet awakened;
and no one rendered an account to the people of the
motives of princes, or of their sudden changes from one
party to another: but when the emperor arrived in a
civilised country, where free and virtuous men had a
share in the government, and brought to light the actions
of princes, his conduct, for the most part, seemed stained
with cowardice and perfidy—the more so, that he deceived
without remorse men whom he called deceivers, only
because they were more clever than himself. Louis of
Bavaria gave a meeting at Trento, in the month of
February, 1327, to the principal chiefs of the Ghibeline
party; they advanced him 150,000 florins, to pay the
expenses of his expedition to Italy: three months afterwards he entered that country with a suite of not more
than 600 horsemen; but the lords of Milan, Mantua,
Verona, and Ferrara met him, with their men at arms,
for the most part German mercenaries, who thus formed
for him a fine army. He received the iron crown at
Milan, on the 30th of May; Galeazzo Visconti, the
richest and most powerful of the Lombard lords, entertained him hospitably: but at the same time that he
excited the jealousy of the other Ghibeline chiefs, his fine
German cavalry and his treasure awakened the cupidity
of Louis. Having secured the obedience of these mercenaries, and feigning to lend an ear to the reports made
against Galeazzo by the other Ghibeline lords, he arrested
Visconti, together with his sons and his two brothers,
in his palace at Milan, on the 6th of July, 1327; and
threatened to put them to the torture if they did not

deliver to him their fortresses and their treasure. He detained them eight months in dungeons, without trial, and without assigning any reason for this severity. After eight months he liberated them, at the intercession of Castruccio. He then offered to sell them the sovereignty, of which he had himself deprived them: but they were not rich enough; for he had deprived them of the means by which they could profit by his offer. In the month of September, Louis passed into Tuscany, at the head of the army which he had seduced from the Visconti. The Pisans, exhausted with the war against Lucca and Sardinia, and desirous of preserving the peace which they had concluded with the Guelphs, sent to offer the emperor 60,000 florins, on that condition. Louis arrested their ambassadors, and threatened to put them to death by torture, if their country did not implicitly obey his will; after one month of hesitation, Pisa acknowledged him sovereign, and was forced to advance him 150,000 florins.

From the moment Louis of Bavaria was joined by Castruccio, he listened to no other counsel; and under the direction of this able politician, he showed a vigour and intelligence that promised to give him the dominion over all Italy, in spite of the excommunications which the pope poured on him with redoubled irritation, upon seeing him defeat all the intrigues of his favourite, Bertrand de Poiet. Castruccio persuaded Louis of the importance of confirming his right to the empire by his coronation at Rome; he delayed, therefore, the war on Florence, near which the duke of Calabria had assembled a numerous army, till his return. It is not improbable that Castruccio meant to reserve for himself the conquest of that city. Louis had named him duke of Lucca, Pistoia, Volterra, and the Lunigiana, on the 11th of November, 1327; and he flattered himself with the hope of uniting all Tuscany to this dukedom, after the departure of the emperor. Castruccio accompanied Louis to Rome; he was made senator of that city, and count palatine of St. John de Lateran. He carried the imperial sword at the coronation, which took place on the 17th of January, 1328, at the Vatican: the ceremony was performed by schismatic bishops, and in contempt of the excommunications of John XXII. Louis in his anger commenced a process in law to depose the pope and appoint a successor; but at this moment he was deprived of the counsel of Castruccio, who had been recalled to Tuscany by news of the taking of Pistoia by the Florentines, on the 28th of January, 1328. On his return he took Pisa by surprise; besieged Pistoia, and made himself master of it on the 3rd of August of the same year; but not till after such fatigue as to occasion an illness, of which he died, on the 3rd of September following. The death of this formidable and ambitious captain saved Florence from the greatest danger which she had yet incurred; and, to complete her good fortune, the sovereign she had chosen to oppose Castruccio, the duke of Calabria, died also about the same time. He had distinguished himself only by his vices, his want of foresight, and his depredations. Louis of Bavaria, too, ceased to be formidable: he completed his discredit by his perfidy towards those who had been the most devoted to him. Salvestro de' Gatti, lord of Viterbo, had been the first Ghibeline chief to open a fortress to him, in the states of the church; Louis arrested him, and put him to the torture, to force him to reveal the place where he had concealed his treasure. The emperor had rendered himself odious and ridiculous at Rome, by the puerility of his proceedings against John XXII., and his vain efforts to create a schism in the church. Having returned to Tuscany, he deprived the children of Castruccio of the sovereignty of Lucca, on the 16th of March, 1329, and sold it to one of their relatives, who, a month afterwards, was driven out by a troop of German mercenaries, which had abandoned the emperor to make war on their own account, that is to say, to live by plunder. Louis passed the summer of 1329 in Lombardy. Towards the end of the autumn he returned to Germany, carrying with him the contempt and detestation of the Italians. He had betrayed all who had trusted in him; and completely disorganised the Ghibeline party, which had relied on his support.

That party had just lost another of their most distinguished chiefs, Can' Grande della Scala. He was the grandson of the first Mastino, whom the republic of

Verona had chosen for master after the death of Eccelino, in 1260. Can' Grande reigned in that city from 1312 to 1329, with a splendour which no other prince in Italy equalled. Brave and fortunate in war, and wise in council, he gained a reputation for generosity, and even probity, to which few captains could pretend. Among the Lombard princes, he was the first protector of literature and the arts. The best poets, painters, and sculptors of Italy, Dante, to whom he offered an asylum, as well as Uguccione dà Faggiuola, and many other exiles illustrious in war or politics, were assembled at his court. He aspired to subdue the Veronese and Trevisan marches, or what has since been called the Terra Firma of Venice He took possession of Vicenza ; and afterwards maintained a long war against the republic of Padua, the most powerful in the district, and that which had shown the most attachment to the Guelph party and to liberty. But Padua gave way to all the excesses of democracy : the people evinced such jealousy of all distinction, such inconstancy in their choice, such presumption, that the imprudence of the chiefs as well as of the mob drew down the greatest disasters on the republic. The Paduans, repeatedly defeated by Can' Grande della Scala from 1314 to 1318, sought protection by vesting the power in a single person ; and fixed for that purpose on the noble house of Carrara, which had long given leaders to the Guelph party. The power vested in a single person soon extinguished all the courage and virtue that remained ; and on the 10th of September, 1328, Padua submitted to Can' Grande della Scala. The year following he attacked and took Treviso, which surrendered on the 6th of July, 1329. He possessed himself of Feltre and Cividale soon after. The whole province seemed subjugated to his power ; but the conqueror also was subdued. Attacked in his camp with a mortal disease, he gave orders on entering Treviso, that his couch should be carried into the great church, in which, four days afterwards, on the 22nd of July, 1329, he expired. He was not more than forty-one years of age : Castruccio was forty-seven at his death. Galeazzo Visconti died nearly about the same age, less than a year before. The Ghibeline party, which had produced such great captains,

thus saw them all disappear at once in the middle of their
career. Passerino de' Bonacossi, tyrant of Mantua, who
belonged to the same party, had been assassinated on the
14th of August, 1328, by the Gonzagas, who thus avenged
an affront offered to the wife of one of them. They took
possession of the sovereignty of Mantua, and kept it in
their family till the eighteenth century. Of all the
princes who had well received Louis of Bavaria in Italy,
the marquis d'Este was the only one who preserved his
power. He was lord of Ferrara; and even this prince,
though Guelph by birth, was forced by the intrigues of
the pope's legate to join the Ghibelines.

The Ghibeline party, which had been rendered so
formidable by the ability of its captains, was now completely disorganised. The Lombards placed no confidence
in those who remained; they had forgotten liberty, and
dared no longer aspire to it; but they longed for a prince
capable of defending them, and who, by his moderation
and good faith, could give them hopes of peace. They
saw none such in Italy: Germany unexpectedly offered
one. John, king of Bohemia, the son of Henry VII.,
arrived at Trent towards the end of the year 1330. The
memory of his father was rendered dearer to the Italians
by the comparison of his conduct with that of his
successor; and John was calculated to heighten this
predilection. He could not submit to the barbarism of
Bohemia; and inhabited, in preference, the county of
Luxemburg, or Paris, and having acquired a spirit
of heroism, by his constant reading, or listening to the
French romances of chivalry, he aspired to the glory of
being a complete knight. All that could at first sight
seduce the people was united in him: beauty, valour,
dexterity in all corporeal exercises, eloquence, an engaging
manner. His conduct in France and Germany, where
he had been, by turns, warrior and pacificator, was noble.
He never sought any thing for himself; he seemed to be
actuated only by the love of the general good or glory.
The Italians, justly disgusted with their own princes,
eagerly offered to throw themselves into his arms; the
city of Brescia sent deputies to Trent, to offer him the
sovereignty of their republic. He arrived there, to take
possession of it, on the 31st of December, 1330. Almost

I

immediately after, Bergamo, Cremona, Pavia, Vercelli, and Novara followed the example of Brescia. Azzo Visconti himself, son of Galeazzo, who, in 1328, had repurchased Milan from Louis of Bavaria, could not withstand the enthusiasm of his subjects; he nominally ceded the government to John, taking henceforth the title of his vicar only. Parma, Modena, Reggio, and, lastly, Lucca also, soon gave themselves to John of Bohemia. John, in all these cities, recalled indiscriminately the Guelph and Ghibeline exiles, restored peace, and made them, at last, taste the first-fruits of good government.

But the Florentines, attached to liberty, and satisfied with their constitution, who saw a foreign prince, a Ghibeline, and the son of Henry VII., whom they had always resisted, arrive on their frontier, could not participate in this infatuation. They knew that, whatever might be the virtue and talents of an absolute prince, his government always degenerated into tyranny; that, if he was not himself corrupted by power, his successors never failed of being so. Numerous examples in Italy, in their own time, sufficiently demonstrated the rapid degeneracy of the race of princes, and the profound pity merited by a people governed by the son of a great man. They were well aware that it was the municipal, democratic, independent constitutions of the cities of Italy, and the constant emulation between them, that had given them such an immense superiority over the rest of Europe. They easily perceived that Italy, in spite of its division, had nothing to fear for its independence from its transalpine enemies; while it had every thing to dread for its liberty, as well as for its civilisation, from the immeasurable growth of an absolute principality formed within its bosom. The Florentines did not undertake to restore liberty to those people who had no longer sufficient elevation of soul to desire or energy to defend it; but they pursued for themselves the noble policy of opposing all usurpation or conquest by any who pretended to domination in Italy; and if they could not preserve to each city its independence, at least of maintaining, through the changes which time necessarily brings, the balance between the different powers, in such

a manner that respect for the rights of all should be
guaranteed by the alliance of those who demanded only
to be free themselves, and to preserve the liberty of
others.   This system of balancing the different powers
in Italy, invented by the statesmen of Florence, was,
during the fourteenth and the greater part of the fifteenth
centuries, the fundamental rule of their conduct.

The Florentines did not find sufficient strength in the
Guelph party to oppose the menacing greatness of the
king of Bohemia.   Robert of Naples was become old;
he wanted energy, and his soldiers courage.   The republic of Bologna, formerly so rich and powerful, had
lost its vigour under the government of the legate,
Bertrand de Poiet; those of Perugia and Sienna had
within themselves few resources, and those few their
jealousy of Florence prevented their liberally employing.
There remained no more free cities in Lombardy ; and
all those, in the states of the church, which, during the
preceding century, had shown so much spirit, had fallen
under the yoke of some petty tyrant, who immediately
declared for the Ghibeline party.   The Florentines felt
the necessity of silencing their hereditary enmities, and
their ancient repugnances, and of making an alliance
with the Lombard Ghibelines against John of Bohemia,
with the condition that, in dividing his spoils, they
should all agree to prevent the aggrandisement of any
single power, and preserve between themselves an exact
equilibrium, in order that Italy, after their conquests,
should incur no danger of being subjugated by one of
them.   The treaty of alliance against the king of
Bohemia, and the partition of the states which he had
just acquired in Italy, was signed in the month of September, 1332.   Cremona was to be given to Visconti;
Parma to Mastino della Scala, the nephew and successor
of Can' Grande; Reggio to Gonzaga; Modena to the
marquis d'Este; and Lucca to the Florentines.   John
did not oppose to this league the resistance that was
expected from his courage and talents.   Of an incon-
stant character, becoming weary of everything, always
pursuing something new, thinking only of shining in
courts and tournaments, he soon regarded all these little
Italian principalities, of which he had already lost some,

as too citizen-like and unlordly : he sold every town
which had given itself to him, to whatever noble desired
to rule over it ; and he departed for Paris on the 15th of
October, 1333, leaving Italy in still greater confusion
than before. The Lombard Ghibelines, confederates of
the Florentines, succeeded, before the end of the summer
of 1335, in taking possession of the cities abandoned by
the king of Bohemia. Lucca, which alone fell to the
share of Florence, was defended by a band of German
soldiers, who made it the centre of their depredations,
and barbarously tyrannised over the Lucchese. Mastino
della Scala offered to treat for the Florentines with the
captains who then commanded at Lucca ; and he succeeded in obtaining the surrender of the town to him, on
the 20th of December, 1335. As soon as he became
master of it, he began to flatter himself that it would
afford him the means of subjugating the rest of Tuscany ;
and, instead of delivering it, as he had engaged, to the
Florentines, he sought to renew against them a Ghibeline
league jointly with the Pisans and all the independent
nobles of the Apennines.

The Florentines, forced to defend themselves against
their ally, who, after they had contributed to his elevation, betrayed them, sought the alliance of the Venetians,
who also had reason to complain of Mastino. A treaty
was signed between the two republics, on the 21st of
June, 1336. The war, to which Florence liberally contributed in money, was made only in Lombardy, and
was successful. Padua was taken from Mastino on the
3rd of August, 1337, and, as that town showed no ardent
desire of liberty, it was given in sovereignty to the Guelph
house of Carrara. The Venetians took possession of
Treviso, Castel-Franco, and Ceneda. It was the first
acquisition they had made beyond the Lagune, their first
establishment on Terra Firma, which henceforward was
to mingle their interests with those of the rest of Italy.
But their ambition at this moment extended no farther.
Satisfied themselves, and sacrificing their allies, they
made peace with Mastino della Scala, on the 18th of
December, 1338, without stipulating that the city of
Lucca, the object of the war, should be given up to the
Florentines, for which these had contracted a debt of

450,000 florins. The Florentines, successively betrayed
by all their allies, saw the danger of their position augment daily ; the Guelphs lost, one after the other, every
supporter of their party: the vigour of the king of
Naples, now seventy-five years of age, was gone. The
pope, John XXII., had died at Avignon, on the 4th of
December, 1334; and his successor, Benedict XII.,
like him a Frenchman, neither understood nor took any
part in the affairs of Italy. A few months previous, on
the 17th of March, 1334, the cardinal Bertrand de Poiet
had been driven by the people from Bologna ; and this
ambitious legate, no longer supported by the pope his
father, had disappeared from the political scene. But the
Bolognese did not long preserve the liberty which they
had recovered. One of their citizens, named Taddeo
de Pepoli, the richest man in all Italy, had seduced the
German guard which they held in pay, and by its aid
took possession of the sovereignty of Bologna, on the
28th of August, 1337. He then made alliance with the
Ghibelines. The number of the free cities, on the aid, or
at least the sympathy, of which Florence could reckon,
continually diminished. The Genoese, from the commencement of the century, had consumed their strength
in internal wars between the great Guelph and Ghibeline
families ; as long as they were free, however, the Florentines, without any treaty of alliance, regarded them as
friendly ; but the long protracted civil wars had disgusted the people with the government: they rose on
the 23rd of September, 1339, and overthrew it, replacing
the signoria by a single chief, Boccanegra, on whom
they conferred the title of doge. It might have been
feared they had only given themselves a tyrant : but the
first doge of Genoa was a friend to liberty ; and the
Genoese people having imitated Venice, in giving themselves a first officer in the state with that title, were not
long before they carried the imitation farther, by seeking
to combine liberty with power vested in a single person.
In the mean while Mastino della Scala suffered a Par-
mesan noble to take from him the city of Parma. As
from that time he had no farther communication with
Lucca, he offered to sell it to the Florentines. The
bargain was concluded in the month of August, 1341 ;

but it appeared to the Pisans the signal of their own servitude, for it cut off all communication between them and the Ghibelines of Lombardy. They immediately advanced their militia into the Lucchese states, to prevent the Florentines from taking possession of the town ; vanquished them in a great battle, on the 2nd of October, 1341, under the walls of Lucca ; and, on the 6th of July following, took possession of that city for themselves.

The people of Florence attributed this train of disasters to the incapacity of their magistrates. The burden of the taxes, and of the debt with which the republic was loaded ; and the jealousy entertained of the rich merchants, who, in spite of the democratic form of the constitution, in fact governed the state, excited a discontent which soon took the darkest hue. The people who in all Italy were regarded as by far the most republican, those who owed all their greatness to liberty, for which they had made such immense sacrifices, the people who carried their love of equality and their jealousy of all distinction to excess, of a sudden appeared wearied of their own sovereignty ; they demanded a master, in order to punish and humiliate those who appeared too great to be reached by the laws of a republic ; they asked to submit to the authority of a single person. At this period, Gaultier de Brienne, duke of Athens, a French noble, but born in Greece, passed through Florence, on his way from Naples to France. The duchy of Athens had remained in his family from the conquest of Constantinople till it was taken from his father in 1312. There remained to him only that of Lecce, in the kingdom of Naples. He had been the lieutenant of the duke of Calabria, at Florence, in 1326, and had then distinguished himself by his bravery and the acuteness of his understanding. It was for this man the Florentines, after their defeat at Lucca, took a sudden fancy. They protested they never should have experienced so many disasters if the duke of Athens had been at the head of their army. On the 1st of August, 1342, they obliged the signoria to confer on him the title of captain of justice, and give him the command of their militia.

The duke of Athens was of that degenerate race of Franks, established in the Levant, whom the people of

the West designated by the name of *Pullani*, to indicate
their small stature, their apparent weakness, and frequently their cowardice. To this physical conformation
they joined the most unbridled love of pleasure, cunning,
perfidy, habits of despotism, and contempt of human
life; the vices, in short, which connection with the East
necessarily communicates to barbarians, always more
disposed to be corrupted than to improve. The duke
of Athens was named president of the tribunals, and
commander of the forces of the republic; offices of
more power than ought to have been given to such a
man, but not enough for his ambition: he aspired to
be absolute sovereign, and to make a single duchy
of Tuscany. He entered into negotiation with those
cities which were subject to or allied with Florence,
with a view to induce them to place themselves under
his rule, and to shake off the yoke and alliance of the
republic. With a rapidity of perception, and a talent
for intrigue, which he had acquired in Greece, he, in a
few days, unravelled all the secret designs, all the jealous
passions, which divided the republic. He perceived that
the first class of citizens, who had the greatest share in
the government, had also the greatest share in the
public hatred; they were objects of execration to the
ancient nobility, whom they had excluded from all the
offices of government; of jealousy to the second class
of citizens immediately under them; and of envy and
anger to the populace, who declared themselves crushed
by the taxes. The duke of Athens sacrificed them to
these various passions; he beheaded many, and ruined
others by fines. He sent to France and Naples for a
troop of cavalry, better suited to intrigue than war. He
ordered them to mix among the people, seduce them into
taverns, and keep them in a constant state of intoxica-
tion, celebrating at the same time the valour and liberality
of the duke, and announcing to them that if he was absolute master, he would make the poorest people in Florence
live in merriment and abundance. Having thus excited
the people to a ferment, he convoked them in parliament
in the public square, on the 8th of September. The
agitators directing the lowest orders proclaimed him
sovereign lord of Florence for his life, forced the public

palace, drove from it the gonfalonier and the priori, and installed him there in their place.

The liberty of Italy had been at an end, if the duke of Athens had succeeded in establishing the despotism of which he had just laid the foundation: all the other republics seemed plunged in a deep lethargy. The desire of investing power in a single person had invaded the proudest and most opulent cities, all those which had before shown the greatest abhorrence of tyranny. As the rest of Europe was not yet ready to profit by the example and instruction of Italy, the slavery of Florence, the destruction of all liberty in the city which gave impulse to the spirit of enquiry, to philosophy, politics, eloquence, poetry, and the fine arts, would have stopped, perhaps for centuries, the civilisation of the world. Gaultier of Athens united all the qualities that Machiavel, 160 years later, enumerated as necessary to a prince, the founder of a despotism. Courageous, dissembling, patient, clear-sighted, perfidious, he knew neither respect nor pity; he was bound by no affection and no principle: accordingly, he sought the alliance of the Ghibeline tyrants of Romagna and Lombardy, whom he had till then combated as enemies to his sovereign the king of Naples. They on their side joyfully coalesced with a despot, who delivered them from an example which might prove contagious to their subjects in the liberty and happiness of Florence: he had no enemies abroad; and his executioners rapidly delivered him from the more dangerous of his enemies at home.

Happily, Florence was not ripe for slavery: ten months sufficed for the duke of Athens to draw from it 400,000 golden florins, which he sent either to France or Naples; but ten months sufficed also to undeceive all parties who had placed any confidence in him; to unite them all in one common hatred, and in a common determination to overthrow his tyranny. Three conspiracies, unconnected with each other, were secretly formed: they soon comprehended almost all the citizens of Florence. The duke, without discovering them, repeatedly defeated them, by the precautions, more rigorous each day, which he took for his security: his cruelty kept pace with his suspicions; he questioned with the torture all those on

whom fell the slightest of his doubts; it was thus he was
led to seize Baldinaccio degli Adimari, who, though the
duke was unaware of it, was the chief of one of the conspiracies.   The universal ferment which this arrest
excited made him sensible that he was in the road to
a discovery; he did not, however, betray his sentiments;
he asked reinforcements from all his allies, and it was
not till those were in motion that, on the 26th of July,
he convoked three hundred of the most distinguished
citizens, professedly to consult them on the affairs of the
republic.   Orders were given in the palace to put every
one to death as soon as he entered; but the people also
were ready.   In each of the massive palaces of Florence,
the citizens were silently assembling : they arrived one
by one, without noise, and unperceived.   The cavalry of
the duke filled the street, where every body seemed
occupied only with their own affairs; no agitation, no
apparent confusion, announced any explosion, when suddenly the cry "To arms!" burst from the old market-
place, and was re-echoed to the gates of St. Peter's.
Instantly from every window, from the roofs of all the
houses, fell a shower of stones and tiles, previously made
ready, on the heads of the duke's cavalry ; every palace
opened and poured forth armed men, who threw chains
across the streets, and made barricades: the cry of
"*Popolo ! popolo ! Libertà !*" resounded from one extremity
of Florence to the other.   The cavalry, surprised, dispersed, and overwhelmed with stones, were soon disarmed; the chains were then taken up, and troops of
citizens united and marched to the Palazzo Vecchio,
where the duke defended himself with 400 transalpine
soldiers.   Gaultier might have long held out in this
massive fortress, if it had been sufficiently victualled;
but hunger forced him to have recourse to the mediation
of the bishop of Florence.   He capitulated, on the
3rd of August, 1343 ; the bishop concealed him till the
6th from the fury of the people, and sent him off secretly
in the night with his cavalry, to whom the duke of
Athens owed their pay ; arrived at Venice, he stole away
from his companions in misfortune, to avoid paying them,
and escaped in a small vessel to Naples, whither he had
previously sent his treasure.

K

CHAPTER VII

THE REVIVAL OF LETTERS — REVOLUTIONS ATTEMPTED BY TWO
LEARNED MEN—ITALY RAVAGED BY THE PLAGUE, AND BY COM-
PANIES OF ADVENTURERS — THE POWER OF THE HOUSE OF
VISCONTI — WAR BETWEEN THE MARITIME REPUBLICS — THE
DANGERS AND FIRMNESS OF THE REPUBLIC OF FLORENCE

THE oppression which weighed upon the rest of Europe
contributed to the maintenance of barbarism, less by
rendering difficult, and sometimes dangerous, the acquisition of knowledge, than by taking away all attraction
from the exercise of the mind.   Thought was a pain to
those capable of judging the state of the human species,
—of studying the past ; of comparing it with the present ;
and of thus foreseeing the future.   Danger and suffering
appeared on all sides.   The men who, in France,
Germany, England, and Spain, felt themselves endued
with the power of generalising their ideas, either
smothered them, not to aggravate the pain of thought,
or directed them solely to speculations the farthest from
real life,—towards that scholastic philosophy which so
vigorously exercised the understanding, without bringing
it to any conclusion.   In Italy, on the contrary, liberty
secured the full enjoyment of intellectual existence.
Every one endeavoured to develop the powers which he
felt within him, because each was conscious that the
more his mind opened the greater was his enjoyment ;
every one directed his powers to a useful and practical
purpose, because each felt himself placed in a state of
society in which he might attain some influence, either
for his own benefit or that of his fellow-creatures.   The
first want which towns had experienced was that of their
defence.   Accordingly, military architecture had taken
precedence in the arts.   From its exercise the transition
was easy to that of religious architecture, at a time when
religion was indispensable to every heart,—to civil
architecture, then encouraged by a government in which
every thing was for all.   The study and pursuit of the
beautiful in this first of the fine arts had paved the way
to all the others.   From the pleasures of the imagination

through the eye, men ascended to those derived from the soul; and hence the birth of poetry.

In the sciences, also, the Italians had begun with the personal protection of man. The consideration of his health presented itself; and the earliest school of medicine was founded at Salerno, in the neighbourhood of the three republics of Gaëta, Naples, and Amalfi. Then followed that of his private rights and property; and the university of Bologna acquired immense celebrity in the teaching of civil and canon law, before any other study was diligently pursued. The rights of all naturally rose out of the rights of each; and politics, as a science, yet existed only in Italy. Statesmen sought, in history, how governments made the happiness or misery of nations, and the study of antiquity was pursued with ardour; while the two Villani wrote history with as much judgment, elevation of soul, and philosophy as Polybius. At the same time, the thinking men in France, who, instead of brutifying themselves in order to suffer less from despotism, anarchy, and the invasion of the English, exercised their understandings, passionately embraced the study of the scholastic theology. They commented on, and developed with subtlety, principles of which they did not permit themselves to judge; and the faculty of the Sorbonne, in the university of Paris, was acknowledged to be the first theological school in Europe; it was that in which the most acuteness and depth of thought were united to the most implicit faith. In Italy, on the contrary, the mind, accustomed to examine the claims of authority, had already produced, since the time of Frederick II., and still more after the translation from the Arabic of the books of Averrhoes, thinkers whom the priests accused not only of heresy, but of incredulity and epicurism.

The popular form of government must have early accustomed the Italians to speak in public; but the example of their preachers was prejudicial to their eloquence: they made discourses, instead of speaking. They supposed that they ought always to begin with what they called *proposing*; that is, taking a text from some celebrated author, either sacred or profane. And this support which they sought in what was said by another, introduced the substitution of pedantry for reason. Accordingly, the fourteenth century, in Italy so fruitful in great men, has left us no model of political eloquence. The Italians were accustomed to express in verse all that strongly moved them. Poetry was for them the language of truth and of persuasion, as much as of the imagination. Lyric poetry, above all, took the place of eloquence: it shone forth with great brilliancy in the fourteenth century. Some of the canzoni of Petrarch express the elevated sentiments of a great soul. A crowd of poets at this epoch obeyed the same inspiration. The name of Petrarch, born in 1304, and that of Boccaccio, in 1313, both Florentines, are the most universally known. The second owes his celebrity to the light, elegant, and easy prose of his novels, more than to his poetry. Both have descended to posterity with their Italian writings alone, which they regarded only as relaxations from their labour, and not with their Latin works, upon which they depended for their glory.

The Italians, in the fourteenth century, discovered, as it were, anew the ancient world: they felt an affinity of thoughts, hopes, and tastes with the best Latin writers, which inspired them with the highest admiration. Petrarch, and particularly Boccaccio, passed from this study to that of Grecian antiquity ; and, on his solicitation, the republic of Florence, in 1360, founded a chair of Grecian literature, the first in the West. A passion for erudition spread from one end of Italy to the other, with an ardour proportionable to the dark ignorance of the preceding centuries. It was imagined that all knowledge consisted in knowing and imitating the ancient masters. The highest glory was attached to classical learning ; and Petrarch and Boccaccio attained a degree of celebrity, credit, and power, unequalled by any other men in the middle ages; not by reason of those merits which we feel at the present day, but as the pontiffs and interpreters of antiquity.

We owe to the learned of the fourteenth century, and to their school, a deep sentiment of gratitude. They discovered, and rendered intelligible to us, all the *chefs-d'œuvre* of antiquity. Fragments only of classic works remained, scattered throughout Europe, and on the point of being lost. Those learned men of Italy collected, collated, and explained them : without their antiquarian zeal, all the experience of past ages, all the models of taste, all the great works of genius, would never have reached us; and, probably, without such guides we should never have attained the point on which we now stand. But they injured their own age by their exclusive bias to erudition. The imagination was extinguished; genius disappeared; and even the language retrograded. It was abandoned, as too vulgar, for the Latin, by all those who attained any distinction for talents : the forms of thinking of the ancients were adopted with those of their language, and pedantry soon smothered all national originality.

Two of these men, learned in the Greek and Latin literature, friends of Petrarch, loving liberty, not like Italians of the middle ages, but like sons of ancient Rome, profited by their celebrity and by their power over their auditors to re-establish a republican government;—Cola di Rienzo, at Rome, in 1347, and Jacopo de' Bussolari, ten years later, at Pavia. The former, though of obscure birth, soon signalised himself by his progress in letters, by his familiarity with all the writers of antiquity, by his knowledge of the manners and laws of the Romans, and of the monuments and inscriptions which still ornamented the capital of the world. No one possessed like him the art of explaining them, and of striking out in his explanations those traits of grandeur and glory which distinguish the ancient republic. Born at Rome, he was a more ardent Roman than republican; seeking rather to restore the sovereignty of the ancient city than the liberty of mankind. He rejected with deep indignation the usurpations of two barbarians; the one a German, calling himself Roman emperor; the other a Frenchman, who called himself the pontiff of Rome. All those who rose to eminence by the study and example of the ancient Romans appeared to him bound to labour to bring back Italy and mankind under the dominion of Rome. Petrarch had also a religious respect for the name of Rome; but living by turns at the court of Avignon, or at those of the tyrants of Lombardy, he had

much less elevation of soul and true enthusiasm than
Cola di Rienzo. The latter was susceptible of all the
emotion which the fine arts give ; and he employed his
own sensibility to act on a susceptible people. Sometimes at the foot of one of the most admirable monuments
of ancient architecture, he explained its purpose to the
crowd, by which he was always attended ; he made them
feel its beauty, and would take occasion to recall the
grandeur and freedom of ancient Rome, which still spoke
to her children from those colossal ruins. He would
contrast it with the state of degradation and suffering to
which Rome was then reduced. He sometimes interpreted
in the public places the inscriptions which he discovered;
and would draw forth proofs of the sovereignty which
Rome exercised over the whole world. Sometimes he
displayed in the capitol allegorical pictures which he had
composed, and, in explaining them, would call upon the
Roman people to quit their state of servitude, and recover
what he emphatically called the *good state*. The pope
had never exercised any sovereign power in Rome ; but
the absence of his court, in ruining the little commerce
of the tradesmen, had contributed to throw the city into
a desolate state of anarchy. The nobles had reduced the
government, composed of a senator and thirteen *caporioni*,
to entire dependence on themselves ; and the nobility of
Rome, as well as of the rest of Italy, believed it beneath
their station to be submissive to the law. The Colonna,
Orsini, and Savelli families, always at war with each
other, garrisoned all the fortresses in Rome with banditti,
their satellites ; and at their head made daily attacks in
the streets upon each other. Cola di Rienzo had a classic
hatred for these turbulent nobles ; a hatred which he
believed he had inherited from the Gracchi. He felt
anxious to be made tribune of the people, in order to
deliver them from the yoke of the patricians ; and on the
20th of May, 1347, while the Colonnas had quitted Rome
with a small body of troops, he summoned the people to
take possession of the government and of the guard of the
city. The Romans appointed him, with the bishop of
Orvieto, the pope's vicar, or depository of his spiritual
power, as tribunes. They ascended the capitol together.
At first the revolution seemed accomplished. The power

of the name of Rome; the joy of men of letters throughout Europe; the hatred provoked by the Roman nobles;
the indifference of the pope, and his distance from Rome,
favoured this revolution. For some weeks it was approved and acknowledged by all Italy. But Cola di
Rienzo, though eloquent, learned, and a poet, was neither
a statesman nor a warrior: he knew not how to consolidate this *good state,* to which he pretended to have
restored the Romans. He continued to occupy them with
allegories, festivals, and processions, while they demanded
of him something more positive. His head was turned
by vanity; and he assumed a degree of pomp which
excited ridicule. He had soon to support a war against
the nobles whom he had exiled; and though several of
the Colonnas perished in an ill-conducted attack on
Rome, Cola in repelling them gave proofs of incapacity
and cowardice. The pope sent a legate to Rome, to
appease the civil war; and this legate, being a French
noble, sided with the nobility. The latter having taken
possession of a division of the town, the tocsin summoned
the people to defend themselves, but it sounded in vain;
and on the 15th of December, 1347, Cola di Rienzo,
obliged to abandon the capitol, retreated to the castle of
St. Angelo, and afterwards sought refuge with Charles IV.,
son of John, king of Bohemia, who gave him up to the
pope in 1352.

The pope Innocent VI., having in the following year
charged his legate, Egidio Albornoz, to recover the
ecclesiastical states from the hands of the tyrants who in
each city had seized the sovereignty, made Cola di Rienzo
accompany him, in order to profit by the influence which
the tribune might still have retained at Rome. The
legate sent him there in the month of July, 1354; declaring at the same time that he made him Roman senator by
the authority of the pope. Cola found again his friends
at Rome, and for a short time succeeded in awakening
th e popular enthusiasm; but he was now only an instrument in the hand of the legate, and it did not depend on
him to realise the hopes which he excited. A new sedition broke forth; and this time the people joined his
enemies the Colonnas: his palace was burnt down, he
was arrested as he endeavoured to escape in disguise,

dragged to the porphyry lion at the foot of the capitol stairs, and there stabbed, on the 8th of October, 1354.

The monk Jacopo de' Bussolari, who in the month of March, 1356, had also restored a sort of ephemeral liberty to Pavia, was, like Cola, a learned man, a poet, and a friend of Petrarch; he was a man of ardent imagination, who had borrowed his love of liberty from the ancients. He was a monk of St. Augustine, and was sent to his birthplace, Pavia, to preach there during Lent. This city had been governed, since the year 1313, by the Ghibeline family of Beccaria, who were supported from abroad by the Viscontis, and the marquis de Montferrat. A war having broken out between the marquis and the lords of Milan, the Beccarias declared against the Viscontis, who had till then regarded the lords of Pavia almost as their lieutenants. The Viscontis in their anger besieged Pavia; and the city would soon have fallen, if Jacopo de' Bussolari had not, by his eloquent sermons, roused the energy of the Pavesans: he preached the reform of morals, faith, liberty and courage; he at the same time animated them by his example. On the 27th of May, 1356, in descending from the pulpit, he placed himself at their head; marched out of the town; attacked the redoubts of the Milanese, took three, one after the other; and forced the Viscontis to raise the siege. It was as important to deliver his country from domestic tyranny as from a foreign yoke. As he often preached against the vices and usurpations of the Beccarias, they endeavoured to get him assassinated; the Pavesans, to protect him, supplied him with a guard; there were several engagements between the faithful troops of their pastor and the satellites of the tyrants. At last Jacopo de' Bussolari issued an order to the Beccarias, to leave the city: they obeyed, but, making an alliance with the Viscontis, renewed the war. In 1358, the monk caused the palaces of the Beccarias to be rased to the ground; in 1359, the Viscontis again besieged the city. An epidemical disease broke out in it with virulence; all the allies which Jacopo de' Bussolari had procured the Pavesans successively abandoned them. The eloquent and courageous monk perceived that he must at last yield to fortune; and in the month of October, 1359, offered

to capitulate with the Viscontis, and to deliver the city to
them, on condition that they should preserve all the
municipal liberties, that the exiles whom he had recalled
should be allowed to remain, and that an amnesty should
be granted the citizens, without a single exception : he
stipulated nothing for himself ; and the Viscontis employing his ecclesiastical superiors against him, he was confined in the prison of his convent at Vercelli, where he
died a miserable death.   They afterwards annulled the
capitulation of Pavia ; declaring that, as they were
imperial vicars, they could not be held to execute any
thing which they promised, contrary to the rights of the
empire.

This empire had passed from Louis of Bavaria, who
died on the 10th of October, 1347, to Charles IV. of
Bohemia.   He had been set up as competitor with the
former by the pope, on the 10th of July, 1346, and was
called the king of the priests : he was, however, soon
after the death of Louis, acknowledged by the whole
empire.   Desirous of obtaining the same acknowledgment
in Italy, he entered it on the 14th of October, 1354, but
without an army ; "appearing," says Villani, " with his
disarmed knights mounted on travelling palfreys, rather
as a merchant going to a fair than an emperor."   He
was crowned at Milan, and afterwards at Rome : and
extracted from the republics, as he passed, a ransom for
their liberty ;   he caused, by his petty intrigues, much
trouble and insurrection, but he at the same time
degraded, in the eyes of the Italians, the imperial majesty,
by his cupidity, and want of dignity and energy.   The
popes who succeeded each other at Avignon also lost the
respect of the faithful by their immoralities, intrigues, and
ambition.   To Benedict XII., an honest but weak man,
possessing a feeble understanding, had succeeded, in 1342,
Clement VI., who lighted the fire of civil war again in
Germany, and signalised himself in his Italian politics by
the most atrocious treachery.   Towards the end of 1352,
he was succeeded by Innocent VI.   This pope formed
the project of recovering the state belonging to the
church ; the sovereignty of which the imperial charters
had abandoned to him.   He made choice, for this purpose, of cardinal Albornoz, a Spaniard, who had already

signalised himself in arms against the Moors; he gave the cardinal little money and few soldiers, but he reckoned, and with some reason, on the favour of the people. These last, in every city of Romagna and of the March, had suffered themselves to be enslaved by the boldest and richest of their fellow-citizens: all were wearied with the yoke of these petty tyrants, and, without any good reason to trust to the government of the church, they were glad of a change. Albornoz, who had still more ability in intrigue than he had military talent, succeeded in setting these tyrants at variance one with the other; in obtaining the assistance of the Guelphs of Tuscany; and, finally, in deposing and subduing them all: but before he terminated these conquests, Innocent VI. died, on the 12th of September, 1362, and was succeeded by Urban V.

The kings of Naples, during this period, had sunk still lower in power and consideration. Robert died on the 19th of January, 1343, at the age of eighty. He had given his grand-daughter, Joan, in marriage to her cousin Andrew, the son of the king of Hungary. Andrew was son of the eldest son of Charles II.; and had a better right than Robert himself to the crown of Naples. The latter, whom his nephew regarded as an usurper, had been desirous of confounding the rights of the two branches of his family, by marrying Joan to Andrew, and crowning them together; but these young people felt towards each other only jealousy and hatred. Andrew was brutal, Joan was elegant in her manners, but depraved. She consented to an assassination, which delivered her from her husband, on the 18th of September, 1345; and two years after, married her cousin, Louis of Tarento, the instigator of the murder. The crown of Hungary had passed to the elder brother of Andrew,—Louis, called the Great. To avenge his brother, he entered Italy, and conquered Naples in 1348. Joan, meanwhile, fled, with her husband, to Provence; and, to conciliate the favour of the pope, abandoned to him the sovereignty of Avignon. It was exactly at the period of the greatest calamity that ever befell mankind. The plague, brought from the East, made the circuit of Italy, and afterwards of all Europe; and in every place it reached carried off,

in seven or eight months, one third of the population.
It is known in history by the name of " the plague of
Florence ;" because, while it mowed down millions of
obscure victims elsewhere, at Florence, where it carried
off nearly a hundred thousand persons, an advanced
civilisation rendered the loss more sensibly felt. Many
distinguished men sank under this scourge; several
philosophers studied it; and a great writer, Boccaccio,
has left of it an admirable description. The terror and
desolation, which an infliction so dreadful caused throughout Italy, superseded all political hatreds,—all wars, however obstinate. Louis of Hungary, in the middle of his
campaign and of his successes, was discouraged, upon
seeing the most flourishing armies swept off by sickness. In 1351, he signed a peace with Joan, who
returned with her husband to her kingdom of Naples,
where both long continued their career of vice and
voluptuousness; abandoning all care of administration,
and of the national defence; permitting their provinces,
in the bosom of peace, to be plundered and laid waste,
in a manner hardly to be feared in the most disastrous
wars.

The most immediate cause of the sufferings of the
kingdom of Naples, and of all Italy, was the formation of
what was called "companies of adventure." Wherever
tyrants had succeeded to free governments, their first
care had been to disarm the citizens, whose resistance
was to be feared; and although a little industry might
soon have supplied swords and lances, yet the danger of
being denounced for using them soon made the subjects
of these princes lose every military habit. Even the
citizens of free towns no longer thought of defending
themselves : their way of life had weakened their corporeal
strength; and they felt an inferiority too discouraging
when they had to oppose, without defensive armour,
cuirassiers on horseback. The chief strength of armies
henceforth was in the heavy-armed cavalry, composed of
men who had all their lives followed the trade of war,
and who hired themselves for pay. The emperors had
successively brought into Italy many of their countrymen,
who afterwards passed into the service of the tyrant
princes. The Viscontis and Della Scalas had sent for

many to Germany, believing that these men—who did not understand the language of the country,—who were bound to it by no affection,—and who were accessible to no political passion,—would be their best defenders. They proved ready to execute the most barbarous orders, and for their recompence demanded only the enjoyments of an intemperate sensuality.

But the Lombard tyrants were deceived in believing the German soldier would never covet power for himself, and would continue to abuse the right of the stronger for the advantage of others only. These adventurers soon discovered that it would be better to make war and pillage the people for their own profit, without dividing the spoil with a master. Some men of high rank, who had served in Italy as *condottieri* (hired captains), proposed to their soldiers to follow them, make war on the whole world, and divide the booty among themselves. The first company, formed by an Italian noble at the moment that the Viscontis dismissed their soldiers, having made peace with their adversaries, made an attack suddenly on Milan, in the hope of plundering that great city; but was almost annihilated in a battle, fought at Parabiago, on the 20th of February, 1339. A German duke, known only by his Christian name of Werner, and the inscription he wore on his breast of "enemy of God, of pity, and of mercy," formed, in 1343, another association, which maintained itself for a long time, under the name of "the great company." It in turns entered the service of princes; and, when they made peace, carried on its ravages and plunderings for its own profit. The duke Werner and his successors,—the count Lando, a German; and the friar Moriale, knight of St. John,—devastated Italy from Montferrat to the extremity of the kingdom of Naples. They raised contributions, by threatening to burn houses and harvests, or by putting the prisoners whom they took to the most horrible tortures. The provinces of Apulia were, above all, abandoned to their devastations; and the king and queen of Naples made not a single effort to protect their people.

There now remained no more than six independent princes in Lombardy. The Viscontis, lords of Milan, had usurped all the central part of that province; the

western part was held by the marquis of Montferrat, and
the eastern by the Della Scala, lords of Verona, Carrara
of Padua, Este of Ferrara, and Gonzaga of Mantua.
These weaker princes felt themselves in danger, and
made a league against the Viscontis, taking into their
service the great company ; but, deceived and pillaged
by it, they suffered greater evils than they inflicted on
their enemies.   When at last the money of the league
was exhausted, and it could no longer pay the company,
this band of robbers entered into the service of the
republic of Sienna, to be let loose on that of Perugia, of
which the Siennese had conceived a deep jealousy.   But
the Florentines would not consent to their entering
Tuscany, where their depredations had been already felt.
They shut all the passes of the Apennines ; they armed
the mountaineers ; they made these adventurers experience a first defeat at the passage of Scalella, on the
24th of July, 1358, and obliged them to fall back on
Romagna.   The legate Albornoz, to deliver himself from
such guests, made them enter Perugia the year following.
Never had the company been so brilliant and so formidable : it levied contributions on Sienna, as well as
Perugia ; but vengeance and cupidity alike excited them
against the Florentines.   They determined on pillaging
those rich merchants, whom they considered far from
warlike, or forcing them to ransom themselves.
    The Marquis de Montferrat, desirous of taking the
company into his service, pressed the republic of Florence,
by his ambassadors, to do what the greatest potentates
had always done,—pay the banditti to be rid of them.
He offered himself for mediator and guarantee, and
promised a prompt and cheap deliverance ; but the
Florentine republic protested it would not submit to any
thing so base ; it assembled an army purely Italian,
placing it under the command of an Italian captain, who
was ordered to advance to the frontier, and offer battle
to the company.   The robbers gave way in proportion
to the firmness of the republic : they made the tour of
the Florentine frontier by Sienna, Pisa, and Lucca,
always threatening, yet never daring to violate it.   On
the 12th of July, 1359, they sent the Florentine commander a challenge to battle, and afterwards failed to

keep the rendezvous which they had given. They escaped at last from Tuscany, without having fought, and divided themselves in the service of different princes, humbled indeed, but too much accustomed to this disorderly life not to be anxious to begin it anew.

The republic of Florence was continually occupied, since the expulsion of the duke of Athens, in guarding against the ambition of the Viscontis, which threatened the subjugation of all Italy. Azzo Visconti, the son of that Galeazzo who had been so treacherously used by Louis of Bavaria, had, in 1328, purchased the city of Milan from that emperor, and soon afterwards found himself master of ten other cities of Lombardy; but he died suddenly, in the height of his prosperity, the 16th of August, 1339. As he left no children, his uncle Luchino succeeded him in the sovereignty. Luchino was false and ferocious, but clever, and possessed in war the hereditary talent of the Viscontis. He was called a lover of justice, probably because he punished criminals with an excess of cruelty, and maintained by terror a perfect police in his states. He died, poisoned by his wife, on the 23rd of January, 1349. His brother John, archbishop of Milan, succeeded him in power. The latter found himself master of sixteen of the largest cities in Lombardy; cities which, in the preceding century, had been so many free and flourishing republics. His ambition continually aspired to more extensive conquests; and on the 16th of October, 1350, he engaged the brothers Pepoli to cede to him Bologna. These nobles, who had usurped the sovereignty of their country, were at this time engaged in a quarrel with the legate, Giles Albornoz, who asserted that Bologna belonged to the holy see. The archbishop was already treated by the pope as an enemy; and preferred exciting still further his wrath, to the renunciation of so important an acquisition. When Clement VI. summoned him to come, and justify himself at the court of Avignon, he answered, that he would present himself there at the head of 12,000 cavalry and 6,000 infantry. The pope, in his alarm, ceded to him the fief of Bologna, on the 5th of May, 1352, on condition of receiving from him an annual tribute of 12,000 florins. Florence saw, with terror, this

city, which had so long been her most powerful and
faithful ally, the Guelph city of letters, commerce, and
liberty, thus pass under the yoke of a tyrant, who had
designs upon her liberty also; who laid snares around
her; who formed alliances against her with all the petty
tyrants of Romagna, and all the Ghibeline lords of the
Apennines. She was at peace with him, it was true;
but she well knew that the Viscontis neither believed
themseves bound by any treaty, nor kept any pledge.

The number of free cities continually diminished. Pisa
was still free, but had, from attachment to the Ghibeline
party, made alliance with the Viscontis. Sienna and
Perugia were free also, but weak and jealous; they
were incessantly disturbed by internal dissensions. The
Florentines could not reckon on them. The archbishop
of Milan suddenly ordered, towards the end of the
summer, 1351, John Visconti da' Oleggio, his lieutenant
at Bologna, to push into Tuscany at the head of a formidable army, without any declaration of war. The
republic had no ally, and but slight reliance on the
mercenaries in its service; but the Florentines, who
showed little bravery in the open field, defended themselves obstinately behind walls; and the great village of
Scarperia, in the Mugello, although so ill fortified that
the walls of many of the houses served instead of a
surrounding wall, and having a garrison of only
200 cuirassiers and 300 infantry, stopped the Milanese
general sixty-one days. He was at last obliged, on the
16th of October, to retire to Bologna.

The republics of Venice and Genoa were, it might have
been thought, the natural allies to whom the Florentines
should have had recourse for their common defence.
Their interests were the same; and the Viscontis had
resolved not to suffer any free state to subsist in Italy,
lest their subjects should learn that there was a better
government than their own. Unhappily, these two
republics, irritated by commercial quarrels in the East,
were then engaged in an obstinate war with each other.
The Genoese had fortified Pera, a suburb of Constantinople, of which they had rendered themselves masters,
as well as of Caffa in the Crimea; and these two colonies
almost equalled the metropolis in wealth and magnificence.

These republicans engaged in a quarrel with the emperor Cantacuzene, besieged his capital, and burnt his fleet. Two years later, they quarrelled also with the Crimean Tartars at Caffa, and attempted to interdict the Latins from carrying on any commerce with them at Tana, now Taganrok. This attempt produced a quarrel with the Venetians, and a war between these two states was the consequence. The Venetians formed an alliance with the Greek emperor, and with Peter IV. of Aragon; formidable fleets, commanded the one by the Genoese admiral, Paganino Doria, the other by the Venetian, Nicolo Pisani, displayed a courage and ability to resist at once man and the elements, which no maritime people have ever since surpassed. On the 13th of February, 1352, Paganino Doria, with sixty-four galleys, attacked, in the straits of the Bosphorus, the Venetians, Catalonians, and Greeks, who had collected, at least, seventy-eight vessels. A violent tempest assailed, in those narrow seas, the two fleets in the midst of their combat: they were overtaken by a dark night; whilst the violence of the winds and tide mixed their vessels, and drove them one against the other. The loss on both sides was prodigious; but the morning discovered to Pisani that he was no longer in a state to continue the combat: he retired to Candia, and the Greeks made peace with the Genoese. A battle, not less bloody, took place in the following year, on the 29th of August, off the coast of Loiera, in Sardinia. Paganino Doria no longer commanded the Genoese; they were defeated with immense loss: in their distress and discouragement, they gave themselves up, on the 10th of October, 1353, to John Visconti, lord of Milan. This tyrant, the richest in Italy, helped them to reestablish their fleet; the command was given anew to Paganino Doria, who attacked and destroyed the Venetian fleet in the Gulf of Sapienza, in the Morea, on the 3rd of November, 1354. The Venetians, exhausted by such great exertions, made peace in the month of May following.

Genoa had sacrificed her liberty to her thirst of vengeance; for although the republic had not conferred the signoria on the archbishop Visconti without imposing conditions, it soon experienced that oaths are not bind-

ing on a prelate and a tyrant. The freedom of Venice
also was in the utmost danger from the consequences of
the same war. It was only a few months after the peace
was signed, that Marino Faliero was elected successor
to Andrea Dandolo, in the ducal chair, on the 11th of
September, 1354. The disorders and calamities of war
had relaxed every social tie; the merchants, and the
workmen employed in the construction of vessels, were
discontented; the nobles conducted themselves with increasing insolence; and the laws were ill observed.
Marino Faliero, who was old, and furiously jealous of
a young and beautiful wife, was insulted, under a mask,
during the carnival, by the president of the quarantia.
He believed the offender in love with his wife. The
offence he received was not punished with the severity
which he demanded. He lent an ear to the complaints
of the plebeians, many of whom had experienced in their
domestic life mortal injuries from the young nobility;
and excited a conspiracy, of which he consented to be
the chief. But just as he was on the point of wreaking
his vengeance on the government of his country, and on
the whole order of nobles, some of his accomplices were
denounced to the Council of Ten: they were seized, and
put to the torture, on the night of the 15th of April,
1355. Their disclosures implicated the doge, who was
also arrested, and on the day after was beheaded.

Though the war of the maritime republics might have
deprived Florence of the aid of Venice or Genoa, it had
at least diverted the attention of John Visconti; made
him direct his exertions elsewhere; and procured some
repose to Tuscany. He died on the 5th of October,
1354, before he could renew his attacks; and his three
nephews, the sons of his brother Stephen, agreed to succeed him in common. The eldest, who showed less talent
for government, and more sensuality and vice, than his
brothers, was poisoned by them the year following. The
two survivors, Barnabas and Galeazzo, divided Lombardy between them; preserving an equal right on
Milan, and in the government. Their relative, Visconti
da' Oleggio, who was their lieutenant at Bologna, made
himself independent in that city nearly about the same
time that the Genoese, indignant at seeing all their con-

ventions violated, rose in insurrection on the 15th of
November, 1356, drove out the Milanese garrison, and
again set themselves free.

The entry of Charles IV. into Tuscany formed also
a favourable diversion by suspending the projects of the
Viscontis against the Florentines; but it cost them
100,000 florins, which they agreed to pay Charles by
treaty on the 12th of March, 1355, to purchase his
rights on their city, and to obtain his engagement that
he should nowhere enter the Florentine territory. The
republics of Pisa and Sienna, who received him within
their walls, paid still dearer for the hospitality which
they granted him. The emperor encouraged the malcontents in both cities; he aided them to overthrow the
existing governments; he hoped by so doing to make
these republics little principalities, which he intended to
bestow as an apanage on his brother, the patriarch of
Aquileia: but after having caused the ruin of his partisans; after having ordered or permitted the execution
of the former magistrates, who were innocent of any
crime, insurrections of the people forced him to quit
both cities, without retaining the smallest influence in
either. After he had quitted Italy, the Viscontis were
engaged in the war to which we have already alluded,
against the marquises of Este, of Montferrat, della Scala,
Gonzaga, and Carrara. The siege of Pavia, and the
ravages of the great company, exhausted their resources,
but did not make them abandon their projects on Tuscany. The influence which they retained in the republic
of Pisa, as chiefs of the Ghibeline party, seemed to facilitate their schemes.

Pisa, in losing its maritime power and its possessions
in Sardinia, had not lost its warlike character; it was
still the state in Italy where the citizens were best exercised in the use of arms, and evinced the most bravery.
It had given proofs of it in conquering, under the eye
of the Florentines, the city of Lucca, which it still retained. Nevertheless, since the peace made by the duke
of Athens on the 14th of October, 1342, commercial
interests had reconciled the two republics. The Florentines had obtained a complete enfranchisement from all
imposts in the port of Pisa; they had established there

their counting-houses, and attracted thither a rich trade. From that time the democratic party predominated in the Pisan republic; at its head was a rich merchant, named Francesco Gambacorta, who attached himself to the Florentines, and to the maintenance of peace. His party was called that of the Bergolini; while that of the great Ghibeline families attached to the counts of la Gherardesca, who despised commerce and excited war, was called the Raspanti party. The Viscontis sought the alliance of the latter; the moment did not appear to them yet arrived in which they could assume to themselves the dominion over all Tuscany. It was sufficient for their present views to exhaust the Florentine republic by a war, which would disturb its commerce; to weaken the spirit of liberty and energy in the Pisans, by subduing them to the power of the aristocracy, in the hope, that when once they had ceased to be free, and had submitted to a domestic tyrant, they would soon prefer a great to a little prince, and throw themselves into his arms. The revolution, which in 1355 had favoured the emperor in restoring power to the Raspanti, facilitated this project.

In pursuance of this view, the party of the Raspanti, at the suggestion of the Viscontis, in 1357 began to disturb the Florentines in the enjoyment of the franchises secured to them at Pisa by the treaty of peace. The Florentines, guessing the project of the Lombard tyrant, instead of defending their right by arms, resolved on braving an unwholesome climate, and submitting to the inconvenience of longer and worse roads, transported all their counting-houses to Telamone, a port in the maremma of Sienna. They persisted till 1361 in despising all the insults of the Pisans, as well as in rejecting all their offers of reconciliation: at length, animosity increasing on both sides, the war broke out, in 1362. The Viscontis supplied the Pisans with soldiers. France during this period had been laid waste by the war with the English; and as the sovereigns were rarely in a state to pay their troops, there had been formed, as in Italy, companies of adventurers, English, Gascon, and French, who lived at the cost of the country, plundering it with the utmost barbarity. The peace of Bretigny permitted

several of these companies to pass into Italy : they carried
with them the plague, which made not less ravages in
1361 than it had done in 1348. The English company
commanded by John Hawkwood, an adventurer, who
rendered himself celebrated in Italy, was sent to the
Pisans by Barnabas Visconti. After various successes,
the two republics, at last exhausted by the plague, and
by the rapacity, and want of discipline of the adventurers
whom they had taken into pay, made peace on the 17th
of August, 1364. But the purpose of the Viscontis was
not the less attained. The Pisans having exhausted
their resources, were at a loss to make the last payment
of 30,000 florins to their army ; they were reduced to
accept the offer made them by Giovanni Agnello, one of
their fellow citizens, of advancing that sum, on condition of being named doge of Pisa. The money had
for this purpose been secretly advanced by Barnabas
Visconti, to whom Agnello had pledged his word never
to consider himself more than his lieutenant at Pisa.
Thus the field fertilised by liberty became continually
more circumscribed ; and Florence, always threatened by
the tyrants of Lombardy, saw around her those only who
had alienated their liberty, and who had no longer any
sentiment in common with the republic.

CHAPTER VIII

THE FLORENTINES SUMMON THE CITIES BELONGING TO THE STATES
    OF THE CHURCH TO RECOVER THEIR LIBERTY—GREAT WESTERN
    SCHISM—WAR OF CHIOZZA—INSURRECTIONS OF THE POPULACE
    AGAINST THE CITIZENS—CONQUESTS OF GIAN GALEAZZO VIS-
    CONTI, DUKE OF MILAN—HIS DEATH

THE chief magistrates of the Florentine republic could
not conceal from themselves the danger which now
menaced the liberty of Italy. They found themselves
closed in,—blockaded, as it were,—by the tyrants, who
daily made some new progress. The two brothers Visconti, masters of Lombardy, had at their disposal immense
wealth and numerous armies ; and their ambition was
insatiable. They were allied, by marriage, to the two

houses of France and England: their intrigues extended throughout Italy, and every tyrant was under their protection. At the same time, their own subjects trembled under frightful cruelties. They shamelessly published an edict, by which the execution of state criminals was prolonged to the period of forty days. In it the particular tortures to be inflicted, day by day, were detailed, and the members to be mutilated designated, before death was reached. On the other hand, their finances were in good order; they liberally recompensed their partisans, and won over traitors in every state inimical to them. They pensioned the captain of every company of adventurers, on condition that he engaged to return to their service whenever called upon. Meanwhile, these captains, with their soldiers, over-ran, plundered, and exhausted Italy, during the intervals of peace; reducing the country to such a state as to be incapable of resisting any new attack. All the Ghibelines, all the nobles who had preserved their independence in the Apennines, were allied to the Viscontis. The march of these usurpers was slow, but it seemed sure. The moment was foreseen to approach when Tuscany would be theirs, as well as Lombardy; particularly as Florence had no aid to expect either from Genoa or Venice. These two maritime republics appeared to have withdrawn themselves from Italy, and to place their whole existence in distant regions explored by their commerce.

For a moment, the few Italian states still free were led to believe that the succour, now so necessary, to enable them to resist the Viscontis, would arrive both from France and Germany. The pope and the emperor announced their determination to deliver the country, over which they assumed a supreme right, from every other yoke. Urban V., moved by the complaints of the Christian world, declared that his duty, as bishop of Rome, was to return and live there; and Charles IV. protested that he would deliver his Roman empire from the devastations of the adventurers, and from the usurpations of the Lombard tyrants. In 1367, Urban returned to Italy; and the same year formed a league with the emperor, the king of Hungary, the lords of Padua, Ferrara, and Mantua, and with the queen of Naples,—

against the Viscontis. But when Charles entered Italy, on the 5th of May, 1368, he thought only of profiting by the terror with which he inspired the Viscontis, to obtain from them large sums of money; in return for which he granted them peace. He afterwards continued his march through the peninsula, with no other object than that of collecting money. His presence, however, caused some changes favourable to liberty. A festival was prepared for him at Lucca, on the 7th of September; on which day he intended confirming, by his investiture, the sovereignty of the doge Gian Agnello over Pisa and Lucca. But the stage on which Agnello had mounted gave way, and in the fall he broke his leg. The Pisans profited by this accident to recover their freedom, and the emperor kept Lucca for himself. At Sienna, he favoured a revolution which overthrew the ruling aristocracy; intending, on his return to that city, after a devotional visit to Rome, to take advantage of the disturbance, and get himself appointed to the signoria: but a sedition against him broke forth on the 18th of January, 1369. Barricades were raised on all sides; his guards were separated from him, and disarmed; his palace was broken into. No attempt, indeed, was made on his person; but he was left alone several hours in the public square, addressing himself in turn to the armed troops which closed the entrance of every street, and which, immovable and silent, remained insensible to all his entreaties. It was not till he began to suffer from hunger, that his equipages were restored to him, and he was permitted to leave the town. He returned to Lucca, where he had already lived, in the time of his father, as prince royal of Bohemia. The Lucchese were attached to him, and placed in him their last hope to be delivered from a foreign yoke, which had weighed upon them since the year 1314. They declared themselves ready to make the greatest sacrifices for the recovery of their freedom; and they, at the same time, testified to him so much confidence and affection as to touch his heart. By a diploma, on the 6th of April, 1369, Charles restored them to liberty, and granted them various privileges; but, on quitting their city, he left in it a German garrison, with orders not to evacuate that town till the Lucchese had paid the

price of their liberty. It was not till the month of April,
1370, and not without the aid of Florence and their other
allies, that they could acquit the enormous sum of
300,000 florins, the price of the re-establishment of their
republic. The Guelph exiles were then immediately
recalled; a close alliance was contracted with Florence;
and the signoria, composed of a gonfalonier and ten
anziani, to be changed every two months, was reconstituted.

Urban V., on his arrival in Italy, endeavoured also to
oppose the usurpations of the Viscontis, who had just
taken possession of San Miniato, in Tuscany, and who,
even in the states of the church, were rendering themselves more powerful than the pope himself. Of the two
brothers, Barnabas Visconti was more troublesome to
him, by his intrigues. Urban had recourse to a bull of
excommunication, and sent two legates to bear it to him;
but Barnabas forced these two legates to eat, in his
presence, the parchment on which the bull was written,
together with the leaden seals and silken strings. The
pope, frightened at the thought of combating men who
seemed to hold religion in no respect, and wearied, moreover with his ill successes, was glad to return to the
repose of Avignon, where he arrived in the month of
September, 1370; and died the November following.

Gregory XI., who succeeded him, was ambitious,
covetous, and false. He joined the Florentines in their
war against the Viscontis; but the legates, to whom he
had entrusted the government of the ecclesiastical states,
and who had rendered themselves odious by their rapacity
and immorality, formed the project of seizing for themselves Tuscany, which they had engaged to defend. All
the troops of the Florentines had been placed at their
disposal, for the purpose of carrying the war into
Lombardy. The cardinal legate, who commanded the
combined army, resided at Bologna; the church having
rescued that city from the grasp of Visconti da' Oleggio,
on the 31st of March, 1360. He signed a truce with
Barnabas Visconti, in the month of June, 1375; and,
before the Florentines could recall their soldiers, sent
John Hawkwood with a formidable army to surprise
Florence. The Florentines, indignant at such a shame-

less want of good faith on the part of the church, whose most faithful allies they had always been, vowed vengeance on the see of Rome.   They determined to rouse the spirit of liberty in every city belonging to it, and drive out the French legates,—more odious and perfidious than the most abhorred of the Italian tyrants.   They, in the month of June, 1375, without placing any confidence in Barnabas Visconti, made an alliance with him against the priests, who had just deceived them under the faith of the most solemn oaths.   They admitted the republics of Sienna, Lucca, and Pisa into this league ; they formed a commission of eight persons, to direct the military department, called " the eight of war ;" they assembled a numerous army, and gave it colours, on which was inscribed, in golden letters, the word " LIBERTY."   This army entered the states of the church, proclaiming that the Florentines demanded nothing for themselves,—that not only would they make no conquests, but would accept dominion over no people who might offer themselves : they were desirous only of universal liberty,—and would assist the oppressed with all their power, solicitous for the recovery of their freedom.

The army of liberty carried revolution into all the states of the church with an inconceivable rapidity : eighty cities and towns, in ten days, threw off the yoke of the legates.   The greater number constituted themselves republics ; a few recalled the ancient families of princes, who had been exiled by Egidio Albornoz, and to whom they were attached by hereditary affection. Bologna did not accomplish her revolution before the 20th of March, 1376.   This ancient republic, in recovering its liberty, vowed fidelity to the Florentines, to whom it owed the restoration of its freedom.   The legates, besides themselves with rage, endeavoured to restrain the people by terror.   John Hawkwood, on the 29th of March, 1376, delivered up Faenza to a frightful military execution : 4,000 persons were put to death, property pillaged, and women violated.   The pope, not satisfied with such rigour, sent Robert of Geneva, another cardinal legate, into Italy, with a Breton company of adventurers, considered as the most ferocious of all those trained to plunder by the wars of France.   The new legate treated

Cesena, on the 1st of February, 1377, with still greater barbarity. He was heard to call out, during the massacre, "I will have more blood!—kill all!—blood, blood!" Gregory XI. at last felt the necessity of returning to Italy, to appease the universal revolt. He entered Rome on the 17th of January, 1377; although the Florentines, who had sent the standard of liberty to the senators and bannerets of Rome, and had made alliance with the Romans, expostulated on the danger they incurred, if they admitted the pontiff within their walls.

The two parties, however, began to be equally weary of the war. Some of the cities enfranchised by the Florentines were already detached from the league. The Bolognese had made, on the 21st of August, 1377, a separate peace with the pope, who had agreed to acknowledge their republic. Barnabas Visconti carried on with the holy see secret negotiations, in which he offered to sacrifice to the church his ally, the republic of Florence. This republic was then pressed for its consent to the opening of a congress for restoring peace to Italy, to be held at Sarzana, in the beginning of the year 1378: the presidency of the congress was given to Barnabas Visconti. The conference had scarcely opened when the Florentines perceived, with more indignation than surprise, that the Lombard tyrant, who had fought in concert with them, intended that they should pay to him and to the pope the whole expenses of the war. The negotiations took the most alarming turn, when the unexpected news arrived of the death of Gregory XI., on the 27th of March, 1378; and the congress separated, without coming to any decision. The year which now opened was destined to bring with it the most important revolutions throughout Italy. Amidst those convulsions, the peace of Florence with the court of Rome, weakened by the great western schism, was not difficult to accomplish.

The pontifical chair had been transferred to France since the year 1305. Its exile from Italy lasted seventy-three years. The Christian world, France excepted, had considered it a scandal; but the French kings hoped by it to retain the popes in their dependence; and the French cardinals, who formed more than three fourths of the sacred college, seemed determined to preserve the

L

pontifical power in their nation. They were, however, thwarted in this intention by the death of Gregory XI. at Rome;—for the conclave must always assemble where the last pontiff dies. The clamour of the Romans, and the manifestation of opinion throughout Christendom, were not without influence on the conclave. On the 8th of April, 1378, it elected—not, indeed, a Roman, whom the people demanded; but an Italian,—Bartolomeo Prignani; who, having lived long in France, seemed formed to conciliate the prejudices of both parties. He was considered learned and pious. The cardinals had not, however, calculated on the developement of the passions which a sudden elevation sometimes gives; or on the degree of impatience, arrogance, and irritability of which man is capable, in his unexpected capacity of master, though in an inferior situation he had appeared gentle and modest. The new pope, who took the name of Urban VI., became so violent and despotic, so confident in himself, and so contemptuous of others, that he soon quarrelled with all his cardinals. They left him; assembled again at Fondi; and, on the 9th of August, declared the holy see vacant; asserting that their previous election was null, having been forced by their terror of the Romans. Consequently, on the 20th of September, they elected another pope. Their choice, no better than the former, fell on Robert, cardinal of Geneva, who had presided at the massacre of Cesena: he took the name of Clement VII. He was protected by queen Joan, with whom Urban had already quarrelled. Clement established his court at Naples; but an insurrection of the people made him quit it the year following, and determined him on returning, with his cardinals, to Avignon. Urban VI., meanwhile, deposed, as schismatics, all the cardinals who had elected Clement, and replaced them by a new and more numerous college; but he agreed no better with these than with their predecessors. He accused them of a conspiracy against him; he caused many to be put to the torture in his presence, and while he recited his breviary; he ordered others to be thrown into the sea in sacks, and drowned; he quarrelled with the Romans, and the new sovereign of Naples, whom he had himself named; he paraded his incapacity and rage through all Italy; and finally took refuge at Genoa, where he died, on the 9th of November, 1389. The cardinals who acknowledged him named a successor on his death, as the French cardinals did afterwards on the death of Clement VII., which took place on the 16th of September, 1394. The church thus found itself divided between two popes and two colleges of cardinals, who reciprocally anathematised each other. Whilst the catholic faith was thus shaken, the temporal sovereignty of the pope, founded by the conquests of the cardinal Albornoz, was over-thrown. Several of the cities enfranchised by the Florentines in the war of liberty, preserved their re-publican government; but the greater number, particu-larly in Romagna, fell again under the yoke of petty tyrants.

The part which Joan of Naples had taken in the schism, by protecting what the orthodox called the revolt of Robert of Geneva and the cardinals, awakened the resentment which Louis of Hungary still entertained for the murder of her first husband; she had since succes-sively married three others, without having a child: her natural heir was the last prince of the race of Charles of Anjou, named Charles da Durazzo, the grandson of king Robert's brother, and cousin to the king of Hungary, at whose court he had been brought up. The aged Louis, learning that Urban VI. had excommunicated and deposed Joan, charged Charles da Durazzo to execute the sentence. He entrusted him with an army, with which the young prince traversed Italy, without meeting any resistance; he entered Naples on the 16th of July, 1381, and pro-claimed himself king, under the name of Charles III. The queen, who could not arm a single person in her defence, was constrained to surrender to him five weeks afterwards. After detaining her nine months in prison, he caused her to be smothered under a feather bed. Louis of Hungary did not long survive this revolution: he died on the 11th of September, 1382, leaving heiress to his dominions a daughter, with whom Charles da Durazzo soon disputed the crown of Hungary. The emperor Charles IV. had died before Louis, at Prague, on the 29th of November, 1378, and had been succeeded by his son, the debauched Wenceslaus. About the same period (1380) the crown of France had passed to a minor, Charles VI., who afterwards became mad. Italy had little to fear from abroad; the danger sprang up in her own bosom.

The republics of Venice and Genoa, on every occasion mutually opposed, regarded each other as rivals. The Genoese carried on a considerable commerce in Cyprus, but had excited there the resentment of the people, who in 1372 rose, and at a public festival massacred all the Genoese on whom they could lay hands. The republic avenged this outrage committed on its citizens; and in 1373 conquered the isle of Cyprus: but, using its victory with moderation, restored the island in fief to the house of Lusignan. The Venetians, notwithstanding, offered their alliance to the Cypriots, and in 1378 they, in concert, besieged the Genoese at Famagosta. In the many quarrels of the Venetians with Louis of Hungary, and with Francesco da Carrara, lord of Padua, they had always found the Genoese siding with their adversaries. The two republics finally attached themselves to the two opposite factions which disputed the remains of the empire of Constantinople, now arrived at its last term. Mutual animosity went on continually increasing. At last the Venetian and Genoese fleets met before Antium, in the month of July, 1378. They attacked each other in the height of a tempest; and the Genoese were vanquished. It was the first battle of a fearful war: Lucian Doria was charged, in the month of May, 1379, to avenge the Genoese. Having entered the Adriatic, on the 29th of that month he met the Venetian fleet, commanded by Vittor Pisani, before Pola. Lucian was killed early in the engagement; but that only served to redouble the animosity of the Genoese; and the Venetian fleet was almost annihilated. The senate threw Vittor Pisani, the greatest admiral the republic ever had, into prison, to punish him for a disaster which would have been avoided had his counsel been taken; for he had given battle by the express order of the senate, contrary to his own judgment. Pietro Doria, who succeeded Lucian in the command of the Genoese fleet, arrived on the 6th of August, to attack the canal or port of Chiozza, twenty-five miles south of Venice. It is one

of the numerous openings which cut the *Aggere*, or long
bank formed by nature between the *Lagune* and the sea.
Francesco da Carrara sent at the same time a flotilla of
Paduan boats, to attack in rear the Venetians, who
defended this opening. The port of Chiozza was forced,
and the town taken, on the 16th of August. Chiozza,
like Venice, is in the bosom of the *Lagune*. The Genoese
fleet, having arrived thus far, could pass up to the canals
of Venice. Never had the republic been in such imminent danger; never had she offered to purchase peace
by greater or more humiliating sacrifices. But the
Genoese, the king of Hungary, and the lord of Padua,
rejected all advances: Pietro Doria declared that he
would not make peace, before he had bridled, with his
own hand, the bronze horses in the square of St. Mark
(the same which have since been seen in the Place du
Carrousel at Paris). The Venetians, driven to the last
extremity, redoubled their patriotic exertions: they drew
Vittor Pisani from his dungeon, to place him in the
command of a new fleet; they shut their canals with
stockades; they recalled their many vessels dispersed in
the Levant, and gave the command of them to Carlo
Zeno, another of their greatest citizens. The defence of
Venice was, notwithstanding, so far doubtful, that the
signoria had made preparations to remove to Candia on
the first reverse of fortune.

On the 1st of January, 1380, Carlo Zeno arrived with
the fleet which he had collected in the eastern seas; the
Venetians, instead of waiting to be besieged, proposed
blockading the Genoese fleet in the *Lagune* of Chiozza,
into which it had so victoriously entered. They succeeded
in first shutting the canal of Chiozza, and afterwards all
the other ports or canals which cut the *Aggere*: each of
these advantages was, however, purchased by an obstinate
battle. Forty-eight galleys, and 14,000 Genoese mariners
or soldiers, were shut in at Chiozza; but they were not
abandoned by their country: it sent a new fleet into the
Adriatic for their deliverance, while the lord of Padua
made the utmost exertions to open a communication
with them. The Venetians, always investing the besieged
still closer, succeeded in avoiding the battle continually
offered them. The Genoese at last perceived that there

was no possibility of saving their galleys; they constructed boats, in which they intended to escape, and
gain the fleet which awaited them in the high seas.   The
moment these boats were transported to the sea-shore,
they were attacked and burnt by the Venetians. Deprived
of all resource, and pressed by famine, the Genoese at
last surrendered at discretion, on the 21st of June, 1380.
Notwithstanding this great reverse of fortune, Genoa
was not cast down.   The Venetians, hard pressed by
land, were obliged to abandon Treviso, and shut themselves up anew in their *Lagune*.   But the two republics,
equally exhausted by the war, were glad to sign, on the
8th of August, 1381, a treaty of peace, which re-
established their former relations, nearly as they stood
before it commenced.   The treaty of peace with the king
of Hungary was more disadvantageous to the Venetians:
they ceded to him the whole of Dalmatia; but as he
died the year following, they took advantage of the
embarrassment into which his daughter was thrown,
to recover their possessions in that province.

The discord which had so long fermented in Florence
between the higher citizens who administered the government, and the lower orders, who demanded a more complete equality, broke out in 1378; a year fruitful in events
to Italy.   The form of the Florentine constitution was
entirely democratic, the only sovereign was the people;
the nobles and the Ghibelines were excluded from all
participation in the government; but a perfect equality
appeared to exist in the rest of the nation, which was
rendered more complete by the citizens being called by
lot to the highest dignities in the state.   Nevertheless, if
government is instituted for the good of all, to invest all
indiscriminately with power, would be very far from
obtaining that good, the object of the common effort.
Education, and the leisure which gives time for reflection,
are two conditions equally necessary to man, in order to
attain the complete developement of his understanding,
and the knowledge, if ever he should arrive at the administration of public affairs, of what would constitute
the happiness of all.   Those who have not learnt to
think, those to whom manual labour leaves no time for
meditation, ought not to undertake the guidance of their

fellow-citizens, by entering the difficult career of government. There was at Florence, as there is every where, a distinction to be made between families whose fortune gives them the means of intellectual improvement, and those who, to live, are obliged to devote themselves to mere labour, so much calculated to render the faculties of the mind obtuse. This distinction was marked by the division of citizens into twenty-one corporations of arts and trades; the seven higher arts were distinguished by the name of *arti maggiori*. In those alone the magistrates were always chosen; and they comprehended families sometimes so enriched by commerce as to rival princes in magnificence: they were designated by the new appellation of *nobili popolani*, nobles of the people, and produced men distinguished in the government of the republic for as much virtue as talent.

There was, however, a want of union among these great families; they had been divided between the two parties, which were at first headed by the Albizzi and Ricci: the Albizzi were among the number of those families which the same revolution that drove out the Ghibelines had, for more than a century, placed at the head of the republic. They made it a part of their religion to maintain the Guelph party in all its purity, and they caused the law of admonition, which excluded from the magistracy every descendant of the ancient Ghibelines, and under that pretext every *new man*, to be executed in all its rigour. Their faction, then, was essentially aristocratic. The Ricci, and with them the Scali, Strozzi, Alberti, and the Medici, had attained later their immense opulence. The name of Medici was never pronounced before the middle of this century: their adversaries profited by the obscurity of their origin, to pretend that their ancestors were Ghibelines. The interest of new families led them to support democratic opinions, and to demand that the distinction between Guelph and Ghibeline, which no longer related to any thing real, should be annihilated. The commission of eight, for the department of war, which had directed, with such courage and ability, the attack on the holy see, were all of the Ricci faction. In arming the republic against the church, it appeared as if they had made it adopt all the principles of the Ghibelines; but when the citizens, impatient of the weight of taxes, began to sigh for peace, the Albizzi took advantage of their discontent, to revive against their adversaries the accusation of Ghibelinism. They even intended, under this pretext, to exclude them from their country. The increasing ill-will between the two factions made it obvious that the quarrel must soon break out. When Salvestro de Medici was, in the month of June, 1378, made by lot gonfaloner, he proposed a law to suspend the proceedings called *admonition*, which the Albizzi directed against his party. The college or little council of the signoria rejected it, as too favourable to the Ghibelines. Salvestro appealed, on the 18th of June, to a council of the people, and after-wards to the people themselves. Violent indignation was immediately manifested against this small oligarchy, which, under pretext of maintaining the ancient Guelph party in all its purity, had branded so many honourable names with exclusion, had encouraged divisions in a republic to which union was necessary, and had thrown doubts on the civic rights of half Florence. The law proposed by Salvestro de' Medici passed by an immense majority.

But this first victory awakened more violent disputes upon the rights and equality of the citizens; on the privi-leges of the *nobili popolani*; on the artifices by which they reserved among themselves the nomination to the magis-tracies; on the prerogatives of the major in opposition to the minor arts; and upon the dependent condition of the numerous artificers who must range under the banner of the major arts, without being permitted to form them-selves into a corporation, or to enjoy any of the ad-vantages attached to these associations. The law which the Medici had just carried, provided only that no new family should be excluded from the magistracies under the pretext that their ancestors were Ghibelines. The people soon demanded that those who had previously been excluded by the admonition should be reinstated in all their rights; that the minor arts should be admitted to furnish members for the magistracies in the same pro-portion as the major arts; finally, that three new corpora-tions should be formed, to include workmen, dyers, weavers, fullers, and others employed in the woollen trade. These men, belonging to the *woollen art,* having no participation in the government, regarded themselves as excluded from every political right. They formed a numerous portion of the population at Florence, called in derision by the name of *ciompi.* The signoria, so far from yielding to these demands, reckoned on restraining the people by terror; on the 20th of July they caused one of the chiefs of the ciompi to be put to the torture, as having been found guilty of a plot against the state; but this only proved a signal for explosion. The ciompi, and all the poorer classes of artisans, flew to arms. The signoria called the urban guard to their aid; but those dared not assemble. On the 22nd of July the ciompi laid siege to the palace of the podestà, and took it on the 23rd; they attacked and made themselves masters also of the palace of the signoria: at that moment a carder of wool, named Michele Lando, in a short waistcoat and barefooted, marched at the head of the people, carrying in his hand the gonfalon of the state, which he had seized in the palace of the podestà: an acclamation suddenly resounded from the crowd who followed him, proclaiming him gonfaloner. During the three preceding days, the populace, masters of the city, had committed many crimes and disorders; but they had no sooner given a new chief to the state, than the chief thus chosen laboured, with admirable courage and capacity, to restore order and peace. He ordained that for the future the supreme magistracy should be composed of three members of the major arts, three of the minor, and three of the ciompi. He put an immediate end to pillaging, burning, and every other disorder. He restored authority to the tribunals, security to the citizens; and exhibited by his own example how much a free government spreads sound sense and elevated sentiments among even the lowest classes of society. The ciompi, it is true, did not long submit to a government which they had themselves created. They rose anew; but Michele Lando vigorously attacked and vanquished them: a vast number were exiled from the city.

The popular party, however, is near its defeat when the moderate chiefs are forced to subdue the spirit of the

M

more ardent. Frightened at some blamable excesses committed by their partisans, they deprive themselves of all vigour in order to suppress them ; they disarm those by whose strength they have conquered ; they distrust their friends, and confide in their enemies. A man of the lower order had vanquished the anarchists whom no other than himself could have subdued : but immediately afterwards, Florence blushed to have entrusted so much power to a man of his class ; and on the next drawing of lot for the magistracy, the three ciompi drawn for the priori were not permitted to sit in the signoria. Giorgio Scali, Salvestro de' Medici, and Benedetto Alberti were placed at the head of the republic : although belonging themselves to the aristocracy, they were the enemies of that order. On discovering a plot of the Albizzi, their ancient rivals, to effect a revolution, with the aid of the troops of Charles III. king of Naples, which then traversed Tuscany, they caused men who had so long administered the republic with glory to die on the scaffold. The public, notwithstanding the confession of the accused, were not convinced that they were really guilty, or justly punished. But division soon sprang up in the new administration : some, no longer fearing any rival, insolently abused their power. Giorgio Scali, learning that one of his creatures, accused of bearing false witness, was in the prison of the captain of the people, who prosecuted him, forced the palace of that judge, on the 13th of January, 1382, at the head of a troop of armed men ; gave it up to pillage; and set its prisoner free. Benedetto Alberti, who had always acted honestly, and in the principles of an austere republican, was indignant at the conduct of his ancient associate. He summoned the people to avenge the insulted honour of the tribunals : for that purpose, he made advances to the major arts and the party of the Albizzi. Giorgio Scali was placed at the bar, and received sentence of death, which was immediately executed. The aristocracy felt, meanwhile, that it had recovered power. On the 21st of January, the city rose at the cry of " Long live the Guelph party !" The nobles, the rich merchants, and the higher citizens comprehended in the major arts, took possession of the public places, created a *balia*, or supreme commission, to reform the state; abolished all the laws which had arisen from the revolution, or the tumult of the ciompi; exiled Michele Lando, Benedetto Alberti, and all those who had in any way signalised themselves in the insurrection; and, finally, reconstituted the aristocracy of the nobili popolani more firmly than it had ever yet stood.

Similar revolutions broke out at the same time in the other Italian republics: in every one the same progress was to be distinguished. The party which in all had risen to power, as democratic, no sooner felt themselves in possession of it than they turned towards aristocracy. The leaders of the rising generation presented themselves as hereditary tribunes of the people, at the same time that they impugned hereditary rights. At Genoa, men of new families completely usurped from the ancient houses of Doria, Spinola, Grimaldi, and Fieschi, all power in the government; and ranged themselves, soon after the middle of the century, under the standard of two plebeian families,—the one named Adorni, and Guelphs; the other Fregosi, and Ghibelines. While they proclaimed their hatred of the aristocracy, and their determination not to allow the doge to be taken from a noble family, they combated for the Adorni and Fregosi, with the same enthusiasm and spirit of clientelage with which their ancestors had fought for a Doria or a Fiesco. The ruinous civil wars into which the republic was precipitated by the rivalry between these two families, and the fear that the Viscontis might profit by these troubles to enslave it, at last determined Antoniotto Adorni, the doge, in 1396, to confer, on the 25th of October, the signoria on Charles VI. king of France, in the hope that a distant monarch might lend the support of his name to the government, without having either the power or the inclination materially to injure the liberty of the republic.

At Sienna, after the nobles had been excluded from the magistracies, several plebeian aristocracies succeeded each other. The signoria, composed of nine members, renewed every two months, had found means of reserving to themselves the nomination of those by whom they were to be replaced. From that time, the election ran among not more than ninety families of rich merchants,

M 2

who, from 1283 to 1355, remained the real rulers of the
republic. This first burgher aristocracy was called "the
order," or "monte," of "nine." The jealousy it excited
in the rank next below it caused the revolution, which
Charles IV. encouraged, in the hope of becoming master
of Sienna, on his first passage through that city. The
Nine, like the nobles, were excluded from all participation in the government. It was agreed to replace them
by a popular magistracy of twelve members, chosen
from the burghership; but these men were no sooner
in power, than, affecting to observe an exact medium
between the aristocracy just excluded and the democracy
whose invasion they feared, they created an order or
monte of twelve, out of those burgher families who
aspired only to a respectable mediocrity. This order,
once in possession of the magistracy, became not less
exclusive than its predecessors, and consequently not
less odious. When Charles returned in 1368, for the
second time, to Sienna, the twelve were deprived of
power; and a third order was created, named "the
reformers," taken from among the classes inferior in
wealth and education to the monte of nine and of twelve.
This order did not, at first, usurp all the power of the
republic,—it demanded only an equal partition with the
other two; but soon betrayed irritation, because, being
by far the most numerous, it had not the most influence.
Its pretensions often occasioned commotions, and changes
in the constitution. When the ciompi seized the government at Florence, the reformers, who regarded themselves as holding the same rank in life, made alliance
with them; but, frequently giving way to sudden bursts
of passion, they were accused of failing in good faith as
well as prudence. They were at length driven out of
Sienna, on the 24th of March, 1385, after an obstinate
battle between them and the other orders of citizens.
Four thousand were exiled; and Sienna remained, from
that time, weakened and shaken in her principles of
liberty.

The terror in which the house of Visconti had held
Florence and the other Italian republics began some-
what to subside. Barnabas, grown old, had divided the
cities of his dominions amongst his numerous children.

His brother, Galeazzo, had died on the 4th of August,
1378; and been replaced by his son, Gian Galeazzo,
called count de Virtus, from a county in Champagne,
given him by Charles V., whose sister he had married.
Barnabas would willingly have deprived his nephew of
his paternal inheritance, to divide it among his children.
Gian Galeazzo, who had already discovered several plots
directed against him, uttered no complaint, but shut himself up in his castle of Pavia, where he had fixed his
residence. He doubled his guard, and took pains to
display his belief that he was surrounded by assassins.
He affected, at the same time, the highest devotion: he
was always at prayers, a rosary in his hand, and surrounded with monks; he talked only of pilgrimages and
expiatory ceremonies. His uncle regarded him as pusil-
lanimous, and unworthy of reigning. In the beginning
of May, 1385, Gian Galeazzo sent to Barnabas to say,
that he had made a vow of pilgrimage to our Lady of
Varese, near the Lago Maggiore; and that he should be
glad to see him on his passage. Barnabas agreed to meet
him at a short distance from Milan, accompanied by his
two sons. Gian Galeazzo arrived, surrounded, as was
his custom, by a numerous guard. He affected to be
alarmed at every sudden motion made near him. On
meeting his uncle, however, on the 6th of May, he hastily
dismounted, and respectfully embraced him; but, while
he held him in his arms, he said, in German, to his
guards, "strike!" The Germans, seizing Barnabas, disarmed and dragged him, with his two sons, to some
distance from his nephew. Gian Galeazzo made several
vain attempts to poison his uncle in the prison into
which he had thrown him; but Barnabas, suspicious of
all the nourishment offered him, was on his guard, and
did not sink under these repeated efforts till the 18th of
December of the same year.

All Lombardy submitted, without difficulty, to Gian
Galeazzo. His uncle had never inspired one human
being with either esteem or affection. The nephew had
no better title to these sentiments. False and pitiless, he
joined to immeasurable ambition a genius for enterprise,
and to immovable constancy a personal timidity which
he did not endeavour to conceal. The least unexpected

motion near him threw him into a paroxysm of nervous terror. No prince employed so many soldiers to guard his palace, or took such multiplied precautions of distrust. He seemed to acknowledge himself the enemy of the whole world. But the vices of tyranny had not weakened his ability. He employed his immense wealth, without prodigality; his finances were always flourishing; his cities well garrisoned and victualled; his army well paid; all the captains of adventure scattered throughout Italy received pensions from him, and were ready to return to his service whenever called upon. He encouraged the warriors of the new Italian school: he well knew how to distinguish, reward, and win their attachment. Many young Italians, in order to train themselves to arms, had, from about the middle of this century, engaged in the German, English, and French troops, which inundated Italy; and they soon proved, that Italian valour, directed by the reflection and intelligence of a highly civilised nation, who carried their arms as well as tactics to perfection, had greatly the advantage over the brute courage of barbarians. Alberic, count of Barbiano, a Romagnole noble, and an ancestor of the princes Belgiojoso, of Milan, formed a company, under the name of St. George, into which he admitted Italians only, and which, in 1378, he placed in the service of Urban VI. This company defeated, at Ponte Molle, that of the Bretons, attached to Clement VII., and regarded as the most formidable of the foreign troops. From that time, the company of St. George was the true school of military science in Italy. Young men of courage, talent, or ambition flocked into it from all parts; and all the captains who, twenty years later, attained such high renown, gloried in having served in that company.

Gian Galeazzo was no sooner firmly established on the throne of Milan, than he resumed his project of subjugating the rest of Italy: the two principalities of the Della Scala at Verona, and of the Carrara at Padua, were the first to tempt his ambition. The house of La Scala had produced, in the beginning of the century, some great captains and able politicians; but their successors had been effeminate and vicious,—princes, who hardly ever attained power without getting rid of their brothers by poison or the dagger. The house of Carrara, on the contrary, which gloried in being attached to the Guelph party, produced princes who might have passed for virtuous, in comparison with the other tyrants of Italy. Francesco da Carrara, who then reigned, his son and grandson, were men of courage, endued with great capacities, and who knew how to gain the affection of their subjects. The republic of Venice never pardoned Carrara his having made alliance against her, with the Genoese and the king of Hungary. After the death of the last named, Venice engaged Antonio della Scala to attack Padua, offering him subsidies to aid him in the conquest of that state. Carrara did all in his power to be reconciled to the prince, his neighbour, whom, in 1386, he repeatedly vanquished; as well as with the republic,— always ready to repair the losses sustained by the lord of Verona. Unable to obtain peace, he was at last reduced to accept the proffered alliance of Gian Galeazzo Visconti, who took Verona on the 18th of October, 1387. Instead of restoring to Carrara the city of Vicenza, as he had promised, he immediately offered his assistance to the Venetians against Padua: that republic was imprudent enough to accept the offer. Padua, long besieged, was given up to Visconti, on the 23rd of November, 1388. A few days afterwards, Treviso was surrendered to him ; so that the frontiers of the lord of Milan's dominions extended even to the edge of the *Lagune*. He had no sooner planted his standard there, than he menaced Venice, which had so unwisely facilitated his conquests.

All the rest of Lombardy was dependent on the lord of Milan. The marquis of Montferrat was brought up at the court of Galeazzo, who governed his states as guardian of this young prince. Albert, marquis d'Este, had, on the 26th of March, 1388, succeeded his brother in the sovereignty of Ferrara, to the prejudice of his nephew Obizzo, whom he caused to be beheaded with his mother. He put to death by various revolting executions almost all his relations, at the suggestion of Gian Galeazzo, whose object was, by rendering him thus odious to the people, to make the lord of Ferrara feel that he had no other support than in him. According to the same infernal policy, Gian Galeazzo accused the wife of the lord of Mantua, daughter of Barnabas, and his own cousin and sister-in-law, of a criminal intercourse with her husband's secretary. He forged letters by which he made her appear guilty, concealed them in her apartment, and afterwards pointed out where they were to be found to Francesco da Gonzaga, who, in a paroxysm of rage, caused her to be beheaded, and the secretary to be tortured, and afterwards put to death in 1390: it was not till after many years that he discovered the truth. Thus all the princes of Lombardy were either subdued or in discredit for the crimes which Visconti had made them commit, and by which he held them in his dependence; he then began to turn his attention towards Tuscany. In the years 1388 and 1389, the Florentines were repeatedly alarmed by his attempts to take possession of Sienna, Pisa, Bologna, San Miniato, Cortona, and Perugia: not one attempt had yet succeeded; but Florence saw her growing danger, and was well aware that the tyrant had not yet attacked her, only because he reserved her for his last conquest.

The arrival at Florence of Francis II. of Carrara, who came to offer his services and his hatred of Gian Galeazzo to the republic, determined the Florentines to have recourse to arms. The lord of Milan, in receiving the capitulation of Padua, had promised to give in compensation some other sovereignty to the house of Carrara; but he had either poisoned Francis I., or suffered him to perish in prison. Several attempts had been made to assassinate Francis II. in the province of Asti, whither he had been exiled. In spite of many dangers, he at last escaped, and fled into Tuscany, taking his wife, then indisposed, with him. He left her there, and passed into Germany, in the hopes of exciting new enemies against Gian Galeazzo; while the Florentines made alliance with the Bolognese against the lord of Milan, and placed their army under the command of John Hawkwood, who ever afterwards remained in their service. Carrara, seconded by the duke of Bavaria, the son-in-law of Barnabas, whose death the duke was desirous of avenging, re-entered Padua on the 14th of June, 1390, by the bed of the Brenta, and was received with enthusiasm by the inhabitants, who regarded him more as a fellow-citizen

than a master. He recovered possession of the whole
inheritance of his ancestors.

The extensive commerce of the Florentines had accustomed them to include all Europe in their negotiations;
and, as they liberally applied their wealth to the defence
of their liberty, they easily found allies abroad. After
having called the duke of Bavaria from Germany, in
1390, they in the year following sent to France for the
count d'Armagnac with a formidable army; but the
Germans as well as the French found, with astonishment,
that they could no longer cope with the new Italian
militia, which had substituted military science for the
routine of the transalpine soldier. Armagnac was vanquished and taken prisoner, on the 25th of July, 1391, by
Giacomo del Verme; and died a few days afterwards.
John Hawkwood, who, in the hope of joining him, had
advanced far into Lombardy with the Florentine army,
had great difficulty in leading it back in safety through
plains inundated by the Adige. After this campaign, the
republic, feeling the want of repose, made peace with
Galeazzo, on the 28th of January, 1392; well knowing
that it could place no trust in him, and that this treaty
was no security against his intrigues and treachery.

These expectations were not belied; for one plot
followed another in rapid succession. The Florentines
about this time reckoned on the friendship of the Pisans,
who had placed at the head of their republic Pietro
Gambacorta, a rich merchant, formerly an exile at
Florence, and warmly attached to peace and liberty:
but he was old, and had for his secretary Jacopo Appiano,
the friend of his childhood, who was nearly of his own
age. Yet Galeazzo found means to seduce the secretary:
he instigated him to the assassination of Gambacorta
and his children, on the 21st of October, 1392. Appiano,
seconded by the satellites furnished him by the duke of
Milan, made himself master of Pisa: but, after his death,
his son, who could with difficulty maintain himself there,
sold the city to Gian Galeazzo, in the month of February,
1399; reserving only the principality of Piombino, which
he transmitted to his descendants. At Perugia, Pandolpho
Baglione, chief of the noble and Ghibeline party, had, in
1390, put himself under the protection of Gian Galeazzo,

who aided him in changing the limited authority conferred on him into a tyranny : but three years afterwards
he was assassinated ; and the republic of Perugia, distracted by the convulsions of opposing factions, was
compelled to yield itself up to Gian Galeazzo, on the
21st of January, 1400.

The Germans observed with jealousy the continually
increasing greatness of Visconti ; which appeared to them
to annihilate the rights of the empire, and dry up the
sources of tribute, on a partition of which they always
reckoned. They pressed Wenceslaus to make war on
Gian Galeazzo. But that indolent and sensual monarch,
after some threats, gave it to be understood that for
money he would willingly sanction the usurpations of
Gian Galeazzo : and, in fact, on the 1st of May, 1395, he
granted him, for the sum of 100,000 florins, a diploma
which installed him duke of Milan and count of Pavia ;
comprehending in this investiture twenty-six cities and
their territory, as far as the *Lagune* of Venice. These
were the same cities which, more than three centuries
before, had signed the glorious league of Lombardy. The
duchy of Milan, according to the imperial bull, was to
pass solely to the legitimate male heir of Gian Galeazzo.
This concession of Wenceslaus caused great discontent
in Germany : it was one of the grievances for which the
diet of the empire, on the 20th of August, 1400, deposed
the emperor, and appointed Robert elector palatine in his
stead. Robert concluded a treaty of subsidy with the
Florentines, or rather entered into their pay, to oppose
Gian Galeazzo : but when, on the 21st of October, 1401,
he met the Milanese troops, commanded by Jacopo del
Verme, not far from Brescia, he experienced, to his
surprise and discomfiture, how much the German cavalry
were inferior to the Italian. He was saved from a
complete defeat only by Jacopo da Carrara, who led a
body of Italian cavalry to his aid. Robert found it
necessary to retreat, with disgrace, into Germany, after
having received from the Florentines an immense sum of
money.

Gian Galeazzo Visconti continued his course of
usurpation. In 1397, he attacked, at the same time,
Francesco da' Gonzaga at Mantua, and the Florentines,

without any previous declaration of war. After having ravaged Tuscany and the Mantuan territory, he consented, on the 11th of May, 1398, to sign, under the guarantee of Venice, a truce of ten years, during which period he was to undertake nothing against Tuscany. That, however, did not prevent him, in 1399, from taking under his protection the counts of Poppi and Ubertini, in the Apennines; or from engaging the republic of Sienna to surrender itself to him, on the 11th of November in the same year.

The plague broke out anew in Tuscany, and deprived the free states of all their remaining vigour. The magistrates, on whose prudence and courage they relied, in a few days sank under the contagion, and left free scope to the poorest intriguer. This happened at Lucca to the Guelph house of Guinigi, which had produced many distinguished citizens, all employed in the first magistracies. They perished under this disease nearly about the same time. A young man of their family, named Paulo Guinigi, undistinguished either for talent or character, profited by this calamity, on the 14th of October, 1400, to usurp the sovereignty. He immediately abjured the Guelph party, in which he had been brought up, and placed himself under the protection of Gian Galeazzo. At Bologna, also, the chief magistrates of the republic were, in like manner, swept away by the plague. Giovanni Bentivoglio, descended from a natural son of that king Hensius so long prisoner at Bologna, took advantage of the state of languor into which the republic had fallen, to get himself proclaimed sovereign lord, on the 27th of February, 1401. He at first thought of putting himself under the protection of the duke of Milan; but Gian Galeazzo, coveting the possession of Bologna, instead of amicably receiving, attacked him the year following. Bentivoglio was defeated at Casalecchio, on the 26th of June, 1402. His capital was taken the next day by the Milanese general, he himself made prisoner, and two days afterwards put to death. Another general of Galeazzo, in May, 1400, took possession of Assisa: the liberty of Genoa, Perugia, Sienna, Pisa, Lucca, and Bologna had, one after the other, fallen a sacrifice to the usurper. The Cancellieri, in the mountains of Pistoia, the Ubaldini, in those of the Mugello, had given themselves up to the duke of Milan. The Florentines, having no longer communications with the sea, across the territories of Sienna, Pisa, Lucca, and Bologna, saw the sources of their wealth and commerce dry up. Never had the republic been in more imminent danger; when the plague, which had so powerfully augmented its calamities, came to its aid. Gian Galeazzo Visconti was seized with it at his castle of Marignano, in which he had shut himself up, to be, as he hoped, secure from all communication with man. He was carried off by the pestilence, on the 3rd of September, 1402.

CHAPTER IX

ANARCHY IN THE DUCHY OF MILAN—THE VENETIANS MAKE THE CONQUEST OF PADUA AND VERONA—THE FLORENTINES OF PISA —FLORENCE, MENACED IN TURN BY LADISLAUS KING OF NAPLES AND FILIPPO MARIA VISCONTI, MAINTAINS AGAINST THEM THE BALANCE OF ITALY

THE regeneration of liberty in Italy was signalised still more, if it were possible, by the developement of the moral than by that of the intellectual character of the Italians. The sympathy existing among fellow-citizens, from the habit of living for each other and by each other,—of connecting every thing with the good of all,— produced in republics virtues which despotic states cannot even imagine. Man must have a country, before he can conceive the duty of sacrificing himself for it. The arts of intrigue and flattery are recommendations to a master; his favour is gained by encouraging his vices: and, in his turn, he recompenses those who serve him at the expense of morality, by dividing with them his power. But to please the people, to rise by the people, virtues must be exhibited to them, not vices: the sympathy of all is gained only by that which is most honourable in each. A popular assembly is swayed only by an appeal to its virtues: even in its errors, some frankness, probity, and generosity, by which men sympathise together, are always to be found; while, if a dark

deed be but conceived, it is a secret carefully kept, with
conscious shame, from every eye—it would be easier to
execute than to announce or recommend it to the public.
Tyrants act on men by terror, corruption, venality,
espionnage, envy. Free governments can lead the people
only by exciting their more honourable passions. Eloquence, to move men in masses, must make its appeals
to honour, pity, justice, and courage. Accordingly, how
rich in virtues was Italy in the twelfth century, when
covered with republics, and when every city simultaneously
fought for liberty! These virtues, the most precious of
all treasures, diminished with the progress of time, and
in exact proportion with the diminution of free states.
From the moment a man entered one of those republics,
he might reckon with certainty on finding good faith in
treaties and negotiations; zeal for the common advantage
in all alliances; courage and fortitude in adversity; an
unbounded liberality from the rich to the poor; in all
great calamities, an eagerness, in every one who had
property, to devote it to the salvation of all; finally, an
energy in the people to resist, by common exertion, every
act of injustice or violence. Even their excesses arose
most commonly from some virtuous indignation. From
the moment, on the contrary, that a man entered the
states of one of the tyrants of Lombardy or Romagna,
he found a government hostile to public opinion, supporting itself only by perfidy and crime. Spies watched and
denounced every expression of generous feeling; they
insinuated themselves into families to betray them; they
abused the sacred ties of kindred, home, and neighbourhood, to convert them into snares; they made all feel
that the wisdom of the subject consisted in distrusting
every one, and not meddling in the affairs of another.
Assassination and poison were common means of government. Every Italian tyrant was stained with the blood
of his kindred; paid murderers despatched the objects
of his suspicions; he outraged public virtue, and could
maintain order only by fear. Death itself at length failing to inspire terror, he combined with capital punishment protracted tortures, the exhibition of which only
rendered men more hardened and fierce.

But the field of virtue in Italy contracted from age to

age, while that of crime enlarged itself. The inhabitants of the kingdom of Naples, from its foundation in the twelfth century,—from the subjugation of the three republics of Naples, Gaëta, and Amalfi,—had been dead to every feeling of association, sympathy, or patriotism: they had since that time been governed by a corrupt court and nobility, which offered examples only of vices. In the thirteenth century, Lombardy also had been detached from the domain of liberty. During the convulsions occasioned either by the violence of the Guelph and Ghibeline factions, or by the contempt of the nobles for all law, every republic, in its turn, fell repeatedly under the yoke of some tyrant; and, however short his reign, it sufficed to familiarise the mind with violence instead of justice, and with the success of crime. At the same time, the devotion of factions to their chiefs, the reference of patriotism to party, and not to the common weal, perverted morality, and confounded the rules of right and wrong.

In the fourteenth century it was still worse: power in Lombardy had passed to those who made of it the uses most destructive of public virtue. Men rose to be princes by crime: their perfidy towards their neighbours, and their domestic treachery, marked the commencement and duration of every reign. Tyrants were so numerous, so constantly under the observation of every citizen, that their example was always operating to corrupt the people. No father of a family could hide from his children the fact, that the prince they must obey had attained power only by betraying his friends or his fellow-citizens, by poisoning or poniarding his uncle or his brother. The states of the church exhibited not fewer examples of the success of crime: every city of Romagna, of the March, of the patrimony of St. Peter, had its tyrant; and every tyrant reigned only to tread under foot every moral duty. Nay, more: Barnabas and Gian Galeazzo Visconti had, in some sort, kept a school of treachery for Tuscany and the states of the church. They had always encouraged every usurpation; and promised beforehand their alliance to whoever could smother the voice of a free people, and seduce them from the sway of morality to that of crime.

These causes of immorality, all which in Italy conspired against public virtue, operated in the beginning of the 15th century with redoubled force. When Gian Galeazzo unexpectedly died of the plague, in the height of his successful career, he divided his estates between his two sons,—Gian Maria, then thirteen years of age, whom he declared duke of Milan; and Filippo Maria, twelve years old, whom he left count of Pavia. But, as these princes were too young to reign, he recommended them to the condottieri in his service, whom he introduced into the council as part of the regency: these were the captains of that new militia which had so well served him in the accomplishment of his projects, and in whom he placed the greatest confidence. The school of Alberic Barbiano, which had formed such brave soldiers and able generals, could not, in like manner, produce good citizens and virtuous men; and Gian Galeazzo, for the protection of his children, needed counsellors guided by principles that would have stood in his way as long as these men were his servants. Jacopo del Verme, Pandolpho Malatesta, Facino Cane, Ottobon Terzo, and the other captains in whom he trusted, were soldiers of fortune, who made of their valour a trade of carnage and plunder; who, indifferent to what was just or unjust, were ready to fight for whoever would pay them, and to betray those for any other who would pay them more. They did not long remain faithful guardians to the trust which their master had reposed in them. They shared it with Catherine, widow of Gian Galeazzo, and with Francesco Barbavara, supposed to be her lover, and known to have commenced his career as valet-de-chambre to the duke. Warriors disdained to obey a woman and her valet; the chiefs, too, of the ancient parties in the cities which Visconti had subdued, rose with their partisans to recover the sovereignty of their fathers. The condottieri resisted them, but resisted them for themselves: Facino Cane made himself tyrant at Alexandria; Ottobon Terzo at Parma; Pandolpho Malatesta at Brescia. Amidst this anarchy, the duchess Catherine believed herself energetic in proportion as she was violent and cruel. She caused several Milanese nobles to be beheaded without trial; she gave up many cities to be sacked by the soldiers;

and thus only redoubled the hatred which she excited: she was thrown into prison, where she died by poison on the 16th of October, 1404; and Francesco Barbavara was obliged to fly. The rest of the duchy of Milan was divided into as many principalities as there were cities. In some, it was the ancient chiefs of the Guelph or Ghibeline party who recovered power; in others, the captain of adventure who happened to be in garrison there: in several it was some daring villain, such as Giovanni da Vignate at Lodi, or Gabrino Fondolo at Cremona, who, profiting by the friendship and confidence of some other usurper, assassinated him, and took his place. Never, even in that country so fertile in tyrants, was power stained with so many crimes.

Gian Maria Visconti, who had seen almost all the cities subdued by his father detached from his dominion, still continued to bear the title of duke of Milan ; while his power, even in that city, passed from one ambitious chief to another, and was at last assumed by Facino Cane, one of the best generals of his father. All that Gian Maria Visconti preserved of sovereign power was an unbounded indulgence in every vice. His libertinism would hardly have been remarked; he was chiefly signalised by the frightful pleasure which he sought in the practice of cruelty. He was passionately devoted to the chace; but such sports soon failed to quench his thirst for cruelty. The tortures inflicted on mute animals, not finding expression by speech, did not come up to his ferocious ideas of enjoyment. He therefore resolved to substitute men for brute animals; and caused all the criminals condemned by the tribunals to be given up to him as objects of this inhuman sport. He had his hounds fed with human flesh, in order to render them more ferocious in tearing the victims; and, when ordinary convicts were scarce, he denounced to the tribunals even the crimes in which he had participated, to obtain the condemnation of his accomplices: after which he delivered them to his huntsman, Squarcia Giramo, charged with providing for the ducal chace. He was at last, on the 16th of May, 1412, assassinated by some Milanese nobles.

The virtue and elevation of soul which had done such

honour to the Italian nation became obscured even in the republics of Genoa, Lucca, Pisa, Sienna, Perugia, and Bologna. These republics, in the course of the fourteenth century, had all more than once fallen under the power of some tyrant: accordingly, the examples of cruelty, perfidy, and the success of those usurpers to whom they had been forced to submit, had had a corrupting influence on their citizens. Neither had Venice preserved the true Italian virtue: its citizens often gave proofs of an unbounded devotion to their country, of an unreserved submission to its most severe ordinances; but it was a narrow-minded and jealous aristocracy, which, according to the spirit of that government, substituted national selfishness for patriotism. The Venetians took not into the least consideration any other people: they fancied they gave proofs of heroism, when the advantage of their republic was in question, in suppressing every human sentiment, in silencing every moral duty. Venice was governed by secret councils, where the voice of the people was never heard: its foreign policy was administered by the Council of Ten; which, in its mysterious meetings, took interest only for a guide. The decemvirs dared unblushingly propose to their colleagues deliberating under the sanction of an oath, and animated with the same spirit as themselves, the sacrifice of what was honest and just to what was useful. Italian virtue had taken refuge at Florence: it was there only that the people deliberated; that they associated together either for peace or war, or negotiation, as well as for the common administration of the government. Nothing was proposed to the public, nothing could obtain the assent of all, except what all felt to be just, honourable, and generous. The republic of Florence was always ready to risk its repose and wealth for the equilibrium and independence of Italy; for the common liberty; and for the progress of intelligence and civilisation. During two centuries, it was always seen eager to put itself forward as the champion of all that was good and noble. Italy might justly glory in the fact, that wherever she was free, she was always found constant in the road to virtue: she is not answerable for the crimes with which she was sullied by her tyrants. Several thousand citizens had always contributed, by their vote, to all that Florence did that was grand and noble; while about fifty princes, distributed in as many palaces, with the few wretches which it belongs to tyrannical governments always to bring forward, sufficed to commit, in spite of a whole population, all the crimes which affrighted Italy.

At the moment in which the death of Gian Galeazzo annihilated, at least for a time, the threatening power of the dukes of Milan, the two republics in Italy which alone had survived his intrigues, and which he had in vain menaced, profited by the anarchy into which Lombardy had fallen, to recover their power, and aggrandise themselves by conquest. Venice, which had shut itself up in its *Lagune*, issued forth to extend its frontiers to the Lake of Garda; and Florence, to which Gian Galeazzo had interdicted all approach to the sea, conquered Pisa, whose ports were necessary to its commerce, and almost to its existence.

Francesco da Carrara, re-established in the sovereignty of Padua in the year 1390, had from that period remained faithful to the Guelph party and to Florence: he hoped to profit by the confusion in which the death of Gian Galeazzo had left all Lombardy; and he invited Gulielmo della Scala to join him, and recover together the sovereignties of Verona and Vicenza. Gulielmo was the son of that Antonio della Scala who, by his alliance with the Venetians fifteen years before, had caused the ruin of Carrara and his own; but a community of misfortune had reconciled them. On the 7th of April, 1404, they, in conjunction, took Verona. On the 21st of the same month Della Scala died; and the report was spread that Carrara had poisoned him. Be that as it may, Carrara, on the 17th of May following, arrested the two sons of Della Scala, and took possession of the city and fortress of Verona. Vicenza, in the mean time, yielded to the Venetians. The latter had hitherto sought their grandeur only in commerce, in their navy, and in their possessions beyond sea; but the confusion into which Lombardy was thrown gave birth in them to a new ambition: they resolved on extending their dominion in a country which seemed to offer itself for their conquest.

They entered into treaty with the duchess Catherine
Visconti, who renounced all right which her son might
have on Verona and Padua; and they set on foot an
army of 9,000 cavalry. Their immense wealth permitted
them to choose the most distinguished captains and the
best soldiers in Italy. The republic, in taking them into
pay, made it one rule, never to confide the command of
its armies to one of its own citizens, that they might
have nothing to fear from his power or glory; and
another, not to allow the soldiers to enter the city of
Venice, the defence of which needed no more than its
Lagune, galleys, and sailors. Two senators, distinguished
by the title of procurators of St. Mark, were charged to
attend in the camp, and watch over the foreign general
whom the signoria had chosen.

War between Venice and the lord of Padua was
declared on the 23rd of June, 1404. Francesco da Carrara
carried it on with the utmost valour; but opposed, without allies, to forces infinitely superior to his own, he saw
successively forced the passage of several canals which
intersected his territory, and behind which he had raised
fortifications. The whole of the Paduan territory was
ravaged by the Venetian army, and almost all its fortresses
taken before the end of the campaign of 1404. A division
of the army arrived to besiege Carrara in his capital, on
the 12th of June, 1405; at the same time that another
division besieged his second son, Jacopo da Carrara, in
Verona, and forced him to capitulate, on the 23rd of June.
The whole rural population had taken refuge in Padua;
and the privations and sufferings experienced in consc-
quence occasioned a contagious malady, which carried
off 40,000 persons. Carrara and his son continued to
fight at the head of the survivors with determined
bravery, till the Venetians made themselves masters of
the first entrenchment. On the 19th of November, 1405,
a capitulation became necessary. Carrara always flattered
himself that the Venetians would grant him some re-
muneration for the principality which they wrested from
him. He repaired to Venice, with his eldest son, on the
faith of the general with whom he had capitulated. On
their arrival, they were thrown into prison; where they
found Jacopo da Carrara, who had been taken prisoner

at Verona. The Council of Ten, putting in practice the advice given later by Machiavelli, of annihilating the whole race of dethroned tyrants, in order to destroy with them the zeal, hopes, and plots of their partisans, caused Francesco da Carrara and his two sons to be strangled in prison, on the 16th of January, 1406. They, at the same time, set a price on the head of the youngest princes, who had escaped from them, and on those of all the survivors of the house of Della Scala: not one fell under the dagger of the assassin, notwithstanding the great recompence shamelessly promised by the Venetians; but, on the other hand, not one ever recovered the states of his fathers.

The Florentines regarded Francesco da Carrara as one of the firmest champions of the Guelph party in Lombardy: they valued his alliance; but they did not think themselves obliged to plunge into war for him, whom they accused of having provoked it by his unjust aggression on Verona. All their efforts, also, were then directed against Pisa: they regarded the conquest of that city as a necessary condition of their existence, ever since the blockade which Gian Galeazzo had made them experience, by subjugating all the states that opened to them any communication with the sea. Gian Galeazzo had left the lordship of Pisa to his natural son, Gabriel Maria, who had, with his mother, taken possession of that city. That of Sienna had recovered its freedom in the month of March, 1404, and had renewed its alliance with Florence. Perugia and Bologna had also, in the preceding month of September, thrown off the yoke of the Viscontis, and voluntarily submitted to the church; which had left them their republican form of government. The Cancellieri, the counts Guidi and Ubertini, and the other feudal nobles of the Apennines, who had placed themselves under the protection of Gian Galeazzo, had been punished for it by the Florentine republic, which had again subdued them to its power. Lucca remained subject to Paulo Guinigi, who governed that ancient republic with moderation, and desired only to be forgotten by his neighbours. Pisa alone, in Tuscany, remained the enemy of Florence. As Gabriel was sensible that his brothers, the Viscontis, were then in

no state to defend him, he purchased the protection of
the marshal Boucicault, the representative of the king of
France at Genoa. Boucicault exercised only the limited
authority assigned by the constitution to the doge. The
Genoese were far more zealous than the marshal in the
support of the independence of Pisa. They feared the
competition of the Florentines in their maritime commerce,
if once they were masters of Pisa, Leghorn, and Porto
Pisano. Boucicault, on the contrary, after having taken
Gabriel Maria under his protection, soon thought of
making them an article of trade. He offered to sell Pisa
to the Florentines, in the month of June, 1405, for the
sum of 400,000 florins; which he agreed to divide with
Gabriel Maria. The Pisans, informed of this negotiation,
rose on the 21st of July; disarmed the garrison of their
tyrants; made themselves masters of the gates of the
city; but failed in their attack on the citadel. Boucicault,
informed of these matters, moderated his demand; and
asked the Florentines no more than 206,000 florins for
the Pisan citadel, and the castles which he still held in
the territory of Pisa. The Florentines paid him that
sum: he was engaged to divide it with Gabriel Maria;
but, to rid himself of this claim, he accused Gabriel of a
plot against the king of France, and caused him to be
beheaded.

The Florentines hoped to induce the Pisans to submit
to them by negotiations; and they offered the most
advantageous conditions: but the Pisans, who proudly
regarded themselves as the most ancient and illustrious
of the Tuscan republics, and as having preserved, more
than any other, their warlike courage, vigorously besieged
their citadel, and retook it on the 6th of September.
They afterwards demanded peace of the Florentines,
offering to reimburse them the money they had paid: to
facilitate the negotiation, they recalled from exile Giovanni
Gambacorta, whose family had been always favoured by
Florence, and named him captain of the people. But
their offers were all rejected; and the Pisans, forced to
have recourse to arms, not only fought valiantly themselves, but eagerly sacrificed their whole fortune to
purchase the services of the condottieri, whom they called
to their aid from all parts of Italy. The war continued

for more than a year: the Pisans successively lost all
their fortresses and territory: their city was blockaded
during the campaign of 1406; and they courageously
supported privations, maladies, and, finally, famine.   But
the chief whom they had elected did not show a like
heroism: Giovanni Gambacorta secretly treated with the
Florentines; and obtained the gift of 50,000 florins, and
the county of Bagno, to open to them the gates of Pisa;
which was done in the night of the 8th and 9th of
November, 1406.   The Florentines did all in their power
to reconcile the Pisans to the yoke which they forced on
them: their army was preceded into the famished towns
by wagon-loads of bread, which the soldiers distributed
themselves to all that demanded it.   Gino Capponi, the
commissioner of Florence, promised, not only the strictest
attention to justice, but privileges, and even friendship,
to the conquered people.   These advances were all in
vain; the Pisans were too haughty to submit to rivals
whom they had so long combated.   The most ancient
and opulent families removed to Lucca, Sardinia, and
Sicily.   The young men almost all engaged in the companies of adventure, to find in the camp an independence
which they could no longer hope for in their own country:
and Pisa, in losing its liberty, lost its commerce, population, and every remnant of prosperity.

The Florentines endeavoured to relieve Pisa from its
state of poverty, by filling it with foreigners: they offered
it to the church for the meeting of the council which was
to terminate the great western schism.   This schism had
lasted since the year 1378.   Pietro di Luna, an Aragonese,
one of the cardinals who had given rise to it, had succeeded
Clement VII., who died at Avignon in 1394.   The succession of popes in the other division of the church had been
more rapid.   Boniface IX., who had succeeded the
turbulent Urban VI., in 1389, was a better warrior than
churchman; he reconquered successively all the states
which his predecessor had lost: he entered Rome, and
consolidated his power by executions.   Innocent VII.,
who succeeded him, in 1404, was a gentle and moderate
man; but as he abandoned the exercise of power to his
brother, who governed only by terror, the number of
executions drove the Romans to revolt.   The pope was

anew driven from his capital; but, returning in 1406, he
died a few months afterwards, and Gregory XII., a
Venetian, was named his successor.

In both divisions of the church, the prolongation of
the schism was considered dishonourable and calamitous
to Christendom: in both the sovereigns were zealous to
suppress it; but on both sides the popes opposed an
obstinate resistance. They had been each elected by
the two colleges of cardinals, under the express condition
that each would be ready to cede his rights, and abdicate
at the same time with his competitor. They either
refused, or by a thousand artifices delayed, to do so.
Benedict XIII. was besieged in his palace at Avignon
by the troops of the king of France, in order to constrain
him to yield: but, after he had declared himself ready
to abdicate, his adversary, Gregory XII., refused.
Benedict, however, advanced as far as La Spezzia, and
Gregory as far as Lucca, to meet in conference with their
two colleges; but both persisted in not taking the last
step. Towards the end of 1408, their cardinals, losing all
patience, left them, and assembled at Leghorn; whence
they issued a summons to convoke the oecumenical
council at Pisa, in the month of March following. This
council, in which were assembled almost all the prelates
of Christendom, after long discussion, condemned and
deposed the two popes, on the 5th of June, 1409; and,
on the 7th of July, the assembled cardinals of the two
" obediences " named in their place a third, Alexander V.
The deposed popes would not submit to the sentence of
the council: both preserved a small flock of the faithful,—
the one in Aragon, the other at Rimini and Naples.
Gregory had retired to the first-mentioned town; so that,
instead of two, there were three popes in the western
church. To terminate the schism, it became necessary
to assemble a second general council; which, sitting at
Constance, on the 1st of November, 1414, forced two of
the popes to abdicate, and deposed the third. The church,
at the same time, implored a reform; to accomplish
which, a third council was assembled at Basle, on the
23rd July, 1431, and this laid the foundation of a new
schism.

While two or three pretenders to the pontifical chair

were thus obliged to defend themselves against each
other, as well as against their own cardinals and against
all Christendom, the king of Naples profited by the
confusion to take possession of nearly all the states of
the church. That king was Ladislaus, son of Charles III.
da Durazzo, whom he had succeeded in 1386, being at
that time only ten years old. Louis II. of Anjou, a
minor, like Ladislaus, disputed the throne with him.
The queen, Joan, when pressed by the Hungarians, had
adopted Louis I., duke of Anjou, the brother of Charles V.;
who had entered the kingdom of Naples in 1382, and
died there in 1384. He left one son, Louis II., then
under age, to whom his mother and her partisans gave
the title of king of Sicily. The war between these two
children, directed by their mothers, ruined the kingdom
of Naples during the latter part of the fourteenth century,
and destroyed its influence over the rest of Italy. It was
not till 1399 that Ladislaus succeeded in driving out the
princes of Anjou, and subduing the kingdom. He had
grown up amidst civil war, receiving the hardening education of privation and danger, alternately seconded or
obstructed by intrigue and treachery. He was brave,
and had studied the art of war; but was still more
expert in dissimulation and perfidy. His ambition was
unbounded, and his passions unrestrained by any one
moral principle. After short attempts to preserve
Provence, and to acquire the crown of Hungary, to
which his birth gave him a title, he judged it more
advantageous to direct all his efforts against the states
which bounded his dominions in Italy. In April, 1408,
he took possession of Rome; and soon afterwards of
Perugia. He conquered almost all the cities of the
March, and of the duchy of Spoleto; from thence he
entered Tuscany, ravaged the territories of Arezzo and
of Sienna, and took possession of Cortona.

The Florentines, when they saw themselves thus
attacked, without any subject of quarrel, by this ambitious
and faithless prince, resolved on opposing to him Louis II.
of Anjou. They recalled Louis from France, in 1409;
and offered a subsidy to aid him in recovering the crown
of Naples. At the same time, they formed a closer connection with one of the two generals who then attracted

the attention of all Italy. Among the numerous captains who had been formed in the school of Alberic da Barbiano, there were two regarded as infinitely superior to all others, from the progress which they had made in the art of war. Braccio da Montone, a noble of Perugia, had studied how to render his army manageable, by augmenting the number of officers, and by accustoming it to fight in detached bodies, which dispersed and rallied at will. The other was Sforza Attendolo, a peasant of Cotignola, in Romagna, who at first distinguished for prodigious strength of body and undaunted bravery, soon became equally distinguished in military tactics; but, instead of adopting the new method of Braccio, he applied himself to bringing the ancient system to perfection. He continued to move his army in large masses; which no one conducted with such unison and steadiness. Braccio distinguished himself by impetuous valour, by prompt and decisive action, and sometimes by trusting to chance: Sforza, by prudent, steady, and cool conduct. All the soldiers of fortune in Italy soon attached themselves to one or other of these two captains; who, nearly of the same age, and having made their first campaigns together, now found themselves opposed to each other in a rivalry of interest and glory. The name of the Bracceschi school was given to the band of soldiers of the one, and Sforzeschi to the other; and, when a state called one of these into its service, it was nearly sure of having the other opposed to it.

The Florentines formed a close connection with Braccio: they placed him at the head of their army; and they settled on him a considerable pension, which was to continue even when out of their service, provided he always returned to it when called upon. Louis of Anjou rendered them but little service: he was engaged in a war on their account in the states of Rome, when he received news that the Genoese had, on the 6th of September, 1409, risen against the French, and driven them out of Genoa. Apprehending that his communication with France might be interrupted, he hastily returned to Provence. After his departure, Braccio carried on the war successfully against the Neapolitans. With the Florentine army he made himself master of Rome, on

N

the 2nd of January, 1410. Florence, however, had no sooner gained a signal advantage over Ladislaus, than it offered him peace, which he eagerly accepted: he bound himself by treaties in terms the most precise, and confirmed them by oaths the most solemn; which were no sooner taken than unblushingly violated by him. The war was interrupted only for the time necessary for the repose of the troops; each year forced them to a new campaign. Louis of Anjou was twice called into Italy by the Florentines: he gained over Ladislaus, at Roccasecca, on the 19th of May, 1411, a great victory, of which he knew not how to take advantage. He again retired, and left Ladislaus to finish the conquest of the ecclesiastical states; while John XXIII., successor of Alexander V., only struggled to prevent the convocation of the council of Constance, which deposed him. Ladislaus, who owed his success chiefly to the talents and bravery of Sforza, then in his pay, made every year some fresh conquest in Tuscany. The Florentine republic, attacked by him on all sides, and exhausted by continual exertion, found no longer any resource by which to resist him, and began to lose all hope; when the king of Naples was seized in his camp with a violent and painful malady, attributed to his debaucheries. He was conveyed in a litter to Naples; and died on arriving there, on the 6th of August, 1414. His sister, Joan II., widow of the son of the duke of Austria, succeeded him. She was forty years of age; and, like her brother, abandoned to the most unrestrained libertinism. She left the government of her kingdom to her lovers, who disputed power by arms: they called into her service, or into that of her second husband, or of the rival princes whom she in turn adopted, the two armies of Sforza and Braccio. The consequence was the ruin of the kingdom of Naples; which ceased to menace the rest of Italy.

The moment Ladislaus disappeared, a new enemy arose to disturb the Florentines—Filippo Maria Visconti, the brother of Gian Maria, and third duke of Milan. He was received in that capital on the 16th of June, 1412, four days after the murder of his brother. Filippo immediately married the widow of Facino Cane, the power-- ful condottiere, who had retained Gian Maria in his dependence; and who died the same day that Gian Maria was assassinated. By this sudden marriage he secured the army of Facino Cane,—which was, in fact, master of the greater part of the Milanese: with its aid he undertook, without delay, to recover the rest of his states from the hands of those tyrants who had divided amongst them the dominions of his father. Filippo Maria, like him, united immeasurable ambition with extreme timidity. During the first year of his reign, which was to decide his existence as prince or subject, he fought with determined courage; but from that time, though he continually made war, he never showed himself to his armies. Even in his palace and garden, he shrank from the eye of man: he never consented to an interview with the emperor Sigismond, who had gone to Milan to exert himself for the extinction of the schism. It is asserted that Filippo Maria was so sensible of his extreme ugliness, that he could not support the humiliation of being looked at. He had the art of discovering great talents, and of attaching the best captains of Italy, in as great a degree as his father; but placed less confidence in those worthy of obtaining it, and possessed less elevation and constancy in his projects. Always as timid as he was ambitious, he became discouraged on the smallest reverse of fortune in the attacks which he continually made on his neighbours: versatile in politics, he no sooner made peace than he renewed war, or contracted an alliance than he broke it. He seemed no less alarmed at the success of his own generals, than at that of his enemies. He was always the first to stop their progress, and to prevent them from profiting by their success; so that his tortuous conduct daily produced some unexpected thwarting result. Without pity for his subjects, he exposed them both to the vexations of his own soldiers and those of the enemy. He would have ruined Lombardy, if the fertility of that rich province had not exceeded his power of mischief.

In the battle of Monza, by which he acquired his brother's inheritance, and the only battle in which he was ever present, he remarked the brilliant courage of Francesco Carmagnola, a Piedmontese soldier of fortune, and immediately gave him a command. Carmagnola soon justified the duke's choice by the most distinguished talents for war, the most brilliant victories, and the most noble character. Francesco Carmagnola was, after a few years, placed at the head of the duke's armies; and, from the year 1412 to that of 1422, successively attacked all the tyrants who had divided the heritage of Gian Galeazzo, and brought those small states again under the dominion of the duke of Milan. Even the republic of Genoa submitted to him, in 1421, on the same conditions as those on which it had before submitted to the king of France,—reserving all its liberties; and granting the duke's lieutenant, who was Carmagnola himself, only those prerogatives which the constitution yielded to the doge.

As soon as Filippo Maria had accomplished the conquest of Lombardy, he resumed the projects of his father against Romagna and Tuscany. He confirmed the treaties of alliance which Gian Galeazzo had contracted with all the Ghibeline tyrants of the first-named province; renewed his intrigues against the republic of Florence, and combined them with those which he at the same time carried on in the kingdom of Naples. Joan, who had sent back to France her second husband, Jaques, count de la Marche, and who had no children, was persuaded, in 1420, by one of her lovers, to adopt Alphonso the Magnanimous, king of Aragon and Sicily, to whom she entrusted some of the fortresses of Naples. She revoked this adoption in 1423; and substituted in his place Louis III. of Anjou, son of Louis II. The former put himself at the head of the ancient party of Durazzo; the latter, of that of Anjou. The consequence was a civil war, in which the two great captains, Sforza and Braccio, were opposed to each other, and acquired new titles to glory. The duke of Milan made alliance with Joan II. and Louis III. of Anjou: Sforza, named great constable of the kingdom, was their general. The Florentines remained constant to Braccio, whom Alphonso had made governor of the Abruzzi; and who had seized, at the same time, the signoria of Perugia, his native city. He found a warlike disposition in the Perugians, associated them in his glory, and made them sharers in the wealth which his arms had procured him. He subdued several of the small neighbouring states, and seemed to be forming a military principality; which Florence accepted as an ally, to defend, in concert, the independence of Tuscany. But Sforza and Braccio both perished, as Italy awaited with anxiety the result of the struggle about to be commenced. Sforza was drowned at the passage of the Pescara, on the 4th of January, 1424; Braccio was mortally wounded at the battle of Aquila, on the 2nd of June of the same year. Francesco, son of the former, succeeded to his father's name and the command of his army, both of which he was destined to render still more illustrious. The son of Braccio, on the contrary, lost the sovereignty of Perugia, which resumed its freedom on the 29th of July of the same year; and the remnant of the army formed by this great captain elected for its chief his most able lieutenant, Nicolo Piccinino.

This was the moment which Filippo Maria chose to push on his army to Romagna, and vigorously attack the Florentines, after he had acknowledged their right to defend that province. The Florentines, having no tried general at the head of their troops, experienced, from the 6th of September, 1423, to the 17th of October, 1425, not less than six successive defeats, either in Liguria or Romagna. Undismayed by defeat, they re-assembled their army for the seventh time: the patriotism of their rich merchants made up for the penury of their exhausted treasury. They, at the same time, sent their most distinguished statesmen as ambassadors to Venice, to represent to that republic, that if it did not join them while they still stood, the liberty of Italy was lost for ever. Lorenzo Ridolfi, one of the ten commissioners of war, had been sent on this mission to the signoria of Venice: finding great difficulty in persuading it to take part in the war, he exclaimed, " I acknowledge we have been wrong in not opposing Filippo Maria in time; for, by our slowness, we have made him duke of Milan and master of Genoa: but you, by sacrificing us, render him king of Italy. We, in our turn, if we must submit to him, will make him emperor." An illustrious fugitive, Francesco Carmagnola, who arrived about this time at Venice, accomplished what Florence had nearly failed in, by discovering to the Venetians the project of the duke of

Milan to subjugate them. Francesco Carmagnola had, by the victories he had gained, the glory he had acquired, and the influence he obtained over the soldiers, excited the jealousy, instead of the gratitude, of Filippo Maria; who disgraced him, and deprived him of his employment, without assigning any reason. Carmagnola returned to court, but could not even obtain an interview with his master. He retired to his native country, Piedmont: his wife and children were arrested, and his goods confiscated. He arrived at last, by Germany, at Venice; soon afterwards some emissaries of the duke of Milan were arrested for an attempt to poison him. The doge, Francesco Foscari, wishing to give lustre to his reign by conquest, persuaded the senate of Venice to oppose the increasing ambition of the duke of Milan. A league, formed between Florence and Venice, was successively joined by the marquis of Ferrara, the lord of Mantua, the Siennese, the duke Amedeus VIII. of Savoy, and the king Alphonso of Naples, who jointly declared war against Filippo Maria Visconti, on the 27th of January, 1426. Carmagnola was charged to raise an army of 16,000 cuirassiers and 8,000 infantry in the states of Mantua.

The good fortune of Carmagnola in war still attended him in the campaign of 1426. He was as successful against the duke of Milan as he had been for him: he took from him the city and whole province of Brescia. The duke ceded this conquest to the Venetians by treaty on the 30th of December: but he employed the winter in assembling his forces; and in the beginning of spring renewed the war. He equipped a considerable fleet on the Po, in order to take possession of the states of Mantua and Ferrara, the allies of the two republics. This fleet was attacked by the Venetians, and, after an obstinate battle, burnt, near Cremona, on the 21st of May, 1427. The duke of Milan had given the command of his army to Nicolo Piccinino, the pupil of Braccio, who had brought with him the flower of the Bracceschi army. Nicolo attacked Carmagnola on the 12th of July, at Casalsecco; but the heat was so intense, and the dust rose in such clouds from under the horses' feet, that the two armies, enveloped in nearly the darkness of night, could no longer distinguish each other, or discern the signals: they separated without claiming advantage on either side. A third battle took place, on the 11th of October, 1427, in a marsh near Macalo: Carmagnola here completely defeated the Milanese army, commanded by Carlo Malatesta, in which were united Francesco Sforza, Nicolo Piccinino, and all the most illustrious captains of Italy. By an imprudent generosity, Carmagnola released these important prisoners; and thus provoked the resentment of the procurators of St. Mark, who accompanied him. A new peace, signed on the 18th of April, 1428, again suspended hostilities without reconciling parties, or inspiring either of the belligerents with any confidence. The Florentines took advantage of this interval of repose to attack Paulo Guinigi, lord of Lucca; whose alliance with the duke of Milan had irritated them, although he had afterwards been abandoned by Filippo Maria. The Lucchese, profiting by this last circumstance, revolted against their lord in the month of September, deposed him, and sent him prisoner to Milan. The Florentines were afterwards driven out of the states of Lucca by Nicolo Piccinino, who defeated them on the borders of the Serchio, on the 2nd of December, 1430; and the general war recommenced.

In this last campaign, fortune abandoned Carmagnola. On the 17th of May, 1431, he suffered himself to be surprised at Soncino, which he had reached with his advanced guard, by Francesco Sforza, who took prisoners 1,600 of his cavalry: he, however, escaped, and rejoined his still brilliant army. On the 23rd of May he approached the Po, to second the Venetian fleet in an attack on Cremona: but the fleet, pushed by that of the Milanese on the opposite shore, was destroyed in his presence, without the possibility of his rendering it any aid. However great his desire to repair these checks, he could not meet the enemy again during the remainder of the summer. A deadly distemper broke out among the horses throughout Italy; his troops were dismounted: and, as the fate of battle depended almost entirely on the cavalry, this calamity reduced him to complete inaction.

The senate of Venice, which made it a rule never to defend the republic but by foreign arms,—never to enlist its citizens under its banners either as generals or soldiers,

—further observed that of governing with extreme rigour those foreign adventurers of whom its armies were composed, and of never believing in the virtue of men who trafficked in their own blood. The Venetians distrusted them: they supposed them ever disposed to treachery; and if they were unfortunate, though only from imprudence, they rendered them responsible. The condottieri were made fully to understand that they were not to lose the armies of the republic without answering for the event with their lives. The senate joined to this rigour the perfidy and mystery which characterise an aristocracy. Having decided on punishing Carmagnola for the late disasters, it began by deceiving him. He was loaded with marks of deference and confidence: he was invited to come to Venice in the month of April, 1432, to fix with the signoria the plan of the ensuing campaign. The most distinguished senators went to meet him, and conduct him in pomp to the palace of the doge. Carmagnola, introduced into the senate, was placed in the chair of honour: he was pressed to speak; and his discourse applauded. The day began to close: lights were not yet called for; and the general could no longer distinguish the faces of those who surrounded him; when suddenly the *sbirri*, or soldiers of police, threw themselves on him, loaded him with chains, and dragged him to the prison of the palace. He was next day put to the torture,—rendered still more painful by the wounds which he had received in the service of this ungrateful republic. Both the accusations made against him, and his answers to the questions, are buried in the profound secrecy with which the Venetian senate covered all its acts. On the 5th of May, 1432, Francesco Carmagnola, twenty days after his arrest, was led out,—his mouth gagged to prevent any protestation of innocence,—and placed between the two columns on the square of St. Mark: he was there beheaded, amidst a trembling people, whom the senate of Venice was resolved to govern only by terror.

CHAPTER X

COSMO DE' MEDICI, CHIEF OF THE REPUBLIC OF FLORENCE—DEATH
OF THE LAST VISCONTI—EFFORTS OF THE MILANESE TO RECOVER
THEIR LIBERTY—THEY ARE ENSLAVED BY FRANCESCO SFORZA—
CONSPIRACY OF STEFANO PORCARI AT ROME

THE fermentation which had manifested itself at Florence
among the lower orders of the people, in the momentary
triumph of the Ciompi, began to subside. Manufacturers,
artisans, men who to live needed their daily labour, themselves renounced the first offices of the republic. They
felt that political equality did not exclude a certain degree
of subordination: they acknowledged the power of capital,
by which they lived; of knowledge, which discovered
outlets for the productions of their industry; and they
were disposed to obey the rich merchants who employed
them. Accustomed by the habits of private life to trust
to the intelligence of their superiors for their most important interests,—for those which most constantly occupied their minds,—they regarded them as still more
proper to decide on political questions, which sometimes
excite the passions of the people, but seldom lead them
to prudent counsel. It is from time to time only that
society, even in the freest states, is universally agitated
by some abstract question, which makes the deeper im-
pression the less it is understood: experience comes afterwards to disabuse people of an exaggerated or unreason-
able expectation. Thus, false ideas of equality made the
Florentines first demand that every citizen should have
an equal share in the government: after they had experienced the violences and depredations caused by the
anarchy of the Ciompi, they unhappily forgot the advantages of true equality. They did not sufficiently seek to
procure to all equal protection and equal justice, to
awaken in all that interest in public affairs which should
excite the developement of their faculties. The flame
which burnt too fiercely in 1378 had consumed the
materials which should have nourished it; and, fifty
years later, the Florentine people no longer evinced any

o

jealousy of those who, by their position, seemed naturally destined to rule them.

General ideas exercise a durable influence only on minds capable of comprehending them. Let liberty exist for all; but let power remain with those who comprehend its objects,—with those who can distinguish the means by which to attain them,—with those who are too proud to acknowledge masters, and too generous to desire subjects,—with those who, anxious for the intellectual progress and for the material well-being of their kind, would give up all their time and attention to obtain both,—with those who, enjoying the advantages of a liberal education, have minds neither irritated by jealousy, narrowed by prejudice, nor disturbed by chimerical apprehensions. Let all, however, have some share in political power; such a share as may be necessary to preserve them from oppression,—to raise their minds and feelings in emergency above material interests,—to divest them of selfishness, that they may, when called upon, comprehend the great questions of morality: but let them participate in this political power as citizens, not as magistrates.

The number of republics had so much diminished in Italy, that the lower orders ran a far greater risk of being corrupted by the example of servility, than by that of the excesses of democracy. In the kingdom of Naples, in Romagna, and Lombardy, those orders remained without protection, exposed to the outrages of the soldier and the oppression of the fiscal officer. Nevertheless, with the exception of the calamities inflicted by the passage of companies of adventure, the burden imposed on them was subject to rules of equal distribution: they were unacquainted with the personal vexations, the domestic oppression, which the nobles inflicted on the plebeians in the west of Europe. Accordingly, in spite of frequent calamities, and of a great diminution of productive energy, Italy, which had ceased to be free, had not ceased to be prosperous. In Lombardy, especially, agriculture and husbandry being well understood, the natural fertility of the soil was turned to the most profitable account; while innumerable manufactures and extensive commerce animated and enriched the towns.

After the kingdom of Naples and the duchy of Milan, the republic of Venice was, in power, the third state of Italy. The people of Venice were deprived, almost as much as those of Milan, of all participation in political power. Their suffrages were never demanded, their voice was never heard; they never thought even of questioning the wisdom of their government. But the senate, far wiser in its administration than the tyrants of Lombardy, never allowed their subjects to bear any other burdens than those imposed by itself; and those were always moderate, always equally distributed, in a spirit of justice. All that the Venetians paid the state was employed scrupulously, and with economy, either for the common defence, or for the ornament of their country. The government cost the people nothing. The people, themselves, looked with pride upon the employment of their money in the public works. The provinces of the Terra Firma were carefully secured from the vexations of the soldier, and as much as possible from the invasion of the enemy. The city of Venice from the period of its foundation had never been invaded,—had never seen the Rialto soiled by the feet of foreign armies,—had never suffered even the temporary domination of a tyrant. The riches of commerce and industry, fostered by such constant security, had grown beyond all precedent. The provinces of the Terra Firma, forgetting all pretension to independence, found themselves happy by comparison with their neighbours. The peasantry, in particular, were ready to give their lives for St. Mark:—it was thus they always designated the state. The only possessions of the republic that had reason to complain were those of the Levant: there the Venetian merchants sacrificed their industry to the narrow spirit of monopoly.

The republic of Florence was the fourth state of Italy in wealth and importance. More generous than Venice, it had more frequently endangered itself by wars, which exposed it often to invasion. Less prudent in its internal administration, it had more than once experienced the convulsions of contending factions, and sometimes even those of temporary tyranny. On the other side, the Florentines owed to the nature of their government a degree of energy, activity, and intelligence which put them in a state to repair their losses much more rapidly. They had in their city manufactures renowned through the western world, particularly that of woollen stuffs, which occupied more hands than any other, and those of silk and gold brocade. Their merchants were the greatest capitalists of Europe; their counting-houses were scattered throughout the commercial parts of the world; and their funds were often lent to princes at enormous interest. The territory of the Florentines was enriched by the most industrious agriculture. In it was concentrated, on a given space, the most labour and the largest capital. The citizens submitted of their own accord to heavy imposts; but the peasantry were treated with more consideration. A moderate and equable partition of the taxes was sought to be maintained; and it was in this view that the Florentines, in 1429, invented the *catasto*,—an enumeration and description of property of every kind, with an estimate of its value, to serve as a basis to taxes always imposed in due proportion. The subjects of Florence must have found themselves at least as happy as those of Venice: but the memory of liberty and independence was more recent; and Pisa, Pistoia, Arezzo, Volterra, and even less important towns, made repeated efforts to recover their liberty. Not one town could yet resign itself to be subject to the Florentines. Within the circle of Tuscany, too, Lucca, which did not lose its liberty from the time of Paulo Guinigi until our day, and Sienna, which preserved hers till 1555, seemed to invite these cities to govern themselves as independent republics. In the two above mentioned, however, the democratic fermentation which had agitated all free states during the latter half of the fourteenth century began to subside, and the government had returned to the hands of those who were fitted for it by their education and talents.

The democratic party at Florence, directed by the Alberti, Ricci, and Medici, were deprived of power in 1381, in consequence of the abuse which their associates, the Ciompi, had made of their victory. From that time their rivals, the Albizzi, directed the republic for the space of fifty-three years, from 1381 to 1434, with a happiness and glory till then unexampled. No triumph

of an aristocratic faction ever merited a more brilliant
place in history. The one in question maintained itself
by the ascendency of its talents 'and virtues, without
ever interfering with the rights of the other citizens, or
abusing a preponderance which was all in opinion. It
was the most prosperous epoch of the republic,—that
during which its opulence acquired the greatest developement,—that in which the arts, sciences, and literature
adopted Florence as their native country,—that in which
were born and formed all those great men, of whom the
Medici, their contemporaries, have reaped the glory,
without having had any share in producing them,—that,
finally, in which the republic most constantly followed
the noblest policy : considering itself as the guardian of
the liberty of Italy, it in turns set limits to the ambition
of Gian Galeazzo Visconti ; of Ladislaus, king of Naples ;
and of Filippo Maria, duke of Milan. Tomaso degli
Albizzi, and after him Nicolo da Uzzano, had been the
chiefs of the aristocracy at this period of glory and wisdom.
To those succeeded Rinaldo, son of Tomaso degli Albizzi ;
who forgot, a little more than his predecessors, that he
was only a simple citizen. Impetuous, arrogant, jealous,
impatient of all opposition, he lost the pre-eminence
which his family had so long maintained.

Rinaldo degli Albizzi saw, with uneasiness, a rival
present himself in Cosmo, son of Giovanni de' Medici,
who revived a party formerly the vanquishers of his
ancestors. This man enjoyed an hereditary popularity
at Florence ; because he was descended from one of the
demagogues who, in 1378, had undertaken the defence of
the minor arts against the aristocracy : he, at the same
time, excited the jealousy of the latter by his immense
wealth, which equalled that of the greatest princes of
Italy. Although the Albizzi saw with distrust the family
of their rivals attain the supreme magistracy, they could
not exclude from it Giovanni de' Medici, who was
gonfalonier in 1421. His son Cosmo, born in 1389, was
priore in 1416 : he was the head of a commercial establishment which had counting-houses in all the great cities of
Europe, and in the Levant : he, at the same time, cultivated literature with ardour. His palace, one of the
most sumptuous in Florence, was the resort of artists,

poets, and learned men; of those, among others, who about this time introduced the Platonic philosophy into Italy. The opulence of Cosmo de' Medici was always at the service of his friends. There were very few poor citizens at Florence to whom his purse was not open.

Cosmo de' Medici had no thought of reviving the doctrine of his ancestors, respecting the right of the lowest order of citizens to enter the magistracy. He expressed no democratic opinions, although he severely criticised the government and its measures, whilst under the direction of Rinaldo degli Albizzi. He wished to have seen adopted other alliances and another policy. He asserted that, since the death of Nicolo da Uzzano, in 1427, the security of the state had been endangered by imprudent wars, and the finances dilapidated by the robbery of the commissaries, particularly in the expedition against Lucca. Constant opposition and accusation at last so provoked Rinaldo, whose character was impetuous and violent, that he determined on proceeding against Cosmo as a state criminal. In the month of September, 1433, a signoria, drawn by lot, was found to be composed of the most devoted creatures of the Albizzi. Bernardo Guadagni presided at it as gonfalonier. On the 7th of September, he summoned Cosmo de' Medici to present himself at the palace, and render an account of his conduct; and, on his arrival there, committed him prisoner to the tower of the clock. The people were immediately called to a parliament by the tolling of the great bell. The Florentines had preserved, from the first period of their republic, the custom of these parliaments, in which the whole population assembled in the public square. Without its being necessary to make those present prove that they were citizens, and without securing any guarantee to the feeble against the powerful, they voted by acclamation on what was proposed by the signoria. In consequence of the sovereignty of the people, the parliament was regarded as superior to all law, to the constitution itself, and even to justice; when warned of some great national danger which justified revolutionary measures, it was supposed to be invested with the whole power of the state, to be raised above all rule: but experience proved that the parliament always sanctioned every revolution, and that the sovereignty of the people lent its name to every act of tyranny. As such a parliament could not deliberate, it was required to transmit its power to a *balia*, or commission, which it invested with all the rights possessed by the Florentine people themselves. Rinaldo degli Albizzi presented a list of the names of those of whom he wished the balia to be composed; about two hundred in number. The balia obtained the purses from which were to be drawn the names of the magistrates. They excluded whom they pleased; they entered new names; they condemned to exile Cosmo de' Medici and his friends. Albizzi had reckoned on Cosmo's being executed: he accused Bernardo Guadagni of having received money from his enemy to spare him; and regarded as a defeat the incomplete vengeance which he had just wreaked.

The event justified his fears. Precisely a year afterwards, in the month of September, 1434, a new signoria was drawn, with Nicolo Donati president, and entirely favourable to Cosmo de' Medici. The balia, notwithstanding its partiality, had not dared to exclude from the magistracy all the eminent men attached to that great citizen. Donati, in his turn, summoned to the palace, Rinaldo degli Albizzi and his friends; who, instead of obeying, endeavoured to defend themselves: but the same people who had voted for them in the last parliament, so far from taking arms at their call, appeared at a new one convoked by Donati,—where they showed the same docility,—where they approved in the same manner by their acclamation another balia presented by the gonfalonier: and this was no sooner constituted, than Cosmo de' Medici, with all his friends, were recalled; and Rinaldo Albizzi, with all his party, exiled.

Albizzi sought an asylum with Filippo Maria, duke of Milan, on whom, as long as he had directed the republic, he had always made war. Forgetting the danger which he had often foretold to liberty in the aggrandisement of the Visconti, and believing, like all exiles, that his country could never submit to be without him, but would rise in his favour on his approach, he pressed Filippo to make war on Florence. The war actually broke out in the same year. Nicolo Piccinino, the successor of Braccio, whom the duke of Milan had placed at the head of his armies, repeatedly penetrated into Tuscany: but the presence of Albizzi, who accompanied him, produced no effect. Francesco Sforza was opposed, on the side of the Florentines, to Piccinino. Sforza had formed an intimate friendship with Cosmo de' Medici; he had often in his need had recourse to the purse of the rich banker; and he already laboured to rise from the rank of condottiere to that of sovereign. In 1443, he had made the pope, Eugenius IV., cede to him the March of Ancona, in recompence for his services against the pope's subjects; and he purposed, in making himself feared by Filippo Maria, to obtain in marriage his only but illegitimate daughter, who would bring him in dower at least some fragments of the duchy of Milan.

During the remainder of the reign of Filippo Maria, he was habitually at war with the two republics of Venice and Florence. He was desirous of recovering from the former the Brescian and Bergamasque territory, which he had been forced to cede to the Venetians; and he resumed against the Florentines the project of his ancestors, to extend the dominion of the Viscontis over Tuscany. Francesco Sforza and Bartolomeo Coleoni gave many proofs of their great talents in the service of the two republics. Nicolo Piccinino and his two sons, Francesco and Jacomo, showed not less ability in the service of the duke of Milan. The last named, however, almost always lost ground by his distrust of his own generals, his versatility, his taste for contradictory intrigues, his eagerness to sign peace every year, and to recommence hostilities a few weeks afterwards. The history of this war is rendered so confused by the secret practices of Filippo Maria, which most commonly seemed in opposition to his own interest, that we do not attempt to fix it in the memory. The duke of Milan, in making peace with the two republics, on the 21st of October, 1441, granted their general, Francesco Sforza, his daughter Bianca in marriage, ceding with her in dower the lordships of Cremona and Pontremoli. It seemed to be his purpose thus definitively to reconcile himself with Sforza : but it was impossible for this prince to remain firm in one resolution, or to preserve his confidence in those

whom he had rendered powerful.   He soon entered into
the most complicated intrigues to deprive his son-in-law
of all his lordships.   The war was renewed between him
and the two republics; and Sforza was again the general
whom the republics put at the head of their combined
army.   He was still their commander in 1447, when
Filippo Maria, pressed by the Venetians, menaced even
in the country around Milan, and fearing to lose his
sovereignty, implored the aid of his son-in-law, promising
him a sincere reconciliation.   Francesco Sforza, who had
just lost the March of Ancona by the secret practices of
the duke of Milan, yet accepted these last offers.   He
renounced his ancient alliance with the Florentines and
Venetians; and, on the 9th of August, he set forward
with his army from Romagna, where he then was, to the
succour of his father-in-law.   Arrived at Cotignola, the
village of his family,—the village in which his father,
after having thrown his pickaxe into the branches of an
oak, to be decided either by its ominous fall, or by its
remaining fixed, had seized the sword to engage in a
company of adventure,—he there learned the death of
the duke of Milan, which had taken place at his capital,
on the 13th of August, 1447.

The war of Lombardy was complicated by its connection with another war which at the same time ravaged
the kingdom of Naples.   The queen, Joan II., had died
there, on the 2nd of February, 1345; three months after
the death of her adopted son, Louis III. of Anjou: by
her will she had substituted for that prince his brother
René, duke of Lorraine.   But Alphonso, king of Aragon
and Sicily, whom she had primarily adopted, and who
had advanced as far as Ischia, the more effectually to
observe the events which might occur at Naples, claimed
the succession, on the ground of this first adoption, as
well as of the ancient rights of Manfred, to whom he had
succeeded in the female line.   The kingdom of Naples
was divided between the parties of Aragon and Anjou.
The Genoese, who had voluntarily ranged themselves
under the protection of the duke of Milan, offered their
assistance to the duke of Anjou; their ancient enmity to
the Catalonians and Aragonese being further quickened
by commercial jealousies.   On the 5th of August, 1435,

their fleet met that of Alphonso, before the island of Ponza. They defeated it in a great battle; in which Alphonso had been made prisoner, with his brother, and all the first nobles of his kingdom. These prisoners were conducted to Milan, and there in a little time set at liberty, by an unexpected generosity of Filippo Maria; whom Alphonso had made sensible how much the subjection of the kingdom of Naples tó the French would endanger the independence of the duchy of Milan, as well as of all Italy. Visconti contracted not only a close alliance with his prisoner, whom he liberated, but promised to aid him in ascending the throne of Naples. This alliance, however, cost him the lordship of Genoa; for the Genoese, indignant at seeing the fruits of their victory carried off by the prince whom they had chosen, rose on the 27th of December, 1435, drove out the Milanese garrison, and recovered their freedom. Alphonso, seconded by the duke of Milan, recommenced the war against René of Anjou with greater advantage. On the 2nd of June, 1442, he took from him the city of Naples: from that time peace was re-established in that kingdom, and Alphonso signalised himself by a liberality which gained for him the surname of "the Magnanimous." No monarch ever showed more zeal in literature, or granted a more constant and more enlightened protection to men of letters. He proved, by many noble actions, that he had profited by the lessons of antiquity which he admired and studied with so much ardour. He established himself amidst a people which he had conquered, but whose hearts he gained; and returned no more either to Sicily or Aragon. He died at Naples, on the 27th of June, 1458.

Filippo Maria Visconti, at his death, left no legitimate successor: the distant relatives who bore his name were not descended from the princes his ancestors, who had usurped the seigniory of Milan; and they had not been even thought of in the imperial bull which had instituted the Milanese duchy in favour of Gian Galeazzo. This bull had expressly excluded women from the succession; who had, besides, never inherited any Italian seigniory. Accordingly, Valentina Visconti, sister to the last duke, and married to the duke of Orleans, and Bianca Visconti, the natural daughter of Filippo Maria, married to Francesco Sforza, had neither of them any right to succeed to the last duke. Upon the extinction of the male line of Visconti, on whom the republic of Milan had conferred the seigniory, the sovereignty legitimately returned to the republic itself, which claimed its restoration. Four illustrious citizens, Antonio Trivulzio, Teodoro Bossi, Giorgio Lampugnani, and Innocenzio Cotta, on the 14th of August, 1447, excited the people to insurrection; and, with their support, reconstituted the Milanese republic. They, at the same time, engaged all the captains of adventure and men at arms who had been in the service of the duke of Milan to declare for them. The most illustrious among these were the two brothers Piccinino, sons of Nicolo, who had died on the 15th of October, 1444; the three brothers San Severino, natural children of a princely house at Naples; but, above all, Francesco Sforza, who, with his brilliant army, entered the service of the republic, upon condition that the republic should confirm the cession of Cremona, which his wife had brought to him in dower, and add to it the seigniories of Brescia and Verona, if Sforza succeeded in taking either or both those towns from the Venetians.

An excellent opportunity then presented itself of restoring to Italy liberty and independence. In the country most exposed to the invasion of the transalpine nations there were three rich and powerful republics— Milan, Venice, and Florence,—supported on one side by the warlike republics of Switzerland; on the other, by the more feeble ones of Genoa, Lucca, Sienna, and Bologna. An equitable alliance between them would have sufficed to secure Italy for ever from the barbarians who menaced it on the side of France and Germany. The opulence of these three republics, their numerous population, and the devotion with which the citizens of free states always concur, with their whole power, in the defence of their country, would have been sufficient to render vain every foreign attack. Unhappily, the two men at the head of the republics of Florence and Venice considered only a present and sordid advantage; they had not the elevation of soul to prefer the future liberty of Italy; and they refused to admit the republic of Milan into a confraternity so desirable for the three states.

Francesco Foscari, who was doge of Venice from 1423 to 1457, had communicated to the republic, of which he was the chief, his own warlike ambition. He had made it achieve the conquest of the Brescian and Bergamasque territory. He judged the opportunity favourable to detach new provinces from the duchy of Milan, or perhaps to subjugate the whole; and he rejected all the advances of the Milanese republic, which ardently desired peace. Cosmo de' Medici, at Florence, also, so far from having, like the preceding chiefs of that republic, a true love of liberty, began to aspire to become the prince of a country in which he had risen as head of the democratic party. He was so superior to his former associates, in wealth, in the number of dependants, in the deference shown him by foreign powers; he was likewise so elated by the flattery of all the most distinguished men of letters; that he believed himself formed to govern without opposition, and without a rival. Almost all the Italian republics had successively submitted to the influence of some family, which had raised itself above every other. The turn of Florence seemed at last come; Cosmo was determined the Medici should take the same rank there which the Bentivogli held at Bologna. He had himself contributed to retain that republic, the ally of Florence, under the domineering power of an usurping family. When Annibal Bentivoglio fell, on the 24th of June, 1445, by the hand of assassins, armed by the pope and the duke of Milan, Cosmo de' Medici supplied the Bolognese with another Bentivoglio, by disclosing an affair of gallantry which one of that name had with a Florentine lady of burgher family. The fruit of that intrigue was a son, named Santi Cascese, whom Cosmo de' Medici caused to be received as the head of the Bolognese republic. The moment was, in fact, come when the credit of the Medici was to prevail over the legal power of the Florentine signoria; and in which they might, like the Bentivogli, transmit their usurped power, not only to their legitimate children, but to their spurious descendants. Cosmo felt no kind of sympathy for the newly forming republic at Milan, which vainly endeavoured to awaken in Italy the

ancient enthusiasm for liberty: he was jealous, too, of
the republic of Venice, which appeared to him to aspire
to the dominion of the whole peninsula. By way of
counterpoise, he promised Francesco Sforza his support
to mount the throne which had been filled by the duke of
Milan.

Francesco Sforza, who had evinced talents for war
superior to those of the most distinguished captains of
the age, possessed, at the same time, the frankness and
the liberality which military habits produce. He was
considered a man eminently true and generous; his
friends felt devotion to him, his soldiers enthusiasm.   But
it is not in the trade of captains of adventure that men
can be formed to true honour. Francesco Sforza showed
himself, more than once, perfidious even to his own
lieutenants; some of whom he put to death with great
cruelty, for having only excited his suspicion. But what,
above all, revealed his character, and, at the same time,
his cleverness, was the address with which he, in turn,
deceived the two republics which trusted him; rendering
their subsidies and soldiers subservient to his own elevation, and betraying them, one after the other, when he
had gained his object. It was thus he won at once the
admiration of his friend and disciple, Louis XI., and lost
the esteem of all honourable men.

The duke of Orleans, in the name of his mother,
Valentina Visconti, advanced pretensions to the duchy of
Milan; and caused it to be attacked by French troops on
the side of Asti. Sforza, not to commit himself with
France, left the care of repelling them to Bartolomeo
Coleoni, who served the Milanese, but not under the
command of Sforza. Sforza, himself, in the mean while,
on the 16th of November, 1447, took by assault Placentia,
then the second city of Lombardy, and pillaged it with a
barbarity from which it never recovered. He also employed himself in exasperating the dissension which
began to manifest itself in the Milanese council. Trivulzio
was a Guelph, Bossi and Lampugnani were Ghibelines;
and the hereditary hatred between their families en-
venomed their mutual jealousy. Trivulzio engaged the
Venetians to offer peace to the republic of Milan, on
condition of ceding to them Crema and the Ghiara d'Adda.

The Ghibelines, excited by Sforza, refused to accede to the treaty, and caused it to be rejected by the council of 800 : he, at the same time, strengthened their confidence by his victories. In the month of May, 1448, he took from the Venetians all they had conquered on the right of the Adda. On the 17th of July, he burnt their fleet on the Po, near Casal Maggiore ; and, on the 15th of September, he gained a great and last victory over them at Caravaggio, where he made nearly their whole army prisoners of war.

Sforza, after these victories, thought the Venetians sufficiently subdued to prevent them from attempting to conquer a state which offered such vigorous resistance. He feared likewise that the Milanese might be too much elated to submit to him. He therefore released all the Venetian prisoners taken by him at Caravaggio ; and on the 18th of October, 1448, signed a treaty with the Venetians, by which he guaranteed to them Brescia and Bergamo, and ceded Crema and the Ghiara d'Adda, on condition that they should aid him in making the conquest of the duchy of Milan, with all the territory attached to it under Filippo Maria. The Milanese, indignant at this treachery, soon perceived the extremity of their danger. Several of the condottieri in their pay, imagining they might derive greater advantages from an ambitious usurper than from a republic, preferred following the fortune of a captain so able and so fortunate as Sforza. Among the subject cities, also, there were many that, despairing of setting themselves free, desired, at least, that Milan, of which they were jealous, should, like them, be subject to a master. Placentia was the first to yield to Sforza ; Abbiate-Grasso, Varese, Tortona, Alexandria, soon after successively opened their gates to him. Pavia had submitted to him in the preceding year, while he was still in the service of the Milanese. In the month of February, 1449, he took possession of Parma ; in the September following, of Lodi and Crema. The Milanese, however, though so hardly pressed, were not wanting to themselves. They obtained some succour from the duke of Savoy ; and the richest citizens placing their whole fortunes at the service of the state, it was enabled to supply its militia with firelocks, then a recent invention, and a costly arm, but inspiring the cavalry with great terror.

The republic of Venice perceived at last, but too late, that its own interests, and the independence of Italy, equally demanded of them to save the republic of Milan. On the 27th of September, 1449, they signed a treaty with the Milanese, by which they acknowledged the new republic, and assigned as limits to it the Adda, the Tessin, the Po, and the Swiss Alps: at the same time, they abandoned to Sforza seven of the largest cities of Lombardy, with their fertile provinces. Sforza believed himself too near attaining his object to renounce it: he, however, sent his brother to Venice to declare his acceptance of the treaty; and, in conformity with the orders which he had received, he removed his army from Milan. The events occurred in the sowing season; and he was desirous of inspiring the Milanese with confidence, to finish the sowing of their land, and thus consume the greater part of their grain. As soon as this operation was over, he hastily recalled his army; he stopped the supplies of provisions, which the Milanese sent for in every direction; and he renewed hostilities. The Venetians attempted to succour Milan; but he defeated them, on the 28th of December. The famine which he produced soon became extreme: the people, incapable of supporting it, rose on the 25th of February, 1450; and, on the 26th, they opened the gates to Francesco Sforza, proclaiming him duke of Milan. The Venetians still attempted, for some years after, to dispute his newly acquired greatness: in this view, they made alliance with Alphonso, king of Naples, and the duke of Savoy. But Cosmo de' Medici, who became daily more powerful at Florence, and who substituted private affection for the generous and ancient love of liberty, drew closer his alliance with Sforza, and sent him aid. Meanwhile, the taking of Constantinople by the Turks, on the 29th of May, 1453, spread terror throughout Christendom. The Italians began to feel the necessity of re-establishing peace among themselves, for the sake of their common defence against barbarians: and a treaty was accordingly signed at Lodi, on the 9th of April, 1454. Bergamo and Brescia, with the territory thereunto belonging, fell to the Venetians; but to Fran-

cesco Sforza was secured the duchy of Milan, in which
Crema and the Ghiara d'Adda were comprehended.

The consent of the emperor was wanting to legitimatise
the title of duke of Milan to Francesco Sforza. But
Frederick III. of Austria, who reigned since the 2nd of
February, 1440, positively refused to acknowledge him.
The new duke, however, felt not the least uneasiness : he
despised Frederick as a weak and indolent prince, incapable either of defending Germany or his hereditary states;
and who thought of Italy only as a fair, in which to sell
at auction titles, dignitaries, and investitures to the
vanity of the great.   In 1432, Sigismond had sold the
title of marquis of Mantua to Giovanni Francesco da
Gonzaga, for 12,000 florins ; on the 15th of May, 1452,
Frederick III. sold, at a higher price, the title of duke
of Modena and Reggio to Borso d'Este. This family
did not obtain from pope Paul II. till nineteen years
later the title of duchy for the seigniory of Ferrara,
which they held from the church.   Sigismond, and after
him Frederick, sold, with the utmost effrontery, the titles
of counts, barons, knights, imperial notaries, and the
legitimatising of bastards, to all who would purchase
them ; and Francesco Sforza, believing himself sure of
obtaining a vain diploma whenever he asked for one,
did not esteem it worth the price.

Almost at the same time that the last attempt of the
Lombards to recover their liberty failed at Milan, the last
attempt of a Roman citizen to restore liberty to Rome
was punished with death by pope Nicholas V.   The
liberties of Rome, as well as those of all the states of the
church, had been lost, without the possibility of marking the exact moment of their destruction.   The senator
and caporioni, or bannerets of Rome, had long administered
the government of the republic, without having the
limits of their authority, and of that of the pope, the
first citizen of the state, properly defined.   The former,
in the oaths taken on entering office, instead of swearing
obedience to the pope, promised him protection : they
swore not to allow any one to touch his life or limb, or
to infringe his liberty.   These magistrates, as well as
those of the other states of the church, were always
elected by the people.   The church was regarded as the

protector of popular liberty ; and, when a city returned
under its sovereignty, it always considered that it had
recovered freedom. The pope, however, often made the
people transfer to him the right of naming the senator of
Rome, or the rectors of the other cities of the church.
During the long residence of the popes at Avignon, the
court of Rome had forgotten its ancient principles of
liberty : its legates had assumed absolute power. The
anarchy of Rome, the outrages committed by the nobles,
the tyranny of several usurpers, had accustomed the
people to the loss of liberty. They had frequently
sought refuge, from a tyranny more cruel, in the absolute
power of the prelates. Perugia, Bologna, and other cities,
had often conferred the signoria on the legate, or the
Roman people on the pope, with the suspension of all
the rights of the citizen. The great western schism again
shook the power of the pontiffs in the states of the
church, a few years after they had been conquered by
the cardinal Albornoz. The popes, unacknowledged by
one half of the church, impoverished, and endangered,
lived, nearly the whole duration of the schism, exiled
from Rome, and most frequently dependent on the
sovereign lord of Rimini. Martin V., who was elected
at the conclusion of the schism by the council of Constance, did not immediately recover the obedience of the
Roman states : he passed the greatest part of his pontificate at Florence. Eugenius IV., who succeeded him
on the 3rd of May, 1431, again lost, in consequence of
his turbulent, ambitious, and despotic character, several
of the states that Martin V. had recovered. His prime
minister, the patriarch Vitelleschi, stained his reign with
numerous acts of cruelty and perfidy : not one of the
liberties of Rome, or of the states of the church, were
any longer respected.

Nicholas V., who succeeded Eugenius IV. on the 6th
of May, 1447, was known at Florence under the name of
Tomaso da Sarzana. He had been preceptor to Rinaldo
degli Albizzi, and afterwards the daily guest of Cosmo de'
Medici. His knowledge in ancient literature, and in
the fine arts, and philosophy, caused him to be ranked
among the most distinguished members of the society
that assembled at the house of that illustrious citizen.

But the studies of Tomaso da Sarzana had not destroyed the servile habits of his mind and education. Grammarians, poets, and rhetoricians were, in this century, too much accustomed to regard themselves as clients or dependents on the rich and great; to live by their bounty, and at their table; to receive from their mouths the word of command for their opinions and sentiments. Tomaso da Sarzana could not learn, in the palace of Cosmo de' Medici, to love or respect a liberty which his patron was secretly undermining, and of which he was labouring to deprive his country. After he had obtained the pontificate, he showed the same zeal for the progress of ancient learning, for collections of manuscripts, for translations of Greek works, for the restoration of the monuments of antiquity, and for the encouragement of comtemporary artists, that had distinguished him in a more humble career. But Nicholas V. rejected impatiently all opposition, all control of his will : he determined on seeing in the Romans only submissive subjects, to whom he denied all participation in the government. Stefano Porcari, a Roman noble, willing to profit by the interregnum which preceded the nomination of Nicholas V., to make the Roman citizens demand the renewal and confirmation of their ancient rights and privileges, was denounced to the new pope as a dangerous person; and, so far from obtaining what he had hoped, he had the grief to see the citizens always more strictly excluded from any participation in public affairs. Those were entrusted only to prelates, who, being prepared for it neither by their studies nor sentiments, suffered the administration to fall into the most shameful disorder.

In an insurrection of the people in the Piazza Navona, arising from a quarrel which began at a bull-fight, Stefano Porcari endeavoured to direct their attention to a more noble object, and turn this tumult to the advantage of liberty. The pope hastily indulged all the fancies of the people, with respect to their games or amusements ; but firmly rejected all their serious demands, and exiled Porcari to Bologna. The latter hoped to obtain by conspiracy what he had failed to accomplish by insurrection. There were not less than 400 exiled Roman citizens : he persuaded them all to join him, and appointed them a rendezvous at Rome, for the 5th of January, 1453, in the house of his brother-in-law. Having escaped the vigilance of the legate of Bologna, he proceeded there himself, accompanied by 300 soldiers, whom he had enlisted in his service. The whole band was assembled on the night of the appointed 5th of January; and Stefano Porcari was haranguing them, to prepare them for the attack of the capitol,—in which he reckoned on re-establishing the senate of the Roman republic,—when, his secret having been betrayed, the house was surrounded with troops, the doors suddenly forced, and the conspirators overcome by numbers before their arms had been distributed. Next morning, the body of Stefano Porcari, with those of nine of his associates, were seen hanging from the battlements of the castle of St. Angelo. In spite of their ardent entreaties, they had been denied confession and the sacrament. Eight days later, the executions, after a mockery of law proceedings, were renewed, and continued in great numbers. The pope succeeded in causing those who had taken refuge in neighbouring states to be delivered up to him; and thus the last spark of Roman liberty was extinguished in blood.

CHAPTER XI

ITALY LOSES THE GREAT MEN WHO GAVE LUSTRE TO THE PRECEDING PERIOD—THE REPUBLIC OF FLORENCE ENSLAVED BY THE MEDICI —WAR OF THE VENETIANS AGAINST THE TURKS—CONQUEST OF CYPRUS

THE generation which witnessed the taking of Constantinople by the Turks, was absorbed by the danger with which this terrible calamity menaced Italy. That country saw on its confines the dominion of the Turks: the banner of the crescent floated over the whole eastern coast of the Adriatic; from the extremity of the Morea to the rugged mountains of Bosnia. Italy was alarmed every year by the conquest and destruction of some Christian kingdom, or by the taking and sacking of some flourishing city. It became filled with emigrants, from the palaces or convents of the whole eastern world. These emigrants were still full of the recollections of a civilisation not inferior to that of Italy herself. They felt the same ardour for ancient literature and science; they were equally habituated to the luxuries and charms of life; while, at the same time, they had escaped from scenes of desolation, massacre, and martyrdom, which their imagination vividly retraced as being about to be repeated in the country which gave them hospitality. On this plea, they implored pity and aid from those to whom they exposed their wretchedness; and their benefactors themselves felt that the hour of Italy was near when the knell of Greece had tolled.

The Turks arrived in Europe with an organisation wholly military, that seemed to ensure them a continuation of new conquests. Still intoxicated with the religious fanaticism of their prophet, which had been revived by communicating it to a new nation and monarchy, they believed that they secured their salvation by the destruction of infidels. Always aggressors, they marched to battle to gain heaven rather than the riches of the earth. The Turkish horseman was unequalled in the use of his scimitar, and in the precision with which he managed his horse; which, running at full speed, stopped, turned, and returned, with a docility which the Latin cavalry could never attain. The new militia of the janissaries was, at the same time, the best infantry in Europe; the most steady and the most intrepid; the only disciplined force at a period when there were no troops of the line in the west. Finally, the artillery of the Turks was more numerous, and better served, than that of the western nations. Industry was not annihilated in the countries which they had conquered: they knew how to profit by the arts which had been carried to perfection in those countries; and thus united the knowledge of civilised people with the courage of barbarians. The report soon spread at Rome, that the same Mahomet who had conquered Constantinople, had vowed to enter also as conqueror the ancient capital of the world, in order to destroy there what he called the idolatry of the Christians.

The fears of Italy were augmented by the conscious-
ness of the want of great leaders.   During the first
quarter of the century after the taking of Constantinople,
all those who had directed with so much glory the
powerful states of that country had disappeared, one
after the other, without being any where replaced by
successors worthy of them.   No great name any longer
inspired confidence; no great character undertook the
direction of government; no generous sentiment animated the people, who passed alternately from fear to
languor; and the country, which had till then presented a scene glowing with so much life, exhibits a continual conflict of selfish interests, to the entire exclusion
of every nobler passion.

The first among the eminent men who quitted the
scene in Italy was the old doge, Francesco Foscari.
He had directed the republic of Venice for the space of
thirty-four years; and, by communicating his ambition
to his fellow-citizens, had excited them to the conquest
of a part of Lombardy.   The council of ten did not,
it appears, pardon Foscari an influence and glory which
had changed the spirit of the republic, and had drawn
it into the whirlpool of Italian politics, of which till then
it had kept clear.   The jealous aristocracy of Venice
could not endure that the chief of the state should
acquire the respect and affection of the people; he was
made to expiate by domestic grief the lustre attached
to his name.   Jacopo Foscari, the son of the doge, was
accused, in 1445, of having received money from the
duke of Milan.   The informer was a Florentine exile
of bad repute: nevertheless, as it was the rule of Venice
to act upon every suspicion, however slight, in matters
concerning the safety of the state, the son of the doge
was put to the torture.   His sufferings forced from him
an avowal; and he was condemned to exile.   A confession thus extorted leaves the guilt of the accused
uncertain, while the barbarous means by which such
evidence is obtained places beyond doubt the criminality
of the judges.   Jacopo Foscari was, probably, as guiltless
on this occasion as he was five years later, when he was
again tortured and condemned.   One of the judges who
presided at his first trial was assassinated in 1450, and

it was suspected that the murderer was an emissary of
Jacopo. Jacopo was accordingly declared guilty, and
the period of his exile prolonged. His innocence, however, was soon afterwards proved, the assassination having
been acknowledged by another person, who declared that
Jacopo had no share in the murder. On receiving the
news of this disclosure, the son of the doge, in exile
at Canea, entreated his judges to allow him to return
to Venice. He preserved for a country, where he had
twice been put to the torture, and twice branded with
infamy, the passionate attachment so characteristic of the
Venetians. He had only one wish, one hope,—that of
carrying back to Venice his bones broken by the executioner, and dying beside his aged father, his mother, his
wife, and children, on the spot which had given him
birth. Unable to soften his judges, he wrote to beg
the duke of Milan to intercede for him : the letter was
intercepted, and transferred to the council of ten. He
declared, that this was what he expected ; that he wished
to awaken fresh suspicion, as the only means of being
restored to home. He was brought back to Venice, as he
desired. His third criminal prosecution began, like the
two others, with torture ; and it was at this terrible price
that he purchased the happiness of once more embracing
his parents, wife, and children. He was again sent back
to die at Canea. Fifteen months afterwards, on the
23rd of October, 1457, his father was deposed from his
functions of doge, on the ground of incapacity from
extreme age. The old man died while listening to the
tolling of the bell for the inauguration of his successor.
No one who succeeded to the ducal throne ever ventured,
from that time, to provoke the jealousy of the aristocracy.

The next great man whom Italy lost, after the doge
Foscari, was Alphonso of Aragon, king of Naples : he
died on the 27th of June, 1458, in the sixty-fourth year
of his age. He had constantly inhabited Italy, or the
adjoining isles, since the year 1420, when he was adopted
by queen Joan II., and became completely Italian. He
proved it by his zeal for reviving literature ; by the protection which he granted to men of letters ; by his
admiration of the ancients. He deserved the title of
Magnanimous, which had been given him by his people.

No sovereign of Naples had been so much beloved, or had done so much good to that fine country. Alphonso left to his brother John, king of Navarre, his kingdoms of Aragon, Valencia, Catalonia, Sardinia, the Balearic Isles, and Sicily. But he regarded the kingdom of Naples, which he had conquered, as belonging immediately to himself; and he left it to Ferdinand, the offspring of his love. The queen, wife of Alphonso, believed that this son was born of Marguerite de Hijar; and put her to death by smothering. The victim was said to have sacrificed her reputation to save that of a more illustrious person. Alphonso never forgave his wife this atrocity; he did not punish her, but he bade her an eternal adieu. He sent her back to Spain, whither he vowed never to return. He legitimatised Ferdinand and caused him to be acknowledged his successor by the three orders of the Neapolitan nation assembled in parliament, and by the pope, lord paramount of the kingdom. Ferdinand had scarely mounted the throne before he showed he in no ways merited the predilection of his father. He was avaricious, cruel, and perfidious. He soon alienated all the Neapolitan barons; and his long reign was passed in repressing the conspiracies of his vassals. These last called to their aid John, duke of Calabria, the son of René of Anjou, who had been formerly the competitor of Alphonso. The duke of Calabria, in his enterprise to place his father on the throne of Naples, believed that he should be assisted both by Francesco Sforza,—who, before he was duke of Milan, had long fought, as his father had done before him, for the party of Anjou,—and by the Florentine republic, which had always been devoted to France. But Sforza judged that the security and independence of Italy could be maintained only so long as the kingdom of Naples did not fall into the hands of France. The French were already masters of Genoa and the gates of Italy: they would traverse in every direction, and hold in fear or subjection every state in the peninsula, if they should acquire the sovereignty of Naples. For these reasons Sforza resisted all his friends, dependents, and even his wife, who vehemently solicited him for the house of Anjou: he also brought Cosmo de' Medici over to his opinion ; and thus prevented the republic of Florence from seconding a party towards which it found itself strongly inclined. The duke of Calabria, who had entered Naples in 1459, had begun successfully ; but, receiving no assistance from abroad, he soon wearied and exhausted the people, who alone had to furnish him with supplies. He lost, one after the other, all the provinces which had declared for him ; and was finally, in 1464, constrained to abandon the kingdom.

Ferdinand, to strengthen himself, kept in dungeons, or put to death, all the feudatories who had shown any favour to his rival : above all, he resolved to be rid of the greatest captain that still remained in Italy, Jacopo Piccinino, the son of Nicolo, and head of what was still called the militia, or school of Braccio. He sent to Milan, whither Piccinino, who had served the party of Anjou, had retired, and where he had married a daughter of Sforza, to invite him to enter his service, promising him the highest dignities in his kingdom. He gave the most formal engagements for his safety to Sforza, as well as to Jacopo himself. He received him with honours, such as he would not have lavished on the greatest sovereign. After having entertained him twenty-seven days in one perpetual festival, he found means to separate him from his most trusty officers, caused him to be arrested in his own palace, and to be immediately strangled. This happened on the 24th of June, 1465.

A few months after the duke of Calabria had quitted the kingdom of Naples, the great citizen, Cosmo de' Medici, who governed Florence, died, in his seventy-fifth year, on the 1st of August, 1464. It was then thirty years since he had been recalled to his country, by the same revolution that had banished the Albizzi. By his authority during that long space of time, he had completely allayed the fermentation which formerly agitated that republic. The constitution had not apparently changed : the executive power was still entrusted to a gonfalonier and eight priori ; who, during the two months they were in office, did not quit the public palace. The judicial power was still exercised by two or three *rectors*, aliens to the state, who, under the titles

of Captain of the people, of Podestà, and of Bargello, were
invested with unlimited power over the lives of the
citizens.   They were chosen each year from some
friendly city ; they arrived with their judges, serjeants,
and all their officers of justice ; they received a munificent
salary : but, on leaving office, they were obliged to render
an account of their administration before a syndicate
charged with the examination of their conduct.   Finally,
the laws could not be executed without the triple sanction
of the college, of the council of the people, and of the
common council.   But the Florentines had in vain preserved all this outward scaffolding of popular power.
Inequality took birth from the immeasurable progress
of wealth ; and the citizens felt the distance between
individuals among them too enormous to retain the
sentiment of equality even in their political rights.   The
revenues of many Florentine citizens surpassed those
of the greatest monarchical princes.   Their palaces, which
are to this day the object of our admiration, already
displayed all the prodigies of art ; at the same time that
they presented, with the crowd of servants who filled
them, the aspect of fortresses, within which public justice
dared not penetrate.   Artisans no longer claimed any
participation in political power ; and even citizens of easy
fortune no longer felt themselves independent.   They
knew that the credit and protection of their richer fellow-
citizens had become necessary to the prosperity of their
industry.

It was in consequence of this great inequality that a
close aristocracy possessed itself of the whole direction
of the state.   It acknowledged as chiefs Cosmo de'
Medici, the richest of the Italians, and Neri Capponi,
the ablest statesman of Florence.   The former made
the most liberal use of his fortune : he built palaces,
churches, and hospitals on all sides.   He was profuse
of gifts, loans, and his credit to the poorest of the citizens.
He granted pensions to the learned, and to artists.   He
collected manuscripts from the Levant and all parts of
Europe, and had them copied.   Men celebrated his taste
and acquirements.   Without having written any thing
himself, he passed for a man of letters ; and the revival
of the Platonic philosophy was attributed to him, in

P

consequence of the translations made by his direction. While Cosmo de' Medici thus fixed the public attention by his private life, Neri Capponi gained the suffrages of the people by his public conduct. Charged, as ambassador, with every difficult negotiation,—in war, with every hazardous enterprise,—he participated in all the brilliant successes of the Florentines, as well during the domination of the Albizzi as during that of the Medici. From the year 1434 to 1455, in which Neri Capponi died, these two chiefs of the republic had six times assembled the parliament to make a balia ; and, availing themselves of its authority, which was above the law, they obtained the exile of all their enemies, and filled the ballotting purses of the magistracy with the names of their own partisans, to the exclusion of all others. It appears that all the efforts of their administration were directed towards calming the passions of the public, and maintaining peace without, as well as repose within, the state. They had, in fact, succeeded in preventing Florence from being troubled with new factions, or engaged in new wars ; but they drew on the republic all the evils attending an aristocratic government. Medici and Capponi had not been able to find men who would sacrifice the liberties of their country without allowing them to gratify their baser passions. These two heads of the republic, therefore, suffered their subordinate agents to divide among themselves all the little governments of the subject cities, and every lucrative employment ; and these men, not satisfied with this first injustice, made unequal partitions of the taxes, increasing them on the poor, lowering them on the rich, and exempting themselves. At last they began to sell their protection, as well with respect to the tribunals as the councils : favour silenced justice ; and, in the midst of peace and apparent prosperity, the Florentines felt their republic, undermined by secret corruption, hastening to ruin.

When Neri Capponi died the council refused to call a new parliament to replace the balia, whose power expired on the 1st of July, 1455. It was the aristocracy itself, comprehending all the creatures of Cosmo de' Medici, that, from jealousy of his domination, wished to return to the dominion of the laws. The whole republic was rejoiced, as if liberty had been regained. The election of the signoria was again made fairly by lot,— the catasto was revised,—the contributions were again equitably apportioned,—the tribunals ceased to listen to the recommendations of those who, till then, had made a traffic of distributive justice. The aristocracy, seeing that clients no longer flocked to their houses with hands full, began to perceive that their jealousy of Cosmo de' Medici had only injured themselves. Cosmo, with his immense fortune, was just as much respected as before: the people were intoxicated with joy to find themselves again free ; but the aristocracy felt themselves weak and abandoned. They endeavoured to convoke a parliament without Cosmo; but he baffled their efforts, the longer to enjoy their humiliation. He began to fear, however, that the Florentines might once more acquire a taste for liberty ; and when Lucas Pitti, rich, powerful, and bold, was named gonfalonier, in July, 1458, he agreed with him to reimpose the yoke on the Florentines. Pitti assembled the parliament ; but not till he had filled all the avenues of the public square with soldiers or armed peasants. The people, menaced and trembling within this circle, consented to name a new balia, more violent and tyrannical than any of the preceding. It was composed of 352 persons, to whom was delegated all the power of the republic. They exiled a great number of the citizens who had shown the most attachment to liberty, and they even put some to death.

Cosmo de' Medici was at this period sixty-nine years of age ; he reckoned that his two sons, now in the prime of life, would support his declining years : but Pietro, the eldest, was absolutely incapacitated by hereditary gout. He could neither walk nor ride, but was carried about in an arm-chair : he was, besides, undistinguished by intellect or force of character. Giovanni, the second, was endued with much more talent: it was on him that Cosmo had placed the hopes of his house ; but he died, in the month of November of the year 1463. Lucas Pitti, rising to the eminence from which they fell, looked on himself henceforth as the only chief of the state. It was about this time that he undertook the building of that magnificent palace which now forms the residence of the grand dukes. The republican equality was not only offended by the splendour of this regal dwelling ; but the construction of it afforded Pitti an occasion for marking his contempt of liberty and the laws. He made of this building an asylum for all fugitives from justice, whom no public officer dared pursue when once he took part in the labour. At the same time individuals, as well as communities, who would obtain some favour from the republic, knew that the only means of being heard was to offer Lucas Pitti some precious wood or marble to be employed in the construction of his palace.

When Cosmo de' Medici died, at his country house of Careggi, on the 1st of August, 1464, Lucas Pitti felt himself released from the control imposed by the virtue and moderation of that great citizen; on whose tomb the signoria inscribed, in the following year, the title of " Father of his Country." His son, Pietro de' Medici, then forty-eight years of age, supposed that he should succeed to the administration of the republic, as he had succeeded to the wealth of his father, by hereditary right : but the state of his health did not admit of his attending regularly to business, or of his inspiring his rivals with much fear. To diminish the weight of affairs which oppressed him, he resolved on withdrawing a part of his immense fortune from commerce; recalling all his loans made in partnership with other merchants; and laying out this money in land. But this unexpected demand of considerable capital occasioned a fatal shock to the commerce of Florence; at the same time that it alienated all the debtors of the house of Medici, and deprived it of much of its popularity. The death of Sforza also, which took place on the 8th of March, 1466, deprived the Medicean party of its firmest support abroad. Francesco Sforza, whether condottiere or duke of Milan, had always been the devoted friend of Cosmo. His son, Galeazzo Sforza, who succeeded him, declared his resolution of persisting in the same alliance ; but the talents, the character, and, above all, the glory of his father, were not to be found in him. Galeazzo seemed to believe that the supreme power which he inherited brought him the

right of indulging every pleasure—of abandoning himself
to every vice without restraint. He dissipated by his
ostentation the finances of the duchy of Milan ; he
stained by his libertinism the honour of almost all the noble
families ; and he alienated the people by his cruelty.

The friends of liberty at Florence soon perceived that
Lucas Pitti and Pietro de' Medici no longer agreed
together ; and they recovered courage when the latter
proposed to the council the calling of a parliament, in
order to renew the balia, the power of which expired on
the 1st of September, 1465 : his proposition was rejected.
The magistracy began again to be drawn by lot from
among the members of the party victorious in 1434.
This return of liberty, however, was but of short
duration. Pitti and Medici were reconciled : they agreed
to call a parliament, and to direct it in concert ; to
intimidate it, they surrounded it with foreign troops.
But Medici, on the nomination of the balia, on the 2nd of
September, 1466, found means of admitting his own
partisans only, and excluding all those of Lucas Pitti.
The citizens who had shown any zeal for liberty were all
exiled ; several were subjected to enormous fines.   Five
commissioners, called accoppiatori, were charged to open,
every two months, the purse from which the signoria
were to be drawn, and choose from thence the names
of the gonfalonier and eight priori, who were to enter
office. These magistrates were so dependent on Pietro de'
Medici, that the gonfalonier went frequently to his palace
to take his orders ; and afterwards published them as the
result of his deliberations with his colleagues, whom he
had not even consulted.   Lucas Pitti ruined himself in
building his palace.   His talents were judged to bear no
proportion to his ambition : the friends of liberty, as
well as those of Medici, equally detested him ; and he
remained deprived of all power in a city which he had
so largely contributed to enslave.

Italy became filled with Florentine emigrants: every
revolution, even every convocation of parliament, was
followed by the exile of many citizens.   The party of
the Albizzi had been exiled in 1434 ; but the Alberti,
who had vanquished it, were, in their turn, banished in
1466 ; and among the members of both parties were to

be found almost all the historical names of Florence,—
those names which Europe had learned to respect, either
for immense credit in commerce, or for the lustre which
literature and the arts shed on all belonging to that
renowned city. Italy was astonished at the exile of so
many illustrious persons. At Florence, the citizens
who escaped proscription trembled to see despotism
established in their republic ; but the lower orders were
in general contented, and made no attempt to second
Bartolomeo Coleoni, when he entered Tuscany, in 1467,
at the head of the Florentine emigrants, who had taken
him into their pay. Commerce prospered ; manufactures
were carried on with great activity ; high wages supported
in comfort all who lived by their labour ; and the Medici
entertained them with shows and festivals, keeping them
in a sort of perpetual carnival, amidst which the people
soon lost all thought of liberty.

Pietro de' Medici was always in too bad a state of
health to exercise in person the sovereignty he had
usurped over his country : he left it to five or six
citizens, who reigned in his name. Tomaso Soderini,
Andrea de' Pazzi, Luigi Guicciardini, Matteo Palmieri,
and Pietro Minerbetti, were the real chiefs of the state.
They not only transacted all business, but appropriated
to themselves all the profit; they sold their influence and
credit ; they gratified their cupidity or their vengeance :
but they took care not to act in their own names, or to
pledge their own responsibility ; they left that to the
house of Medici. Pietro, during the latter months of
his life, perceived the disorder and corruption of his
agents. He was afflicted to see his memory thus stained,
and he addressed them the severest reprimands ; he
even entered into correspondence with the emigrants,
whom he thought of recalling, when he died, on the
2nd of December, 1469. His two sons, Lorenzo and
Giuliano, the elder of whom was not twenty-one years of
age, were presented by Tomaso Soderini to the foreign
ambassadors, to the magistrates, and to the first citizens
of the ruling faction ; which last he warned, that the
only means of maintaining the influence of their party
was to preserve the respect of all for its chiefs. But the
two young Medici, given up to all the pleasures of their

age, had yet no ambition. The power of the state remained in the hands of the five citizens who had exercised it under Pietro.

While the republic of Florence thus lost its liberty, that of Bologna fell equally under the domination of the family of Bentivoglio. Its subjugation was still more disgraceful. No lustre whatever was attached to the name of Giovanni II. (Bentivoglio), who governed that state from 1462 to 1508. Having been left an infant by his father Annibal, killed in 1445, he was brought up by the illegitimate son of one of his relations, whom Cosmo de' Medici had discovered at Florence ; and received from him, as a paternal inheritance, the sovereignty of his country. The republics of Sienna and Lucca, taking advantage of peace, had sunk into profound and obscure tranquillity : that of Genoa, wearied with internal convulsions, which followed each other incessantly, had lost all influence over the rest of Italy ; continually oppressed by faction, it no longer preserved even the recollection of liberty. In 1458, it had submitted to the king of France, then Charles VII. ; and John of Anjou, duke of Calabria, had come to exercise the functions of governor in the king's name. He made it, at the same time, his fortress, from whence to attack the kingdom of Naples. But this war had worn out the patience of the Genoese : they rose against the French ; and, on the 17th of July, 1461, destroyed the army sent to subdue them by René of Anjou.

The Genoese had no sooner thrown off a foreign yoke, than they became divided into two factions,—the Adorni and the Fregosi : both had, at different times, and more than once, given them a doge. The more violent and tyrannical of these factious magistrates was Paolo Fregoso, also archbishop of Genoa, who had returned to his country, in 1462, as chief of banditti ; and left it again, two years afterwards, as chief of a band of pirates. The Genoese, disgusted with their independence, which was disgraced by so many crimes and disturbances, had, on the 13th of April, 1464, yielded to Francesco Sforza, duke of Milan ; and afterwards remained subject to his son Galeazzo.

The Venetians alone, at this epoch, preserved in honour

the name of republic in Italy; but it was a republic
without liberty.   Their internal policy remains in the
shade : their efforts for the defence of Italy against the
Turks is all that is consigned to history.   These efforts
would have been more glorious, if they had better known
how to govern their eastern subjects.   Their possessions
on the Illyrian coast, up to the extremity of Greece,
were so extensive,—they comprehended countries the
productions of which were so rich, the positions of
which were so strong; of which one part of the population were so brave, the other so industrious; that if the
Venetians had frankly put themselves at the head of the
Illyrian nation,—if they had governed them only with
as much equity, with a protection as intelligent, as that
with which they governed their conquered provinces
in Lombardy, they would have founded an imperishable
empire, in which civilisation would not have been lost:
but the Venetians always regarded these establishments
beyond Italy as the Spaniards, English, and Dutch, at a
later period, have regarded their possessions in the two
Indies.   They not only did not allow the inhabitants
the enjoyment of political rights, but they denied them
those of humanity : if they allowed that they were men,
they at least never permitted them to forget that they
were considered as an inferior race to the Italian.
Instead of turning to account the superior intelligence
and industry of the Greeks, they were determined to see
in them no other qualities than those of cunning and
perfidy; and they appropriated to themselves, at the
expense of the natives, and in their own towns, the
monopoly of commerce.   The Albanians and Illyrians,
very different from the Greeks, were impatient of control,
and despised the restraints of regular industry ; but they
were energetic and brave.   The republic would have
found in them its best soldiers and sailors, if it had
received them into its armies and navies on an equal
footing; but it persisted in considering them only as
savages, to whom it yielded no confidence, always
restricting them to the lowest ranks in the army ; and,
when at last it consented to raise among them the light
cavalry of the Stradiots, they were destined more to
over-run and ravage than to defend the country.

The Venetians sent an ambassador to Mahomet II. immediately after the taking of Constantinople, to redeem those of their countrymen who had been made captive in the capital of the Greek empire. On the 18th of April, 1454, this ambassador signed a treaty of peace and good neighbourhood with the sultan, by virtue of which the republic was to support at Constantinople, as in the time of the Greek empire, a *baile*, who was to be at the same time its ambassador there, and the judge of all the Venetian subjects in the Levant. Mahomet II. took advantage of this peace to subdue successively the Illyrian or Greek princes whose independence had survived the fall of Constantinople. In 1458, he conquered the kingdoms of Rascia and of Servia; in the same year he over-ran the duchy of Athens, causing the last duke, Francesco Acciaiuolo, a Florentine, to be strangled. In 1460, he despoiled the two Paleologi, brothers of the last emperor, bearing the title of despots of the Morea. In 1462, he conquered Sinope, Cerasus, and Trebisond, little Greek states which maintained their independence on the borders of the Euxine sea. In 1463, he subdued Wallachia and Moldavia, afterwards the kingdom of Bosnia, and the bannat of Sclavonia. During the same year, the war again broke out in the Morea, between the Venetians and Turks. The former had possessed, for a long period, several strong places in the peninsula, Coron, Modon, Argos and Napoli di Malvagia. The commandant of Coron had received within his fortress a slave, who had stolen the treasury chest of the Turkish commander at Athens, and had divided the money with him : he refused to surrender the culprit, under the pretence of his having turned Christian. The Turks immediately commenced hostilities. Luigi Loredano, captain general of the Venetians, excited to revolt the Greeks of the Peloponnesus, and undertook jointly with them to defend the isthmus of Corinth; but he suffered himself to be driven out of it the following year. He abandoned the Greeks who had joined him : they were all massacred, while he returned to seek refuge in his fortresses.

The Venetians, notwithstanding this check, used their endeavours to form a powerful league against the

Mussulmans. On the 12th of September, 1463, they concluded an alliance with Matthias Corvinus the liberator of Hungary : they reckoned on the powerful assistance of a crusade which the duke of Burgundy had promised to lead against the infidels, and which the pope Pius II. had caused to be preached in all the Latin countries. But when the pope visited the army, which he had ordered to assemble at Ancona, he found only a disorderly and cowardly troop, greedy of gain, clamorous for money and arms, on receiving which they immediately deserted. Pius II. himself, worn down by illness, expired at Ancona, on the 14th of August, 1464. The few remaining crusaders immediately dispersed ; the pope had engaged the valiant George Castriot, surnamed Scanderbeg, on the occasion of this crusade, to break the treaty of peace which he had made with the Turks, after twenty years of victories gained over them, from 1442 to 1462. Abandoned alone to those enemies whom he had so long braved, he lost, in 1465, nearly the whole of Epirus, which he had excited to insurrection against the Turks : he himself died on the 17th of January, 1466, in the Venetian town of Alessio, to which he had been driven to take refuge. Matthias Corvinus alone remained to the Venetians : by combating the Turks in Hungary, he prevented them from concentrating their forces against the republic : but the pope, Paul II., who had succeeded Pius II., feared the reformers of Bohemia still more than the Mussulmans. He engaged Matthias Corvinus to turn his arms against the king of Bohemia, and depose him for having tolerated the Hussites. The Turks took advantage of the absence of this formidable antagonist to invade Croatia, in 1469, and to massacre almost all the inhabitants. The year following they, for the first time, equipped a fleet, with which they drove that of the Venetians out of the Grecian seas ; attacked Eubœa, which belonged to the republic ; took Negropont by assault, on the 12th of July, 1470, and put all the inhabitants to the sword.

The Venetians, whose commerce extended through the known world, now attempted to find allies against Mahomet in the distant regions of Asia, situated to the east of Turkey. Their ambassadors, on this occasion,

have written relations of their travels, which have been
handed down to us; and they, for the first time, revealed
the eastern world to the Latins. Hassan Beg, or
Hussun Cassan, who had conquered Persia from the
descendants of Timour, in the year 1468, then threatened
the Turkish empire. He had married a Greek princess
of Trebisond: the Venetians sent to him as ambassador
a relation of that princess, named Catterino Zeno, who,
on his way to him, traversed with infinite danger
Caramania, the little Armenia, and the country of the
Curds. This route was soon shut by the Turks against
other Venetians disposed to follow him: and Josaphat
Barbaro, Ambrosio Contarini, and others whom the
republic successively sent to Hussun Cassan, attempted
alternately either to join the caravans of the Mamelukes
in Egypt, and traverse with them Syria up to the Persian
Gulf; or to arrive by Germany and Poland at the
Black Sea, and from thence enter Persia by Georgia
and Mingrelia. When Contarini wanted to return to
Europe, he was cut off from both these routes by the
Turks, and obliged to venture along the whole length
of the Caspian Sea, to pass the gates of Derbend, and
reach Poland by Astracan and Muscovy. But these
travels, wonderful for the fifteenth century, and giving
a great impulse to geography, were of little advantage
in the war: the communications were too slow and
uncertain to admit the possibility of any concert in
action between the Persians and Venetians. Their
efforts to meet had no other effect than the ruin and
pillage of several Greek cities of Asia. In 1472, Pietro
Mocenigo laid waste Caria and the Isle of Cos; he
pillaged Satalia, Pamphylia, Smyrna, and Ionia. The
following year he burnt Myra in Lycia, every where
seeking news of Hussun Cassan, of whose defeat, near
Trebisond, he at last heard. These two campaigns were
stained with atrocious cruelties inflicted on the Greek
Christians, subjects of the Turks, whom the Venetians
pretended to deliver.

At this period the Venetian admiral was diverted from
the war against the Turks, by the part which he took
in the civil wars that for twelve years desolated the
island of Cyprus. James III. de Lusignan, king of

Cyprus, at his death in 1458, left only one legitimate
child—a daughter—who, in the following year, married
Louis, the second son of the duke of Savoy: he had
also a natural son named James, who, with the aid of the
soudan of Egypt, whose vassal he acknowledged himself
to be, seized the crown from his sister and the duke.
James de Lusignan was repeatedly called upon to defend
himself against his sister, to do which he stood in great
need of money. A rich Venetian merchant gave him his
daughter Caterina Cornaro in marriage, with a dower
of 100,000 ducats. To render this simple citizen's
daughter worthy a royal alliance, the republic adopted
Caterina Cornaro, and pronounced her daughter of Saint
Mark. The marriage was celebrated in 1471; and on
the 6th of June, 1473, James de Lusignan died, leaving
his wife pregnant. The republic hastened to proclaim
itself guardian of its adopted daughter, and of the child
she might bear. This child died in a year after its birth;
and the republic again proclaimed that Caterina Cornaro
inherited from her son, and that the republic, in its turn,
should inherit from its daughter: regarding itself as
eternal, it was sure of surviving Caterina, but it was not
equally certain that she might not marry again, and
have other children. To secure their guardianship, the
Venetians had garrisoned all the cities of the island, since
the year 1473; but this precarious possession did not
satisfy them. In 1489, they engaged the queen Caterina
Cornaro to abdicate, and to retire to Asolo in the
Trevisan. It was thus the Venetian republic gained the
kingdom of Cyprus, the crown of which it united with
those of Candia and the Morea. The isle of Cyprus,
rich in wine, corn, oil, and copper, was the most
important of the three.

The Turks vainly besieged Scutari in the year 1474,
and Lepanto the year following; but in the same year
(1475) Mahomet II. took and ruined the city of Caffa,
the flourishing colony of the Genoese, in the Crimea.
The Turks, afterwards masters of Bosnia, began, in
1477 and 1478, to threaten the states of the Terra Firma
of the Venetians. They passed the Isonzo, and even
the Tagliamento; they laid waste the fertile countries
of the patriarchate of Aquilea and of Friuli; they

massacred the people, or led them away captive; and
thus began to make the Italians experience the horrors
of those wars of barbarians which depopulated before
they enslaved the Eastern Empire. On the 15th of
June, 1478, they took Croia, which had been the
capital of Scanderbeg, and massacred the inhabitants,
in contempt of a capitulation. They afterwards renewed
the siege of Scutari. The republic of Venice, abandoned
by all Christendom, exhausted by long exertions, and
fearing soon to see the Turkish armies enter Lombardy,
accounted itself fortunate in purchasing peace by giving
up to the Mussulmans Scutari, together with several
fortresses which it possessed in Illyria and the Morea.
Such were the conditions on which peace was signed
between the sultan and the republic, on the 26th of
January, 1479.

CHAPTER XII

FREQUENCY OF CONSPIRACIES—THE LAST RESOURCE OF THE ITALIAN
PATRIOTS—THEIR ILL SUCCESS—CONSPIRACY OF THE PAZZI—
THE ADMINISTRATION OF LORENZO DE' MEDICI—HIS DEATH

ITALY had reached the fatal period at which liberty can
no longer be saved by a noble resistance, or recovered
by open force. There remained only the dangerous and,
most commonly, the fatal resource of conspiracy. So
long as habits of liberty are preserved amongst a whole
people; so long as every class has an equal horror of
slavery; a sudden explosion of the sentiment which fills
every heart suffices to accomplish a revolution—to render
vain the effort of usurpers, or to overthrow a recent
tyranny, though at the moment it may have succeeded
in establishing itself. The despot, even when he has
silenced by terror the people whom he has oppressed and
disarmed, always feels at war with them; he has too
much to fear from every class, to hope, with any chance
of success, to attach any of them to his cause. But when
absolute power has been established long enough for the

violence of its first origin to be forgotten; when the majority of the men in the prime of life have been born under its yoke, and have never known a better state; the usurper finds himself supported by the inert part of the nation—by those who, incapable of thinking, or of investigating for themselves, must be contented with borrowed ideas, and with blindly assenting to every doctrine which the government may promulge. With the loss of liberty is lost also that free and animated intercourse which warms the soul, and diffuses noble sentiments even among classes unenlightened by the knowledge of the past, or by the experience of foreign nations. In slavish countries, the prince alone speaks, amidst universal silence: he dictates the proclamations of authorities, the sentences of the tribunals; he even inspires the language to be uttered from the pulpit or the confessional: because the disposal of the revenue is at his will, he appears as a dispensing providence; and makes the people believe he gives all that he does not take from them. The indigent are grateful to him for the public charities; the labourer, for the justice and police which protect his property. The populace of towns applaud the rigour which falls on the higher classes. The national pride takes offence at the foreigner who expresses his pity for an unhappy and ill-governed people; and the vanity of the vulgar is interested in the support of what exists. If any memory of the period of liberty is preserved amongst the ignorant classes, it only refers to unhappiness and pain. They have heard of the efforts, the sacrifices, made by their fathers in defence of the people's rights; but they see only the evils of the struggle, while the result, because it is not of a material nature, escapes their imagination. They conclude that bread was as dear, and labour as painful, in the days of liberty as in their times; and to the privations they endure were then added dangers and violent catastrophes, of which fathers transmitted to their children some terrible details. Slavery, it is said, so debases man as to make him love it; and experience confirms the maxim. Nations every where appear attached each to its government in proportion to its imperfections; what is most vicious in institutions is every where most liked; and the most

obstinate resistance is that which the people oppose to
their moral advancement.

Such, in particular, was the state of Italy towards the
end of the fifteenth century. The lower orders in the
cities of Lombardy preserved no other memory of the
period of liberty than that impressed on the imagination
by some ruin, which their forefathers pointed out as
monuments of ancient battles or of ancient violence.
The peasantry, having never enjoyed any political rights,
feared nothing but the scourge of war ; and prized a
government in proportion only to its pacific disposition.
Galeazzo Sforza, the more to excite the attachment of
the people, moved more by the senses than by reflection,
surrounded himself with the magnificence of the richest
monarch. The Milanese people were grateful to him for
the spectacle, without considering that they paid for it
themselves. The Medici, whose authority at Florence
was more recent, endeavoured still more to render themselves popular, by keeping their fellow-citizens in a state
of continual festivity ; the expense of which, at least in
part, was supplied from their own patrimony. The
sovereigns of the other states of Italy, also, in various
ways succeeded in gaining the affection of the peasantry
and of the populace of towns. The protection against
the law extended to the guilty was one of the great means
of seduction. The law threatened criminals with the
most terrible punishment : prosecutions began with torture, and ended with the wheel. Nevertheless every
village festival produced a murder ; and those who committed it were exactly the sort of determined men whom
the tyrant most desired to have about him. By shielding
them from justice, he obtained from them and their
families a grateful attachment, proportioned to the cruelty
of the punishment which they escaped. These men, the
most dangerous leaders of a rabble, were therefore all
devoted to the prince ; and a call to the overthrow of his
tyranny found no response either in the towns or in the
country. On the other hand, all those who had any
elevation of soul—who knew what their country had
been, and what it had become—who could compare the
servitude at home with the liberty abroad,—all those
whom philosophy enlightened on the increasing moral

degradation of men subject to absolute power,—could not resign themselves to the loss of liberty, which they knew would be followed by the loss of virtue. They would willingly have resisted ; but soldiers, paid with their own money, shielded the tyrant within walls which their fathers had raised to protect their freedom. Social organisation, founded for the common good, was directed by an usurping hand for the oppression of all. The right of the tribunals to punish, and that of the prince to pardon, were exercised in concert only to provide resolute assassins for the latter. Alliances contracted in the name of the country established a mutual guarantee of the usurpers against the people. No power existed which could be invoked by the enlightened citizen : though he had been assured that all endued with intelligence and virtue were on his side—that the whole of the wealthy part of the nation desired liberty—he knew that the tyrant could arm against it the whole ignorant and brutal mass of the people. It was resentment for the triumph of injustice and brutality—for the oppression exercised by men governed only by the senses over all those actuated by the nobler sentiments of the soul,—that so frequently in this century obliged the latter to resort to conspiracy. The study of the works of the ancients, also, then pursued with so much ardour, conciliated universal approbation, almost admiration, for conspirators. Harmodius, Timoleon, Brutus, who with the dagger had restored liberty to Athens, Corinth, and Rome, were pointed out to youthful pupils as the avengers of abused law and justice—as the saviours of humanity ; murder, on the other hand, was so common, even men of honour felt so little scrupulous respecting it, that conspiritors were never stopped by any repugnance to shed blood: not only every prince and noble, but every magistrate and citizen, throughout Europe, was ready to kill, in order to defend the smallest right, to overcome any obstacle, to inspire fear, to give proof of energy, or to blot out an offence. Whoever kept servants, demanded above all that they should be brave, and that they should wear arms for the execution of any sanguinary order in case of need. It was because murders were generally committed by them, that domestic service did not degrade. Persons well born placed their children

with nobles, as pages, footmen, and grooms, because they
carried a sword, and their service was ennobled by the
chance of spilling blood.

So far from experiencing the repugnance we now feel
to assassination as a means of delivering our country,
men of the fifteenth century perceived honour in a
murder, virtue in a sacrifice, and historic grandeur in
conspiracy. Danger alone stopped them; but that
danger must be terrible. Tyrants, feeling themselves at
war with the universe, were always on their guard; and
as they owed their safety only to terror, the punishment
which they inflicted, if victorious, was extreme in its
atrocity. Yet these terrors did not discourage the
enemies of the existing order, whether royalist or republican. Never had there been more frequent or more
daring conspiracies than in this century. The ill success
of some never deterred others from immediately treading
in their steps.

The first plot was directed against the Medici. Bernardo Nardi, one of the Florentine citizens, who had
been exiled from his country in the time of Pietro de'
Medici, accompanied by about a hundred of his partisans,
surprised the gate of Prato, on the 6th of April, 1470.
He made himself master of the public palace, and arrested
the Florentine podestà; he took possession of the citadel;
and afterwards, traversing the streets, called the people
to join him, and fight for liberty. He intended to make
this small town the strong hold of the republican party,
whence to begin his attack on the Medici. But although
he had succeeded by surprise in making himself master
of the town, the inhabitants remained deaf to his voice,
and not one answered his call,—not one detested tyranny
sufficiently to combat it, at the peril of the last extremity
of human suffering. The friends of the government,
seeing that Nardi remained alone, at last took arms,
attacked him on all sides, and soon overpowered him by
numbers. Nardi was made prisoner, led to Florence,
and there beheaded with six of his accomplices; twelve
others were hanged at Prato.

The conspiracy, which broke out at Ferrara on the
1st of September, 1476, was directed by a monarchical
party. The house of Este, sovereign of Ferrara, Modena,

and Reggio, had successively for its chiefs two natural
sons of Nicholas III.;—Lionel, who reigned from 1441
to 1450 ; and Borso, who reigned from 1450 to 1470. It
was not till after the death of the latter, that their brother,
Hercules I., legitimately born in marriage, succeeded to
an inheritance which had been strengthened and augmented under the reigns of the two bastards. It was
Borso, in fact, who had caused an authority which his
ancestors held from the people, to be sanctioned by the
heads of the empire and the church. Frederic III. had
named him duke of Modena and Reggio, and Paul II.
duke of Ferrara. Borso had no children ; but Lionel
left a son, named Nicolo, who, when Hercules took
possession of the sovereignty, sought refuge at Mantua.
Of all the princes of the house of Este, Lionel and Borso
had been the most beloved by their subjects. The
gentleness of their dispositions, their generosity, talents,
activity, and love of letters, had won every heart. Those
who, for thirty years, had served these two princes, made
it a point of duty to transmit their crown to the son of
Lionel, and regarded the succession of Hercules as an
usurpation. They plotted to establish the rights of one
whom they considered the legitimate heir of the throne.
On the 1st of September, 1476, they introduced Nicolo
d'Este, with 600 infantry, into Ferrara, and, immediately
dispersing themselves through the streets, called upon
the people to take arms for the son of their benefactor.
But the people were indifferent between their masters,
and would not incur the risk of punishment by declaring
for either in preference to the other : instead of flocking
to their call, they fled, and shut themselves up in their
houses. The satellites of Hercules, who, for a moment,
had believed the revolution accomplished, recovered
courage, and attacked and vanquished Nicolo, who, with
one of his cousins, was immediately beheaded : twenty-five
of his accomplices were hanged.

Girolamo Gentile, the same year, organised a conspiracy at Genoa to throw off the yoke of the duke of
Milan : it failed in like manner, because the people
hesitated to join him, though he had already made himself master of the gates. Notwithstanding these fatal
examples, another conspiracy was formed the same year,

at Milan, against Galeazzo Sforza, whose yoke became insupportable to all who had any elevation of soul. There was no crime of which that false and ferocious man was not believed to be capable. Among other crimes, he was accused of having poisoned his mother. It was remarked of him, that, enjoying the spectacle of astonishment and despair, he always preferred to strike the most suddenly and cruelly those whom he had given most reason to rely on his friendship. Not satisfied with making the most distinguished women of his states the victims of his seduction or his violence, he took pleasure in publishing their shame—in exposing it to their brothers or husbands. He not unfrequently gave them up to prostitution. His extravagant pomp exhausted his finances, which he afterwards recruited by the most cruel extortion on the people. He took pleasure in inventing new and most atrocious forms of capital punishment; even that of burying his victims alive was not the most cruel. At last, three young nobles, of families who had courageously resisted the usurpation of Francesco Sforza, and who had themselves experienced the injustice and outrages of his son, resolved to deliver their country from this monster; not doubting that, when he had fallen, the Milanese would joyfully unite in substituting a free government for a tyranny. Girolamo Olgiati, Carlo Visconti, and Andrea Lampugnani, resolved, in concert, to trust only to themselves, without admitting one other person into their secret. Their enthusiasm had been excited by the lessons of their literary instructor, Colas di Montano, who continually set before them the grandeur of the ancient republics, and the glory of those who had delivered them from tyranny. Determined on killing the duke, they long exercised themselves in the handling of the dagger, to be more sure of striking him, each in the precise part of the tyrant's body assigned to him. Animated with a religious zeal, not less ardent than their republican enthusiasm, they prepared themselves by prayer, by vows to St. Stephen, and by the assistance of the mass, for the act which they were about to perform. They made choice of the 26th of December, 1476, St. Stephen's day, on which they knew that the duke Galeazzo would go in state to the church of the saint.

They waited for him in that church ; and when they saw him advance between the ambassadors of Ferrara and Mantua, they respectfully approached him, their caps in hand. Feigning to keep off the crowd, they surrounded him, and struck him all at the same instant, in the midst of his guards and courtiers. Galeazzo Sforza fell dead under their weapons ; and the crowd which filled the church saw the tumult, and heard the cries, without comprehending the cause.

The three conspirators endeavoured to escape from the church, to call the people to arms and liberty ; but the first sentiments which they encountered were astonishment and terror. The guards of the duke drew their swords only to avenge him. Lampugnani, in attempting to avoid them, got entangled in the trains of the kneeling women, was thrown down, and killed by an esquire of Galeazzo : a few steps from him, Visconti also was put to death by the guards. But Olgiati had the misfortune to escape, in this first moment, from all who pursued him ; and, running through the streets, called loudly to arms and liberty: not one person answered the call. He afterwards sought to conceal himself ; but was discovered, seized, and put to the most excruciating torture. In the interval between that infliction and his death, he wrote or dictated the narrative demanded of him, and which has been handed down to us. It is composed in a strain of the noblest enthusiasm, with a deep religious feeling, with an ardent love of liberty, and with the firm persuasion that he had performed a good action. He was again delivered to the executioner, to have his flesh torn with red-hot pincers. At the time of his martyrdom, he was only twenty-two years of age.

The conspiracy of the Pazzi at Florence speedily followed that of Olgiati at Milan. Andrea de' Pazzi, one of the five *accoppiatori*, who had exercised such great power under Pietro de' Medici, was dead; but had left three sons, and several grandsons. One of these last had married a sister of Lorenzo and Giuliano de' Medici. Their fortune was immense; it was engaged in commerce, which they carried on with great success. They considered that they had a right to be reckoned among those who held the first rank in their country; but

Lorenzo and Giuliano de' Medici, on arriving at man's estate, endeavoured to recover all the authority which their father had suffered to escape from his hand : they, in particular, evinced an extreme jealousy of all those who, in his time, had administered the republic; and although the family of the Pazzi then reckoned nine citizens, who, by their age, rank, and talents, were formed to sit in the signoria, the Medici did not permit one of them to be called to it. One of the Pazzi had married the only daughter of Giovanni Borromeo, the richest citizen of Florence, to whose inheritance he was destined to succeed ; but, at the moment of Borromeo's death, the Medici caused a law to be passed, by which the male issue in the collateral line were called to inherit, in preference to daughters; and they thus deprived Giovanni de' Pazzi of a fortune which he had looked upon as already his. Francesco de' Pazzi, his brother, whose temper was hot and impetuous, unable to endure such injustice, quitted Florence, to establish himself at Rome. There the pope, Sixtus IV., made him his banker, and soon gave him his whole confidence.

Sixtus IV. was of the house of Rovere, a plebeian family of Savona, in the states of Genoa. His election to the holy see was tainted with simony ; and he was charged with the most dissolute morals. He had four nephews, whom he had loaded with all the church had to give. He introduced two—Giuliano della Rovere, the son of his brother, and Pietro Riario, his sister's son— into the sacred college. He intended making princes of the two others, who were secular. He married Leonardo della Rovere to a natural daughter of Ferdinand : he made him prefect of Rome and duke of Sora. Girolamo Riario he married to a natural daughter of Galeazzo Sforza, duke of Milan ; after which he purchased for him the city and principality of Imola, to which he purposed to add some principalities of Romagna. This dilapidation of the patrimony of the church, to aggrandise the nephews of the pope, was one of the most scandalous examples of what was afterwards called the nepotism of the court of Rome. But although Sixtus IV. was a corrupt man, he was not destitute of talents, nor even of a certain elevation of sentiment. He had at heart the support of the independence of Italy; and he believed it could be maintained only by republican forms of government, and with the aid of liberty, the value of which he had learned to appreciate at Genoa. He found himself constantly thwarted in his politics by the Medici, whether pursuing no higher object than the elevation of his nephews, or following a nobler one, he endeavoured to engage all the states of Italy to join in a common league for its defence. This continual opposition soon engendered hatred; and Girolamo Riario and Francesco Pazzi laboured to render it more violent. Sixtus IV. finally promised all the pontifical forces to second a conspiracy, the object of which [was to restore liberty to Florence by killing the two brothers Medici. The approbation of the pope alone determined Jacopo de' Pazzi, the eldest of the family, and the uncle of Francesco, to take part in a plot so dangerous.

The Pazzi would not run the risk of being abandoned, as the conspirators of Milan had been, after the execution of the plot, because no one knew their intentions, or were prepared to second them. Accordingly, they admitted vast numbers into their secret: amongst others, Francesco Salviati, whom the pope had named archbishop of Pisa; but the Medici had refused to let him take possession of his see. It was necessary for the success of the conspiracy, that the two Medici should be struck at the same moment; for if one survived, he would instantly be the avenger of the other. It was further advisable that some of the conspirators should occupy the public palace, and intimidate the signoria, while others called the people to liberty: four troops, to act simultaneously, were accordingly requisite. It was judged indispensable, also, that the two brothers should be in the same place, in order that the conspirators might stab them at the same moment. Raphael Riario, a son of the pope's nephew, a young man of eighteen years, whom the pope had just made a cardinal, and sent to Pisa, gave occasion, on his passage through Florence, to many entertainments; in one of which, it was hoped, the brothers might be found together. But Giuliano was neither at the fête given by Jacopo de' Pazzi to the young cardinal at Montughi, nor at that which Lorenzo de' Medici gave at Fiesole. The conspirators were, on both days, ready. The archbishop Salviati, with Jacopo, son of the historian Poggio Bracciolini, and a numerous troop of conspirators, were to make themselves masters of the palace, and force the signoria to approve the revolution ; others, with Jacopo de' Pazzi, were to raise the people. Francesco Pazzi and Bernardo Bandini undertook to kill Giuliano, who, timid and suspicious, generally wore a cuirass under his robe ; and Gian Battista da Montesecco, the captain of a troop of adventurers, was appointed to despatch Lorenzo. The absence of Giuliano on these two occasions obliged the conspirators to defer the execution of their project to a religious ceremony that was to take place in the cathedral, and at which the two brothers must indispensably be present. It was agreed that the assassins should strike them as they knelt, at the moment that the priest, in performing mass, raised the host, and they, with all present, bowed down their heads. But Gian Battista da Montesecco declared, that though he had undertaken with pleasure to kill Lorenzo at a festival—for he was accustomed to murder—he could not offer the conspirators his assistance in a church, for he was not accustomed to sacrilege. All the others then refused to commit what began to appear to them an irreligious act ; so that they were forced to have recourse to two priests, Antonio da Volterra and Stefano di Bagnone, who, accustomed to live in churches, and perform themselves all the offices, felt neither respect nor fear for sacred things. This caused the ruin of all.

Every one was at his post when the Medici entered the temple, on the 26th of April, 1478 : the brothers took their places at some distance from each other. The mass began : at the moment of the elevation of the host, Antonio da Volterra put his hand on the left shoulder of Lorenzo, the better to secure the blow he was to strike on the right side. The touch, however, made Lorenzo start up, and with his arm enveloped in his cloak, he parried the blow ; he drew his sword, as did his two esquires, and the priests fled. At the same instant Giuliano had been killed by Bernardo Bandini. Francesco de' Pazzi, intending also to strike him, deeply

wounded himself in the thigh: Bandini immediately
ran towards Lorenzo, who escaped from him, and shut
himself up in the sacristy. Seeing the people in a state of
tumult, and despairing of success, Bandini immediately
left Florence, and did not think himself safe till he had
reached Constantinople. Salviati, meanwhile, also failed
at the palace of the signoria ; he had concealed his followers near the entry, the door of which shut with a
spring lock, which his satellites were unable to open,
when they were to rejoin him. He afterwards presented
himself to the gonfalonier, but his troubled look and em-
barrassed language so excited suspicion, that, without
listening to him, the gonfalonier sprang to the door,
seized by the hair Jacopo Bracciolini, who was concealed
behind it, delivered him to his sergeants, and was soon
master of the other conspirators in the palace : he had
them all instantly put to death, either by the dagger, or
by precipitating them alive from the windows ; to the
frames of which he hung archbishop Salviati, with two
of his cousins and Jacopo Bracciolini. The two priests,
who had failed in their attempt to kill Lorenzo, were
pursued and cut to pieces by the friends of the Medici :
lastly, Jacopo de' Pazzi, who had put himself at the
head of the troop of conspirators, whose part it was to
summon the people to liberty through the streets, lost all
courage, seeing that no one answered his call. He left
the city by the Romagna gate ; but had not proceeded far
before he was stopped by a party of peasants, and brought
back. In the mean time the friends of the Medici had
called the populace to vengeance ; and to this cry, at least,
they were not slow in answering : Francesco, Rinaldo,
and Jacopo de' Pazzi were hung at the windows of the
palace, beside the archbishop ; all those who had any
relation of blood or connection of friendship with them—
all those who had shown any opposition to the government—were torn from their houses, dragged through the
streets, and put to death. More than seventy citizens
were torn to pieces by the mob, in these first days.
Lorenzo de' Medici afterwards exerted all his activity to
obtain the surrender of those who had sought refuge
abroad : even Bernardo Bandini was sent back by
Mahomet II. from Constantinople. The executioner

did not rest till 200 Florentines had perished in consequence of the conspiracy of the Pazzi.

The ill success of the conspiracy of the Pazzi strengthened, as always happens, the government against which it was directed. The Medici had been content till then to be the first citizens of Florence : from that time Lorenzo looked upon himself as the prince of the city; and his friends, in speaking of him, sometimes employed that title. In addressing him, the epithet of " most magnificent lord " was habitually employed. It was the mode of addressing the condottieri, and the petty princes who had no other title. Lorenzo affected in his habits of life an unbounded liberality, pomp, and splendour, which he believed necessary to make up for the real rank which he wanted. The Magnificent, his title of honour, is become, not without reason, his surname with posterity.

On the failure of the conspiracy, he was menaced by all Italy at once. The pope fulminated a bull against him on the 1st of June, 1478, for having hanged an archbishop. He demanded that Lorenzo de' Medici, the gonfalonier, the priori, and the balia of eight, should be given up to him, to be punished according to the enormity of their crime. At the same time he published a league, which he had formed against them with Ferdinand of Naples and the republic of Sienna. He gave the command of the army of the league to Frederic da Montefeltro, duke of Urbino, and ordered him to advance into Tuscany. Lorenzo de' Medici, who was no soldier, did not join the army raised to defend him ; he was obliged to confine the command of it to Hercules d'Este, duke of Ferrara, who entered the service of the Florentines, but who soon gave them room to think that there existed a secret understanding between him and the enemy. The duchess Bonne of Savoy, the widow of Galeazzo Sforza, regent of Milan, was the only ally on whom Lorenzo could reckon. But the king of Naples, to prevent her from sending troops into Tuscany, undertook to raise enemies against her at home. He began by offering aid to the Genoese, who, wearied of the yoke under which they had voluntarily placed themselves, rose and threw it off in the month of August, 1478. Having recovered their freedom, they restored the title of doge to Prosper Adorno, who had previously borne it.

Sixtus IV. in the month of January, 1479, succeeded in engaging the Swiss of the canton of Uri, to declare war against the duchess of Milan. These formidable mountaineers obtained a victory, at Giornico, over the best Italian troops, to the astonishment, almost more than alarm, of the latter ; who were made, for the first time, to appreciate the corporal strength and unconquerable courage of a race till then unknown to them. On the 7th of September, 1479, the Florentine army was defeated at Poggio Imperiale, by the duke of Calabria, who had there joined his forces with those of the duke of Urbino. Almost at the same time the brothers of Galeazzo Sforza, whom the duchess regent had exiled from Milan, re-entered at the head of their partisans, and accomplished a revolution in that city. They deprived the duchess of the regency ; they punished her ministers and favourites with death, for having, as they said, abandoned the true interests of the state, and of the house of Sforza. They declared her son, Gian Galeazzo Sforza, of full age, though not more than twelve years old ; and the eldest brother, Ludovico, surnamed the Moor, undertook the direction of affairs ; from that time he was in fact the sovereign of Milan.

The situation of Lorenzo de' Medici became critical : he found himself, without allies, attacked by all the forces of Italy. His enemies had successively ravaged the provinces of the Florentine states, and were already masters of his strongest fortresses. Even his friends at Florence began to tire of a war which the pope and the king of Naples declared they made only against him. The people, whose attachment was founded on his prodigality and his public entertainments, showed, when his prosperity declined, that they were ready to abandon him. He felt the full extent of his danger when he was informed by the duke of Urbino, the general of the enemy's army, that, among his adversaries, the king of Naples and Ludovic the Moor were disposed to be reconciled to him. The dukes of Urbino and Calabria had not sufficient authority to make peace with him ; but they strongly advised him to go in person to Naples, and they furnished

him with a Neapolitan galley at Leghorn to convey him.
It was not without fear that Lorenzo put himself into the
hands of such an enemy as Ferdinand, who had so often
shown himself cruel and perfidious. He departed, however, from Florence, on the 5th of December, 1479 ; and
was received at Naples with more friendship and respect
than he had ventured to hope. He frankly acknowledged
to Ferdinand his danger ; but he explained to him also
his resources. Italy abandoned him ; but he placed his
hope in France.   Louis XI. and René II. duke of Lorrain
both pretended to inherit the right of the Angevins to
the kingdom of Naples : they offered their alliance, and
promised to send troops to Tuscany. Lorenzo endeavoured to convince Ferdinand of all the danger he incurred by the introduction of the French into Italy. He
acknowledged that, for himself, he should derive no other
advantage than that of injuring his enemies. He strongly
represented how preferable it would be for both, to seek
an arrangement between themselves, instead of opening
their country to the incursion of barbarians ; and, finally,
he offered him an indemnity in the republic of Sienna,
which the duke of Calabria, son of the king, already
coveted.   That state had made alliance with the pope
and the king of Naples against Florence ; had received,
without distrust, the Neapolitan troops within its fortresses ;
and had repeatedly had recourse to the duke of Calabria
to terminate, by his mediation, the continually renewed
dissensions between the different orders of the republic.
The duke of Calabria, instead of reconciling them, kept
up their discord ; and, by alternately granting succour
to each party, was become the supreme arbitrator of
Sienna.   Lorenzo de' Medici promised to offer no obstacle
to the transferring of that state in sovereignty to the duke
of Calabria.   On this condition, he signed his treaty with
the king of Naples on the 6th of May, 1480.   The republic
of Sienna would have been lost, and the Neapolitans,
masters of so important a place in Tuscany, would soon
have subjugated the rest, when an unexpected event saved
Lorenzo de' Medici from the consequences of his imprudent offer. Mahomet II. charged his grand vizier,
Achmet Giedik, to attempt a landing in Italy, which the
latter effected, and made himself master of Otranto on

the 28th of July, 1480. Ferdinand, struck with terror, immediately recalled the duke of Calabria, with his army, to defend his own states.

Lorenzo de' Medici, on his return from Naples to Florence, rendered still more oppressive the yoke which he had imposed on his country. He determined, above all, to efface from his authority the revolutionary, and consequently transitory, character which it still retained; at the same time to obliterate the memory of the sovereignty of the people, maintained by the periodical assembling of parliaments. He called one, however, on the 12th of April, 1480, which he purposed should be the last. He made that parliament create a balia; destined, likewise, to despoil itself for ever of a power which those extraordinary commissioners had, in fact, constantly abused. The balia transferred to a new council of seventy members the absolute power which had been delegated to them by the Florentine people. That council, henceforth, was to form a permanent part of the constituted authorities. It was charged to exercise a general scrutiny, and to choose only those among the Florentine citizens who were qualified for the magistracies. They were afterwards to distribute their names in the different elective purses of the signoria. They were to make a new division of the taxes; to re-establish an equilibrium in the finances, or rather, to employ the money of the state in acquitting the debts of the Medici, whose immense fortune was deranged, not only by the magnificence of Lorenzo, but by the profusion and disorder of his clerks, who carried on his commerce with the pomp and extravagance which they thought suitable to a prince.

It was not till the 3rd of December, 1480, that the pope, Sixtus IV., reconciled the republic of Florence to the church. He yielded then only to the terror which the conquest of Otranto by the Turks had inspired. Although he had shown talent, and some elevated views for the defence of the independence of Italy, his absolute want of all principle, his impetuosity of character, and his blind partiality to his nephews, rendered him one of the worst popes that ever governed the church.

The Turks had no sooner been driven from Otranto,

by Alphonso, the eldest son of the king of Naples, on the
10th of August, 1481, than Sixtus excited a new war
in Italy. His object was to aggrandise his nephew,
Girolamo Riario, for whom he was desirous of forming a
great principality in Romagna. With that view, he
proposed to the Venetians to divide with him the states
of the duke of Ferrara; but a league was formed in 1482,
by the king of Naples, the duke of Milan, and the
Florentines, to defend the dukedom. The year following,
Sixtus IV., fearing that he should not obtain for his
nephew the best part of the spoils of the duke of Ferrara,
changed sides, and excommunicated the Venetians, intending to take from them the provinces which he destined
for Girolamo Riario. The new allies, without consulting
him, soon afterwards made peace with the Venetians, at
Bagnolo, on the 7th of August, 1484. This news threw
him into a fit of gout, which, falling inward, destroyed
him, on the 13th of August following. Innocent VIII.,
who succeeded him, was quite as corrupt as his predecessor; but endued with far less talent and energy.
After having, in the beginning of his pontificate, made
war without any reasonable motive against Ferdinand
and the Florentines, he made peace with them on the
11th of August, 1486. He married his son, Franceschetto
Cibo, to a daughter of Lorenzo de' Medici; and this
alliance afterwards procured to his posterity the duchy of
Massa-Carrara. In 1489, he gave a cardinal's hat to
Giovanni, son of Lorenzo de' Medici, afterwards Leo X.
By the venality of distributive justice, by monopoly, and
by the ignorance and carelessness of the administration,
he brought Rome into a state of poverty and spoliation
hitherto unexampled. He died at last, on the 25th of
July, 1492, the most despised, but not the most detested,
of the popes who had yet filled the chair of St. Peter.

Lorenzo de' Medici, his friend and counsellor, has been
ranked among the number of great men; and, in fact, he
had some right to the gratitude of posterity, for the constant protection he afforded letters and the arts, and the
impulse which he gave to them himself, as a poet and a
man of taste. He gained the affection of the literary
society which he assembled round him, as much by the
charm of his character as by his liberality. But it is not

as a statesman that he can pretend to glory. He was a bad citizen of Florence, as well as a bad Italian : he degraded the character of the Florentines, destroyed their energy, ravished from them their liberty, and soon further exposed them to the loss of their independence. Fearing the example and contagion of liberty in the rest of Italy, he preferred alliance with the sovereigns who were most odious,—with Ferdinand king of Naples, with Galeazzo Sforza, with his widow, afterwards with Ludovic the Moor; and lastly, with pope Innocent VIII. At the same time he joined in every intrigue against the republics of Sienna, Lucca, and Genoa. He was suspected also of having favoured conspiracies against two petty princes of Romagna, his enemies. Girolamo Riario, whom Sixtus IV. had made sovereign of Forli and Imola, and who had been the chief promoter of the Pazzi conspiracy, was stabbed in his own palace by three captains of his guard, on the 14th of April, 1488. Catherine Sforza, his widow, and the natural daughter of the duke Galeazzo, preserved, however, the principality for her son Octavian. She married, not long afterwards, Giovanni de' Medici, the grandfather of the first grand duke of Tuscany. It was she who gave her name, afterwards so sadly memorable, to her godchild Catherine de' Medici. Galeotto Manfredi, lord of Faenza, was stabbed by his wife on the 31st of May following, as he was about to sell his little principality to the Venetians, and Faenza remained to his son Astor de' Manfredi, under the protection of Lorenzo de' Medici.

The house of Medici had encouraged, at Florence, the taste for pleasure and luxury, as a means of confirming its power; but this corruption of morals began to produce a reaction. All the young men, who had abandoned themselves with enthusiasm to the study of the arts and of letters, who rendered a sort of worship to ancient literature, who studied the Grecian philosophy, and were accused of preferring even the religion of the ancient Romans to that of the church, were, at the same time, devotedly attached to the Medici. This feeling they shared with all the libertines,—all those who thought only of sensual pleasure, and who sacrificed to it the liberty of their country : but those of graver morals, and of a deeper religious conviction,—those who regarded the progress of corruption as certain to draw down the vengeance of Heaven on Florence,—joined to compunctious penitence a love of ancient liberty, and a detestation of a tyranny founded on the triumph of vice. They were called *piagnoni* (the weepers). Girolamo Savonarola, a Dominican monk of Ferrara, and an eloquent orator, had preached to them a double reform, religious and political; for he had himself embraced with equal enthusiasm the cause of piety and that of liberty. He arrived on foot at Florence, in the year 1489, and lodged in the convent of St. Mark. He began immediately to preach there, with a profound conviction on his own part, and with a talent equal to his courage, against the scandalous abuses introduced into the church of Rome, and against the criminal usurpations in the state, which had deprived the citizen of his just rights. The partisans of the double reform soon reckoned in this flock the most respectable citizens of Florence.

In the beginning of the year 1492, Lorenzo de' Medici was attacked by a slow fever, joined to the gout, hereditary in his family: he retired to his country house of Careggi, where, being sensible of his danger, he sent for Girolamo Savonarola, who, till then, had refused to visit him, or to show him any deference; but it was from him that Lorenzo, struck with his reputation for sanctity and eloquence, desired, in dying, to receive absolution. Savonarola refused him neither his consolation nor his exhortations; but he declared that he could not absolve him from his sins till he proved his repentance by reparation, to the utmost of his power. He should forgive his enemies; restore all that he had usurped: lastly, give back to his country the liberty of which he had despoiled it. Lorenzo de' Medici would not consent to such a reparation; he accordingly did not obtain the absolution on which he set a high price, and died, still possessing the sovereignty he had usurped, on the 8th of April, 1492, in his forty-fourth year.

CHAPTER XIII

INVASION OF ITALY BY CHARLES VIII.—PIETRO, SON OF LORENZO
DE' MEDICI, DRIVEN FROM FLORENCE—REVOLT AND WAR OF PISA
—THE POLITICAL AND RELIGIOUS REFORM OF SAVONAROLA AT
FLORENCE—HIS DEATH

THE period was at length arrived, when Italy which had
restored intellectual light to Europe, reconciled civil
order with liberty, recalled youth to the study of laws
and of philosophy, created the taste for poetry and the
fine arts, revived the science and literature of antiquity,
given prosperity to commerce, manufactures, and agriculture,—was destined to become the prey of those very
barbarians whom she was leading to civilisation.   Her
independence must necessarily perish with her liberty,
which was hitherto the source of her grandeur and power.
In a country covered with republics three centuries
before, there remained but four at the death of Lorenzo
de' Medici; and in those, although the word "liberty"
was still inscribed on their banners, that principle of life
had disappeared from their institutions.   Florence, already
governed for three generations by the family of the
Medici, corrupted by their licentiousness, and rendered
venal by their wealth, had been taught by them to fear
and to obey.   Venice with its jealous aristocracy, Sienna
and Lucca each governed by a single caste of citizens, if
still republics, had no longer popular governments or republican energy.   Neither in those four cities, nor in Genoa,
which had surrendered its liberty to the Sforzas, nor
in Bologna, which yielded to the Bentivoglios, nor in any
of the monarchical states, was there to be found throughout Italy that power of a people whose every individual
will tends to the public weal, whose efforts are all combined for the public benefit and the common safety.   The
princes of that country could appeal only to order and
the obedience of the subject, not to the enthusiasm of the
citizen, for the protection of Italian independence and of
their own.
    Immense wealth, coveted by the rest of Europe, was,
it is true, always accumulating in absolute monarchies,

as well as in republics; but if, on the one hand, it furnished the pay of powerful armies, on the other, it augmented the danger of Italy, by exciting the cupidity of
its neighbours.   The number of national soldiers was
very considerable; their profession was that which led
the most rapidly to distinction and fortune.   Engaged
only for the duration of hostilities, and at liberty to retire
every month; instead of spending their lives in the
indolence of garrisons, or abandoning the freedom of their
will, they passed rapidly from one service to another,
seeking only war, and never becoming enervated by idleness.   The horses and armour of the Italian men at arms
were reckoned superior to those of the transalpine nations
against which they had measured themselves in France,
during "the war of the public weal."   The Italian captains
had made war a science, every branch of which they
thoroughly knew.   It was never suspected for a moment
that the soldier should be wanting in courage; but the
general mildness of manners, and the progress of civilisation, had accustomed the Italians to make war with
sentiments of honour and humanity towards the vanquished.   Ever ready to give quarter, they did not strike
a fallen enemy.   Often, after having taken from him his
horse and armour, they set him free; at least, they never
demanded a ransom so enormous as to ruin him.   Horsemen who went to battle clad in steel, were rarely killed
or wounded, so long as they kept their saddles.   Once
unhorsed, they surrendered.   The battle, therefore, never
became murderous.   The courage of the Italian soldiers,
which had accommodated itself to this milder warfare,
suddenly gave way before the new dangers and ferocity
of barbarian enemies.   They became terror-struck when
they perceived that the French caused dismounted horsemen to be put to death by their valets, or made prisoners
only to extort from them, under the name of ransom, all
they possessed.   The Italian cavalry, equal in courage,
and superior in military science, to the French, was for
some time unable to make head against an enemy whose
ferocity disturbed their imaginations.

While Italy had lost a part of the advantages which,
in the preceding century, had constituted her security,
the transalpine nations had suddenly acquired a power

which destroyed the ancient equilibrium. Up to the close of the fifteenth century, wars were much fewer between nation and nation than between French, Germans, or Spaniards among themselves. Even the war between the English and the French, which desolated France for more than a century, sprang not from enmity between two rival nations, but from the circumstance that the kings of England were French princes, hereditary sovereigns of Normandy, Poitou, and Guienne. Charles VII. at last forced the English back beyond sea, and reunited to the monarchy provinces which had been detached from it for centuries. Louis XI. vanquished the dukes and peers of France who had disputed his authority; he humbled the house of Burgundy, which had begun to have interests foreign to France. His young successor and son, Charles VIII., on coming of age, found himself the master of a vast kingdom in a state of complete obedience, a brilliant army, and large revenues; but was weak enough to think that there was no glory to be obtained unless in distant and chivalrous expeditions. The different monarchies of Spain, which had long been rivals, were united by the marriage of Ferdinand of Aragon with Isabella of Castile, and by the conquest which they jointly made of the Moorish kingdom of Granada. Spain, forming for the first time one great power, began to exercise an influence which she had never till then claimed. The emperor Maximilian, after having united the Low Countries and the county of Burgundy, his wife's inheritance, to the states of Austria, which he inherited from his father, asserted his right to exercise over the whole of Germany the imperial authority which had escaped from the hands of his predecessors. Lastly, the Swiss, rendered illustrious by their victories over Charles the Bold, had begun, but since his death only, to make a traffic of their lives, and enter the service of foreign nations. At the same time, the empire of the Turks extended along the whole shore of the Adriatic, and menaced at once Venice and the kingdom of Naples. Italy was surrounded on all sides by powers which had suddenly become gigantic, and of which not one had, half a century before, given her uneasiness.

France was the first to carry abroad an activity unemployed at home, and to make Italy feel the change which had taken place in the politics of Europe. Its king, Charles VIII., claimed the inheritance of all the rights of the second house of Anjou on the kingdom of Naples. Those rights, founded on the adoption of Louis I. of Anjou by Joan I., had never been acknowledged by the people or confirmed by possession. For the space of a hundred and ten years, Louis I., II., and III., and René, the brother of the last, made frequent but unsuccessful attempts, to mount the throne of Naples. The brother and the daughter of René, Charles of Maine and Margaret of Anjou, at last either ceded or sold those rights to Louis XI. His son, Charles VIII., as soon as he was of age, determined on asserting them. Eager for glory, in proportion as his weak frame, and still weaker intellect, incapacitated him for acquiring it, he, at the age of twenty-four, resolved on treading in the footsteps of Charlemagne and his paladins; and undertook the conquest of Naples as the first exploit that was to lead to the conquest of Constantinople and the deliverance of the holy sepulchre.

Charles VIII. entered Italy in the month of August, 1494, with 3,600 men at arms or heavy cavalry; 20,000 infantry, Gascons, Bretons, and French; 8,000 Swiss, and a formidable train of artillery. This last arm had received in France, during the wars of Charles VII., a degree of perfection yet unknown to the rest of Europe. The states of Upper Italy were favourable to the expedition of the French. The duchess of Savoy and the marchioness of Montferrat, regents for their sons, who were under age, opened the passages of the Alps to Charles VIII. Ludovic the Moor, regent of the duchy of Milan, recently alarmed at the demand made on him by the king of Naples, to give up the regency to his nephew Gian Galeazzo, then of full age, and married to a Neapolitan princess, had himself called the French into Italy; and, to facilitate their conquest of the kingdom of Naples, opened to them all the fortresses of Genoa which were dependent on him. The republic of Venice intended to remain neutral, reposing in its own strength, and made the duke of Ferrara and the marquis of Mantua, its neighbours, adopt the same policy; but

southern Italy formed for its defence a league, comprehending the Tuscan republics, the states of the church,
and the kingdom of Naples.

At Florence, Lorenzo de' Medici left three sons; of
whom Pietro II., at the age of twenty-one, was named
chief of the republic. His grandfather, Pietro I., son
of Cosmo, oppressed with infirmities and premature old
age, had shown little talent, and no capacity for the
government of a state. Pietro II., on the contrary, was
remarkable for his bodily vigour and address; but he
thought only of shining at festivals, tilts, and tournaments. It was said that he had given proofs of talent in
his literary studies, that he spoke with grace and dignity;
but in his public career he proved himself arrogant, pre-
sumptuous, and passionate. He determined on governing
the Florentines as a master, without disguising the yoke
which he imposed on them: not deigning to trouble
himself with business, he transmitted his orders by his
secretary, or some one of his household, to the magistrates. Pietro de' Medici remained faithful to the treaty
which his father had made with Ferdinand king of
Naples, and engaged to refuse the French a free passage,
if they attempted to enter southern Italy by Tuscany.
The republics of Sienna and Lucca, too feeble to adopt
an independent policy, promised to follow the impulse
given by Medici. In the states of the church, Roderic
Borgia had succeeded to Innocent VIII., on the 11th of
August, 1492, under the name of Alexander VI. He was
the richest of the cardinals, and at the same time the
most depraved in morals, and the most perfidious as
a politician. The marriage of one of his sons (for he had
several) with a natural daughter of Alphonso son of
Ferdinand, had put the seal to his alliance with the
reigning house of Naples. That house then appeared
at the summit of prosperity. Ferdinand, though seventy
years of age, was still vigorous: he was rich: he had
triumphed over all his enemies; he passed for the most
able politician in Italy. His two sons, Alphonso and
Frederick, and his grandson, Ferdinand, were reputed
skilful warriors: they had an army and a numerous fleet
under their orders. However, Ferdinand dreaded a war
with France, and he had just opened negotiations to avoid

it when he died suddenly, on the 25th of January, 1494.
His son, Alphonso II., succeeded him ; while Frederick
took the command of the fleet, and the young Ferdinand
that of the army, destined to defend Romagna against
the French.

It was by Pontremoli and the Lunigiana that
Charles VIII., according to the advice of Ludovic the
Moor, resolved to conduct his army into southern Italy.
This road, traversing the Apennines from Parma to
Pontremoli, over poor pasture lands, and descending
through olive groves to the sea, the shore of which
it follows at the foot of the mountains, was not without
danger.   The country produces little grain of any kind.
Corn was brought from abroad, at a great expense, in
exchange for oil.   The narrow space between the sea
and the mountains was defended by a chain of fortresses,
which might long stop the army on a coast where
it would have experienced at the same time famine and
the pestilential fever of Pietra-Santa.   Pietro de' Medici,
upon learning that the French were arrived at Sarzana,
and perceiving the fermentation which the news of their
approach excited at Florence, resolved to imitate that act
of his father which he had heard the most praised—his
visit to Ferdinand at Naples.   He departed to meet
Charles VIII.   On his road he traversed a field of
battle, where 300 Florentine soldiers had been cut to
pieces by the French, who had refused to give quarter to
a single one.   Seized with terror, on being introduced
to Charles, he, on the first summons, caused the fortresses
of Sarzana and Sarzanello to be immediately surrendered.
He afterwards gave up those of Librafratta, Pisa, and
Leghorn ; consenting that Charles should garrison and
keep them until his return from Italy, or until peace was
signed ; and thus establishing the king of France in the
heart of Tuscany.   It was contrary to the wish of the
Florentines that Medici had engaged in hostilities against
the French, for whom they entertained an hereditary
attachment; but the conduct of the chief of the state,
who, after having drawn them into a war, delivered
their fortresses, without authority, into the hands of the
enemy whom he had provoked, appeared as disgraceful
as it was criminal.

Pietro de' Medici, after this act of weakness, quitted Charles, to return in haste to Florence, where he arrived on the 8th of November, 1494. On his preparing, the next day, to visit the signoria, he found guards at the door of the palace, who refused him admittance. Astonished at this opposition, he returned home, to put himself under the protection of his brother-in-law, Paolo Orsini, a Roman noble, whom he had taken, with a troop of cavalry, into the pay of the republic. Supported by Orsini, the three brothers Medici rapidly traversed the streets, repeating the war cry of their family,—" Palle ! Palle !"—without exciting a single movement of the populace, upon whom they reckoned, in their favour. The friends of liberty, the Piagnoni, on the other hand, excited by the exhortations of Savonarola, assembled, and took arms. Their number continually increased. The Medici, terrified, left the city by the gate of San Gallo; traversed the Apennines; retired first to Bologna, then to Venice; and thus lost, without a struggle, a sovereignty which their family had already exercised sixty years.

The same day, the 19th of November, 1494, on which the Medici were driven out of Florence, the Florentines were driven out of Pisa. This latter city, which had been eighty-seven years under the dominion of her ancient rival, could not habituate herself to a state of subjection. Pisa had successively lost all that gave her prosperity or made her illustrious. She no longer had shipping, commerce, or wealth; the population diminished; agriculture was neglected throughout the Pisan territory; stagnant water began to infect the air; every profession which led to distinction was abandoned. There were no men of science or letters, no artists; there remained only soldiers; but with them, courage and the military spirit survived at Pisa in all their ancient splendour. Every noble served in the companies of adventure; every citizen and peasant exercised himself in arms, and on every occasion evinced a bravery which was beginning to be rare in Italy, and which commanded the respect of the French. Charles VIII., on receiving from Pietro de' Medici the fortresses of Librafratta, Pisa, and Leghorn, in the Pisan states, engaged to preserve to the

Florentines the countries within the range of these fortresses, and to restore them at the conclusion of the war.
But Charles had very confused notions of the rights of a
country into which he carried war, and was by no means
scrupulous as to keeping his word. When a deputation
of Pisans represented to him the tyranny under which
they groaned, and solicited from him the liberty of their
country; he granted their request without hesitation,
without even suspecting that he disposed of what was not
his, or that he broke his word to the Florentines: he
equally forgot every other engagement with them. Upon
entering Florence, on the 17th of November, at the head
of his army, he regarded himself as a conqueror, and
therefore as dispensed from every promise which he had
made to Pietro de' Medici,—he hesitated only between
restoring his conquest to Pietro, or retaining it himself.
The magistrates in vain represented to him that he was
the guest of the nation, and not its master; that the gates
had been opened to him as a mark of respect, not from
any fear; that the Florentines were far from feeling
themselves conquered, whilst the palaces of Florence
were occupied not only by the citizens but by the soldiers
of the republic. Charles still insisted on disgraceful conditions, which his secretary read as his ultimatum. Pietro
Capponi suddenly snatched the paper from the secretary's
hand, and tearing it, exclaimed, "Well, if it be thus,
sound your trumpets, and we will ring our bells!" This
energetic movement daunted the French: Charles declared himself content with the subsidy offered by the
republic, and engaged on his part to restore as soon as
he had accomplished the conquest of Naples, or signed
peace, or even consented to a long truce, all the fortresses
which had been delivered to him by Medici. Charles
after this convention departed from Florence, by the road
to Sienna, on the 28th of November. The Neapolitan
army evacuated Romagna, the patrimony of St. Peter,
and Rome, in succession, as he advanced. He entered
Rome on the 31st of December, without fighting a blow.
The first resistance which he encountered was on the
frontiers of the kingdom of Naples; and having there
taken by assault two small towns, he massacred the
inhabitants. This instance of ferocity struck Alphonso II.

with such terror, that he abdicated the crown in favour
of his son, Ferdinand II., and retired with his treasure
into Sicily. Ferdinand occupied Capua with his whole
army, intending to defend the passage of the Vulturno.
He left that city to appease a sedition which had broken
out at Naples; Capua, during his absence, was given up
through fear to the French, and he was himself forced,
on the 21st of February, to embark for Ischia. All the
barons, his vassals, all the provincial cities, sent deputa-
tions to Charles; and the whole kingdom of Naples was
conquered without a single battle in its defence. The
powers of the north of Italy regarded these important
conquests with a jealous eye: they, moreover, were
already disgusted by the insolence of the French, who
had begun to conduct themselves as masters throughout
the whole peninsula. The duke of Orleans, who had been
left by Charles at Asti, already declared his pretensions
to the duchy of Milan, as heir to his grandmother, Valentina Visconti. Ludovico Sforza, upon this, contracted
alliances with the Venetians, the pope, the king of Spain,
and the emperor Maximilian, for maintaining the independence of Italy; and the duke of Milan and the Venetians assembled near Parma a powerful army, under the
command of the marquis of Mantua.

Charles VIII. had passed three months at Naples in
feasts and tournaments, while his lieutenants were subduing and disorganising the provinces. The news of
what was passing in northern Italy determined him on
returning to France with the half of his army. He departed from Naples, on the 20th of May, 1495, and passed
peaceably through Rome, whilst the pope shut himself
up in the castle of St. Angelo. From Sienna he went to
Pisa, and thence to Pontremoli, where he entered the
Apennines. Gonzaga, marquis of Mantua, awaited him
at Fornovo, on the other side of that chain of mountains.
Charles passed the Taro, with the hope of avoiding him;
but was attacked on its borders by the Italians, on the
6th of July. He was at the time in full march; the divisions of his army were scattered, and at some distance
from each other. For some time his danger was imminent;
but the impetuosity of the French, and the obstinate
valour of the Swiss, repaired the fault of their general.

A great number of the Italian men at arms were thrown in the charges of the French cavalry, many others were brought down by the Swiss halberts, and all were instantly put to death by the servants of the army. Gonzaga left 3,500 dead on the field, and Charles continued his retreat. On his arrival at Asti, he entered into treaty with Ludovico Sforza, for the deliverance of the duke of Orleans, whom Sforza besieged at Novara. He disbanded 20,000 Swiss, who were brought to him from the mountains, but to whose hands he would not venture to confide himself. On the 22nd of October, 1495, he repassed the Alps, after having ravaged all Italy with the violence and rapidity of a hurricane. He had left his relative, Gilbert de Montpensier, viceroy at Naples, with the half of his army; but the people, already wearied with his yoke, recalled Ferdinand II. The French, after many battles, successively lost their conquests, and were at length forced to capitulate at Atella, on the 23rd of July, 1496.

The invasion of the French not only spread terror from one extremity of Italy to the other, but changed the whole policy of that country, by rendering it dependent upon that of the transalpine nations. While Charles VIII. pretended to be the legitimate heir of the kingdom of Naples, the duke of Orleans, who succeeded him under the name of Louis XII., called himself heir to the duchy of Milan. Maximilian, ambitious as he was inconsistent, claimed in the states of Italy prerogatives to which no emperor had pretended since the death of Frederick II. in 1250. The Swiss had learnt, at the same time, that at the foot of their mountains there lay rich and feeble cities which they might pillage, and a delicious climate, which offered all the enjoyments of life ; they saw neighbouring monarchs ready to pay them for exercising there their brigandage. Finally, Ferdinand and Isabella, monarchs of Aragon and Castile, announced their intention of defending the bastard branch of the house of Aragon, which reigned at Naples. But, already masters of Sicily, they purposed passing the strait and were secretly in treaty with Charles VIII., to divide with him the spoils of the relative whom they pretended to defend. Amidst these different pretensions and intrigues, in which Italian interests had no longer any

s

share, the spirit of liberty revived in Tuscany once more, but only to exhaust itself in a new struggle between the Florentines and Pisans. The French garrisons which Charles had left in Pisa and Librafratta, instead of delivering them to the Florentines, according to his order, had given them up to the Pisans themselves on the 1st of January, 1496. The allies, who had fought Charles at Fornovo, reproached the Florentines with their attachment to that monarch, and took part against them with the Pisans. Ludovico Sforza, and the Venetians, sent reinforcements to the latter, and the emperor Maximilian himself brought them aid. Thus, the only Italians who had at heart the honour and independence of Italy, exhausted themselves in unequal struggles and in fruitless attempts.

At the moment when Florence expelled the Medici, that republic was bandied between three different parties. The first was that of the enthusiasts, directed by Girolamo Savonarola; who promised the miraculous protection of the Divinity for the reform of the church and the establishment of liberty. These demanded a democratic constitution,—they were called the *Piagnoni*. The second consisted of men who had shared power with the Medici, but who had separated from them; who wished to possess alone the powers and profits of government, and who endeavoured to amuse the people by dissipations and pleasures, in order to establish at their ease an aristocracy,—these were called the *Arabbiati*. The third party was composed of men who remained faithful to the Medici, but not daring to declare themselves, lived in retirement,—they were called *Bigi*. These three parties were so equally balanced in the balia named by the parliament, on the 2nd of December, 1494, that it soon became impossible to carry on the government. Girolamo Savonarola took advantage of this state of affairs to urge that the people had never delegated their power to a balia which did not abuse the trust. " The people," he said, " would do much better to reserve this power to themselves, and exercise it by a council, into which all the citizens should be admitted." His proposition was agreed to: more than 1,800 Florentines furnished proof that either they their fathers, or their grandfathers, had

sat in the magistracy; they were consequently acknowledged citizens, and admitted to sit in the general council.
This council was declared sovereign, on the 1st of July,
1495; it was invested with the election of magistrates,
hitherto chosen by lot, and a general amnesty was proclaimed, to bury in oblivion all the ancient dissensions of
the Florentine republic.

So important a modification of the constitution seemed
to promise this republic a happier futurity. The friar
Savonarola, who had exercised such influence in the
council, evinced at the same time an ardent love of mankind, deep respect for the rights of all, great sensibility,
and an elevated mind. Though a zealous reformer of
the church, and in this respect a precursor of Luther,
who was destined to begin his mission twenty years
later, he did not quit the pale of orthodoxy; he did not
assume the right of examining doctrine; he limited his
efforts to the restoration of discipline, the reformation of
the morals of the clergy, and the recall of priests, as well
as other citizens, to the practice of the gospel precepts:
but his zeal was mixed with enthusiasm; he believed
himself under the immediate inspiration of Providence;
he took his own impulses for prophetic revelations, by
which he directed the politics of his disciples, the Piagnoni. He had predicted to the Florentines the coming
of the French into Italy; he had represented to them
Charles VIII. as an instrument by which the Divinity
designed to chastise the crimes of the nation; he had
counselled them to remain faithful to their alliance with
that king, the instrument of Providence, even though his
conduct, especially in reference to the affairs of Pisa, had
been highly culpable. This alliance however ranged the
Florentines among the enemies of pope Alexander VI.,
one of the founders of the league which had driven the
French out of Italy; he accused them of being traitors
to the church and to their country for their attachment
to a foreign prince. Alexander, equally offended by the
projects of reform and by the politics of Savonarola,
denounced him to the church as a heretic, and interdicted
him from preaching. The monk at first obeyed, and procured the appointment of his friend and disciple the
Dominican friar, Buonvicino of Pescia, as his successor

in the church of St. Mark; but on Christmas-day, 1497, he declared from the pulpit that God had revealed to him, that he ought not to submit to a corrupt tribunal; he then openly took the sacrament with the monks of St. Mark, and afterwards continued to preach. In the course of his sermons, he more than once held up to reprobation the scandalous conduct of the pope, whom the public voice accused of every vice and every crime to be expected in a libertine so depraved,—a man so ambitious, perfidious, and cruel,—a monarch and a priest intoxicated with absolute power.

In the mean time, the rivalry encouraged by the court of Rome between the religious orders soon procured the pope champions eager to combat Savonarola: he was a Dominican,—the general of the Augustines; that order whence Martin Luther was soon to issue. Friar Mariano di Ghinazzano signalised himself by his zeal in opposing Savonarola. He presented to the pope, friar Francis of Apulia, of the order of minor observantines, who was sent to Florence to preach against the Florentine monk, in the church of Santa Croce. This preacher declared to his audience that he knew Savonarola pretended to support his doctrine by a miracle. " For me," said he, " I am a sinner ; I have not the presumption to perform miracles, nevertheless, let a fire be lighted, and I am ready to enter it with him. I am certain of perishing, but Christian charity teaches me not to withhold my life, if, in sacrificing it, I might precipitate into hell a heresiarch, who has already drawn into it so many souls."

This strange proposition was rejected by Savonarola ; but his friend and disciple, friar Dominic Buonvicino, eagerly accepted it. Francis of Apulia declared that he would risk his life against Savonarola only. Meanwhile, a crowd of monks, of the Dominican and Franciscan orders, rivalled each other in their offers to prove by the ordeal of fire, on one side the truth, on the other the falsehood, of the new doctrine. Enthusiasm spread beyond the two convents ; many priests and seculars, and even women and children, more especially on the side of Savonarola, earnestly requested to be admitted to the proof. The pope warmly testified his gratitude to the Franciscans for their devotion. The signoria of

Florence consented that two monks only should devote
themselves for their respective orders, and directed the
pile to be prepared. The whole population of the town
and country, to which a signal miracle was promised,
received the announcement with transports of joy. On
the 17th of April, 1498, a scaffold, dreadful to look on,
was erected in the public square of Florence: two piles
of large pieces of wood, mixed with faggots and broom,
which should quickly take fire, extended each eighty feet
long, four feet thick, and five feet high; they were
separated by a narrow space of two feet, to serve as a
passage by which the two priests were to enter, and pass
the whole length of the piles during the fire. Every
window was full; every roof was covered with spectators;
almost the whole population of the republic was collected
round the place. The portico called the Loggia de'
Lanzi, divided in two by a partition, was assigned to the
two orders of monks. The Dominicans arrived at their
station chanting canticles, and bearing the holy sacrament. The Franciscans immediately declared that they
would not permit the host to be carried amidst flames.
They insisted that the friar Buonvicino should enter the
fire, as their own champion was prepared to do, without
this divine safeguard. The Dominicans answered, that
"they would not separate themselves from their God at
the moment when they implored His aid." The dispute
upon this point grew warm. Several hours passed away.
The multitude, which had waited long, and began to feel
hunger and thirst, lost patience; a deluge of rain suddenly fell upon the city, and descended in torrents from
the roofs of the houses,—all present were drenched. The
piles were so wet that they could no longer be lighted;
and the crowd, disappointed of a miracle so impatiently
looked for, separated, with the notion of having been
unworthily trifled with. Savonarola lost all his credit;
he was henceforth rather looked on as an impostor.
Next day his convent was besieged by the Arabbiati,
eager to profit by the inconstancy of the multitude; he
was arrested with his two friends, Domenico Buonvicino,
and Silvestro Marruffi, and led to prison. The Piagnoni,
his partisans, were exposed to every outrage from the
populace,—two of them were killed; their rivals and old

enemies exciting the general ferment for their destruction.
Even in the signoria, the majority was against them;
and yielded to the pressing demands of the pope. The
three imprisoned monks were subjected to a criminal
prosecution. Alexander VI. despatched judges from
Rome, with orders to condemn the accused to death.
Conformably with the laws of the church, the trial opened
with the torture. Savonarola was too weak and nervous to
support it : he avowed in his agony all that was imputed
to him ; and, with his two disciples, was condemned to
death. The three monks were burnt alive, on the 23rd of
May, 1498, in the same square where, six weeks before,
a pile had been raised to prepare them a triumph.

CHAPTER XIV

THE FRENCH MASTERS OF MILAN AND GENOA, AND THE SPANIARDS OF
NAPLES—THE GONFALONIER SODERINI AT FLORENCE—LEAGUE
OF CAMBRAY AGAINST VENICE—THE MEDICI RE-ESTABLISHED AT
FLORENCE

THE expedition of Charles VIII. against Naples had
directed towards Italy the attention of all the western
powers. The transalpine nations had learnt that they
were strong enough to act as masters, and if they pleased
as robbers, in this the richest and most civilised country
of the earth. All the powers on the confines henceforth
aspired to subject some part of Italy to their dominion.
They coveted their share of tribute from a land so
fruitful of impost, from those cities in which industry
employed such numbers, and accumulated so much
capital. Cupidity put arms in their hands, and smothered
every generous feeling. The commanders were rapacious;
the soldiers thought only of pillage. They regarded the
Italians as a race abandoned to their extortions, and
vied with each other in the barbarous methods which
they invented for extorting money from the vanquished,
until at last they completely destroyed the prosperity
which had provoked their envy.

Charles VIII. died at Amboise, on the 7th of April,

1498, the day destined at Florence for the trial by fire of
the doctrine of Savonarola. Louis XII., who succeeded
that monarch, claimed as grandson of Valentina Visconti,
to be the legitimate heir to the duchy of Milan, although,
according to the law acknowledged by all Italy, and
confirmed by the imperial investiture granted to the father
of Valentina, females were excluded from all share in the
succession. This monarch, at his coronation, took with
the title of king of France those of duke of Milan and
king of Naples and Jerusalem. It was to the duchy of
Milan that he seemed particularly attached, apparently
as having been the object of his ambition before he came
to the throne. He preserved during his whole reign,
as if he were simply duke of Milan, a feudal respect
for the emperor as lord paramount, which was as fatal
to France as to Italy.

After having thus announced to the world his pretensions to the duchy of Milan, Louis hastened to secure his
possession of it by arms. He easily separated his
antagonist, Ludovico Sforza, from all his allies. The
emperor Maximilian had married the niece of Ludovico,
to whom he had granted the investiture of his duchy;
but Maximilian forgot, with extreme levity, his promises
and alliances. A new ambition, a supposed offence, even
a whim, sufficed to make him abandon his most matured
projects. The Swiss had just then excited his resentment; and to attack them the more effectually, he signed
with Louis XII. a truce, in which Ludovico Sforza was
not included, and was therefore abandoned to his enemy.
The Venetians were interested still more than the
emperor in defending Ludovico, but were incensed
against him; they accused him of having deceived them,
as well in the war against Charles VIII. as in that for
the defence of Pisa. They suspected him of having
suggested to Maximilian the claims which he had just
made on all their conquests in Lombardy, as having
previously appertained to the empire. They were
obliged, moreover, to reserve all their resources to resist
the most formidable of their enemies. Bajazet II. had
just declared war against them. Bands of robbers
continually descended from the mountains of Turkish
Albania to lay waste Venetian Dalmatia. The Turkish

pachas offered their support to every traitor who
attempted to take from the Venetians any of their
stations in the Levant.   Corfu very nearly fell into the
hands of the Turks: at length hostilities openly began.
The Turks attacked Zara; all the Venetian merchants
established at Constantinople were put into irons, and
Scander Bashaw, sangiak of Bosnia, passed the Isonzo
on the 29th of September, 1499, with 7,000 Turkish
cavalry.   He ravaged all the rich country which extends
from that river to the Tagliamento, at the extremity
of the Adriatic, and spread terror up to the lagune which
surround Venice.   Invaded by an enemy so formidable,
against whom they were destined to support, for seven
years, a relentless war, the Venetians would not expose
themselves to the danger of maintaining another war
against the French.   On the 15th of April, 1499, they
signed, at Blois, with Louis, a treaty, by which they
contracted an alliance against Ludovico Sforza, and
abandoned the conquest of the Milanese to the king of
France, reserving to themselves Cremona and the Ghiara
d'Adda.

Ludovico Sforza found no allies in any other part of
Italy.   Since the execution of Savonarola at Florence,
the faction of the Arabbiati had succeeded that of the
Piagnoni in the administration, without changing its
policy.   The republic continued to guard against the
intrigues of the Medici, who entered into an alliance
with every enemy of their country, in order to bring
it back under their yoke.   Florence continued her efforts
to subdue Pisa; but, fearing to excite the jealousy
of the kings of France and Spain, did not assemble for
that purpose either a numerous army or a great train of
artillery.   She contented herself with ravaging the Pisan
territory every year, in order to reduce that city by
famine.   Even these expeditions were suspended when
those powerful monarchs found it convenient to make
a show of peace.   The cities of Sienna, Lucca, and
Genoa, actuated by their jealousy of Florence, sent
succour to Pisa.   Pope Alexander VI., who had been
always the enemy of Charles VIII., now entered into
an alliance with Louis XII.; but on condition that
Cæsar Borgia, son of Alexander, should be made duke

of Valentinois in France and of Romagna in Italy,—
the French king assisting him against the petty princes,
feudatories of the holy see, who were masters of that
province.   The king of Naples, Frederick, who had
succeeded his nephew Ferdinand on the 7th of September, 1496, was well aware that he should, in his turn,
be attacked by France ; but although he merited, by his
talents and virtues, the confidence of his subjects, he had
great difficulty in re-establishing some order in his
kingdom, which was ruined by war, and had neither
an army nor an exchequer to succour his natural ally, the
duke of Milan.

A powerful French army, commanded by the sires
De Ligny and D'Aubigny, passed the Alps in the month
of August, 1499.   On the 13th of that month they
attacked and took by assault the two petty fortresses
of Arazzo and Annone, on the borders of the Tanaro ;
putting the garrisons, and almost all the inhabitants,
to the sword.   This ferocious proceeding spread terror
among the troops of Ludovico Sforza.   His army, the
command of which he had given to Galeazzo San
Severino, dispersed ; and the duke, not venturing to
remain at Milan, sought for himself, his children, and
his treasure, refuge in Germany, with the emperor
Maximilian.   Louis XII., who arrived afterwards in Italy,
made his entry into the forsaken capital of Ludovico on
the 2nd of October.   The trembling people, wishing to
conciliate their new master, saluted him with the title of
duke of Milan, and expressed their joy in receiving him
as their sovereign.   The rest of Lombardy also submitted
without resistance ; and Genoa, which had placed itself
under the protection of the duke of Milan, passed over to
that of the king of France.   Louis returned to Lyons
before the end of the year : the fugitive hopes which he
had excited already gave way to hatred.   The insolence
of the French,—their violation of all national institutions,
their contempt of Italian manners,—the accumulation of
taxes, and the irregularities in the administration, rendered
their yoke insupportable.   Ludovico Sforza was informed
of the general ferment, and of the desire of his subjects
for his return.   He was on the Swiss frontier, with a considerable treasure : a brave but disorderly crowd of young

men, ready to serve any one for pay, joined him. In a few days 500 cavalry and 8,000 infantry assembled under his banner: and, in the month of February, 1500, he entered Lombardy at their head. Como, Milan, Parma, and Pavia immediately opened their gates to him: he next besieged Novara, which capitulated. Louis, meanwhile, displayed the greatest activity in suppressing the rebellion: his general, Louis de la Tremouille, arrived before Novara, in the beginning of April, with an army in which were reckoned 10,000 Swiss. The men of that nation in the two hostile camps, opposed to each other for hire, hesitated, parleyed, and finally took a resolution more fatal to their honour than a battle between fellow countrymen could have been. Those within Novara not only consented to withdraw themselves, but to give up tc the French the Italian men at arms with whom they were incorporated, and who were immediately put to the sword or drowned in the river. They permitted La Tremouille to arrest in their ranks Ludovico Sforza, and the two brothers San Severino, who attempted to escape in disguise. They received from the French the wages thus basely won, and afterwards, rendered reckless by the sense of their infamy, they in their retreat seized Belinzona, which they ever after retained. Thus, even the weakest of the neighbours of Italy would have their share in her conquest. Ludovico Sforza was conducted into France, and there condemned to a severe captivity, which, ten years afterwards, ended with his life. The Milanese remained subject to the king of France from this period, to the month of June, 1512.

The facility with which Louis had conquered the duchy of Milan, must have led him to expect that he should not meet with much more resistance from the kingdom ot Naples. Frederick also, sensible of this, demanded peace; and, to obtain it, offered to hold his kingdom in fief, as tributary to France. He reckoned, however, on the support of Ferdinand the Catholic, his kinsman and neighbour, who had promised him powerful aid, and had given him a pledge of the future by sending into Sicily his best general, Gonzalvo di Cordova, with sixty vessels and 8,000 chosen infantry. But Ferdinand had previously proposed to Louis a secret understanding, to divide

between them the spoils of the unhappy Frederick. While
the French entered on the north to conquer the kingdom
of Naples, he proposed that the Spaniards should enter
on the south to defend it; and that, on meeting, they,
instead of giving battle, should shake hands on the partition of the kingdom,—each remaining master of one half.
This was the basis of the treaty of Grenada, signed on
the 11th of November, 1500. In the summer of 1501,
the perfidious compact was executed by the two greatest
monarchs of Europe.

The French army arrived at Rome on the 25th of June;
at the same time that the army of Gonzalvo di Cordova
landed in Calabria. The former, from the moment they
passed the frontier, treated the Neapolitans as rebels, and
hanged the soldiers who surrendered to them. Arrived
before Capua, they entered that city while the magistrates
were signing the capitulation, and massacred 7,000 of the
inhabitants. The treachery of Ferdinand inspired the
unhappy Frederick with still more aversion than the
ferocity of the French. Having retired to the island of
Ischia, he surrendered to Louis, and was sent to France,
where he died, in a captivity by no means rigorous, three
years afterwards. The Spaniards and French advanced
towards each other, without encountering any resistance.
They met on the limits which the treaty of Grenada had
respectively assigned to them; but the moment the conquest was terminated, jealousy appeared. The duke de
Nemours and Gonzalvo di Cordova disputed upon the
division of the kingdom: each claimed for his master
some province not named in the treaty. Hostilities at last
began between them on the 19th of June, 1502, at Atripalda.
Louis, while the negotiation was pending, delayed sending reinforcements to his general. After a struggle, not
without glory, and in which La Palisse and Bayard first
distinguished themselves, D'Aubigny was defeated at
Seminara on the 21st of April, and Nemours at Cerignola
on the 28th of the same month, 1503. The French army
was entirely destroyed, and the kingdom of Naples lost
to Louis XII. Louis had sent off, during the same campaign, a more powerful army than the first, to recover it;
but, on arriving near Rome, news was received of the
death of Alexander VI., which took place on the 18th of

August, 1503. The cardinal d'Amboise, prime minister of Louis, detained the army there to support his intrigues in the conclave : when it renewed its march, in the month of October, the rainy season had commenced. Gonzalvo di Cordova had taken his position on the Garigliano, the passage of which he defended, amidst inundated plains, with a constancy and patience characteristic of the Spanish infantry. During more than two months the French suffered or perished in the marshes : a pestilential malady carried off the flower of the army, and damped the courage and confidence of the remainder. Gonzalvo, having at last passed the river himself, on the 27th of December, attacked and completely destroyed the French army. On the 1st of January, 1504, Gaëta surrendered to him ; and the whole kingdom of Naples was now, like Sicily, but a Spanish possession.

Thus the greater part of Italy had already fallen under the yoke of the nations which the Italians denominated barbarian. The French were masters of the Milanese and of the whole of Liguria ; the Spaniards of the Two Sicilies ; even the Swiss had made some small conquests along the Lago Maggiore ; and this was the moment in which Louis XII. called the Germans also into Italy. On the 22nd of September of the same year in which he lost Gaëta, his last hold in the kingdom of Naples, he signed the treaty of Blois, by which he divided with Maximilian the republic of Venice, as he had divided with Ferdinand the kingdom of Naples. Experience ought to have taught him that Maximilian, like Ferdinand, would reserve for himself the conquests made in common. The future ought to have alarmed him ; for Charles, the grandson and heir of Maximilian of Austria, and of Ferdinand of Aragon, of Mary of Burgundy, and of Isabella of Castille, was already born. It was foreseen that he would unite under his sceptre the greatest monarchies in Europe ; and Louis, instead of guarding against his future greatness, had promised to give him his daughter in marriage. It was the thoughtlessness of Maximilian, and not the prudence of Louis, that delayed, during four years, the execution of the treaty of Blois.

During this interval, Genoa—which had never ceased to consider herself a republic, although the signoria had been conferred first on Ludovico Sforza, and next on Louis XII. as duke of Milan—learned from experience that a foreign monarch was incapable of comprehending either her laws or liberty. According to the capitulation, one half of the magistrates of Genoa should be noble, the other half plebeian. They were to be chosen by the suffrages of their fellow-citizens; they were to retain the government of the whole of Liguria, and the administration of their own finances, with the reservation of a fixed sum payable yearly to the king of France. But the French could never comprehend that nobles were on an equality with villains; that a king was bound by conditions imposed by his subjects; or that money could be refused to him who had force. All the capitulations of Genoa were successively violated; while the Genoese nobles ranged themselves on the side of a king against their country: they were known to carry insolently about them a dagger, on which was inscribed, " Chastise villains;" so impatient were they to separate themselves from the people, even by meanness and assassination. That people could not support the double yoke of a foreign master and of nobles who betrayed their country. On the 7th of February, 1507, they revolted, drove out the French, proclaimed the republic, and named a new doge; but time failed them to organise their defence. On the 3rd of April, Louis advanced from Grenoble with a powerful army. He soon arrived before Genoa: the newly-raised militia, unable to withstand veteran troops, were defeated. Louis entered Genoa on the 29th of April; and immediately sent the doge and the greater number of the generous citizens, who had signalised themselves in the defence of their country, to the scaffold.

Independent Italy now comprised only the states of the Church, Tuscany, and the republic of Venice; and even these provinces were pressed by the transalpine nations on every side. The Spaniards and French alternately spread terror through Tuscany and the states of the church; the Germans and Turks held in awe the territories of Venice. The states of the church were at the same time a prey to the intrigues of the detestable Alexander, and his son Cæsar Borgia. More murders, more assassinations, more glaring acts of perfidy, were committed within a short space, than during the annals of the most depraved monarchies. Cæsar Borgia, whom his father created duke of Romagna in 1501, had previously despoiled and put to death the petty princes who reigned at Pesaro, Rimini, Forli, and Faenza. He had, in like manner, possessed himself of Piombino in Tuscany, the duchy of Urbino, and the little principalities of Camerino and Senegallia. He had caused to be strangled in this last city, on the 31st of December, 1502, four tyrants of the states of the church, who followed the trade of condottieri. These princes had served in his pay, and, alarmed by his intrigues, had taken arms against him; but, seduced by his artifices, they placed themselves voluntarily in his power. Cæsar Borgia had made himself master of Città do Castelli, and of Perugia; and was menacing Bologna, Sienna, and Florence, when, on the 18th of August, 1503, he and his father drank, by mistake, a poison which they had prepared for one of their guests. His father died of it, and Borgia himself was in extreme danger. In thirteen months he lost all his sovereignties, the fruits of so many crimes. Attacked in turn by pope Julius II., who had succeeded his father, and by Gonzalvo di Cordova, he was at last sent into Spain, where he died in battle, more honourably than he deserved.

In Tuscany, the republic of Florence found itself surrounded with enemies. The Medici, continuing exiles, had entered into alliances with all the tyrants in the pontifical states: they took part in every plot against their country; at the same time, they sought the friendship of the king of France, who was more disposed to favour a prince than a republic. Pietro de' Medici had accompanied the army sent, in 1503, against the kingdom of Naples, and lost his life at the defeat of the Garigliano. His death did not deliver Florence from the apprehension which he had inspired. His brothers Giovanni and Giuliano carried on their intrigues against their country. The war with Pisa, too, which still lasted, exhausted the finances of Florence. The Pisans had lost their commerce and manufactures; they saw their harvests, each year, destroyed by the Florentines: but they opposed to all these disasters a constancy and courage not to be subdued. The French, Germans, and Spaniards, in turn sent them succour; not from taking any interest in their cause, but with the view of profiting by the struggle which they protracted. Lucca and Sienna also, jealous of the Florentines, secretly assisted the Pisans; but only so far as they could do it without compromising themselves with neighbours whom they feared. Lucca fell, by degrees, into the hands of a narrow oligarchy. Sienna suffered itself to be enslaved by Pandolfo Petrucci, a citizen, whom it had named captain of the guard, and who commanded obedience, without departing from the manners and habits of republican equality.

In the new position of Italy, continually menaced by absolute princes, whose deliberations were secret, and who united perfidy with force, the Florentines became sensible that their government could not act with the requisite discretion and secrecy, while it continued to be changed every two months. Their allies even complained that no secret could be confided to them, without becoming known, at the same time, to the whole republic. They accordingly judged it necessary to place at the head of the state a single magistrate, who should be present at every council, and who should be the depositary of every communication requiring secrecy. This chief, who was to retain the name of gonfalonier, was elected, like the doge of Venice, for life; he was to be lodged in the palace, and to have a salary of 100 florins a month. The law which created a gonfalonier for life was voted on the 16th of August, 1502; but it was not till the 22nd of September following that the grand council chose Pietro Soderini to fill that office. He was a man universally respected; of mature age, without ambition, without children; and the republic never had reason to repent its choice. The republic, at the same time, introduced the authority of a single man into the administration, and suppressed it in the tribunals. A law of the 15th of April, 1502, abolished the offices of podestà and of captain of justice, and supplied their places by the *ruota;* a tribunal composed of five judges, of whom four must agree in passing sentence: each, in his turn, was to be president of the tribunal for six months. This rotation

caused the name of *ruota* to be given to the supreme courts
of law at Rome and Florence.

The most important service expected from Soderini
was that of subjecting Pisa anew to the Florentine
republic: he did not accomplish this until 1509. That
city had long been reduced to the last extremity: the
inhabitants, thinned by war and famine, had no longer
any hope of holding out; but Louis XII. and Ferdinand
of Aragon announced to the Florentines that they must
be paid for the conquest which Florence was on the point
of making. Pisa had been defended by them since 1507,
but only to prevent its surrendering before the amount
demanded was agreed on: it was at length fixed at
100,000 florins to be paid to the king of France, and
50,000 to the king of Aragon. This treaty was signed
on the 13th of March; and on the 8th of June, 1509,
Pisa, which had cruelly suffered from famine, opened its
gates to the Florentine army: the occupying army was
preceded by convoys of provisions, which the soldiers
themselves distributed to the citizens. The signoria of
Florence abolished all the confiscations pronounced
against the Pisans since the year 1494; they restored to
them all their property and privileges. They tried, in
every way, to conciliate and attach that proud people;
but nothing could overcome their deep resentment, and
their regret for the loss of their independence. Almost
every family, which had preserved any fortune, emi-
grated; and the population already so reduced by war,
was still further diminished after the peace.

The republic of Venice was condemned, by the war
which it had to support against the Turkish empire,
from 1499 to 1503, to make no effort for maintaining the
independence of Italy against France and Aragon. It
had solicited the aid of all Christendom, as if for a holy
war, against Bajazet II.; and, in fact, alternately received assistance from the kings of France, Aragon, and
Portugal, and from the pope: but these aids, limited
to short services on great occasions, were of little real
efficacy. They aggravated the misery of the Greeks
among whom the war was carried on, caused little injury
to the Turks, and were of but little service to the Venetians. The Mussulmans had made progress in naval

discipline; the Venetian fleet could no longer cope with theirs; and Antonio Grimani, its commander, till then considered the most fortunate of the citizens of Venice, already father of a cardinal, and destined, long after, to be the doge of the republic, was, on his return to his country, loaded with irons. Lepanto, Pylos, Modon, and Coron, were successively conquered from the Venetians by the Turks; the former were glad at last to accept a peace negotiated by Andrea Gritti, one of their fellow-citizens, a captive at Constantinople. By this peace they renounced all title to the places which they had lost in the Peloponnesus, and restored to Bajazet the island of Santa Maura, which they had, on their side, conquered from the Turks. This peace was signed in the month of November, 1503.

The period in which the republic of Venice was delivered from the terror of the Turks was also that of the death of Alexander VI., and of the ruin of his son Cæsar Borgia. The opportunity appeared to the signoria favourable for extending its possessions in Romagna. That province had been long the object of its ambition. Venice had acquired by treachery, on the 24th of February, 1441, the principality of Ravenna, governed for 166 years by the house of Polenta. In 1463, it had purchased Cervia, with its salt marshes, from Malatesta IV., one of the princes of Rimini; upon the death of Cæsar Borgia, it took possession of Faenza, the principality of Manfredi; of Rimini, the principality of Malatesta; and of several fortresses. Imola and Forli, governed by the Alidosi and the Ordelaffi, alone remained to be subdued, in order to make Venice mistress of the whole of Romagna. The Venetians offered the pope the same submission, the same annual tribute, for which those petty princes were acknowledged pontifical vicars. But Julius II., who had succeeded Borgia, although violent and irascible, had a strong sense of his duty as a pontiff and as an Italian. He was determined on preserving the states of the church intact for his successors. He rejected all nepotism, all aggrandisement of his family; and would have accused himself of unpardonable weakness, if he suffered others to usurp what he refused to give his family. He haughtily exacted the restitution of all that the Venetians possessed in the states of the church; and as he could not obtain it from them, he consented to receive it from the hands of Louis and Maximilian, who combined to despoil the republic. He, however, communicated to the Venetians the projects formed against them, and it was not till they appeared resolved to restore him nothing, that he concluded his compact with their enemies.

The league against Venice, signed at Cambray, on the 10th of December, 1508, by Margaret of Austria, daughter of Maximilian, and the cardinal d'Amboise, prime minister of Louis, was only the completion of the secret treaty of Blois, of the 22nd of September, 1504. No offence had been given, to justify this perfidious compact. Maximilian, who detested Louis, had the same year endeavoured to attack him in the Milanese; but the Venetians refused him a passage; and after three months' hostilities, the treaty between the emperor and the republic was renewed, on the 7th of June, 1508. Louis XII., whom the Venetians defended, and Maximilian, with whom they were reconciled, had no other complaint against them than that they had no king, and that their subjects thus excited the envy of those who had. The two monarchs agreed to divide between them all the *terra firma* of the Venetians, to abandon to Ferdinand all their fortresses in Apulia, to the pope the lordships in Romagna, to the houses of Este and Gonzaga the small districts near the Po; and thus to give all an interest in the destruction of the only state sufficiently strong to maintain the independence of Italy.

France was the first to declare war against the republic of Venice, in the month of January, 1509. Hostilities commenced on the 15th of April; on the 27th of the same month, the pope excommunicated the doge and the republic. The Venetians had assembled an army of 42,000 men, under the command of the impetuous Bartolomeo d'Alviano and the cautious Pitigliano. The disagreement between these two chiefs, both able generals, caused the loss of the battle of Aignadel, fought, on the 14th of May, 1509, with the French, who did not exceed 30,000. Half only, or less, of the Venetian army was engaged; but that part fought heroically, and perished without falling back one step. After this discomfiture,

Bergamo, Brescia, Crema, and Cremona, hastily surrendered to the conquerors, who planted their banners on the border of Ghiaradadda, the limits assigned by the treaty of partition. Louis signalised this rapid conquest by atrocious cruelties : he caused the Venetian governors of Caravaggio and of Peschiera to be hanged, and the garrisons and inhabitants to be put to the sword; he ruined, by enormous ransoms, all the Venetian nobles who fell into his hands; seeking to vindicate to himself his unjust attack by the hatred which he studied to excite.

The French suspended their operations from the 31st of May ; but the emperor, the pope, the duke of Ferrara, the marquis of Mantua, and Ferdinand of Aragon profited by the disasters of the republic to invade its provinces on all sides at once. The senate, in the impossibility of making head against so many enemies, took the generous resolution of releasing all its subjects from their oath of fidelity, and permitting them to treat with the enemy, since it was no longer in its power to defend them. In letting them feel the weight of a foreign yoke, the senate knew that it only rendered more dear the paternal authority of the republic ; and, in fact, those citizens who had eagerly opened their gates to the French, Germans, and Spaniards, soon contrasted, in despair, their tyranny with the just and equal power which they had not had the courage to defend. The Germans, above all, no sooner entered the Venetian cities, than they plunged into the most brutal debauchery ; offending public decency, and exercising their cruelty and rapacity on all those who came within their reach. Notwithstanding this, the native nobles joined them. They were eager to substitute monarchy for republican equality and freedom; but their insolence only aggravated the hatred which the Germans inspired. The army of the republic had taken refuge at Mestre, on the borders of the Lagune, when suddenly the citizen evinced a courage which the soldier no longer possessed. Treviso, in the month of June, and Padua on the 17th of July, drove out the imperialists ; and the banners of St. Mark, which had hitherto constantly retreated, began once again to advance.

The war of the league of Cambray showed the Italians, for the first time, what formidable forces the transalpine nations could bring against them. Maximilian arrived to besiege Padua in the month of September, 1509. He had in his army Germans, Swiss, French, Spaniards, Savoyards ; troops of the pope, of the marquis of Mantua, and of the duke of Modena ; in all more than 100,000 men, with 100 pieces of cannon. He was, notwithstanding, obliged to raise the siege, on the 3rd of October, after many encounters, supported on each side with equal valour. But these barbarians, who came to dispute with the Italians the sovereignty of their country, did not need success to prove their ferocity. After having taken from the poor peasant, or the captive, all that he possessed, they put him to the torture to discover hidden treasure, or to extort ransom from the compassion of friends. In this abuse of brute force, the Germans showed themselves the most savage, the Spaniards the most coldly ferocious. Both were more odious than the French ; although the last mentioned had bands called flayers (écorcheurs), formed in the English wars, and long trained to grind the people.

Pope Julius II. soon began to hate his accomplices in the league of Cambray. Violent and irascible, he had often shown in his fits of passion that he could be as cruel as the worst of them. But he had the soul of an Italian. He could not brook the humiliation of his country, and its being enslaved by those whom he called barbarians. Having recovered the cities of Romagna, the subject of his quarrel with the Venetians, he began to make advances to them. At the end of the first campaign, he entered into negotiations ; and on the 21st of February, 1510, granted them absolution. He was aware that he could never drive the barbarians out of Italy but by arming them against each other ; and as the French were those whom he most feared, he had recourse to the Germans. It was necessary to begin with reconciling the Venetians to the emperor ; but Maximilian, always ready to undertake every thing, and incapable of bringing any thing to a conclusion, would not relax in a single article of what he called his rights. As emperor, he considered himself monarch of all Italy ; and although he was always stopped on its frontier, he refused to renounce the smallest part of what he had purposed conquering.

He asserted that the whole Venetian territory had been
usurped from the empire ; and before granting peace to
the republic, demanded almost its annihilation.

It was with the aid of the Swiss that the pope designed
to liberate Italy. He admired the valour and piety
of that warlike people: he saw, with pleasure, that
cupidity had become their ruling passion. The Italians,
who needed the defence of the Swiss, were rich enough
to pay them ; and a wise policy conspired for once with
avarice ; for the Swiss republics could not be safe if
liberty were not re-established in Italy. Louis XII.,
by his prejudice in favour of nobility, had offended those
proud mountaineers, whom, even in his own army, he
considered only as revolted peasants. Julius II. employed the bishop of Sion, whom he afterwards made
cardinal, to irritate them still more against France. In
the course of the summer of 1510, the French, according
to the plan which Julius had formed, were attacked
in the Milanese by the Swiss, in Genoa by the Genoese
emigrants, at Modena by the pontifical troops, and at
Verona by the Venetians ; but, notwithstanding the
profound secrecy in which the pope enveloped his
negotiations and intrigues, he could not succeed, as he
had hoped, in surprising the French every where at the
same time. The four attacks were made successively,
and repulsed. The sire de Chaumont, lieutenant of
Louis in Lombardy, determined to avenge himself by
besieging the pope in Bologno, in the month of October.
Julius feigned a desire to purchase peace at any price ;
but, while negotiating, he caused troops to advance ; and,
on finding himself the stronger, suddenly changed his
language, used threats, and made Chaumont retire.
When Chaumont had placed his troops in winter
quarters, the pope, during the greatest severity of the
season, attacked the small state of Mirandola, which had
put itself under the protection of France ; and entered
its capital by a breach, on the 20th of January, 1511.

The pope's troops, commanded by the duke of Urbino,
experienced in the following campaign a signal defeat
at Casalecchio, on the 21st of May, 1511. It was called
" the day of the ass-drivers," because the French knights
returned driving asses before them loaded with booty.

The loss of Bologna followed; but Julius II. was not discouraged. His legates laboured, throughout Europe, to raise enemies against France. They at last accomplished a league, which was signed on the 5th of October, and which was called Holy, because it was headed by the pope. It comprehended the kings of Spain and England, the Swiss, and the Venetians. Louis XII., to oppose an ecclesiastical authority to that of the pontiffs, convoked, in concert with Maximilian, whom he continued to consider his ally, an œcumenical council. A few cardinals, who had separated from the pope, clothed it with their authority; and Florence dared not refuse to the two greatest monarchs of Europe the city of Pisa for its place of meeting, although the whole population beheld with dread this commencement of a new schism.

A powerful Spanish army meanwhile advanced from Naples, to the aid of the pope, under the command of Raymond de Cardona; and laid siege to Bologna on the 26th of January, 1512. The French had driven to despair, by their extortions, the people of the provinces which they had seized from Venice. On the 3rd of February, Brescia revolted against them. Gaston de Foix, duc de Nemours, and nephew of Louis XII., had, at the age of twenty-two, been just placed at the head of the French army. With a rapidity ever memorable, he in turn successfully opposed his two enemies. Having, on the 5th of February, entered Bologna, he forced the Spaniards to raise the siege, and make a precipitate retreat through Romagna. He instantly returned to attack the Venetians, and on his road defeated one of their armies. He retook Brescia by assault, on the 19th of February, and punished that unhappy city by a frightful massacre of its inhabitants; but pillage disorganised and corrupted his army, and six weeks elapsed before he could return to Romagna, to oppose the armies of Spain and of the pope, which had again advanced. He forced them to give battle, near Ravenna, on Easter Sunday, the 11th of April, 1512. It was the most murderous battle that Italy had yet seen: nearly 20,000 dead covered the plain on which it was fought. Gaston de Foix, was, for the last time, victorious. The formidable Spanish infantry slowly retreated, without

permitting itself to be broken in any part. Gaston,
furious at its escaping him, made one last effort against
it, and was killed.

The death of Gaston proved the signal of the defeat
of the French in Italy.   The ministers of Louis thought
they might, after the battle of Ravenna, safely dismiss
a part of their army; but Maximilian, betraying all his
engagements, abandoned the French to their enemies.
Without consenting to make peace with Venice, he gave
passage through his territory to 20,000 Swiss, who were
to join the Venetian army, in order to attack the French.
He, at the same time, recalled all the Germans who had
enlisted under the banner of France.   Ferdinand of
Aragon and Henry VIII. of England almost simultaneously attacked Louis, who, to defend himself, was
obliged to recall his troops from Italy.   In the beginning
of June, they evacuated the Milanese; of which the
Swiss took possession, in the name of Maximilian Sforza,
son of Louis the Moor.   On the 29th of the same
month, a revolution drove the French out of Genoa; and
the republic and a new doge were again proclaimed.
The possessions of France were soon reduced to a few
small fortresses in that Italy which the French thought
they had subdued.   But the Italians did not recover
their liberty by the defeat of only one of their oppressors.
From the yoke of France, they passed under that of the
Swiss, the Spaniards, and the Germans; and the last
they endured always seemed the most galling.   To add
to their humiliation, the victory of the Holy League
enslaved the last and only republic truly free in Italy.

Florence was connected with France by a treaty
concluded in concert with Ferdinand the Catholic.   The
republic continued to observe it scrupulously, even after
Ferdinand had disengaged himself from it.   Florence
had fulfilled towards all the belligerent powers the duties
of good neighbourhood and neutrality, and had given
offence to none : but the league, which had just driven
the French out of Italy, was already divided in interest,
and undecided on ¡the plan which it should pursue.   It
was agreed only on one point, that of obtaining money.
The Swiss lived at discretion in Lombardy, and levied
in it the most ruinous contributions : the Spaniards of

Raymond de Cardona insisted also on having a province abandoned to their inexorable avidity ; Tuscany was rich and not warlike. The victorious powers who had assembled in congress at Mantua proposed to the Florentines to buy themselves off with a contribution ; but the Medici, who presented themselves at this congress, asked to be restored to their country, asserting that they could extract much more money by force, for the use of the holy league, than a republican government could obtain from the people by gentler means. Raymond de Cardona readily believed them, and in the month of August, 1512, accompanied them across the Apennines, with 5,000 Spanish infantry as inaccessible to pity as to fear. Raymond sent forward to tell the Florentines, that if they would preserve their liberty, they must recall the Medici, displace the gonfalonier Soderini, and pay the Spanish army 40,000 florins. He arrived at the same time before the small town of Prato, which shut its gates against him : it was well fortified, but defended only by the *ordinanza*, or country militia. On the 30th of August, the Spaniards made a breach in the wall, which these peasants basely abandoned. The city was taken by assault ; the militia, which would have incurred less danger in fighting valiantly, were put to the sword : 5,000 citizens were afterwards massacred, and others, divided among the victors, were put to lingering tortures, either to force them to discover where they had concealed their treasure, or to oblige their kinsmen to ransom them out of pity ; the Spaniards having already pillaged all they could discover in holy as well as profane places.

The terror caused at Florence, by the news of the massacre of Prato, produced next day a revolution. A company of young nobles, belonging to the most illustrious families, who, under the title of Society of the Garden Ruccellai, were noted for their love of the arts, of luxury and pleasure, took possession, on the 31st of August, of the public palace ; they favoured the escape of Soderini, and sent to tell Raymond de Cardona that they were ready to accept the conditions which he offered. But all treaties with tyrants are deceptions. Giuliano de' Medici, the third son of Lorenzo, whose character was gentle and conciliatory, entered Florence on the

2nd of September, and consented to leave many of the liberties of the republic untouched. His brother, the cardinal Giovanni, afterwards Leo X., who did not enter till the 14th of the same month, forced the signoria to call a parliament on the 16th. In this pretended assembly of the sovereign people, few were admitted except strangers and soldiers : all the laws enacted since the expulsion of the Medici in 1494 were abolished. A balia, composed only of the creatures of that family, was invested with the sovereignty of the republic. This balia showed itself abjectly subservient to the cardinal Giovanni de' Medici, his brother Giuliano, and their nephew Lorenzo, who now returned to Florence after eighteen years of exile, during which they had lost every republican habit, and all sympathy with their fellow-citizens. None of them had legitimate children ; but they brought back with them three bastards, — Giulio, afterwards Clement VII., Ippolito, and Alessandro,—who had all a fatal influence on the destiny of their country. Their fortune, formerly colossal, was dissipated in their long exile ; and their first care, on returning to Florence, was to raise money for themselves, as well as for the Spaniards, who had re-established their tyranny.

CHAPTER XV

CALAMITIES WITH WHICH THE FRENCH, SPANIARDS, AND GERMANS OVERWHELMED ITALY—PILLAGE AND RUIN OF THE GREATEST CITIES—OPPRESSION OF THE ITALIAN NATION, AND LOSS OF ITS INDEPENDENCE

THE three destructive wars comprised in the last chapter —viz. that of the French and Swiss in the Milanese, that of the French and Spaniards in the kingdom of Naples, that of the French, Spaniards, Germans, and Swiss, in the states of Venice,—robbed Italy of her independence. The country to which Europe was indebted for its progress in every art and science, which had imparted to other nations the medical science of Salerno, the jurisprudence of Bologna, the theology of Rome, the philo-

T

sophy, poetry, and fine arts of Florence, the tactics and
strategy of the Bracceschi and Sforzeschi schools, the
commerce and banks of the Lombards, the process of
irrigation, the scientific cultivation both of hills and
plains,—that country now belonged no more to its own
inhabitants! The struggle between the transalpine
nations continued, with no other object than that of
determining to which of them Italy should belong; and
bequeathed nothing to that nation but long-enduring,
hopeless agonies. Julius II. in vain congratulated himself on having expelled the French, who had first imposed
a foreign yoke on Italy; he vowed in vain that he would
never rest till he had also driven out all the barbarians;
but he deceived himself in his calculations: he did not
drive out the barbarians, he only made them give way
to other barbarians; and the new comers were ever the
most oppressive and cruel. However, this project of
national liberation, which the pope alone could still
entertain in Italy with any prospect of success, was soon
abandoned. Eight months after the expulsion of the
French from the Milanese, and five months after the
re-establishment of the Medici at Florence, Julius II., on
the 21st of February, 1513, sank under an inflammatory
disease. On the 11th of March, Giovanni de' Medici
succeeded him, under the name of Leo X.; eleven months
after the latter had been made prisoner by the French at
the battle of Ravenna, and six months after the Spanish
arms had given him the sovereignty of his country,
Florence.

It has been the singular good fortune of Leo X. to
have his name associated with the most brilliant epoch
of letters and the arts since their revival. He has thus
shared the glory of all the poets, philosophers, artists,
men of learning and science, his contemporaries. He
has been held up to posterity as one who formed and
raised to eminence men who were in fact his elders, and
who had attained celebrity before the epoch of his power.
His merit consisted in showering his liberality on those
whose works and whose fame had already deserved it.
His reign, on the other hand, which lasted nine years,
was marked by fearful calamities, which hastened the
destruction of those arts and sciences to which alone the

age of Leo owes its splendour. The misfortunes which
he drew down on his successor were still more dreadful.
The pope was himself a man of pleasure, easy, care-
less, prodigal; who expended in sumptuous feasts the
immense treasures accumulated by his predecessor. He
had the taste to adorn his palace with the finest works
of antiquity, and the sense to enjoy the society of philosophers and poets; but he had never the elevation of
soul to comprehend his duties, or to consult his conscience. His indecent conversation and licentious conduct scandalized the church; his prodigality led him
to encourage the shameful traffic in indulgences, which
gave rise to the schism of Luther; his thoughtlessness
and indifference to human suffering made him light up
wars the most ruinous, and which he was utterly unable to carry on; he never thought of securing the
independence of Italy, or of expelling the barbarians: it
was simply for the aggrandisement of his family, that
he contracted or abandoned alliances with the transalpine nations: he succeeded, indeed, in procuring that
his brother Giuliano should be named duc de Nemours,
and he created his nephew duke of Urbino; but he
endeavoured also to erect for the former a new state,
composed of the districts of Parma, Placentia, Reggio,
and Modena; for the latter, another, consisting of the
several petty principalities which still maintained themselves in the states of the church. His tortuous policy
to accomplish the first object, his perfidy and cruelty to
attain the second, deserved to be much more severely
branded by historians.

The sovereign pontiff and the republic of Venice
were the only powers in Italy that still preserved some
shadow of independence. Julius II. had succeeded in
uniting Romagna, the March, the patrimony and campagna of Rome, to the holy see. Amongst all the vassals
of the church, he had spared only his own nephew,
Gian Maria della Rovere, duke of Urbino. On the
defeat of the French, he further seized Parma and
Placentia, which he detached from the Milanese, without
having the remotest title to their possession, as he also
took Modena from the duke of Ferrara, whom he detested. Leo X. found the holy see in possession of all

these states, and was at the same time himself all-powerful at Florence. Even the moment of his elevation to the pontificate was marked by an event, which showed that every vestige of liberty had disappeared from that republic. The partisans of the Medici pretended to have discovered at Florence a conspiracy, of which they produced no other proofs than some imprudent speeches, and some wishes uttered for liberty. The most illustrious citizens were, nevertheless, arrested; and Machiavelli, with several others, were put to the torture. Pietro Boscoli and Agostino Capponi were beheaded; and those who were called their accomplices exiled. The two republics of Sienna and Lucca were in a state of trembling subjection to the pontiff; so that all central Italy, peopled with about 4,000,000 inhabitants, was dependent on him : but the court of Rome, since it had ceased to respect the ancient municipal liberties, never extended its authority over a new province without ruining its population and resources. Law and order seemed incompatible with the government of priests : the laws gave way to intrigue and favour; commerce gave way to monopoly. Justice deserted the tribunals, foresight the councils, and valour the armies. It was proverbially said, that the arms of the church had no edge. The great name of pope still moved Europe at a distance, but it brought no real force to the allies whom he adopted.

The republic of Venice, with a smaller territory, and a far less numerous population, was in reality much more powerful than the church. Venetian subjects, if they did not enjoy liberty, had at least a government which maintained justice, order, and the law; their material prosperity was judiciously protected. They in return were contented, and proved themselves devotedly attached to their government; but the wars raised by the league of Cambray overwhelmed that republic with calamity. The city of Venice, secure amidst the waters, alone escaped the invasion of the barbarians; though, even there, the richest quarters had been laid waste by an accidental fire. The country and the provincial towns experienced in turn the ferocity of the French, Swiss, Germans, and Spaniards. Three centuries and a half had elapsed since this same

Veronese march, the cradle of the Lombard league, had repelled the invasion of Frederick Barbarossa. But while the world boasted a continual progress, since that period, in civilisation,—while philosophy and justice had better defined the rights of men,—while the arts, literature, and poetry, had quickened the feelings, and rendered man more susceptible of painful impressions,—war was made with a ferocity at which men in an age of the darkest barbarism would have blushed. The massacre of all the inhabitants of a town taken by assault, the execution of whole garrisons which had surrendered at discretion, the giving up of prisoners to the conquering soldiers in order to be tortured into the confession of hidden treasure, became the common practice of war in the armies of Louis XII., Ferdinand, and Maximilian. Kings were haughty in proportion to their power; they considered themselves at so much the greater distance above human nature: they were the more offended at all resistance, the more incapable of compassion for sufferings which they did not see or did not comprehend. The misery which they caused presented itself to them more as an abstraction; they regarded masses, not individuals; they justified their cruelties by the name of offended majesty; they quieted remorse by considering themselves, not as men, but as scourges in the hand of God. Three centuries have elapsed, and civilisation has not ceased to march forward; the voice of humanity has continued to become more and more powerful; no one now dares to believe himself great enough to be dispensed from humanity; nevertheless, those who would shrink with horror from witnessing the putting to death of an individual, do not hesitate to condemn whole nations to execution. The crimes which remain for us to relate, do not merit more execration than those of which we are ourselves the witnesses at this day. Kings, in their detestation of freedom, let loose upon unhappy Italy, in the sixteenth century, famine, war, and pestilence; as, from the same motive in our time, they have loosed upon heroic Poland, famine, war, and the cholera.

Louis XII., after having lost the Milanese, through his infatuated ambition to reconquer the small province of the Cremonese, which he had himself ceded to the republic of Venice, felt anew the desire of being reconciled with that republic, his first ally in Italy. The Venetians, who knew that without their money, artillery, and cavalry, the Swiss could never have faced the French, much less have driven them out of Italy, saw that their allies did not appreciate their efforts and sacrifices. Maximilian, who in joining never granted them peace, but only a truce, re-asserted his claims on Verona and Vicenza, and would not consent to allow the Venetians any states in Terra Firma but such as they purchased from him at an enormous price. The pope, to enforce the demands of Maximilian, threatened the Venetians with excommunication ; and their danger after victory appeared as great as after defeat. Andrea Gritti, one of their senators,—made prisoner after the battle of Aignadel, and the same who, during his captivity at Constantinople, had signed the peace of his country with the Turks,—again took advantage of his captivity in France to negotiate with Louis. He reconciled the republic with that monarch, who had been the first to attack it ; and a treaty of alliance was signed at Blois, on the 24th of March, 1513. This was, however, a source of new calamity to Venice. A French army, commanded by La Tremouille, entered the Milanese, and on its approach the Germans and Spaniards retired. The Swiss, who gloried in having re-established Maximilian Sforza on the throne of his ancestors, were, however, resolved not to abandon him. They descended from their mountains in numerous bodies, on the 6th of June, 1513 ; attacked La Tremouille at the Riotta, near Novara ; defeated him, and drove him back with all the French forces beyond the Alps. The Spaniards and the soldiers of Leo X. next attacked the Venetians without any provocation : they were at peace with the republic, but they invaded its territory in the name of their ally Maximilian. They occupied the Paduan state, the Veronese, and that of Vicenza, from the 13th of June till the end of autumn. It was during this invasion the Spaniards displayed that heartless cruelty which rendered them the horror of Italy ; that cupidity which multiplied torture, and which invented sufferings more and more atrocious, to extort gold from their prisoners. The Germans in the next campaign, over-ran the Venetian provinces ; and notwithstanding

the savage cruelties and numerous crimes of which the
country had just been the theatre, yet the German commander found means to signalise himself by his ferocity.

Francis I. succeeded Louis XII. on the 1st of January,
1515; on the 27th of June he renewed his predecessor's
alliance with Venice; and on the 15th of August entered
the plains of Lombardy, by the marquisate of Saluzzo,
with a powerful army. He met but little resistance in
the provinces south of the Po, but the Swiss meanwhile
arrived in great force to defend Maximilian Sforza, whom,
since they had reseated him on the throne, they regarded
as their vassal. Francis in vain endeavoured to negotiate
with them; they would not listen to the voice of their
commanders; democracy had passed from their *lands-
gemeinde* into their armies, popular orators roused their
passions; and on the 13th of September they impetuously
left Milan to attack Francis I. at Marignano. Deep
ditches lined with soldiers bordered the causeway by
which they advanced; their commanders wished by some
manœuvre to get clear of them, or make the enemy change
his position; but the Swiss, despising all the arts of war,
expected to command success by mere intrepidity and
bodily strength. They marched to the battery in full
front; they repulsed the charge of the knights with their
halberds, and threw themselves with fury into the ditches
which barred their road. Some rushed on to the very
mouths of the cannon, which guarded the king, and there
fell. Night closed on the combatants; and the two
armies mingled together fought on for four hours longer
by moonlight. Complete darkness at length forced them
to rest on their arms; but the king's trumpet continually
sounded, to indicate to the bivouac where he was to be
found; while the two famous horns of Uri and Unter-
walden called the Swiss together. The battle was renewed on the 14th at daybreak: the unrelenting obstinacy
was the same; but the French had taken advantage of
the night to collect and fortify themselves. Marshal
Trivulzio, who had been present at eighteen pitched
battles, declared that every other seemed to him children's
play in comparison with this "battle of giants," as he
called it: 20,000 dead already covered the ground; of
these two-thirds were Swiss. When the Swiss despaired

of victory they retreated slowly,—but menacing and terrible. The French did not dare to pursue them.

This horrible butchery, however, hastened the conclusion of the wars which arose from the league of Cambray. The Swiss were not sufficiently powerful to maintain their sway in Lombardy : eight of their cantons, on the 7th of November, signed, at Geneva, a treaty of peace with Francis I., who compensated, with considerable sums of money, all the claims which they consented to abandon. On the 29th of November, the other cantons acceded to this pacification, which took the name of " Paix perpétuelle," and France recovered the right of raising such infantry as she needed among the Swiss. Raymond de Cardona, alarmed at the retreat of the Swiss, evacuated Lombardy with the Spanish troops. The French recovered possession of the whole duchy of Milan. Maximilian Sforza abdicated the sovereignty for a revenue of 30,000 crowns secured to him in France. Leo X., ranging himself on the side of the victors, signed, at Viterbo, on the 13th of October, a treaty, by which he restored Parma and Placentia to the French. In a conference held with Francis at Bologna, between the 10th and 15th of the following December, Leo induced that monarch to sacrifice the liberties of the Gallican church by the concordat, to renounce the protection he had hitherto extended to the Florentines and to the duke of Urbino, although the former had always remained faithful to France. The pope seized the states of the duke of Urbino, and conferred them on his nephew, Lorenzo II. de' Medici. Amidst these transactions, Ferdinand the Catholic died, on the 15th of January, 1516, and his grandson Charles succeeded to his Spanish kingdoms. On the 13th of August following, Charles signed, at Noyon, a treaty, by which Francis ceded to him all his right to the kingdom of Naples as the dower of a newborn daughter, whom he promised to Charles in marriage. From that time Maximilian remained singly at war with the republic of Venice and with France. During the campaign of 1516, his German army continued to commit the most enormous crimes in the Veronese march ; but Maximilian had never money enough to carry on the war without the subsidies of his allies : remaining alone, he could no longer hope to be

successful.   On the 14th of December he consented to
accede to the treaty of Noyon ; he evacuated Verona,
which he had till then occupied, and the Venetians were
once more put by the French in possession of all the
states of which the league of Cambray had proposed the
partition : but their wealth was annihilated, their population reduced to one half, their constitution itself shaken,
and they were never after in a state to make those efforts
for the defence of the independence of Italy, which might
have been expected from them before this devastating war

Had Italy been allowed to repose after so many disasters, she might still have recovered her strength and
population ; and when the struggle should have recommenced with the transalpine nations, she would have
been found prepared for battle ; but the heartless levity
and ambition of Leo did not give her time.   While the
family of the Medici was becoming extinct around him,
he dreamt only of investing it with new dignities ; he
refused the Florentines permission to re-establish their
republic, and offered his alliance to whatever foreign
monarch would aid him in founding on its ruins a principality for the bastard Medici.   His third brother Giuliano duc de Nemours, whom he had at first charged with
the government of Florence, died on the 17th of March,
1516.   Lorenzo II., son of his eldest brother Pietro, whom
he had made duke of Urbino, and whom he sent to command at Florence after Giuliano rendered himself odious
there by his pride and by his contemptible incapacity—
he too died only three years afterwards, on the 28th of
April, 1519.   Leo supplied his place by cardinal Giulio
de' Medici, afterwards Clement VII.   This prelate was
the natural son of the first Giuliano killed in the Pazzi
conspiracy of 1478.   He was considered the most able
of the pope's ministers, and the most moderate of his
lieutenants.   Giuliano II. had also left an illegitimate
son, Ippolito, afterwards cardinal ; and Lorenzo II. had
a legitimate daughter, Catherine, afterwards queen of
France, and an illegitimate son, Alexander, destined to
be the future tyrant of Florence.   Leo, whether desirous
of establishing these descendants, or carried away by
the restlessness and levity of his character, sighed only
for war.

U

The emperor Maximilian died on the 19th of January, 1519, leaving his hereditary states of Austria to his grandson Charles, already sovereign of all Spain, of the Two Sicilies, of the Low Countries, and of the county of Burgundy. Charles and Francis both presented themselves as candidates for the imperial crown; the electors gave it to the former, on the 28th of June, 1519: he was from that period named Charles V. Italy, indeed the whole of Europe, was endangered by the immeasurable growth of this young monarch's power. The states of the church, over which he domineered by means of his kingdom of the Two Sicilies, could not hope to preserve any independence but through an alliance with France. Leo at first thought so, and signed the preliminary articles of a league with Francis; but, suddenly changing sides, he invited Charles V. to join him in driving the French out of Italy. A secret treaty was signed between him and the emperor, on the 8th of May, 1521. By this the duchy of Milan was to be restored to Francesco Sforza, the second son of Louis the Moor. Parma, Placentia, and Ferrara were to be united to the holy see: a duchy in the kingdom of Naples was to be secured to the bastard Alexander de' Medici. The pope united his army to that of the emperor in the kingdom of Naples; the command of it was given jointly to Prospero Colonna and the marquis Pescara: war was declared on the 1st of August, and the imperial and pontifical troops entered Milan on the 19th of November: but in the midst of the joy of this first success, Leo X. died unexpectedly, on the 1st of December, 1521.

Death opportunely delivered Leo from the dangers and anxieties into which he had thoughtlessly precipitated himself. His finances were exhausted; his prodigality had deprived him of every resource; and he had no means of carrying on a war which he had only just begun. He left his successors in a state of distress which was unjustly attributed to them, and which rendered them odious to the people; for the war into which he had plunged them, without any reasonable motive, was the most disastrous of all those which had yet afflicted unhappy Italy. There remained no power truly Italian that could take any part in it for her defence. Venice was so exhausted by the war of the league of Cambray, that she was forced to limit her efforts to the maintenance of her neutrality, and was hardly powerful enough to make even her neutral position respected. Florence remained subject to the cardinal Giulio de' Medici. The republics of Sienna and Lucca were tremblingly prepared to obey the strongest: all the rest depended on the transalpine power; for an unexpected election, on the 9th of January, 1522, had given a Flemish successor to Leo X., under the name of Adrian VI. This person had been the preceptor of Charles V., and had never seen Italy, where he was re-garded as a barbarian. The kingdom of Naples was governed and plundered by the Spaniards. After the French had lost the duchy of Milan, Francesco Sforza, who had been brought back by the imperialists, possessed only the name of sovereign. He had never been for a moment independent; he had never been able to protect his subjects from the tyranny of the Spanish and German soldiers, who were his guards. Finally, the marquis de Montferrat and the duke of Savoy had allowed the French to become masters in their states, and had no power to refuse them passage to ravage oppressed Italy anew.

The marshal Lautrec, whom Francis I. had charged to defend the Milanese, and who still occupied the greater part of the territory, was forced by the Swiss, who formed the sinews of his army, to attack the imperialists on the 29th of April, 1522, at Bicocca. Prospero Colonna had taken up a strong position about three or four miles from Milan, on the road to Monza: he valued himself on making a defensive war,—on being successful, without giving battle. The Swiss attacked him in front, throw-ing themselves, without listening to the voice of their commander, into a hollow way which covered him, and where they perished, without the possibility of resistance. After having performed prodigies of valour, the remainder were repulsed with dreadful loss. In spite of the remon-strances of Lautrec, they immediately departed for their mountains; and he for his court, to justify himself. Lescuns, his successor in the command, suffered the imperialists to surprise and pillage Lodi; and was at last forced to capitulate at Cremona on the 6th of May, and evacuate the rest of Lombardy. Genoa was not compre-hended in the capitulation, and remained still in possession of the French; but, on the 30th of May, that city also was surprised by the Spaniards, and pillaged with all the ferocity which signalised that nation. It was one of the largest depôts of commerce in the west, and the ruin of so opulent a town shook the fortune of every merchant in Europe. The general of Charles then, judging Lombardy too much exhausted to support his armies, led them to live at discretion in the provinces of his ally, the pope. They raised among the states still calling themselves independent, enormous subsidies to pay the soldiers, for which purpose Charles never sent money. The plague, breaking out at the same time at Rome and Florence, added to the calamities of Italy so much the more that Adrian VI. abolished, as pagan superstition, or acts of revolt against Providence, all the sanitary measures of police which had been invented to stop the spread of contagion. The pope died on the 14th of September, 1523; and the Romans, who held him in horror, crowned his physician with laurel, as the saviour of his country.

The death of Adrian, however, saved no one. The cardinal Giulio de' Medici was chosen his successor, on the 18th of November, under the name of Clement VII. This man had passed for an able minister under his cousin Leo X., because prosperity still endured, and the pontifical treasury was not exhausted; but when he had to struggle with a distress which he, however, had not caused, his ignorance in finance and administration, his sordid avarice, his pusillanimity, his imprudence, his sudden and ill considered resolutions, his long indecisions, made him alike odious and contemptible. He was not strong enough to resist the tide of adversity. He found himself without money and without soldiers, engaged in a war without an object : he was incapable of commanding, and nowhere found obedience.

The French were not disposed to abandon their title to Lombardy, the possession of which they had just lost. Before the end of the campaign, Francis sent thither another army, commanded by his favourite, the admiral Bonnivet. This admiral entered Italy by Piedmont; passed the Ticino on the 14th of September, 1523; and marched on Milan. But Prospero Colonna, who had chosen, among the great men of antiquity, Fabius

Cunctator for his model, was admirable in the art of stopping an army, of fatiguing it by slight checks, and at last forcing it to retreat without giving battle. Bonnivet, who maintained himself on the borders of Lombardy, was forced, in the month of May following, to open himself a passage to France by Ivrea and Mont St. Bernard. The chevalier Bayard was killed while protecting the retreat of Bonnivet, in the rear-guard. The imperialists had been joined, the preceding year, by a deserter of high importance, the constable Bourbon, one of the first princes of the blood in France, who was accompanied by many nobles. Charles V. put him, jointly with Pescara, at the head of his army, and sent him into Provence in the month of July; but after having besieged Marseilles, he was soon constrained to retreat. Francis I., who had assembled a powerful army, again entered Lombardy, and made himself master of Milan: he next laid siege to Pavia, on the 28th of October. Some time was necessary for the imperialists to re-assemble their army, which the campaign of Provence had disorganised. At length it approached Pavia, which had resisted through the whole winter. The king of France was pressed by all his captains to raise the siege, and to march against the enemy; but he refused, declaring that it would be a compromise of the royal dignity, and foolishly remained within his lines. He was attacked by Pescara on the 24th of February, 1525; and, after a murderous battle, made prisoner.

For several months, while Francis I. was besieging Pavia, he appeared the strongest power in Italy; and the pope and Venetians, alarmed at his proximity, had treated with him anew, and pledged themselves to remain neutral. The imperial generals, after their victory, declared that these treaties with the French were offences against their master, for which they should demand satisfaction. Always without money, and pressed by the avidity of their soldiers, they sought only to discover offenders, as a pretence to raise contributions, and to let their troops live at free quarters. The pope and the Venetians were at first disposed to join in a league for resisting these exactions; and they offered Louisa of Savoy, regent of France, their aid to set her son Francis at liberty. But Clement VII. had not sufficient courage to sign this league : he preferred returning again to the alliance of the emperor and the duke of Milan, for which he paid a considerable sum. As soon as the imperial generals had received the money, they refused to execute the treaty which they had made with him, and the pope was obliged to go back to the Venetians and Louisa of Savoy. Meanwhile Jerome Morone, chancellor of the duke of Milan, an old man regarded as the most able politician of his time, made overtures, which revived the hope of arming all Italy for her independence. Francesco Sforza found himself treated by the Germans and Spaniards with the greatest indignity in his own palace : his subjects were exposed to every kind of insult from an unbridled soldiery ; and when he endeavoured to protect them, the officers took pleasure in making him witness aggravations of injustice and out-rage. The man, however, who made the German yoke press most severely on him was the marquis Pescara, an Italian, but descended from the Catalonian house of Avalos, established in the kingdom of Naples for more than a century. He manifested a sort of vanity in associating himself with the Spaniards : he commanded their infantry ; he adopted the manners as well as pride of that nation. Morone, nevertheless, did not despair of awakening his patriotism, by exciting his ambition. The kingdom of Naples, which had flourished under the bastard branch of the house of Aragon when the family of Avalos first entered it, had sunk, since it had been united to Spain, into a state of the most grievous oppres-sion. Morone determined on offering Pescara the crown of Naples, if he would join his efforts to those of all the other Italians, for the deliverance of his country. Success depended on him : he could distribute the imperial troops, which he commanded, in such a manner as that they could oppose no resistance. The duke of Milan had been warned that Charles V. intended taking his duchy from him, to confer it on his brother Ferdinand of Austria. The kingdom of· Naples and the duchy of Milan were ready to pass over from the emperor's party to that of France, provided the French king would renounce all his claims to both, acknowledge Pescara

king of Naples, Francesco Sforza duke of Milan ; and
restore to Italy her independence, after having delivered
her from her enemies.

This negotiation was at first successful: each of the
governments to which the proposition of concurring in
the independence of Italy was addressed, seemed to agree
to it.   France renounced all pretensions to Lombardy
and the Two Sicilies ; Switzerland promised to protect,
on its side, the land of ancient liberty, and to furnish it
with soldiers ; Henry VIII. of England promised money ;
Pescara coveted the crown, and Sforza was impatient to
throw off a yoke which had become insupportable to
him; but, unhappily the negotiation was entrusted to too
many cabinets, all jealous, perfidious, and eager to obtain
advantages for themselves by sacrificing their allies.
Clement was desirous of obtaining from the emperor a
more advantageous treaty, by threatening him with France ;
the queen regent of France endeavoured to engage Charles
to relax his rigour towards her son, by threatening him
with Italy ; Pescara, reserving the choice of either betraying his master or his allies, as should prove most profitable to him, had warned Charles that he was engaged in
a plot which he would reveal as soon as he had every clue
to it.   The duchess of Alençon, sister of Francis, sent by
her mother to negotiate at Madrid, spoke still more
clearly.   She offered Charles to abandon Italy, the project
respecting which she disclosed, provided the emperor, in
restoring her brother to liberty, would renounce his purpose of making him purchase it at the price of one of
the provinces of France.   Pescara, finding that his court
knew more than he had told, determined on adopting the
part of provocative agent instead of rebel ; he had only to
choose between them.   On the 14th of October, 1525,
he invited Morone to a last conference in the castle of
Novara.   After having made him explain all his projects
anew, while Spanish officers hid behind the arras heard
them, he caused him to be arrested, seized all the fortresses in the state of Milan, and laid siege to the castle,
in which the duke had shut himself up.   He denounced
to the emperor as traitors, the pope, and all the other
Italians his accomplices; but while he played this odious
part, he was attacked by a slow disease, of which he died

on the 30th of November, 1525, at the age of thirty-six, abhorred by all Italy.

Charles, abusing the advantages which he had obtained, imposed on Francis the treaty of Madrid, signed on the 14th of January, 1526; by which the latter abandoned Italy and the duchy of Burgundy. He was set at liberty on the 18th of March following; and almost immediately declared to the Italians, that he did not regard himself bound by a treaty extorted from him by force. On the 22nd of May, he signed a league for the liberty of Italy with Clement VII., the Venetians, and Francesco Sforza, but still did not abandon the policy of his mother: instead of thinking in earnest of restoring Italian independence, and thus securing the equilibrium of Europe, he had only one purpose,—that of alarming Charles with the Italians; and was ready to sacrifice them as soon as the emperor should abandon Burgundy. At the same time, his supineness, love of pleasure, distrust of his fortune, and repugnance to violate the treaty of Madrid, hindered him from fulfilling any of the engagements which he had contracted towards the Italians; he sent them neither money, French cavalry, nor Swiss forces. Charles, on the other hand, sent no supplies to pay his armies to Antonio de Leyva, the constable Bourbon, and Hugo de Monçada, their commanders. These troops were therefore obliged to live at free quarters, and the oppression of the whole country was still more dreadful than it had ever yet been.

The defection of the duke of Milan, in particular, gave a pretence to Antonio de Leyva to treat the wretched Milanese with redoubled rigour, as if they could be responsible for what Leyva called the treachery of their master. The Spanish army was quartered on the citizens of Milan; and there was not a soldier who did not make his host a prisoner, keeping him bound at the foot of the bed, or in the cellar, for the purpose of having him daily at hand, to force him, by blows or fresh torture, to satisfy some new caprice. As soon as one wretched person died under his sufferings, or broke his bonds and ended his sufferings by voluntary death, either precipitating himself through a window or into a well, the Spaniard passed into another house to recommence on its proprietor the same torture. The Venetians and the pope had united

their forces, under the command of the duke of Urbino,
who, exaggerating the tactics of Prospero Colonna, was
ambitious of no other success in war than that of avoiding
battle.   He announced to the senate of Venice, that he
would not approach Milan till the French and Swiss,
whose support he had been promised, joined him.   His
inaction, while witnessing so many horrors, reduced the
Italians to despair.   Sforza, who had been nine months
blockaded in the castle of Milan, and who always hoped
to be delivered by the duke of Urbino, whose colours
were in sight, supported the last extremity of hunger
before he surrendered to the Spaniards, on the 24th of
July, 1526. The pope, meanwhile, was far from suspecting
himself in any danger; but his personal enemy, Pompeo
Colonna, took advantage of the name of the imperial
party to raise in the papal state 8,000 armed peasants,
with whom, on the 20th of September, he surprised the
Vatican, pillaged the palace, as well as the temple of St.
Peter, and constrained the pope to abjure the alliance of
France and Venice.   About the same time, George de
Frundsberg, a German condottiere, entered Lombardy
with 13,000 adventurers, whom he had engaged to follow
him, and serve the emperor without pay, contenting
themselves with the pillage of that unhappy country.

The constable Bourbon, to whom Charles had given
the chief command of his forces in Italy, determined to
take advantage of this new army, and unite it to that for
which at Milan he had now no further occasion ; but it
was not without great difficulty that he could persuade
the Spaniards, to quit that city where they enjoyed the
savage pleasure of inflicting torture on their hosts.   At
length, however, he succeeded in leading them to Pavia.
On the 30th of January, 1527, he joined Frundsberg, who
died soon after of apoplexy.   Bourbon now remained
alone charged with the command of this formidable army,
already exceeding 25,000 men, and continually joined on
its route by disbanded soldiers and brigands intent on
pillage.   The constable had neither money, equipments,
nor artillery, and very few cavalry ; every town shut its
gates on his approach, and he was often on the point of
wanting provisions.   He took the road of southern Italy,
and entered Tuscany, still uncertain whether he should

pillage Florence or Rome. The marquis of Saluzzo, with a small army, retreated before him; the duke of Urbino followed in his rear, but always keeping out of reach of battle. At last, Bourbon took the road to Rome, by the valley of the Tiber. On the 5th of May, 1527, he arrived before the capital of Christendom. Clement, long alarmed at his march, had, on the 15th of March, signed a truce of eight months with the viceroy of Naples, and dismissed his troops, never imagining that one of the emperor's lieutenants would not respect the engagements of the other. On the approach of Bourbon, however, the walls of Rome were again mounted with engines of war. The next day, the 6th of May, this renegade prince led his troops to the assault of the city. He was killed near the Janiculum, while mounting the first scaling ladder. His fall did not stop the terrific band of robbers which he led. The victorious army scaled the walls, which were ill defended; and spread terror through the quarters of the Borgo, Vatican, and Trastevere. In a few hours they were masters of the whole city, Clement having neglected to destroy the bridges on the Tiber.

The capital of Christendom was then abandoned to a pillage unparalleled in the most calamitous period—that of the first triumph of barbarism over civilisation: neither Alaric the Goth nor Genseric the Vandal had treated it with like ferocity. Not only was all that could be seized in every house and every shop carried off, but the peasants of the fiefs of Colonna took possession of the heavy furniture which did not tempt the cupidity of the soldier. From the day on which these barbarians entered the city all personal protection was withdrawn; women were abandoned to the outrages of the victors; and sanctuaries, enriched by the veneration of Christendom for twelve centuries, were devoted to spoliation. The squares before the churches were strewed with the ornaments of the altar, relics, and other sacred things, which the soldiers threw into the streets after having torn off the gold and silver which adorned them. Men, women, and children were seized, whenever their captors could flatter themselves that they had concealed some treasure, or that there was any one sufficiently interested for them to pay their ransom. Every house resounded with the cries and lamentations of wretched persons thus subjected to the torture; and this dreadful state of crime and agony lasted not merely days, but was prolonged for more than nine months: it was not till the 17th of February, 1528, that the prince of Orange, one of the French lords who had accompanied Bourbon in his rebellion, finally withdrew from Rome all of this army that vice and disease had spared. The Germans, indeed, after the first few days, had sheathed their swords, to plunge into drunkenness and the most brutal debauchery; but the Spaniards, up to the last hour of their stay in Rome, indefatigable in their cold-blooded cruelty, continued to invent fresh torture to extort new ransoms from all who fell into their hands; even the plague, the consequence of so much suffering, moral and physical, which broke out amidst all these horrors, did not make the rapacious Spaniard loose his prey.

The struggle between the Italians, feebly seconded by the French, and the generals of Charles V., was prolonged yet more than two years after the sack of Rome; but it only added to the desolation of Italy, and destroyed alike in all the Italian provinces the last remains of prosperity. On the 18th of August, 1527, Henry VIII. of England and Francis I. contracted the treaty of Amiens, for the deliverance, as the two sovereigns announced, of the pope. A powerful French army, commanded by Lautrec, entered Italy in the same month, by the province of Alexandria. They surprised Pavia on the 1st of October, and during eight days barbarously pillaged that great city, under pretence of avenging the defeat of their king under its walls. After this success, Lautrec, instead of completing the conquest of Lombardy, directed his march towards the south; renewed the alliance of France with the duke of Ferrara, to whose son was given in marriage a daughter of Louis XII., sister of the queen of France. He secured the friendship of the Florentine republic, which, on the 17th of the preceding May, had taken advantage of the distress and captivity of the pope, to recover its liberty, and to re-establish its government in the same form in which it stood in 1512. The pope, learning that Lautrec had arrived at Orvieto, escaped from the castle of St. Angelo on the 9th of December, and took refuge in the

French camp. The Spaniard Alarcon had detained him captive, with thirteen cardinals, during six months, in that fortress; and, though the plague had broken out there, he did not relax in his severity. After having received 400,000 ducats for his ransom, instead of releasing him, as he had engaged to do the next day, it is probable that he suffered him to escape, lest his own soldiers should arrest him in order to extort a second ransom.

Lautrec passed the Tronto to enter the Abruzzi with his powerful army on the 10th of February, 1528. The banditti whom Charles V. called his soldiers, whom he never paid, and who showed no disposition to obedience, were cantoned at Milan, Rome, and the principal cities in Italy: they divided their time between debauchery and the infliction of torture on their hosts; their officers were unable to induce them to leave the towns and advance towards the enemy. The people in the excess of suffering, met every change with eagerness, and received Lautrec as a deliverer. He would probably have obtained complete success, if Francis had not just at this moment withheld the monthly advance of money which he had promised. That monarch, identifying his pride of royalty with prodigality, exhausted his finances in pleasures and entertainments; his want of economy drew on him all his disasters. Lautrec, on his side, although he had many qualities of a good general, was harsh, proud, and obstinate: he piqued himself on doing always the opposite of what he was counselled. Disregarding the national peculiarities of the French, he attempted in war to discipline them in slow and regular movements. He lost valuable time in Apulia, where he took and sacked Melfi, on the 23rd of March, with a barbarity worthy of his adversaries, the Spaniards: he did not arrive till the 1st of May before Naples. The prince of Orange had just entered that city with the army which had sacked Rome, but of which the greater part had been carried off by a dreadful mortality, the consequence and punishment of its vices and crimes. Instead of vigorously attacking them, Lautrec, in spite of the warm remonstrances of his officers, persisted in reducing Naples by blockade; thus exposing his army to the influence of a destructive climate. The imperial fleet was destroyed, on the 28th of May, in the gulf of Salerno, by Filippino Doria, who was in the pay of France. The inhabitants of Naples experienced the most cruel privations, and sickness soon made great havoc amongst them: but a malady not less fatal broke out at the same time in the French camp. The soldiers, under a burning sun, surrounded with putrid water, condemned to every kind of privation, harassed by the light cavalry of the enemy, infinitely superior to theirs, sank, one after the other, under pestilential fevers. In the middle of June, the French reckoned in their camp 25,000 men; by the 2nd of August there did not remain 4,000 fit for service. At this period all the springs were dry, and the troops began to suffer from hunger and thirst. Lautrec, ill as he was, had till then supported the army by his courage and invincible obstinacy; but, worn out at last, he expired in the night of the 15th of August:— almost all the other officers died in like manner. The marquis de Saluces, on whom the command of the army devolved, felt the necessity of a retreat, but knew not how to secure it in presence of such a superior force. He tried to escape from the imperialists, by taking advantage of a tremendous storm, in the night of the 29th of August; but was soon pursued, and overtaken at Aversa, where, on the 30th, he was forced to capitulate. The magazines and hospitals at Capua were, at the same time, given up to the Spaniards. The prisoners and the sick were crowded together in the stables of the Magdalen, where contagion acquired new force. The Spaniards foresaw it, and watched with indifference the agony and death of all; for nearly all of that brilliant army perished—a few invalids only ever returned to France.

During the same campaign another French army, conducted by François de Bourbon, count de St. Pol, had entered Lombardy, at the moment when Henry duke of Brunswick led thither a German army. Henry, finding nothing more to pillage, announced that his mission was to punish a rebellious nation, and put to the sword all the inhabitants of the villages through which he passed. Milan was at once a prey to famine and the plague, aggravated by the cupidity and cold-blooded ferocity of Leyva, who still commanded the Spanish garrison. Leyva seized all the provisions brought in from the country ; and, to profit by the general misery, resold them at an enormous price. Genoa had remained subject to the French, and was little less oppressed ; none of its republican institutions were any longer respected : but a great admiral still rendered it illustrious. Andrea Doria had collected a fleet, on board of which he summoned all the enterprising spirits of Liguria : his nephew Filippino, who had just gained a victory over the imperialists, was his lieutenant. The Dorias demanded the restoration of liberty to their country as the price of their services : unable to obtain it from the French, they passed over to the imperialists. Assured by the promises of Charles, they presented themselves, on the 12th of September, before Genoa, excited their countrymen to revolt, and constrained the French to evacuate the town : they made themselves masters of Savona on the 21st of October, and a few days afterwards of Castelletto. Doria then proclaimed the republic, and re-established once more the freedom of Genoa, at the moment when all freedom was near its end in Italy. The winter passed in suffering and inaction. The following year, Antonio de Leyva surprised the count de St. Pol at Landriano, on the 21st of June, 1529, and made him prisoner, with all the principal officers of the French army. The rest dispersed or returned to France. This was the last military incident in this dreadful war.

Peace was ardently desired on all sides ; negotiations were actively carried on ; but every potentate sought to deceive his ally in order to obtain better conditions from his adversary. Margaret of Austria, the sister of the emperor's father, and Louisa of Savoy, the mother of the king of France, met at Cambray ; and in conference to which no witnesses were admitted, arranged what was called *"Le traité des dames."* Clement VII. had at the same time a nuncio at Barcelona, who negotiated with the emperor. The latter was impatient to arrange the affairs of Italy, in order to pass into Germany. Not only had Soliman invaded Austria, and, on the 13th of September, arrived under the walls of Vienna, but the reformation of Luther excited in all the north of Germany a continually increasing ferment. On the 20th of June, 1529, Charles signed at Barcelona a treaty of perpetual alliance with the pope : by it he engaged to sacrifice the republic of Florence to the pope's vengeance, and to place in the service of Clement, in order to accomplish it, all the brigands who had previously devastated Italy. Florence was to be given in sovereignty to the bastard Alexander de' Medici, who was to marry an illegitimate daughter of Charles V. On the 5th of August following, Louis and Margaret signed the treaty of Cambray, by which France abandoned, without reserve, all its Italian allies to the caprices of Charles; who, on his side, renounced Burgundy, and restored to Francis his two sons, who had been retained as hostages. Charles arrived at Genoa, on board the fleet of Andrea Doria, on the 12th of August. The pope awaited him at Bologna, into which he made his entry on the 5th of November. He summoned thither all the princes of Italy, or their deputies, and treated them with more moderation than might have been expected after the shameful abandonment of them by France. As he knew the health of Francesco Sforza, duke of Milan, to be in a declining state, which promised but few years of life, he granted him the restitution of his duchy for the sum of 900,000 ducats, which Sforza was to pay at different terms: they had not all fallen due when that prince died, on the 24th of October, 1535, without issue, and his estates escheated to the emperor. On the 23rd of December, 1529, Charles granted peace to the Venetians; who restored him only some places in Apulia, and gave up Ravenna and Cervia to the pope. On the 20th of March, Alphonso d'Este also signed a treaty, by which he referred his differences with the pope to the arbitration of the emperor. Charles did not pronounce on them till the following year. He conferred on Alphonso the possession of Modena, Reggio, and Rubbiera, as fiefs of the empire; and he made the pope give him the investiture of Ferrara. On the 25th of March, 1530, a diploma of the emperor raised the marquisate of Mantua to a duchy, in favour of Frederick de Gonzaga. The duke of Savoy and the marquis de Montferrat, till then protected by France, arrived at Bologna, to place themselves under the protection of the emperor. The duke of Urbino was recommended to him by the Venetians, and obtained some promises of favour. The republics of Genoa,

Sienna, and Lucca had permission to vegetate under the imperial protection ; and Charles, having received from the pope, at Bologna, on the 22nd of February and 24th of March, the two crowns of Lombardy and of the empire, departed in the beginning of April for Germany, in order to escape witnessing the odious service in which he consented that his troops should be employed against Florence.

CHAPTER XVI

OPPRESSION OF ITALY DURING THE THREE LAST CENTURIES— SUCCESSIVE FALL OF ALL HER REPUBLICS—HER LAST CON- VULSIONS

THE evil destiny of Italy was accomplished. Charles VIII., when he first invaded that country, opened its gates to all the transalpine nations : from that period Italy was ravaged, during thirty-six years, by Germans, French, Spaniards, Swiss, and even Turks. They inflicted on her calamities beyond example in history ; calamities so much the more keenly felt, as the sufferers were more civilised, and the authors more barbarous. The French invasion ended in giving to the greatest enemies of France the dominion of that country, so rich, so industrious, and of which the possession was sought ardently by all. Never would the house of Austria have achieved the conquest of Italy, if Charles VIII., Louis XII., and Francis I. had not previously destroyed the wealth and military organisation of the nation ; if they had not themselves introduced the Spaniards into the kingdom of Naples, and the Germans into the states of Venice ; forgetting that both must soon after be subject to Charles V. The independence of Italy would have been beneficial to France : the rapacious and improvident policy which made France seek subjects where it should only have sought allies, was the origin of a long train of disasters to the French.

A period of three centuries of weakness, humiliation, and suffering, in Italy, began in the year 1530: from that time she was always oppressed by foreigners, and enervated and corrupted by her masters. These last reproached her with the vices of which they were themselves the authors. After having reduced her to the impossibility of resisting, they accused her of cowardice when she submitted, and of rebellion when she made efforts to vindicate herself. The Italians, during this long period of slavery, were agitated with the desire of becoming once more a nation : as, however, they had lost the direction of their own affairs, they ceased to have any history which could be called theirs ; their misfortunes have become but episodes in the histories of other nations. We should not, however, look upon the task which we have imposed on ourselves as concluded, if we did not distinguish, amidst this general subjugation, the particular calamities which closed the existence of the republics which still remained independent after the coronation of Charles V.

The Florentines, who, from 1512, had been victims of all the faults of Leo X. and Clement VII.,—who had been drawn into all the oscillations of their policy, and called upon to make prodigious sacrifices of money for projects with which they had not even been made acquainted,—were taught under these popes to detest the yoke of the Medici. When the constable Bourbon approached their walls in his march to Rome, on the 26th of April, 1527, they were on the point of recovering their liberty : the cardinal de Cortona, who commanded for the pope at Florence, had distributed arms among the citizens for their defence ; and they determined to employ them for their liberation : but the terror which this army of brigands inspired did the cardinal the service of repressing insurrection. When, however, they heard soon after of the taking of Rome, and of the captivity of the pope, all the most notable citizens presented themselves in their civic dress to the cardinal de Cortona ; declared firmly, but with calmness, that they were henceforth free ; and compelled him, with the two bastard Medici whom he brought up, to quit the city. It was on the 17th of May, 1527, that the lieutenant of Clement obeyed ; and the constitution, such as it existed in 1512, with its grand council, was restored without change, except that the office of gonfalonier was declared annual. The first person invested with this charge was Nicolo Capponi, a man enthusiastic in religion, and moderate in politics: he was the son of Pietro Capponi, who had braved Charles VIII. In 1529, he was succeeded by Baldassare Carducci, whose character was more energetic, and opinions more democratic. Carducci was succeeded, in 1530, by Raffaele Girolami, who witnessed the end of the republic.

Florence, during the whole period of its glory and power, had neglected the arts of war: it reckoned for its defence on the adventurers whom its wealth could summon from all parts to its service; and set but little value on a courage which men, without any other virtue, were so eager to sell to the highest bidder. Since the transalpine nations had begun to subdue Italy to their tyranny, these hireling arms sufficed no longer for the public safety. Statesmen began to see the necessity of giving the republic a protection within itself. Macchiavelli, who died on the 22nd of June, 1527, six weeks after the restoration of the popular government, had been long engaged in persuading his fellow citizens of the necessity of awakening a military spirit in the people: it was he who caused the country militia, named *l'ordinanza*, to be formed into regiments. A body of mercenaries, organised by Giovanni de' Medici, a distant kinsman of the popes, served at the time as a military school for the Tuscans, among whom alone the corps had been raised: it acquired a high reputation under the name of *bande nere*. No infantry equalled it in courage and intelligence. Five thousand of these warriors served under Lautrec in the kingdom of Naples, where they almost all perished. When, towards the end of the year 1528, the Florentines perceived that their situation became more and more critical, they formed, among those who enjoyed the greatest privileges in their country, two bodies of militia, which displayed the utmost valour for its defence. The first, consisting of 300 young men of noble families, undertook the guard of the palace, and the support of the constitution; the second, of 4,000 soldiers drawn only from among families having a right to sit in the council-general, were called the civic militia: both soon found opportunities of proving that generosity and patriotism suffice to create, in a very short period, the best soldiers. The illustrious Michael Angelo was charged to superintend the fortifications of Florence: they were completed in the month of April, 1529. Lastly, the ten commissioners of war chose for the command of the city Malatesta Baglioni of Perugia, who was recommended to them as much for his hatred of the Medici, who had unjustly put his father to death, as for his reputation for valour and military talent.

Clement VII. sent against Florence, his native country, that very prince of Orange, the successor of Bourbon, who had made him prisoner at Rome; and with him that very army of robbers which had overwhelmed the holy see, and its subjects, with misery and every outrage. This army entered Tuscany in the month of September, 1529, and took possession of Cortona, Arezzo, and all the upper Val d'Arno. On the 14th of October the prince of Orange encamped in the plain of Ripoli, at the foot of the walls of Florence; and, towards the end of December, Ferdinand de Gonzaga led on the right bank of the Arno another imperial army, composed of 20,000 Spaniards and Germans, which occupied without resistance Pistoia and Prato. Notwithstanding the immense superiority of their forces, the imperialists did not attempt to make a breach in the walls of Florence; they resolved to make themselves masters of the city by blockade. The Florentines, on the contrary, animated by preachers who inherited the zeal of Savonarola, and who united liberty with religion as an object of their worship, were eager for battle: they made frequent attacks on the whole line of their enemies, led in turns by Malatesta Baglioni and Stefano Colonna. They made nightly sallies, covered with white shirts to distinguish each other in the dark, and successively surprised the posts of the imperialists: but the slight advantages, thus obtained, could not disguise the growing danger of the republic. France had abandoned them to their enemies; there remained not one ally either in Italy or the rest of Europe; while the army of the pope and emperor comprehended all the survivors of those soldiers who had so long been the terror of Italy by their courage and ferocity, and whose warlike ardour was now redoubled by the hope of the approaching pillage of the richest city in the West.

The Florentines had one solitary chance of deliverance. Francesco Ferrucci, one of their citizens, who had learned the art of war in the bande nere, and joined to a mind full of resources an unconquerable intrepidity and an ardent patriotism, was not shut up within the walls of Florence: he had been named commissary-general, with unlimited power over all that remained without the capital. Ferrucci was at first engaged in conveying provisions from Empoli to Florence: he afterwards took Volterra from the imperialists; and, having formed a small army, proposed to the signoria to seduce all the adventurers and brigands from the imperial army, by promising them another pillage of the pontifical court, and succeeding in that, to march at their head on Rome, frighten Clement, and force him to grant peace to their country. The signoria rejected this plan as too daring. Ferrucci then formed a second, which was little less bold. He departed from Volterra, made the tour of Tuscany, which the imperial troops traversed in every direction, collected at Leghorn, Pisa, the Val di Nievole, and in the mountains of Pistoia, every soldier, every man of courage, still devoted to the republic; and, after having thus increased his army, he intended to fall on the imperial camp before Florence and force the prince of Orange, who began to feel the want of money, to raise the siege. Ferrucci, with an intrepidity equal to his skill, led his little troop, from the 14th of July to the 2nd of August, 1530, through numerous bodies of imperialists, who preceded, followed, and surrounded him on all sides, as far as Gavinana, four miles from San Marcello, in the mountains of Pistoia. He entered that village about mid-day, on the 2nd of August, with 3,000 infantry and 500 cavalry. The prince of Orange, at the same time, entered by another gate, with a part of the army which besieged Florence. The different corps, which had on every side harassed Ferrucci in his march, poured in upon him from all quarters: the battle instantly began, and was fought with relentless fury within the walls of Gavinana. Philibert de Challon, prince of Orange, in whom that house became extinct, was killed by a double shot, and his corps put to flight; but other bands of imperialists successively arrived, and continually renewed the attack on a small force exhausted with fatigue : 2,000 Florentines were already stretched on the field of battle ; when Ferrucci, pierced with several mortal wounds, was borne bleeding to the presence of his personal enemy, Fabrizio Maramaldi, a Calabrese, who commanded the light cavalry of the emperor. The Calabrese stabbed him several times in his rage ; while Ferrucci calmly said, " Thou wouldst kill a dead man !" The republic perished with him.

When news of the disaster at Gavinana reached Florence, the consternation was extreme. Baglioni, who for some days had been in treaty with the prince of Orange, and who was accused of having given him notice of the project of Ferrucci, declared that a longer resistance was impossible, and that he was determined to save an imprudent city, which seemed bent upon its own ruin. On the 8th of August he opened the bastion, in which he was stationed, to an imperial captain, and planted his artillery so as to command the town. The citizens, in consternation, abandoned the defence of the walls, to employ themselves in concealing their valuable effects in the churches ; and the signoria acquainted Ferdinand de Gonzaga, who had succeeded the prince of Orange in the command of the army, that they were ready to capitulate. The terms granted on the 12th of August, 1530, were less rigorous than the Florentines might have apprehended. They were to pay a gratuity of 80,000 crowns to the army which besieged them, and to recall the Medici. In return, a complete amnesty was to be granted to all who had acted against that family, the pope or the emperor. But Clement had no intention to observe any of the engagements contracted in his name. On the 20th of August, he caused the parliament, in the name of the sovereign people, to create a balia, which was to execute the vengeance of which he would not himself take the responsibility : he subjected to the torture, and afterwards punished with exile or death, by means of this balia, all the patriots who had signalised themselves by their zeal for liberty. In the first month 150 illustrious citizens were banished ; before the end of the year there were more than 1,000 sufferers : every Florentine family, even among those most devoted to the Medici, had some one member among the proscribed.

Alexander, the bastard Medici, whom Clement had appointed chief of the Florentine republic in preference to his cousin Hyppolito, did not return to his country till the 5th of July, 1531: he was the bearer of a rescript from the emperor, which gave Florence a constitution nearly monarchical; but, so far from confining himself within the limits traced, Alexander oppressed the people with the most grievous tyranny. Cruelty, debauchery, and extortion marked him for public hatred. On the 10th of August, 1535, he caused to be poisoned his cousin, the cardinal Ippolito, who undertook the defence of his fellow-countrymen against him. He at last, on the 6th of January, 1537, was himself assassinated by his kinsman and companion in licentiousness, Lorenzino de' Medici.

But the death of Alexander did not restore freedom to his country. The agents of his tyranny, the most able but also the most odious of whom was the historian Guicciardini, needed a prince for their protector. They made choice of Cosmo de' Medici, a young man of nineteen, descended in the fourth generation from Lorenzo, the brother of the former Cosmo. On the 9th of January, 1537, they proclaimed him duke of Florence, hoping to guide him henceforth at their pleasure; but they were deceived. This man, false, cold-blooded, and ferocious, who had all the vices of Filippo II., and who shrank from no crime, soon got rid of his counsellors, as well as of his adversaries. Cosmo I., in 1569, obtained from the pope Pius V. the title of grand duke of Tuscany; a title that the emperor would not then acknowledge, though he afterwards, in 1575, granted it to the son of Cosmo. Seven grand dukes of that family reigned successively at Florence. The last, Gian Gastone, died on the 9th of July, 1737.

It was Cosmo I. who abolished the name of republic at Sienna, as he had done at Florence. That city, so long faithful to the Ghibeline party, had evinced the same devotion to the emperor in the wars of the beginning of the century. Charles V. took advantage of it to introduce into Sienna a Spanish garrison, destined to overawe Tuscany and the court of Rome; but the Spaniards showed there, as every where else, the characteristic pride, cupidity, and ferocity which had rendered them universally odious.   On the 11th of August, 1552, the Siennese, unable to bear with them any longer, rose against them, drove them out, and introduced a French garrison in their stead.   Cosmo pledged himself to remain neutral in the war lighted up anew between the French and the imperialists : he, nevertheless, on the 27th of January, 1554, attacked, without any declaration of war, the Siennese, whose city he hoped to take by surprise. Having failed in this attack, he gave the command of his army to the ferocious marquis de Marignano, who undertook to reduce it by famine.   The first act of Marignano was to massacre without mercy all the women, children, aged, and sick, whom the Siennese, beginning to feel the want of provisions, had sent out of the town : every peasant discovered carrying provisions into Sienna was immediately hung before its gates.   The villages and fortresses of the Siennese, for the most part, attempted to remain faithful to the republic ; but in all those which held out until the cannon was planted against their walls, the inhabitants were inhumanly put to death.   It was then that the edge of the sword or famine destroyed the rustic population, particularly that of the coast of Maremma, covered with forests at this day.   The Maremmane fever over-ran that desolate district ; and those who at the peace returned there to reap the inheritance of the victims of Marignano, soon fell themselves the victims of that disease.   The city of Sienna at last capitulated, on the 2nd of April, 1555 ; and its capitulation was not better respected than that of Florence.   Death and exile were the lot of those generous citizens to whom an amnesty had been promised.   The Spaniards retained possession of Sienna for two years ; and did not surrender it to the duke of Florence until the 19th of July, 1557.

After the subjugation of Sienna, there remained in Italy only three republics, Lucca, Genoa, and Venice, unless it may be permitted to reckon San Marino, a free village, situated on the summit of a mountain of Romagna, which has alike escaped both usurpation and history until our own time.

In 1546, Lucca had a gonfalonier, named Francesco Burlamachi, who formed the bold project of restoring liberty to all the republics of Tuscany. The militia of Lucca, in number only 2,000, were to be reviewed by him on a given day, after which he was to lead them suddenly across the mountains to Pisa, in order to rouse that warlike city to revolt: detachments were, at the same time, to be sent to excite similar insurrections at Pescia, Pistoia, Florence, Bologna, Sienna, and Perugia. Popular governments were every where to be organised, and the different towns were to form one confederation.

Charles V., then engaged in Germany in combating the league of Smalkalde, was supposed not to be in a situation to defend Italy. But the spies of Cosmo discovered the plot. The duke of Florence demanded the punishment of the conspirators from the magistrates of Lucca; who, trembling at the emperor's displeasure, delivered Burlamachi to the lieutenant of Charles at Milan. The first magistrate of a republic, calling itself still free, was tortured, and afterwards beheaded, by order of a foreign governor. From that period Lucca was ruled by a narrow aristocracy, called in derision *i signori del cerchiolino;* because the magistracies passed among them from one to the other in rotation as in a circle. The Martiniana law, proposed on the 9th of November, 1556, by the gonfalonier Martin Bernardini, excluded from office every man who was not descended from families which had an hereditary share in the sovereignty of the republic: of those there were not, in the year 1600, more than 168; and at the last enumeration, made in 1797, there more than 88. They were, nevertheless, to furnish a signoria, composed of a gonfalonier, nine anziani, a senate of thirty-six members, and a grand council of ninety. This jealous aristocracy, hated by the people, could not maintain itself from the moment it came in contact with the French of the revolution. These last took possession of Tuscany, on the 15th of October, 1800 ; on the 25th of December, 1801, the Lucchese gave themselves a representative constitution ; and on the 4th of June, 1805, they demanded of Napoleon a sovereign of his family. His sister, the princess Elise, was, on the 23rd of June following, invested with the principality of Lucca, but with laws which secured to the citizens and people more equality and freedom than they had for a long period enjoyed.

Andrea Doria restored the name of republic to Genoa, his native country, but with it he restored neither liberty nor independence. He constituted for the government of the republic a narrow aristocracy, which he continued to rule with his nephew Giannettino. He, at the same time, attached his country to the house of Austria, with a submission which the greater number of Genoese felt as the deepest humiliation. It was to throw off the double yoke of the Spaniards and of Doria that Gian Luigi de' Fieschi formed a conspiracy, celebrated alike in history and poetry. Fieschi brought down the vassals of his vast fiefs in the mountains; he had roused and inflamed the partisans of ancient freedom : he combined with all these the restless spirits which desired only confusion and a change. In fine, he secured the aid of France; and on the 2nd of January, 1547, seized the port, fleet, and gates of the city. Giannettino Doria was killed as he endeavoured to appease the sedition. The aged Doria fled; the revolution was accomplished : but Gian Luigi de' Fieschi, who should direct its course, was nowhere to be found. In passing from one galley to another, he had fallen unperceived into the sea, and, being loaded with heavy armour, was drowned. His companions, without a chief, knew no longer what was to be done. Though victors, they already treated with the signoria as if vanquished; and contented themselves with the promise of an amnesty. The Dorias did not observe this pledge; all the conspirators whom they could seize were executed. It was not till after the death of Andrea Doria, which took place only on the 25th of November, 1560, that the Genoese limited, though in a small degree, the rights of the aristocracy; they admitted, on the 17th of March, 1576, a body of new nobles into the government. They also preserved, with jealousy, the little that remained of their independence. The court of Spain repeatedly endeavoured to suppress the name of republic, and to overawe them by a citadel : but they twice defeated its attempts, in 1548 and 1571.

The aristocracy of Genoa was again, in 1628, endangered by a conspiracy. The families inscribed on the golden book, and having the right to sit in council, including the new as well as ancient nobility, did not exceed in number 170; but there were in Liguria at least 450 families equally noble, decorated with titles, possessing fiefs, prelacies, commanderies, and hereditary wealth, who were excluded from all share in the government. Julius Cesar Vachero persuaded these to aid him in seizing a sovereignty from which they thought themselves unjustly excluded. Vachero was a merchant of immense wealth, who had adopted the Spanish manners, then predominant in Italy. His palace was always filled with bravos; he never walked out without having numbers in his train; whoever offended him immediately fell under the dagger of the assassin, who escaped from justice by intimidating the judges or witnesses with fresh crimes. All the families not inscribed on the golden book promised to unite their bravos to those of Vachero. On the 1st of April, 1628, they were to make a joint attack upon the public palace, massacre all the ancient nobility and new-model the government, under the protection of the duke of Savoy: but the plot was discovered the evening preceding that destined for its execution. Vachero and several of his accomplices were arrested and executed.

The Genoese in the same century experienced a great calamity. On the 18th of May, 1684, their capital was bombarded by the fleet of Louis XIV.; who felt his royal dignity offended by so small a people daring to resist his will. He demanded the establishment of a depôt at Savona, to provision with salt and ammunition of war his fortress of Casal de Montferrat. The senate of Genoa refused their consent to an establishment alike contrary to their neutrality and independence. The marquis de Siegnelay punished them, by pouring on this city 14,000 bombs in three days: the public palace was more than half destroyed; and the whole town would have been ruined, if the doge had not consented to proceed to Paris with four senators to make his apology to the king.

Dignity and grandeur still characterised the doge, even in his humiliation: but this proud, and perhaps noble, merit was all that remained to the Genoese aristocracy;

it became more and more narrow and exclusive. It adopted the manners of the Spaniards, under whose protection it had risen. The Genoese nobles, like the grandees of Spain, always kept a band of assassins in their pay ; and it was by the dagger alone that they sought to make themselves feared or respected. The sovereign nobility, prodigal and voracious, created by their pomp wants beyond their resources : accordingly, they stooped to the most disgraceful depredations to obtain money. The state could make no contract without being robbed ; it was cheated in the victualling of fortresses, and of the navy, and in the payment of troops ; every place was an object of sale, and justice was venal in the tribunals. The subjects of the eastern and western coasts, called the two *Riviere*, and of Corsica, frequently revolted in order to throw off a yoke which had become odious to them. In the eighteenth century, the Corsicans redoubled their efforts to rid themselves of the tyranny of Genoa. From the year 1730 to the 15th of May, 1768, Corsica maintained an obstinate war against the republic ; which esteemed itself fortunate in prevailing on France to accept all its rights to that island in payment of a debt contracted with the French for the purpose of subduing its revolted subjects.

But the spirit of the ancient Italian republicans was not extinguished among the people of Genoa as among the nobles. The two branches of the house of Austria in Spain and Germany had become extinct ; and, in the war of the Austrian succession, the Genoese had made alliance with the house of Bourbon, which disputed with Maria Theresa the inheritance of her father Charles VI. In this war the French, united with the Spaniards, were defeated and driven out of Lombardy. The Austrians appeared before Genoa ; and the senate, which dared not arm the population, opened their gates to them, on the 6th of September, 1746. The Austrians abused, as they have ever done, the favours of fortune. They exacted from Genoa a contribution of 9,000,000 of florins of the empire, a sum which that city was not in a condition to pay. They seized all the money at the bank, all the plate of the churches, and even the property of individuals. They emptied the arsenals : and destined the artillery of

Genoa to be employed in an attack which they meditated against Provence. They made the Genoese themselves draw the cannon of which they robbed them; and expecting to find in the Italians Austrian baseness and servility, they urged them in their labour with blows. A heavy mortar had stuck fast amidst the ruins of a narrow street, and a German serjeant raised his cane on a Genoese to make him draw with more force; the latter, seizing a stone, threw it at the head of the Austrian. The people collected, calling out, not "to arms!" for they had none, but to attack the Austrians with stones. The Genoese from every window showered on them the stones of walls which they demolished, or the tiles of houses which they unroofed. In those narrow and winding streets the soldiers could find no shelter. They could present themselves in no imposing masses. They fired on their assailants; and more than one house was full of dead: but as they could not see the fall of those whom they struck, they were not cheered by their success. Meanwhile the streets were soon covered with Austrian dead. The Austrians tried in vain to set fire to houses, in the construction of which there happened to be but few combustible materials. Terror at length seized them: they fled from the city. It was the 5th of December, 1746. The populace which had expelled them lost no time in lining the ramparts and gates with cannon. The marquess Botta Adorno, general of the Austrians, had established in Genoa all his magazines, with his park of artillery. The revolt which drove him out deprived him both of arms and provisions; and in the barren mountains which surround Genoa, nothing was to be procured: he was accordingly, on the 10th of December, obliged to repass the Apennines. The peace of Aix-la-Chapelle, concluded two years afterwards, on the 18th of December, 1748, secured to the republic of Genoa the integrity of its territory, under the protection of France.

The expulsion of the Austrians was the last glorious event in the history of Genoa, as well as the last display of energy by the Italian nation, till the universal convulsion caused by the revolution of France. In the years 1794 and 1795, the senate of Genoa availed itself of the importance of its position to preserve its neutrality: its inclinations, however, sometimes prevailed over its interest, and not unfrequently exposed the French to outrages. These last postponed their demand of reparation, till the victory of Monte Notte, gained by Bonaparte over the Piedmontese and Austrians, on the 11th of April, 1796, placed Genoa at their discretion. From that time partisans of democracy began to claim as a right that all the inhabitants of Liguria should participate in the sovereignty. The nobles, seconded by the clergy, had a numerous party on their side among the people. On the 22nd of May, 1797, they resorted to arms; and 10,000 of the lowest class, collected by the cry of *Viva Maria!* for a moment triumphed over the friends of liberty. But this event itself furnished Bonaparte with an opportunity of interfering: he supported the rights of the nation against the aristocracy, and made the deputies of the senate sign, on the 6th of June, 1797, the convention of Monte Bello, which obliged the Genoese to adopt the name of the Ligurian republic; the inhabitants of Liguria being all admitted to a share in the sovereignty. The constitution of this republic was proclaimed on the 14th of June, 1797; it was modified on the 26th of June, 1802; and abolished on the 8th of October, 1805, by the union of the state of Genoa to France. Bonaparte had engaged the members of the government themselves to make the demand, on the 4th of June, 1805.

We have now to speak only of the decline and fall of the republic of Venice, the state in Italy whose existence was of longest duration. As this republic was the most powerful, the most wealthy, and the most wisely administered of all the Italian states, it appeared, even after the year 1530, when all Italy fell under the yoke of Charles V., to have preserved some vigour and independence. But the signoria of Venice did not share in the illusion which it created abroad: it felt the nation's weakness and danger, and knew too well that the vital principle was gone.

The whole of the sixteenth century was employed by the Venetians in repairing the disasters of the league of Cambrai. They had to rebuild all the walls of their city; to recover their reduced population; to re-establish their manufactures and agriculture, and to liquidate the enormous debt with which they were loaded; besides being always menaced by the Turks, against whom they had to support two disastrous wars : one from 1537 to 1540, which cost them their islands in the Archipelago, and their last fortresses in the Morea ; the other from 1570 to 1573, which deprived them of the isle of Cyprus. They appeared in some degree sacred to the western people, who regarded them as their defenders against the infidels ; they were moreover united by an identity of interests to the Roman empire,—like them, menaced by the Mussulmans : they, consequently, drew closer their alliance with the house of Austria, and under that pretext withdrew themselves from every other participation in the general affairs of Europe.

But in the beginning of the seventeenth century the Mussulman empire no longer inspired so much terror. The yoke of Spain continued to grow more insupportable to Italy ; while the development of the protestant party in Europe showed some prospect of throwing it off. The policy of the Venetian republic was, in fact, constantly to throw off the yoke of the house of Austria. But knowing its own weakness, and justly suspicious of allies who would abandon after compromising them, the Venetians contented themselves with giving succour to those whom they considered the defenders of European liberty, without openly making themselves a party to their leagues.

Venice was the first to acknowledge Henry IV., rejected by the catholic powers, and to negotiate his reconciliation with the pope. In 1617, it made alliance with the Dutch. During the thirty years' war, it gave succour to the protestants of Germany, to Bethlem Gabor, and to Ragotski, in Hungary. It supported the duke of Savoy against the king of Spain, and the protestant Grisons against the catholics of that canton.

At this period, when the republic was come almost to open hostility with the court of Spain, Phillip III. was represented in Italy by three powerful noblemen, ambitious, intriguing, and faithless—Don Pedro de Toledo, governor of Milan ; the duke d'Ossuna, viceroy of Naples ; and the marquis de Bedmar, ambassador at Venice. In 1618, a project was formed between these three lords to destroy a republic which stood in the way of their ambition, and which had always thwarted the

enterprises of Spain.   Some French adventurers, who
had signalised themselves in the armies and fleets of the
republic, of whom the most illustrious were the corsair
Jaques Pierre and Jaffier, dissatisfied with the rewards
which they had obtained, offered their services to the
marquis de Bedmar.   The marquis encouraged them
to enlist in their service the assassins, bravos, and
robbers who, under the Spanish rule, always formed
a part of the household of men of quality.   It was agreed
that, at a given signal, they should massacre the doge,
senators, and nobles ; that the city should afterwards
be abandoned to their pillage ; and that a general fire
should veil their crimes.   On the other side, it appears
that Jaques Pierre gave early notice of this plot to the
senate; that he carried it on by its order ; that the
senate made use of it to hide its secret intelligence with
the duke d'Ossuna, with whom a project was entered into
of nearly the same nature with that which had been
proposed in the preceding century by Morone to Pescara.
It was intended, with the aid of the senate, to re-establish
the independence of all Italy, by driving the Spaniards
out of Lombardy, and giving Ossuna the crown of
Naples.   Fresh disclosures of Antoine Jaffier apparently
discovered to the Council of Ten that the conspirators
preferred the pillage of Venice to the doubtful chances
of a revolt at Naples ; and that the information which
they had given of their plot was destined only to deceive
the vigilance of the state inquisitors.   The republic,
however, had embarked itself in intrigues which could
not bear the light.   On a certain morning, the inhabitants
of Venice saw with horror the bodies of Jaques Pierre,
Regnault, Boulant, and several others, hanging in the
square of St. Mark.   One hundred and sixty others were,
it was affirmed, drowned in the grand canal ; among
them was Jaffier.   No motive was assigned for these
executions ; no explanation was given to the public ;
no recrimination was addressed to the court of Spain.
The Council of Ten desired, above all, the silence of
terror ; and the romantic history of this conspiracy,
published by St. Réal in 1674, and the tragedy of " Venice
Preserved," by Otway, in 1682, were the only public
documents of this catastrophe for a long time.

The Venetians were afterwards forced by the attacks
of the Turks to make advances to the house of Austria,
the enemy of their enemies. On the 23rd of June, 1645,
the sultan Ibrahim unexpectedly attacked the isle
of Candia. The war which thus began was the longest
and most ruinous that the republic had yet sustained
against the Ottoman empire : it lasted twenty-five years.
The Venetians displayed obstinate valour in defence
of Candia. Courageous adventurers arrived from every
part of the west to fight under their banner, as in a holy
war. Their fleet twice destroyed that of the Mussulmans ;
but the forces of the republic were too disproportioned
to those of the Turkish empire. Candia was forced
to surrender on the 6th of September, 1669 ; and the
senate of that colony, the reflected image of the republic,
returned into the grand council of Venice, which had
given it birth : peace followed this capitulation.
    A second war between the Venetians and the Porte
was, before the end of the century, crowned with more
success. The republic engaged in it, in 1682, in concert with the emperor Leopold and John Sobieski, king
of Poland. It conquered the Morea, Egina, Santa
Maura, and several fortresses in Dalmatia, which were
secured to it by the treaty of Carlowitz, signed on the
26th of January, 1699 : but the Turks could not suffer
so feeble an enemy to take from them one of their finest
provinces. They might soon visibly convince themselves
that the Venetians were no longer in a state to make
a last effort to protect their conquests : the supreme power
was concentrated in an oligarchy becoming daily more
distracted. Half the nobility admitted to the grand
council were reduced to the most extreme poverty.
They lived on the bounty of the great, to whom they sold
their suffrages. The families from among whom alone
was selected the Council of Ten made every other tremble
and obey. They regarded the state as a prey to be divided
amongst themselves. Justice was venal ; the finances
dilapidated ; the fortifications falling into ruin ; the
effective force of the army did not amount to one half
of what appeared on the roll : every thing was to the
Venetian noble an object of embezzlement and robbery.
The oppression of the distant provinces was so great,

that the eastern Christian subjects of the republic regretted the dominion of the Ottomans. The sultan, Achmet III., informed of this universal disorganisation, sent his army, on the 20th of June, 1714, into the Morea; and in a month conquered that peninsula, covered with fortresses, of which not one made any resistance. On the 27th of June, 1718, the republic abandoned, under the peace of Passarowitz, all its claims on the Morea. From that period it had no further war with the Turks.

The republic abstained, with the same timidity, from taking any part in the war of the succession, either in Spain or Austria, in the quadruple alliance, or in that of the election of Poland, which disturbed Italy during the first half of the eighteenth century. It could not even make its neutrality respected. Its territory, always open to every belligerent power, was often the theatre of their most obstinate warfare. Venice, with 3,000,000 of subjects, 14,000 troops of the line (of which one half was composed of excellent Sclavonian soldiers), twelve vessels of war, and the means of arming 50,000 men, was incapable of making herself respected, or of protecting her subjects, either by sea or land. Her debt, even in the bosom of peace, was always increasing; her manufactures always in decay; her territory was infested with robbers; every city was divided into factions, which the senate encouraged, in order to weaken its subjects. A suspicious and cruel government, which maintained itself only by the vigilance of spies, which had promoted immorality to enervate the people, which made the most profound secrecy its only safeguard,—which did not tolerate even a question on public affairs,—which deprived the accused of every protection before the tribunals,—which acknowledged no other limit to the right of punishing by the dagger, by poison, or by the axe of the executioner, than that of the terror of its rulers;—a government such as this became execrated by its subjects. It stained with the most odious tyranny the very name of republic.

The French revolution appeared to the Venetian aristocracy an enemy destined to destroy it : of all the governments which divided Europe, the Venetian was the most opposite in principle to that of the French; nevertheless, the senate refused to enter into the coalition

against France, in 1792. Any display of force would
have augmented its expenses, and diminished the spoils
of provinces which the patricians divided amongst themselves. The same parsimony, the same sacrifice of the
public to private interests, hindered Venice, when the
victories of Bonaparte opened Lombardy to him, in
April, 1796, from augmenting her army or provisioning
her fortresses, in order to protect her territory from the
two belligerent powers. The government, adopting a
vacillating policy between the two parties, and awaiting
events, laid aside its arms : this soon brought war into
the states of the republic. The Austrians, always the
first to violate neutral ground, traversed them in every
direction : Beaulieu occupied Peschiera and Verona ;
Wurmser threw himself into Bassano, and passed through
Vicenza and Padua ; Alvinzi and the archduke Charles
occupied Friuli and Palma Nova, up to the eastern
limits of the republic. Napoleon successively drove the
Austrians from each of these provinces ; but, as the
French occupied them, the spirit of reform in the tribunals
and the laws, the spirit of publicity and equality, an
impatience of every yoke,—the spirit, in short, of the
French,—manifested itself, and the republic was at last
made to understand how much it was detested by all
those who had the least elevation of soul or cultivation
of mind.

Others, it is true, of the lowest class, (day-labourers in
towns, and peasants in the country,) completely under
the influence of priests, comprehending only what exists,
fearing all change, and still deeply excited by the name
of St. Mark, regarded France and every thing French
with horror. The senate, relying on this party, whose
fanaticism it excited, and hearing that Napoleon had
passed the Piove on his march to Germany, on the 11th
of March, 1797, gave orders to arrest at Bergamo fourteen
of the principal inhabitants, who had declared themselves
the most earnest in favour of the new doctrines. The
patriots, warned in time, arrested the proveditor himself,
raised the standard of revolt, and proclaimed the liberty
of Bergamo : a few days afterwards, a similar revolution
broke out at Brescia. Bonaparte had just defeated the
archduke Charles at the Tagliamento, and was marching

on Vienna. An Austrian column, commanded by Laudon, had meanwhile penetrated by the Tyrol into Italy; which he inundated with proclamations, announcing the defeat and destruction of the French army, and inviting the Italians to take arms to crush its fugitive remains. The senate, feeling that its position became daily more critical, believed the moment come for throwing off the mask and joining the Austrians. Emili, the proveditor of Verona, after having conferred with Laudon, ordered the tocsin to be rung, on the 17th of April, throughout the whole province ; and joining 30,000 insurgents to 3,000 soldiers, whom he commanded, every where attacked the French, massacred all those within his reach, and suffered the infuriated people to murder 400 sick in the hospitals. The next day preliminaries of peace between Austria and the French republic were signed at Leoben ; and, on the 3rd of May, 1797, Bonaparte, informed of the insurrection which had been organised in the rear of his army, and of the massacre of his sick, declared war against Venice from Palma Nova. The oligarchy, in consternation, implored the court of Vienna, which had drawn it into this imprudent attack, to include Venice in the suspension of arms and the negotiations for peace ; but Austria refused all assistance : she had her own views on her ally, and Venice fell. The French general Baraguai d'Hilliers entered the city on the 16th of May, and planted unopposed the tricolour banner on St. Mark. The negotiations for peace, however, continued. Austria, beginning to recover from her panic, disputed the concessions demanded, and asked compensation out of the states of her ally. Hostilities were on the point of recommencing ; but France did not yet find herself strong enough to liberate all Italy. On the 17th of October, 1797, Napoleon signed the treaty of Campo Formio, by which he secured the liberty of one half of the Venetian territory up to the Adige, which was united to the Cisalpine republic. The Ionian isles were, at the same time, united to France. Austria, on her side, took possession of Venice and the remainder of the Venetian states. The loss of liberty sustained by that part of the republic was, however, of no long duration : at the expiration of eighteen months the war was renewed ; and, after the French had made themselves masters of Vienna, they obliged Austria to restore Venice and all her territory to the kingdom of Italy, under the treaty of Presburg, signed on the 26th of December, 1805.

It was thus that the invasion of the French, at the end of the eighteenth century, restored to Italy all the advantages of which their invasion at the end of the fifteenth had deprived her. When Charles VIII. entered Naples with his victorious army, on the 22nd of February, 1495, and overthrew the ancient system of Italian politics, he gave the signal for all the calamities which afterwards precipitated the peninsula under the yoke of the trans-alpine nations. The Italians continued to regard themselves as the first people in Europe, but they had almost everywhere lost their liberty : of the five republics which they could still reckon, four were narrow aristocracies. When Napoleon Bonaparte was appointed to the command of the French army in Italy, on the 23rd of February, 1796, he began to effect a regeneration which gave to the Italian nation more liberty than it had lost. It is the participation of numbers in the government, and not the name of republic as opposed to monarchy, that constitutes liberty : it is, above all, the reign of the laws; publicity in the administration, as well as the tribunals; equality ; the removal of all shackles on thought, on education, and on religion. Five millions and a half of inhabitants in the kingdom of Italy were put in possession of a constitution which secured to them all these advantages, with a participation in the legislature and in the vote of taxes. They had recovered the glorious name of Italians ; they had a national army, the bravery of which rendered it daily more illustrious. Six millions and a half inhabitants of the kingdom of Naples received institutions less advanced, it is true; but even there the law had succeeded arbitrary power; public and oral evidence had succeeded secret information and the torture ; equality, the feudal system ; education, instead of retrograding, had been rendered progressive, and thought, as well as religious conscience, had recovered freedom: finally, 2,000,000 of Piedmontese, 500,000 Genoese, 500,000 Parmesans, and 2,500,000 Tuscans and Romans,—in all, 5,500,000 Italians,—were temporarily united to France. They partook of all the privileges of the conquerors: they became with them accustomed to the dominion of the law, to freedom of thought, and to military virtue,— secure that at no very distant period, when their political education should be accomplished, they would again be incorporated in that Italy to the future liberty and glory of which they now directed their every thought.

Such was the work which the French accomplished by twenty years of victory: it was doubtless incomplete, and left much to be desired; but it possessed in itself the principle of greater advancement: it promised to revive Italy, liberty, virtue, and glory. It has been the work of the coalition to destroy all; to place Italy again under the galling yoke of Austria; to take from her, with political liberty, civil and religious freedom, and even freedom of thought; to corrupt her morals; and to heap upon her the utmost degree of humiliation. Italy is unanimous in abhorring this ignominious yoke: Italy, to break it, has done all that could be expected of her. In a struggle between an established government and a nation, the former has all the advantages: it has in its favour rapidity of communication, certainty of information, soldiers, arsenals, fortresses, and finances. The people have only their unarmed hands and their masses accustomed to act together: nevertheless, in every struggle during these fifteen years in Italy, between the nation and its oppressors, the victory has remained with the people. At Naples, in Sicily, in Piedmont, in the states of the church, at Modena and Parma, unarmed masses have seized the arms of the soldiers; men chosen by the people have taken the places of the despots in their palaces. The Italians, every where victorious over their own tyrants, have, it is true, been every where forced back under the yoke with redoubled cruelty by the league of foreign despots. Attacked before they could have given themselves a government or formed a treasury, arsenals, or an army, by the sovereign of another nation, who reckons not less than 30,000,000 of subjects, they did not attempt a hopeless resistance, which would have deprived them of every chance for the future. Let those who demand more of them begin by doing as much themselves.

Italy is crushed; but her heart still beats with the love

of liberty, virtue, and glory : she is chained and covered with blood ; but she still knows her strength and her future destiny : she is insulted by those for whom she has opened the way to every improvement ; but she feels that she is formed to take the lead again : and Europe will know no repose till the nation which, in the dark ages, lighted the torch of civilisation with that of liberty, shall be enabled herself to enjoy the light which she created.

INDEX

THE END

*9 7 8 1 4 3 4 4 6 0 6 5 3 *